VISIONS
OF
CALIBAN

CALIBAN
as played by H. Beerbohm Tree
(painting by Charles A. Buchel, 1904)

CHIMPANZEE
an adult male in Tanzania
(photograph by Geza Teleki)

Other books by
DALE PETERSON

———

A Mad People's History
of Madness

Big Things from Little Computers

Genesis II

Intelligent Schoolhouse

COCO Logo *(with Don Inman
and Ramon Zamora)*

The Deluge and the Ark

◆

Other books by
JANE GOODALL

———

Innocent Killers
(with Hugo van Lawick)

In the Shadow of Man

Grub the Bush Baby
(with Hugo van Lawick)

The Chimpanzees of Gombe:
Patterns of Behavior

Through a Window

My Life with Chimpanzees

The Chimpanzee Family Book

Jane Goodall's Animal World:
Chimpanzees

Dale Peterson and Jane Goodall

VISIONS
OF
CALIBAN

On Chimpanzees and People

HOUGHTON MIFFLIN COMPANY

Boston · New York

1993

For information about permission to reproduce selections from
this book, write to Permissions, Houghton Mifflin Company,
215 Park Avenue South, New York, New York 10003.

Library of Congress Cataloging-in-Publication Data

Peterson, Dale.
Visions of Caliban : on chimpanzees and people / Dale Peterson
and Jane Goodall.
p.   cm.
Includes bibliographical references (p.   ) and index.
ISBN 0-395-53760-6
1. Chimpanzees.   2. Human-animal relationships.   I. Goodall,
Jane, date.   II. Title.
QL737.P96P47   1993   92-38757
599.88'44 — dc20   CIP

Printed in the United States of America

Book design by Robert Overholtzer

BP 10 9 8 7 6 5 4 3 2 1

For Dwight ("Pete") Peterson
— D.P.

For Grégoire and all the other chimpanzees
suffering under our human dominion
— J.G.

Contents

VISIONS
OF
CALIBAN

Introduction

PROSPERO:

> Then was this island
> (Save for the son that she did litter here,
> A freckled whelp, hagborn) not honored with
> A human shape.

— William Shakespeare, *The Tempest* (1611)

DURING THE WINTER OF 1610–11, William Shakespeare created his vision of Caliban. Caliban is a "monster," simultaneously man and beast, and he serves as a central character in the last play wholly written by Shakespeare, a comedy called *The Tempest*, first performed in the fall of 1611.

In *The Tempest*, several Europeans engage in a social and moral struggle on a tropical island. The island includes one very troublesome original inhabitant, Caliban, enslaved by the most powerful of the Europeans, a man named Prospero.

Who or what is Caliban? We know that Caliban is shaped like a human. Before the Europeans came, Prospero declares, the magical island was "not honored with a human shape" — except, he is quick to add, for the shape of Caliban, the "freckled whelp," the unfortunate son of a witch and a devil. Caliban was there, honoring the island with his shape. He possessed a shape capable of honoring, itself an *honored shape*.

Every new production of *The Tempest* creates a new vision of Caliban. He has been variously portrayed as a primitive man, the missing link, a noble savage, a natural man, a representative of oppressed Third World peoples, and so on. The play's cast of characters describes him as a "savage and deformed slave," possibly implying that Shakespeare intended his "monster" (a word repeated some forty times in the play) to be fundamentally human, perhaps debased by inhumane treatment at the hands of the Europeans. To be sure, the Europeans treat Caliban like an animal, yet he can speak, just like a person. And he experiences dreams and visions, just like a person. Our usual vision presumes that Caliban *is* a person. But, of course, it is possible to possess a human shape without actually being human, and the play's text is finally ambiguous about whether Caliban is an animalized human or a humanized animal.

The newly arrived Europeans dominate the play's social action, but that "freckled whelp" Caliban dominates the moral action. Caliban, though possessing the honored shape, nonetheless endures as an abused and despised lost sibling of humankind, huddled beyond the edge of humanity's moral island.

I first crossed paths with Jane Goodall during the early 1970s, when she was a professor at Stanford University and I was a doctoral candidate there. We were headed in very different directions. She taught ethology. I studied literature. In a normal sequence of events we might never have met.

But in 1984 I read a newspaper article describing the impending extinction of a stunningly beautiful South American monkey, the muriqui (sometimes called the woolly spider monkey). The largest monkey of Central and South America, once a common species in the once vast Brazilian Atlantic coastal forests, the muriqui had been reduced by the time I read that article to perhaps three hundred fifty individuals. I had never thought much about extinctions before then, had never conceived of a species diminishing to such a small number and fragile state. I was horrified, and as a result I set out on a journey of body, mind, and soul that led me to study primates and tropical forests in scientific libraries and to travel by myself around the world searching for endangered primates in their forest habitats. I found monkeys in southeastern Brazil and the Amazon, in West and East Africa, and in India; gorillas in East Africa; lemurs in Madagascar; gibbons in Southeast Asia; orangutans in Borneo. And I wrote a book about the subject, *The Deluge and the Ark*. What I learned from that study and from those travels is both simple and terrible: we are killing the planet, and we are extinguishing the most wonderful forms of life and consciousness that share the planet with us.

Chimpanzees are an endangered species from the order of primates, and while working on *The Deluge and the Ark*, I briefly considered including them in that book. But chimpanzees, so complex, so thoroughly studied, so hauntingly close to human, require a book of their own; and to write such a book, I needed the collaboration of an expert. So it was that Jane Goodall and I crossed paths again, and this time we were proceeding in the same direction. We decided to co-author a book about the relationship between chimpanzees and people, a book that would touch on both the conservation situation of chimpanzees in the wild and the ethical issues associated with our treatment of them in captivity.

I knew something about people, but what did I know about chimpanzees? I was forced to do some basic research. I spent three months traveling in Africa, scouting out the issues across thousands of miles in nearly a dozen countries on that continent, and I spent at least an equal amount of time investigating the particular circumstances of people and chimpanzees throughout the United States. In Africa I ran in panic from the crashing and rumbling of a spooked herd of forest elephants; I was warned away from stepping onto a very poisonous snake by the screams of wild chimpanzees; I returned home with malarial plasmodia swimming in my blood. But I discovered that the real dangers lurk back here in the temperate zone. People's treatment of chimpanzees and the other great apes in captivity arouses extreme passions and, moreover, is partly driven by powerful commercial interests. Probably a criminal element is involved in some peripheral aspects of my story. Certainly, major lawsuits have been directed at several others who have tried to tell parts of the same story I wish to tell. Early on, however, I resolved simply to seek the truth and to tell it precisely as I see it. I resolved to consider every issue with a mind as open as possible, and to approach with respect and compassion every person associated with the issues, regardless of stripe or gripe. It is true that I have omitted some names and disguised the identities of a few people I write about in this book, to protect them, and I have altered the details of one or two places — but with the exception of such occasional alterations I have written my best and most careful vision of what is true.

The Shakespearean connection arose when I began conceptualizing the story of people in Western cultures meeting chimpanzees. Long before Shakespeare's time, Europeans had discussed "apes" in their zoological literature, but what they meant by "apes" is not what we mean now. "Apes" then simply referred to some of the more human-looking monkey species, particularly the tailless Barbary macaques. Knowledge of the humanoid great apes may first have come to Europe during the late Renaissance, in 1607 to be precise, when an English sailor named Andrew Battell returned to England and began telling his amazing tales. Battell had been held prisoner by the Portuguese in Africa for several years; upon returning home at last, he described what he had learned about that new world and provided a very specific account of two sorts of half-human, half-bestial "monsters." Clearly, we recognize now, Battell was speaking of chimpanzees and gorillas.

The date of Battell's arrival in England, 1607, is interesting partly because it is framed by Copernicus' declaration of a new understanding of the universe (1543) and Galileo's famous confirmation of that idea (1632). While astronomy and the achievements of Copernicus and Galileo finally removed humanity from an isolated and splendid centrality in the celestial world, biology and the discovery of the great apes would begin to remove humanity from an isolated, splendid centrality in the natural world.

But 1607 is an interesting date also because it falls so close to the winter of 1610–11, when Shakespeare wrote his wonderful comedy, *The Tempest*, based on themes of exploration into the New Worlds and featuring as a central character a "monster" named Caliban. Was William Shakespeare's vision of Caliban inspired by Andrew Battell's reports of the African great apes? I have begun to believe it was, although the question may not be finally answerable or even important. What *is* important is that Shakespeare imagined with astonishing brilliance and foresight how people might behave toward a being they considered to be neither quite beast nor quite human. Eventually I came to recognize that *The Tempest* would provide a perfect template for the structure of this book. I realize that many of my readers will not have read or seen a performance of *The Tempest* lately, and I have tried to make all my references to the play self-contained and transparent enough that they won't need to.

When Jane Goodall and I first thought of writing this book, we conceived of it as a collaboration between two people with divergent backgrounds and approaches — Dale Peterson, who during recent travels into nearly a dozen countries in Africa and during extensive travel and research in the United States has asked some questions, and Jane Goodall, who after three decades of studying wild chimpanzees in Africa has reached some conclusions. Rather than pretend, as co-authors often do, that we were actually sitting in the same room and working furiously with four hands on the same keyboard, we decided to clarify that our collaboration was taking place over space and time, that we were actually sitting in at least two rooms and working furiously on at least two keyboards — and, more important, that we were grappling with our subject from differing viewpoints and with distinctive voices. Thus, we decided to emphasize whose voice is actually speaking, who is writing what, with the help of different typefaces: Dale Peterson's writing is printed in this typeface; *Jane Goodall's looks like this.* I expect the reader will soon adjust to this mildly unusual arrangement and ultimately find that the mixture achieves some satisfactory integration.

Certainly this book is more Dale's than mine. It is he who has done so much work and traveled so widely, watching with his writer's eye, scribbling in his little notebook, facing all the problems that beset the solitary traveler in Africa. It is he who has done the necessary reading and research, who has spent hour after hour setting his impressions and deliberations on paper. And his was the brilliant idea of weaving the various strands of this book together with the Shakespearean vision of Caliban. I have brought to the joint venture my long years of working with chimpanzees; my concern for their plight in captivity, which has resulted in so many visits to zoos and medical research laboratories; and my growing understanding of their situation in Africa gained from recent travels through East and Central Africa. During the time we have spent together, thinking through this book, we have realized how very closely our philosophies mesh. We have had no major disagreements. And so, whether the following pages appear in Peterson or Goodall typeface, they represent our joint opinion.

— Dale Peterson (in Cambridge, Massachusetts)
— *Jane Goodall (in Dar es Salaam, Tanzania)*

1 • Sounds and Sweet Airs

CALIBAN:
> *Be not afeard; the isle is full of noises,*
> *Sounds and sweet airs that give delight and hurt*
> *not.*

IT HAD RAINED during the night in Uganda, and in the early morning a mist moved in dense waves across the meadow and filtered into trees at the forest's edge. We had seen several chimpanzees yesterday feeding in a tree near the swamp. This morning Kevin wanted to look elsewhere. We entered a forest with water dripping from leaves and moss and ferns growing on trunks and limbs.

As we walked, I listened to water dropping from leaves onto leaves and to the relaxed and regular calls of two obscure birds: one whistling with pure tone a short and rising three-note do-re-mi, the other warbling in five notes. I heard a world of sounds beyond, calls and counter-calls of hidden insects and birds buzzing and grinding, twittering and chirping.

We walked, sat and listened, then walked some more. Kevin whooped once, and bodies went flying through the air, crashing into leaves: monkeys. He whooped once more, and we paused in silence for an answering whoop from the Ugandans, B.J. and Peter, who were also looking for chimpanzees. Nothing. An hour, perhaps two, passed. The mist burned off, and as the day's heat rose, we moved closer to where B.J. and Peter had gone into the forest.

We found the Ugandans at last, standing on a trail and looking up into a low tree. A large chimpanzee lay on his back little more than a dozen feet above the ground in a nest of folded-over green branches, lolling back, a sybarite in a saggy mattress. He turned his head and gazed our way. After a few moments he sat up, flipped over the edge of the nest, dangling for a moment by one arm, then dropped to the ground and walked slowly and silently on all fours down the trail, his rump swaying heavily as he walked. Following him, we soon came upon two other chimpanzees, both males. They walked along the trail in the same direction, slow and swaying, just ahead of the one we had followed. Then all three left the trail and entered a thorny undergrowth. We followed them, but they tucked themselves down low and rolled right into and through the undergrowth, while we, struggling and bethorned, hacked with machetes. We stopped, listening for a long time.

Then we heard a tremendous explosion — BOOM! — followed by a terrible screaming and wailing and tremulous moaning. Another BOOM! More screams and wails and moans. Then a double explosion — BOOM! BOOM! More screams, and then an orgiastic burst of hoots — hooooooo, hoooooooo, hoooooooo — rising higher and faster and louder, crescendoing into a terrific din of screams, followed by more explosions and more screams and hoots. A short list of possibilities passed quickly through my mind. The explosions weren't sharp and final like gunshots, but sounded more like the crashing of one solid object against another, as in a traffic accident — or perhaps the booming of a drum, someone pounding on a massive drum. Finally sense resolved confusion, and I knew what we heard: chimpanzees kicking and punching tree roots.

(The roots of some tropical forest trees grow high and wide, becoming large triangles of wood at the base, looking like fins of a rocket or buttresses of a cathedral. The day after this incident, I examined some tree buttresses and found them as thin as four inches, as thick as a foot, roots of solid green wood. I struck one with my fist and could barely generate any sound at all. I reckoned a sledge-hammer might turn such flanges of wood into vibrating drums, and I marveled at the power of these animals.)

The explosions and screams continued, and we navigated through the forest toward the sounds until we found a tree holding three quiet chimpanzees — no, four, I realized, as I noticed a tiny infant clinging to its mother. Sitting on a branch, the mother was plucking and eating leaves. A young chimpanzee, not yet adolescent, also plucked and ate leaves in that tree. An adolescent male was there, too, but he was on the move. Climbing, walking, swinging, using a branch as a pendulum, he left that tree and entered another.

As we observed these four, the explosions and screams continued

somewhere in the forest behind us; at the same time we heard movement in the trees and brush closer behind us, a crackling and rustling
through leaves and branches, and then we saw, high in the trees to one
side, a dark shape appear behind leaves. The shape emerged as a
chimpanzee, a big adult male, who stood upright on a branch perhaps
twenty-five feet above the ground, looking at us; soon a second adult
male emerged from behind the first and stood in the same tree. Pausing, they looked down at us with serious and shadowed faces, and then
began moving toward the tree with the feeding chimps. The feeding
tree was three trees away, and many of the branches in between
looked flimsy, but those two big creatures hardly hesitated.

The first one walked out as far as he could on a thin, now sagging
branch, holding onto his fragile perch with curled feet and grasping
toes, bracing himself with both hands on a higher branch; then he
reached far, far out with a foot, stretching his leg, and he wrapped
some toes around a thin branch of the adjacent tree, pulling that tree
to him with one foot, now both feet — and simultaneously pulling
himself to the tree, so that his body began tilting, feet first, tilting
until he was hanging out almost like a flag. He let go of the first tree
with his hands and threw his weight quickly onto the flimsy branch of
the second. That flimsy branch suddenly dipped way down and would
have broken or dropped him, I imagine, had he not within an instant
thrown his weight even farther toward the center of the tree and
clambered up into swirling branches and a small rainstorm of leaves.
The second male casually followed with the same feet-first procedure,
and from this tree they steadily made their way over to the feeding
tree.

More and more chimpanzees appeared from behind leaves, high in
the branches, and after a while I sat down beneath a tree filled with
chimpanzees, with chimpanzees in trees on either side, while eventually the booming and screaming from a hidden place in the forest
behind us ceased, and the forest itself became quiet, with only a minor
tooting and warbling of birds and the small sounds of chimpanzees
plucking and eating leaves, of twigs and husks and other detritus
dropping now and then, of leaves sometimes brushing against each
other with the dreamy sibilation of distant surf.

2 ✦ Man or Fish?

TRINCULO (seeing CALIBAN for the first time):
What have we here? A man or a fish?

ANOTHER TIME IN UGANDA, I watched several chimpanzees high up in the vast domed network of limbs and branches of a giant fig tree, and in some adjacent trees. One of the females was in estrus, her bottom swollen and pink as a result, and at least three males had been sitting around with erections sticking out. It appeared that the female had already mated with one of the males; the other two seemed to be quietly submitting résumés.

At that point, a fourth male, very large, appeared from some hidden green place in the higher outer branches of the fig tree. He climbed across those outer branches like a monkey, on all fours, and then, upon reaching a broad main limb of the fig tree, he stood up on his hind legs and presented himself as a horrific sight. The hair on his shoulders and back and neck bristled, making him look even bigger and more powerful than he was, and he walked down that branch upright, quite like a human, steadying himself as he walked with hands reaching into higher branches, and he burst forth with a parox-ysm of pant-hoots — noisily inhaling air, exhaling with hoots, faster, higher, louder, into a climax of fierce braying hoots merging into screams. While producing this extended sequence of noises, he walked down the branch to the tree trunk, perhaps forty feet above the ground, turned back onto another main branch and walked out again, then jumped into a nearby tree where a young female bystander had been situated. Screaming, she scrambled into another tree. Other chimps added to the commotion with a chorus of wails and grunts and screams, while this big displaying male clambered into an area of trees where one of the hopeful males with erections was sitting. There was no fight, no physical contact, but the hopeful male turned aside, the tumescence between his legs wilting, and the big newcomer then turned back toward the estrous female. His résumé was accepted.

1

If chimpanzees can be profoundly noisy, more typically they are very quiet. Humans, by comparison, can barely restrain themselves from vocalizing. I've several times walked through a forest with one or two companions, talking casually, and only by luck or someone else's skill discovered the silent, dark clump of an ape obscured by leaves or vines. They can be elusive. You can walk right under them, right next to them, and never know they're there. And if they decide to avoid you by skittering off into the underbrush through a tangle of vines and thorns, you'll likely see dark shapes receding fast and hear only a slight crackling that quickly dies.

Once, in Tanzania, three of us followed a young female chimpanzee up a ridge along a steep, switchback trail. My two companions, walking some distance ahead of me, were experienced ape trackers. One of them, a zoologist, had spent several months studying chimps in that very forest. Yet halfway up the ridge, just after she reached an abrupt switch in the trail, this young ape quietly squeezed off into the brush; her first two trackers, hot and panting, walked right by. By the time I reached that turn in the trail, the chimp had reemerged from her hiding place and was standing upright, silently watching the first two of her followers walk away — ready, I imagined, to follow them.

Chimpanzees are superb gymnasts in the trees. I have been amazed, watching them. They will run four-legged along a branch, like monkeys, and leap in a horizontal crouch, like monkeys. They will hang beneath branches and brachiate, swinging from branch to branch, like gibbons. They will stand upright, slightly crouched, and jump out and down, like humans, onto a lower branch or cluster of foliage. They will shinny fast up or down a thick tree trunk, like bears, hands and feet grasping widely on either side of the bole, then walk out onto a steeply sloping branch, walking on all fours perhaps, grasping with their feet, pulling up with their hands. They will change directions in an instant by spinning one-handed around a vertical branch or trunk, as if it were a pole. They will hang upside down if necessary, and dangle by one hand when appropriate. They will swing on a vine; use a convenient branch or small tree as a pendulum; create a temporary bridge out of three or four branches, each of which would be unreliable if used separately; make an instant and satisfactory decision when a thin branch breaks high above the ground. They are intuitive physicists, predicting with all necessary accuracy where a particular branch will drop and sway once their weight has been added at a particular distance from the fulcrum. A human gymnast of Olympic caliber may be capable of performing many chimpanzee routines, but with two major distinctions. Human gymnasts become fatigued within minutes, and they perform in stereotyped routines. Chimpanzees, by contrast, make instant and spontaneous decisions, and they carry them through with mastery for extended periods.

Have I mentioned nerve? Chimpanzees hardly hesitate before committing themselves to very difficult situations with unpredictable results, thin branches at great heights. I remember this: An adult female chimpanzee, a mother with a baby clinging to her belly, having spent some time in the top of a palm tree, decided to move on. She climbed down the cushiony cluster of fronds until, feet dangling loosely, she was hanging by both hands, grasping the slick ends of two palm fronds thirty feet above the ground. An adjacent tree, approximately the same height, was several feet to her left. She proceeded to move into that tree by shifting her weight, back and forth, back and forth, until she had swung far enough to reach a branch with one foot and then pull the tree closer. The event was unexceptional to her, but I remember it — this hanging of full body weight by grasping the slippery blades of two palm fronds — as a discovery of nerve.

These daring performances are possible because of the innate strength of chimpanzees and because they can grasp with their feet as well as with their hands. Chimpanzee strength must have been recognized from the time the first individual was taken captive, but it was not quantified until the 1920s when John E. Bauman of Augustana College in Sioux Falls, South Dakota, sought out caged chimpanzees and induced them to pull on a rope attached to a dynamometer. Suzette, an adult female of 135 pounds, with both hands scored a 1,260-pound pull on the dynamometer; a second time she scored, "without appearing to exert herself notably," a pull of 905 pounds.

Boma, an adult male weighing 155 pounds, rated 847 pounds with a single one-handed pull on the device! For comparison, Bauman tested seven male college students, most of them football players in peak condition, with the same equipment. They averaged 375-pound pulls with both hands. Five of the seven attempted one-handed pulls and averaged 175 pounds per attempt. If we match the average weight of the college students with the chimpanzee weights, pound for pound an obese and out-of-shape female chimpanzee, Suzette, was more than three and a half times as strong as human males in a two-handed pull. The unconditioned male chimp, Boma, in the one-handed pull, demonstrated himself to be nearly four and a half times as strong as well-conditioned human males, pound for pound.

Life in the forest demands strength for a variety of purposes. I am always impressed to see how an adult chimpanzee can reach out and, with just one hand, bend over and snap a great branch to add to the formation of a sleeping platform or nest, or to feed on fruits or blossoms growing at the end of the branch. As part of an intimidation display an adult male may pick up and throw, with apparent ease, a rock of more than four pounds — or he may hurl or flail a large bough. Each day the chimpanzees' muscles are used and developed as they climb trees and move from branch to branch. I suspect that a wild chimpanzee male in his prime would be considerably stronger, pound for pound, than a caged individual of similar weight — but even caged chimpanzees are astonishingly powerful.

In one respect humans are stronger, for while chimpanzees have extremely long and powerful fingers, they have small, weak thumbs. If a chimpanzee grabs your wrist, you can sometimes escape by twisting against that weak thumb. Otherwise their hands resemble ours. I remember when villagers found the newly dead body of an adolescent male chimpanzee near the northern boundary of Gombe National Park. They were so impressed by the chimpanzee's physical likeness to humans that, practicing Muslims though they are, the villagers decided to give him a proper burial. They were amazed at his eyelashes, his ears, his hands and feet, and the nails on his fingers and toes.

For all the similarities of hand and foot, there are differences, too. The nails are coarser than ours, and black. A chimpanzee's big toe operates like a human thumb: it is opposable, and therefore (as we have seen) the foot can be used like a hand for grasping branches or holding objects. When walking, chimpanzees place the soles of their feet on the ground, as we do, and the middle sections of the backs of the first three fingers. For this reason they are described as "knuckle walkers," and the parts of the fingers used in this way are calloused. The skin on the palm of the hand, usually black except in infants, is amazingly soft and warm to the touch.

Despite their small size, chimpanzee thumbs are opposable, like ours, and these apes can grasp small objects with great precision. They can pick tiny flakes of dry skin from each other's skin during social grooming. They can use little stems to fish for termites, inserting them delicately into tunnels in the nest. And in captivity they can learn to manipulate almost everything that we can — from keys for opening locks to pencils for drawing. To grasp and manipulate heavy objects, however, chimpanzees rely on the strength of their fingers.

2

When chimpanzees stand upright, as they do to emphasize their size in an aggressive display, or to see over a barrier such as high grass or brush, or to carry food in their hands, then the human quality of their form becomes most apparent. Standing upright, crouching slightly, looking across high grass perhaps, we discover these apes as the mirror to ourselves. Our eyes rise to a face: low forehead, big ears, bulging mouth, bridgeless nose, prominent ridge at the brow. And we look into eyes that look back with a steady and inquisitive fix. "Monkeys are threatened by the gaze of others," David and Ann Premack have written in *The Mind of an Ape*. "Apes and humans, in contrast, enjoy being the focus of attention. Humans regard being looked at as an honor, as proof of personal achievement. Far from averting its eyes, the chimpanzee appears to be asking the very questions about us which we ask about it as we gaze into its eyes."

The questions we ask tend to be fundamental. I recall that big chimpanzee in Uganda appearing from a hidden green place high in the giant fig tree, bristling his hair, staggering, swaying with strength, bursting into a paroxysm of sound, walking upright quite like a man along that great limb. Who or what is this being that touches two worlds, recognizably beast yet somehow approaching human — a pe-

culiar hybrid that, like Caliban, the despised slave of Shakespeare's
The Tempest (1611), repels yet intrigues?

In one of that play's most successful comic scenes, Trinculo, a
jester, stumbles upon the "savage and deformed slave" Caliban, who
is lying low and playing possum. Trinculo speculates: "What have we
here? A man or a fish? Dead or alive? A fish!" Caliban resembles a fish,
according to Trinculo, because he stinks like one. On further examination, however, Trinculo notes that this strange "fish" has "fins" that
look like arms. Indeed, the "monster" has legs like a man. So perhaps,
Trinculo thinks, perhaps after all he is not a fish but a native of the
island recently struck by lightning. Perhaps he is a man.

Man or fish? This anatomical and behavioral debate rages throughout the play. Caliban is at times described in human terms (albeit
uncomplimentary ones): he is a "villain," a "man-monster," a "mis-
shapen knave," and so on. Yet he is also a "tortoise," a "puppy-headed
monster," a "howling monster," a "mooncalf," and a "plain fish and
no doubt marketable." People often insult other people by describing
them as animals, but in the case of Caliban the hurled epithets are so
pointed and persistent, so fully woven into the play's broader tapestry,
that they move beyond mere insult into the realm of debate. The
problem might be stated this way: Is Caliban a man or an animal?

One approach to the Caliban problem is to see *The Tempest* as
Shakespeare's critical allegory of European imperialism. The "brave
new world" of the magical island is a marvelous representation of the
new world or worlds being exploited in Shakespeare's time. The Europeans of the play come to a rich wilderness island, conquer it with
superior technology, and enslave the native inhabitants. Yoking the
dual powers of technology and slavery, the Europeans transform this
wilderness into a productive garden. As for Caliban (whose name is a
variant of "cannibal"), he embodies the despised and abused slave and
thereby represents slavery, the buying and selling and fundamental
exploitation of non-Europeans by Europeans. His social brilliance and
verbal eloquence mark for any audience Caliban's heroic stature; but
for the European characters of the play, he is a "thing most brutish"
who stinks like a fish and can never be trusted. Slavery requires,
morally and psychologically, that a slaveholder dehumanize the slave,
and Caliban is the image of that dehumanization in progress.*

* At various times, Caliban has been played on stage as a besotted beast, a noble savage
(during the Romantic period), and the missing link (during the Darwinian half of the
nineteenth century and into the twentieth). In response to more recent intellectual

Without denying the rightness of that particular reading, I would like to imagine an alternate vision for Caliban. I would like to see Caliban as the humanized nonhuman, the despised ambassador from animal to man, the missing link seen and denied.

It is true that Caliban shares his tempestuous island with monkeys and that he worries that Prospero will magically transform him into an ape with a forehead "villainous low." But those primates belong to an Aristotelian zoology, closed before the opening of Africa, polished and antique, lacking any reference to the humanoid great apes of that continent: the chimpanzees, bonobos (sometimes called pygmy chimps), and gorillas. The "apes" mentioned by Aristotle, in fact, are not what we today would properly call apes at all. They were probably Barbary macaques, atypically tailless monkeys of Mediterranean Africa. Aristotelian zoology survived well into the Renaissance; Shakespeare used it in his play. Yet two centuries before he wrote *The Tempest*, the Portuguese were sending ships down the West African coast, ultimately marking two thousand miles of coastline with fortified settlements and trading posts and entering the territory of the African great apes. The Portuguese preoccupied themselves with ivory, gold, and slaves; but Andrew Battell, the Englishman held prisoner by the Portuguese in West Africa, returned to England in 1607 to provide for Europeans (in an account anthologized in 1625) probably the earliest detailed description of gorillas and chimpanzees. Battell described "two kinds of Monsters, which are common . . . and very dangerous. The greatest of these two Monsters is called, Pongo, in their Language: and the lesser is called, Engeco. This Pongo is in all proportion like a man, but that he is more like a Giant in stature, then a man: for he is very tall, and hath a mans face, hollow eyed, with long haire upon his browes. His bodie is full of haire, but not very thicke, and it is of a dunnish colour . . . They sleepe in the trees, and build shelters for the raine. They feed upon Fruit that they find in the Woods, and upon Nuts, for they eate no kind of flesh. They cannot speake, and have no understanding more than a beast."

Did Battell's "two Monsters" influence Shakespeare's creation of

---

fashions, Caliban has been portrayed as a prehistoric man and as the embodiment of sexuality. Peter Hall's 1974 production of *The Tempest*, featuring Sir John Gielgud as a forceful Prospero, gave Caliban a two-sided face: one side monstrous, the other noble. The vision of Caliban as a Third World victim of colonialism seems to be our modern, postcolonialist construction. It is a tribute to the brilliance of Shakespeare's evocative vision that many interpretations seem legitimate.

that "howling monster" Caliban? It is entirely possible. We know
Battell arrived in England three years before Shakespeare began work
on *The Tempest*. Freed from imprisonment at the hands of an exotic
enemy in an even more exotic land, Battell must have stimulated
significant public attention with his dramatic appearance in England.
We also know that Shakespeare consulted contemporary travelers'
accounts while writing the play, since, for one thing, reports and
letters appearing in England in 1610 that told of a remarkable shipwreck in the Bermuda Islands certainly influenced the language and
imagery of the play. The most thorough modern scholarship on the
possible origins of Caliban, Alden T. Vaughan and Virginia Mason
Vaughan's book entitled *Shakespeare's Caliban: A Cultural History*,
overlooks Battell's report entirely (even though that report suggests
the image of Caliban more particularly than any other), possibly because the only surviving version does not seem to have been published
until around 1625, in Samuel Purchas' twenty-volume encyclopedia of
explorers' narratives. That late publication date, however, tells us
very little about the earlier currency of Battell's account. In fact,
Purchas may have begun acquiring such narratives as early as 1604,
when, as curate, he took up residence in the vicarage of Eastwood, a
mere two miles distant from the flourishing seaport of Leigh on the
Thames. During Purchas' early years in Eastwood, he worked with
and for a second, better-known enthusiast named Richard Hakluyt.
Both Purchas and Hakluyt regularly sought out and talked with sailors
and sea captains returning from unusual voyages; both would have
been actively collecting travelers' tales in 1607. Either one would have
been eager to interview Andrew Battell and write down his fascinating
account in 1607 or soon thereafter.

How might Shakespeare have acquired a copy of the report? Hakluyt
had already distinguished himself as one of England's foremost collectors and publishers of such narratives. Shakespeare, an "apparently
avid reader of histories and travel accounts," would have been familiar
with much of Hakluyt's published collections. Since both men were
established literary figures in the relatively small city of London, and
since both men were interested in travelers' tales, Shakespeare could
well have known Hakluyt or at least known someone who knew him.
One has reason enough to imagine that materials Hakluyt acquired
(either directly or by way of his continuing association with Purchas)
but did not publish would still have been passed on to a famous

dramatist looking for stories about recent explorations into exotic worlds.

Whether we finally think of Caliban as an animalized human or a humanized animal, for the other characters of the play he lurches, anatomically and behaviorally, somewhere in between, a disturbing specimen of continuity between human and animal. The image of Caliban suggests that we are not alone, that we endure on an island-planet troubled, pestered, shadowed by a bestial double. And the chimpanzee, I will argue, has provoked for us much the same anatomical and behavioral debate that Caliban provokes in *The Tempest*.

3

In 1640 the first live chimp arrived in Europe, a gift to the Prince of Orange. England's first live chimpanzee was shipped from Angola at century's end, in 1698. He soon died, and was dissected in 1699 by a London physician, Edward Tyson, who described "a sort of *Animal* so much resembling *Man*, that both the Ancients and the Moderns have reputed it to be a Puny Race of Mankind." By 1758 the great Swedish botanist and taxonomist Linnaeus had acknowledged the strong anatomical affinity of humans and apes, as well as monkeys, lemurs, and bats, by placing them all in the same order of *primates*. Except for bats, which have since flown elsewhere, Linnaeus' original clustering remains. A century later Charles Darwin confirmed the general validity of Linnaeus' matchmaking by indicating that anatomy is history, that physical similarity suggests common descent.

All biologists now agree that Darwin's *On the Origin of Species* (1859) describes accurately a principle of genetic continuity linking all living things; but Darwin's later claim, in *The Descent of Man* (1871), that "there is no fundamental difference between man and the higher mammals in their mental faculties," has proved more problematic. The anatomical continuity between humans and great apes is clear, as it has been for some time. Even the brains are hardly distinguishable (though ape brains are smaller). But we have only lately begun to appreciate that the continuity between humans and chimpanzees extends well beyond mere physical structure and very deeply into the structures of behavior and mind.

*

It was the late Louis S. B. Leakey, paleontologist and anthropologist, who enabled me to fulfill my lifelong dream of working with wild animals in Africa and who gave me the opportunity to study not just any animal but the one most like us. When in 1960 I set off for Gombe National Park (in those days, Gombe Stream Reserve), paleontologists knew quite a bit about the appearance of early humans. Fossil skulls and limb bones, whole or fragmented, had been compared to those of modern humans, and comparative anatomists were able to map out the "honored shape," the form of flesh and sinew that had once clothed the fossil bones. The teeth of our earliest known ancestors and the patterns of wear on the teeth had been compared to those of modern animals. This comparison had yielded information about the diet of early humans. And of course many stone tools and other artifacts had been found that illuminated some aspects of their life.

But social patterns do not fossilize. For years Louis had wondered about the behavior of the people whose skeletons he sought, tirelessly, across the vast miles of their African birthplace. At the forefront of innovative thinking, he believed that understanding the behavior of modern apes would enable him to make informed guesses about the probable behavior of Stone Age humans. If we find behaviors shared by modern chimpanzees and modern humans, he argued, we can assume that those same patterns were present in the common ancestor and so, of course, in the earliest true humans.

That Leakey was far ahead of mainstream scientific thinking I discovered when I went to university. When, for example, I mentioned behaviors shown by the Gombe chimpanzees such as begging and embracing, I was told in no uncertain terms that while those patterns certainly looked like begging and embracing in humans, the chimpanzees were only performing a series of mechanical movements triggered by specific circumstances. Any attempt to compare the motivations underlying chimpanzee begging and embracing to human motivations was anthropomorphic. And the sin of anthropomorphism was to be avoided at all costs. At that time, only thirty years ago, it would have been impossible for me to write a dissertation on the mind of the chimpanzee. Animals, it was held, did not have minds; only humans did. It was the same when I wanted to discuss the personality of the different chimpanzees I was studying. Animals did not have personalities. Idiosyncrasies in the behavior of different individuals did occur, it was admitted, but such matters were seldom relevant and were best ignored.

I find it hard to imagine that those who espoused such notions really believed them. But ethologists were desperate to have their discipline regarded as a "hard" science, as opposed to a "soft" social science. Well and good when this meant more stringent methods of observation — the use of check sheets and time sampling as opposed to random note taking. Unfortunately, many of the attempts to improve the image of ethology were, and still are, made at the expense of the animal subjects. Experiments all too often are invasive and painful. Scientists have license to perform procedures on animals that in any other context would be condemned as unacceptable cruelty. As a scientific attempt to distinguish the innate from the learned nature of bird song, for example, hundreds of birds have been surgically deafened in laboratories. To determine facts about sexual behavior, male and female animals of many species, from rats to monkeys, have been injected with a variety of hormones, castrated, ovariotomized, raised in varying degrees of social isolation, and so on.

Many of these experiments have yielded little worthwhile information. For example, in the early 1920s Henry Nissen, a respected scientist from the original Yerkes Laboratory at Orange Park, Florida, kept an infant chimpanzee for two years with his arms encased in plaster cylinders. This was an attempt to discover if certain responses, such as scratching, or grabbing something to keep from falling, were innate or learned — Nissen believed he was preventing the chimp from learning those motor patterns. When after two years the animal's arms were freed, not surprisingly there was a good deal of muscle atrophy, and the chimp did not initially move his hand to push away objects poked into him. Was this any fair measure of whether such movements were learned or innate? I think not. Obviously, Nissen's chimp could have failed to learn such behaviors (suggesting that they were ordinarily learned, rather than innate), or he could have learned that doing such things was useless under the circumstances (suggesting that they could have been innate).

The list of torments inflicted on millions of animals of a whole variety of species in the name of acquiring knowledge would fill many pages and would not make good reading. It is not at all surprising that ethologists performing such experiments, like their colleagues in medical laboratories, found it convenient if not essential to believe that the subjects were merely bundles of stimuli and responses, mindless and quite without feelings. Unfortunately for the ethologists involved in such experiments today, it is becoming increasingly difficult to deny the fact that animals have minds and feelings, particularly the higher animals. And especially, as I know directly from my own life's work, chimpanzees.

The "hard" attitude of ethologists began to soften, I believe, in response to information collected from field researchers studying various species of primates during the 1960s. The evidence suggested that primate societies were extremely complex; the more we learned, the clearer it became that mechanistic explanations of sophisticated social interactions were often not appropriate. It became increasingly obvious that high levels of social intelligence have evolved in all the higher primates, not only humans.

The original observations of tool using (fashioning and using twigs for termite fishing at Gombe) sparked some controversy because they challenged one of the main criteria long held to differentiate "man" from "beast" — we could use and make tools, they could not. When I wrote to tell Louis Leakey about my first glimpses of this activity, he made his famous response, "Ah! Now we must redefine Man, redefine Tool, or accept chimpanzees as humans." No wonder this discovery was perceived, by some, as a challenge to our human supremacy. The termite-fishing behaviors ultimately suggested other intellectual skills. For example, after a period of rest a chimpanzee might first gaze in different directions (as though making up his mind what to do), then walk over to a clump of grass, pick a stem, trim it to a suitable length, and carry it to a termite mound. That mound might be a hundred meters or more away — and it might have been invisible when the chimp selected and trimmed the tool. These larger observations suggested that chimpanzees could conceptualize out-of-sight situations and make simple plans for the immediate future.

It is not surprising that a few scientific voices were raised in disbelief and belittlement when these and other examples of intelligent behavior were reported in the early 1960s. But the response of the "establishment" then was by no means as vicious as during the 1920s, when Robert Yerkes and Wolfgang Köhler published, independently, the results of their work on chimpanzee mentality. Both men insisted that chimpanzees were capable of reason, able to solve problems not just through trial and error, but also through insight — ideation, as Yerkes called it. Köhler related that his chimpanzee Sultan, when shown a fruit out of reach beyond the bars of his cage, sat and looked at it for a moment, glanced around as though seeking a handy tool to *extend his reach, then suddenly ran into a neighboring room to seize a stick that he obviously had noticed earlier in the day. A large segment of the scientific community was appalled by the interpretation Yerkes and Köhler placed on these kinds of observations. Indeed, the famous Russian physiologist Ivan Pavlov denounced Köhler's interpretation of the chimpanzee's behavior as "disgusting."*

Similarly, many scientists seemed initially outraged by the early published results of the language acquisition experiments conducted on chimpanzees. The very first attempt to teach a chimpanzee language failed. That was in the late 1940s, when Keith and Catherine Hayes tried to teach a baby chimpanzee named Viki to speak. Even after three years of training she could utter only four words, breathy exhalations that were almost unrecognizable — nor is that surprising, because the anatomy of chimpanzees' vocal apparatus makes it impossible for them to pronounce consonants. In the mid-1960s another husband and wife team, R. Allen and Beatrix Gardner, wondered whether it might not be easier to teach chimpanzees to use signs rather than words (especially since the chimpanzees' natural communication repertoire relies so heavily on postures and gestures).* The Gardners and their chimpanzee, Washoe, began a whole series of brilliant and rewarding studies on chimpanzee communication with human sign language.

There can be little doubt that the language work with apes has taught us a great deal about the working of the chimpanzee mind. And it is not just from the formal training and testing that we have learned. On one occasion a student who worked with Washoe happened to be reading a book by the fire on a chilly day. Apparently Washoe wanted to walk in the garden; she repeatedly produced the signs she had been taught to indicate her wish. The student paid no attention. Finally the chimpanzee, exasperated, approached her lazy human companion and, seizing the poker from the hearth, proceeded to lever his feet off the ground, one at a time.

During this same period other scientists became interested in whether chimpanzees could recognize themselves in mirrors, not merely as members of their own species but as individuals — whether, in other words, chimpanzees possessed self-awareness or self-consciousness. Washoe had already demonstrated the ability

---

* Robert Yerkes had wondered about this possibility too, but had never followed up on it.

when she spontaneously identified herself in the mirror, staring at her image and making her name sign. Of course, that account was merely anecdotal. But in the late 1960s psychologist Gordon Gallup, Jr., tested self-recognition with primates using a series of ingenious mirror experiments. He began with chimps and monkeys that were raised in laboratory cages but happened to be unacquainted with mirrors or other reflective surfaces. He exposed them individually, in isolation, to mirrors at varying distances from their cages, and he and his assistants monitored the animals' behavior from a hidden vantage point. Four young chimpanzees (two males and two females) were the first subjects in this test; they were exposed to mirrors for a total of about eighty hours during a period of ten days. Gallup found that the chimpanzees' individual behaviors during the first few days of exposure to the mirrors were almost entirely *social* — bobbing, vocalizing, threatening. The chimpanzees were acting as if the creature in the mirror was a member of their species, yet not themselves. After those first few days a remarkable change took place. The social behavior rapidly decreased and was replaced by unequivocably self-directed behavior. The chimpanzees began grooming parts of their bodies that could not be seen without a mirror; they began exploring their genital-anal areas with the help of the mirror, picking food from their teeth, picking at their noses, making faces, blowing spit-bubbles, manipulating wads of food with their lips — all actions directed to the self, yet done with the assistance of an image separate from the self.

Once his four chimpanzees had been exposed to mirrors for eighty hours, Gallup rendered them unconscious with an anesthetic and painted spots of an odorless, tasteless dye on the forehead and one ear of each ape. He did the same with six monkeys — two male and two female stump-tailed macaques and two male rhesus macaques — all of whom had been similarly exposed to mirrors over several days. All ten primates were allowed to regain consciousness in isolation, with mirrors placed before their cages, and they were secretly observed. What happened? The six monkeys looked at their own dye-spotted images in the mirrors, but continued to behave socially, as if they were looking at dye-spotted other members of their species. The four chimpanzees, however, upon regaining consciousness and looking at themselves in the mirrors, immediately found the red spots on their own foreheads and ears. They touched the spots several times, examined their fingers, and even in one instance smelled the finger.

Gallup concluded that he had demonstrated a "decisive difference between monkeys and chimps" and that "these data would seem to qualify as the first experimental demonstration of a self-concept in a subhuman form." We who are so used to mirrors, to recognizing ourselves in images, may find such self-recognition ordinary and unremarkable. Yet it can be argued that self-recognition in mirrors is evidence of a very sophisticated mentality. After all, self-recognition demonstrates the existence of a *self*, that remarkable sense of *I* that so powerfully and peculiarly motivates all humans.

When we come to a comparison of chimpanzee and human emotions, we may stand on somewhat shaky ground. Emotions are difficult to study, even in humans. If I tell you I am happy, how do you know that my feelings are like yours when you are happy? Equally, how do I know that because you tell me you feel sad, you feel as I do when I feel sad? Sometimes, of course, people show outward signs of inward emotions. If you smile, laugh, hug me spontaneously, jump up and down, I assume you are happy because I may do the same things when I am happy. Still, you do not necessarily feel exactly the way I feel, but it is reasonable to assume that the emotion triggering such similar responses is itself similar — particularly when these behaviors are shown in similar contexts: if we both act this way when we receive a letter with wonderful news.

When young chimpanzees smile, laugh, hug you, jump up and down, it looks as if they are happy. And these actions occur in contexts likely to trigger similar behaviors in human children. Is it not reasonable to suppose that the underlying emotions are similar? They may be identical.

There are, similarly, behaviors shown by humans and chimps alike that suggest unhappiness: crying sounds, drooping or puckering of the mouth, a certain look in the eyes. Expressions of fear are also very similar in humans and chimps — staring eyes, grinning, a need to hug someone. The hair of chimpanzees bristles when they are frightened, and they may defecate uncontrollably. Do we not talk about the hair rising on the back of our neck during extreme fear, and a certain "loosening of the bowels"? Given the dramatic similarities in physiology between ourselves and chimpanzees, particularly similarities in the brain and central nervous system, it seems absurd to suppose that the emotions underlying these similar behaviors are not themselves similar.

4

Culture, clothes, and civilization obscure our place within the natural world. History is marked by an amnesia about human origins and dependence. This great forgetting might be compared with an adult's powerful amnesia about infancy and very early childhood. Without photographs, without bronzed shoes, without the anecdotes of our parents and siblings, would we now fully believe who once lay in that cradle?

Although humankind has emerged from the rest of the natural world quite recently on the earth's calendar, we have been quick to forget and slow to remember. After tens of thousands of years of spoken language, approximately five thousand years of written language, five hundred years of printing, a century of electronic communications, a generation of computers, we take the human drama most seriously. Only lately have we begun to see that drama as it unfolds on the larger stage of biological history. Until recently the common presumption has been quite simple: the barrier separating humans from even the most interesting of other animals is uncrossable. A good deal of recently acquired knowledge now suggests otherwise. We now know that humans are very much part of the natural world and that our relationship with that organic whole converges as well as diverges. We share so much with the natural world; most particularly, we share with our nearest biological relatives, the chimpanzees, much more than we might have imagined even a quarter of a century ago. The great amnesia is penetrated by a realigned understanding.

As best we can determine, partly from the evidence of hundreds of "missing link" bones and skulls and partly from genetic comparisons, gorillas were the earliest to diverge from the ancestral African ape line. The ape line divided again, six million to eight million years ago, into two significant populations. One major group evolved into the modern chimpanzees and bonobos, a second eventually produced *Homo sapiens.* The divergences were probably at first geographical. A river, a line of mountains, perhaps some other physical barrier, separated expanding groups of the ancestral ape, physically preventing further genetic interchange. Thus the genetic definition of the various groups began a slow separation; environmental pressures would combine with genetic change to produce increasingly distinct populations.

The African apes now include three surviving species: gorillas, bonobos, and chimpanzees. Earlier populations of the protohuman line became extinct, but by about two hundred thousand years ago some were anatomically close enough to modern humans to be recognizably *Homo sapiens*. In spite of an impressively large brain, however, the *Homo sapiens* of two hundred thousand years ago may not have been much more remarkable than their ape relatives. Archaeological studies demonstrate that these early humans used crude stone tools, as had their ancestors for a couple of million years; but they had yet to develop handles for their tools, bows and arrows, fish hooks, rope nets, and so on. The cultural and technological changes that mark the rise of modern humans may have occurred later, perhaps with the evolutionary development of a larynx to provide the physical capacity for spoken language. The start of language, the development of a vast symbolic world to engage our mentality, may have been the start of our amnesia. The natural world became separate and gradually forgotten. Mother became Other.

Although a gap of at least six million years — the point of divergence between us and our nearest surviving relative, the chimpanzee — may seem vast, on the scale of evolutionary time it is not. Recent genetic studies demonstrate that our human gene code has diverged from that of the chimpanzee by less than 2 percent. We still share with this species more than 98 percent of our genetic heritage, which means that chimpanzees are closer to us than zebras are to horses. How strange, then, that we still think of chimps as very interesting dogs and still assign them the approximate legal status of mice.

A good measure of the power of an idea is the negation it engenders. Martin Luther declared himself to be mightily provoked by Copernicus and his new theories: "The fool will turn the whole science of astronomy upside down." At almost exactly the same time Shakespeare was placing dramatic flesh on his vision of Caliban (a vision that may have arisen in response to astonishing new reports from Africa), Galileo was gazing through his new telescope to examine craters on the moon and to peer more fully into the rest of the heavens. The Inquisition was peeved enough by Galileo's later *Discourse* to place him under house arrest and force him to recant — for Galileo had threatened the noble position of man at the center of God's universe. In a similar way, I like to imagine, Caliban excites a disgust worthy of Inquisitors among the tempestuous island's human visitors because he, brilliantly, monstrously, threatens to burst through the barrier between man and beast.

I like to see Caliban as a monstrous Engeco, slowly taking shape behind leaves, powerfully staggering upright along a branch high in a giant fig tree, or rising, numinous as a dream, from the dark and backward abysm of time.

3 ◆ To Snare the Nimble Marmoset

CALIBAN:
> I'll show thee every fertile inch o' th' island;
>
> I'll show thee the best springs; I'll pluck thee berries;
>
> I'll fish for thee, and get thee wood enough.
>
> I prithee let me bring thee where crabs grow;
> And I with my long nails will dig thee pignuts,
> Show thee a jay's nest, and instruct thee how
> To snare the nimble marmoset.

When I first went to study chimpanzees in Africa, little was known of their behavior in the wild. Henry Nissen's pioneering work in West Africa had yielded few data — partly because he stayed in the field for less than three months and partly because he was everywhere accompanied by a line of porters. A few anecdotes had told of chimpanzees using tools and eating meat. But science would not accept such tales. Even though Africans, particularly hunters, must have known a great deal about chimpanzees for a very long time, science was not interested in their stories either. Because most people believed that wild chimpanzees were very dangerous, the early scientist-explorers always traveled with guns. One nineteenth-century researcher even built himself a cage to sit inside while he looked out in safety at any apes who chose to approach.

So dangerous were chimpanzees thought to be that the British government in what was then Tanganyika would not allow a young English girl to go into the forest alone. I had to have a companion, they said. It was my mother who volunteered to accompany me and remained in my camp for the first four months.

In fact, my worst fear during those early months was that the meager amount of money that Louis Leakey had managed to obtain for me would be exhausted before I had made any worthwhile observations. Every time I got anywhere near chimpanzees they fled, terrified of the alien presence in their forest. I wrote many despairing letters to Louis. And he always wrote back, saying, "I know you can do it." This response made me feel even worse. Suppose I failed? I would not only lose my dream, I would let down my mentor as well.

That I did not fail was due in part to patience: I sat on open ridges, observing through binoculars, not trying to get too close, so that the chimpanzees gradually got used to seeing me. But it was one adult male chimpanzee (whom I named, because of the white hair on his chin, David Greybeard) who helped me to open the door into the world of the wild chimpanzee. He had a calm nature, and for some reason he accepted my presence long before any of the others. Almost every time that I got close to chimps during my first year in the field, David Greybeard was there. Sometimes he was alone, sometimes with one or more of his companions — reassuring them, when they would have run off, by his calm reaction to my presence.

It was David who provided me with two critically important observations, material that enabled Louis to obtain the money I so desperately needed — funding from the National Geographic Society for another year in the field. I made both of those observations nearly half a century ago, yet they remain vividly in my mind.

Once I stood at one of the peaks of Gombe, looking to the east across a receding series of hills, when I happened to see, about forty or fifty meters away, some chimpanzees sitting high in a big mbula tree. I recognized one of the chimps as David, and he was accompanied by a female and a youngster. Because I was a little higher than they were, I looked slightly downward through my binoculars as I watched an incredible scene unfold over the next three hours. The three chimpanzees in the tree held and manipulated a pink object — I soon realized it was a piece of meat — and they squabbled from time to time as they ate. David kept the best of the meat for himself, but on occasion would allow the female to bite from the carcass too, and at least once he actually handed her a small piece. The meat was probably a baby bushpig, already partially eaten; below those chimps in the tree were two adult bushpigs and three small, striped baby bushpigs on the ground. The pigs raised a fuss, snorting and charging toward the tree.

The chimpanzees above would rather serenely pull away pieces of the meat with their teeth, then would pluck leaves and stuff them into their mouths to chew with the meat — perhaps in the way we combine a piece of bread with juicy things we eat. A scrap of meat would fall out of the tree from time to time, and when that happened the juvenile chimp clambered down the trunk after it. Every time he did, one of the pigs would charge violently, and the chimp, screaming in response, would escape back up the tree. It was an amazing scene, and one had the sense that the pigs were enraged because the chimps had just snatched away one of their babies.

Not very long after that observation, I witnessed another exciting episode. Again, I believe, the chimpanzee David Greybeard allowed me to get close enough. It was October, when the rains had started after a long dry season, bringing their lovely, rich smell to the parched land. The new buds on the trees gave the distant hills a golden red tinge. Where there had been dry-season fires, the ground was black; new green grass and occasional flowers had begun to sprout up through the ashy blackness.

This time I was traveling from a peak into one of the valleys and moving through an area of fairly flat land of low bushes and trees. I saw one of the termite hills — a big, rather smooth, reddish-colored mound — and I saw a black object. When you're walking through the forest and woodlands in Gombe, you see so many black objects — tree stumps, small hollows, and so on — that you expect to be chimps. But in those days I always froze and looked through my binoculars. Indeed, this time the black object was a chimp, David Greybeard again. It took quite a long time for me to work around cautiously to a place where I could see better, and I tried to hide myself behind a bush. In retrospect, I believe David realized perfectly well that I was there; but I didn't know it at the time. Looking through a screen of foliage, I could see his hand moving with a piece of grass in it. I wasn't close enough to see the termites adhering to the piece of grass, as they do. I did see David drop that piece of grass, reach out to pick up another, and poke that into the mound. After he left, I went over. The pieces of grass lay on the ground, and termites were running over the surface of the mound. I poked a piece of grass into the termite hill, and when I pulled it out, some termites had bitten onto it and were clinging with all their might.

During none of that observation did I have a really clear view. It

wasn't until the next occasion, again with David Greybeard and this
time also his usual companion, Goliath, that I saw the tools being
fashioned: the leaves stripped, the ends bitten off.

Earlier, when I had been at Gombe for about two months, I was
visited by field biologist George Schaller, who had just finished his
pioneering study of mountain gorillas. As he left, he had said: "Well,
Jane, wild gorillas don't use tools and they don't eat meat. That is
interesting for those people studying human evolution. If you see your
chimps doing either of those things it will all be worthwhile." So when
I saw both I could hardly believe it! Of course, what I saw then has
since been confirmed hundreds of times; but I still feel deep gratitude
to David Greybeard, for it was he who gave me those first glimpses
into his remarkable world.

1

Caliban, desperate to foment a mutiny against his powerful master,
Prospero, offers allegiance and service to Stephano, the drunken butler. Caliban promises to kiss Stephano's foot and swear fealty. More
important, he promises not only to supply sufficient wood but to show
the butler "every fertile inch" of the island. Caliban offers, in short, to
deliver the knowledge necessary for survival on the island. He will
reveal the best springs, pick berries and catch fish, show where the
crab apples ("crabs") grow, dig earth nuts ("pignuts"), find the jay's
nest, demonstrate how to trap monkeys ("snare the nimble marmoset")*, and so on.

Caliban is the island's practical botanist and zoologist. He is an
expert, and his expertise becomes all the more significant as the
Europeans abruptly dismiss it and him. Stephano simply tells Caliban
to stop talking and keep walking. In a brief soliloquy later in the play,
Prospero dismisses Caliban as "a devil, a born devil, on whose nature
Nurture can never stick." That formula — *nature without nurture* —
succinctly summarizes what the Europeans think of Caliban. He is, for

* The word "marmoset" derives from the Old French *marmouset*, meaning a grotesque
creature. In Shakespeare's time, the word was used to describe monkeys then being
imported from South America; currently, marmoset refers to several species of small
South American monkeys.

them, entirely a creature of instinct. He is able to learn, perhaps, in a primitive and rote fashion, yet surely this "puppy-headed monster" cannot acquire complex knowledge or possess culture.

Nature without nurture. The formula reminds one of the traditional Platonic distinction between animals and people. Animals are infused with vegetative and sensitive souls, Plato asserted, but only people are lucky enough to have rational souls. By the mid-twentieth century, laboratory animals were doing all sorts of interesting things inside their cages. Yet laboratory studies are artificial situations; for "real" animals, really existing in nature, the Platonic distinction seemed to hold. Animals, it was thought, instinctually react to their environments; they cannot intelligently interact. Animals, it was thought, do not make or use tools. Animals do not acquire knowledge, in any sophisticated sense, and they certainly do not possess culture in any sense of the word. We had come to distinguish ourselves from the rest of the natural world as the sole possessors of *nurture* — of learned controls and habits stored in the cerebral cortex, of knowledge and culture.

Jane Goodall's discovery more than thirty years ago that chimpanzees were fashioning and using tools for termite fishing was one of a series of discoveries that have profoundly expanded our appreciation for the complexity of animal behavior and intelligence. We have learned, for example, that polar bears will pick up objects and throw them as weapons; they have been seen attempting to kill or capture lounging seals by hurling pieces of ice at them. We have discovered that sea otters swim and dive with stones tucked under their limbs. When they find abalone attached to rocks and difficult to dislodge, they may hammer the shellfish loose with their stones; if, back on the surface, they find the abalone shell hard to pry open, they will swim on their backs, hold shell against chest with one paw, and with the other paw smash stone against shell.

Even birds use objects as tools. Egyptian vultures break open small eggs by picking them up and throwing them onto the ground; they break open ostrich eggs by picking up small rocks and hurling them at the thick shells. Crows and herring gulls regularly open shellfish by dropping them from above onto hard surfaces. Some species of Darwin's finches in the Galápagos Islands probe into crevices for insects with cactus spines or twigs held in their beaks; sometimes they first modify the tool, making it shorter or breaking off awkward protrusions. Even among bird species that do not commonly use objects as tools, occasional creative individuals do. In the mid-1970s Steward Janes, climbing some rocky cliffs in the northwestern United States to inspect raven nestlings, was bombed with small rocks dropped by one of the disturbed parents. H. B. Lovell in 1958 reported the remarkable sighting of a green heron that dropped pieces of bread onto a surface of water and then caught fish that had been lured to the floating bread. The bird carried the bread from some considerable distance and dropped it in that particular spot, where the fish were; when the bread drifted away from the spot, the bird picked it up and brought it back. Ornithologist Greg Roberts described a somewhat similar case. A black kite he was observing dropped bread onto the flowing surface of a river, then perched above the bread and swooped down after crayfish began to probe the floating lure.

Hermit crabs take on empty snail shells for protection, after examining the shells' exteriors to determine their suitability. Furthermore, they sometimes will pick up sea anemones, which have protective nematocysts, and place them on their shells, thereby acquiring a stinging shield against predators. One marine crab species, *Melia tessellata*, plucks anemones from the sea bottom and will hold two of them forward, one in each claw, to threaten potential predators.

Entomologist Elizabeth McMahan has described the tool-using tactics of *Salyavata variegata*, otherwise known as the assassin bug, a species of predatory insect that inhabits the rain forests of Central and South America. The assassin bug likes to eat a particular species of termite. But soldiers of this termite species, though blind, easily recognize most predators by their distinctive odor and feel, and they will vigorously attack, spraying a sticky toxin produced by glands inside their heads. As a countermeasure, the assassin bug disguises his own telltale smell and feel by covering his entire body with crumbs of the termite nest material, scraped off the nest and adhered to his gluey body hairs. The assassin then positions himself at an opening to the termite nest, confuses the normally aggressive soldier termites with his glued-on camouflage, and undetected and unopposed reaches into the nest and seizes a worker termite. With a sharp mouthpart, the predator injects an enzyme that liquefies the worker termite's internal organs; he then sucks out the liquids, leaving the victim's exoskeleton intact. So far, so good. But the assassin bug has just begun. Now he takes the empty termite exoskeleton, pushes it back in front of the nest's opening, and jiggles it slightly. Normally, worker termites will eat the bodies of dead siblings as a way of conserving nutrients, so when this body shell is dangled before the nest, it becomes a lure. A worker grabs it — whereupon the assassin yanks the exoskeleton back out with the live termite still attached, then proceeds to devour the next victim, liquefying and sucking out its internal organs. The assassin may continue with this fishing behavior for an extended period, each time using the exoskeleton of his most recent victim as a lure to capture another. McMahan observed one assassin eat thirty-one termites in succession this way, although the average meal is more like seven or eight.

Only recently has Western science begun to accept just how sophisticated nonhuman animal behavior can be, even in the so-called lower forms of life. But we must be careful in our use of words such as "awareness" and "intelligence." For most of us, intelligence implies rational thought, the ability to cope with new situations and solve problems. There is a world of difference in the assassin bug's termite-fishing behavior and that of the chimpanzee. Impressive though the insect's performance may be, it is less flexible, more rigid and preprogrammed, than that of the ape. Which is hardly surprising if we compare the size and complexity of the brains of the two species.

Perhaps the most remarkable aspect of the chimpanzee's performance is that which I have already mentioned — the careful selection, even preparation, of a tool for use at a termite mound that is some distance away and out of sight. Sometimes the material selected needs no preparation — a grass stem, for example. At other times leaves must be stripped from twigs, narrow strips of bark peeled from thick stems, edges trimmed from a wide blade of grass. Some chimpanzees are very particular about the type of material they select, and it varies at different times, presumably in relation to the nature of the task. Some passages are wider than others; sometimes the termites are close to the surface, at other times much deeper down. There are individuals who will go quite a distance from where they are working to collect a special kind of material, even climbing into a nearby tree for pieces of vine. On these occasions they usually select several tools, taking back "spares" to be used when the current one becomes bent or frayed.

There are clear-cut differences in the termite-fishing performances of different chimpanzees; some are much better at it than others. They will be more careful about the selection and fashioning of their tools, or more patient, prepared to spend ten minutes or so searching for a productive tunnel in a mound that others reject after a cursory examination. Over the years the best termite fishers at Gombe have been two females, Pom and Gremlin. I still remember watching Gremlin work one particularly tricky mound. The termites were way down below the surface, so that only the longest tools offered any help. She persisted for well over an hour, and her tools got more and more remarkable. By the end she was using a piece of flexible vine, carefully stripped of all protuberances, that was at least 1.5 meters long. With skillful twists of her wrist and infinite concentration, she managed to insert at least two-thirds of this vine into the passage — and was rewarded with a crunchy mouthful. After she had moved on, I stayed behind for a moment. I picked up the same long tool and, using a technique as similar to hers as possible, undertook to put it into the same passage. Try as I would, I could not insert more than half of the piece of vine!

It is fascinating to see how infants gradually acquire termite-fishing skills. We know today that young chimpanzees, like young human children, can learn new behaviors by watching the performances of others, imitating that behavior, and then practicing. At first an infant simply plays around while the mother works — often getting in the way and having to be pushed gently aside. Then isolated parts of the performance appear in the child's growing repertoire of behaviors: stripping leaves from twigs; poking sticks (much too thick) into holes in the mound (not necessarily passages); investigating the heap, scratching at little holes with the index finger, sniffing the entrance; "mopping" at the surface of the mound with the back of the wrist, just as the mother does to gather up termites that have dropped from her tool; and, from about eighteen months old, occasionally eating one of the small worker insects, those usually discarded by the mother. Often, too, the infants spend time watching their mothers very closely.

By the time an infant is about two years old, the first real fishing attempts are seen. A proper tool — usually very short indeed — is poked into a proper hole. Sometimes, if the termites are close to the surface, the infant may succeed in catching one of the soldier termites with the big red heads, the kind the adult chimpanzee is actually fishing for. At first the infant is fearful of such a prize, for these soldiers have long, sharp jaws and a painful nip. Sometimes the diminutive fisher drops the tool with its clinging termite and flicks it away violently. Once a female infant held out her catch toward her mother, who was fishing nearby. The mother bent her head, picked off the termite with her lips, and continued working. Her infant continued too and soon caught another soldier. This time she picked it off and chewed it vigorously, her face screwed up, her sensitive lips drawn back in a grin of fear!

What intrigues me most about termite fishing is the sense that it is a traditional or cultural behavior. This "culture" would obviously differ from many examples of human culture if only because wild chimps do not have language; but it is still behavior resulting from nurture, not nature. It is a learned, not instinctual, activity in which the learning is transmitted from one generation to the next. As Caliban would pass on his knowledge and skills — the location of fruits and nuts and birds' nests, how to snare the nimble marmoset — so field scientists have begun to see that much of a chimpanzee community's tremendously detailed repertoire for survival, and much of the community's complex knowledge of its environment, is passed on as a tradition or a cultural heritage. Chimpanzees are cultural animals.

If chimpanzees truly possess cultural traditions, passed from one generation to the next through observational learning, we would expect that chimpanzee populations in different parts of Africa would demonstrate different tool-using techniques. Adaptive behaviors that originated with, perhaps, a chance performance by one individual in response to a particular environmental challenge (and these will differ from one habitat type to another) would become incorporated into the repertoire of the individual's community. And this is exactly what we find.

Chimpanzees in the Mahale Mountains of Tanzania fish for termites in much the same way as those at Gombe. So do the chimpanzees of the Mount Asserik region in Senegal, far away in the west of Africa. By contrast, the chimpanzees of Mbini (Río Muni) use stout sticks to acquire a meal of termites, utilizing these sticks to break open the termite mounds rather than as fishing tools. Chimpanzees in the Bossou region of Guinea occasionally capture termites by poking sticks into little holes in trees and pounding them up and down. Sometimes they acquire mashed insects this way! The technique is clearly inefficient, but it is used effectively to feed on sticky (and presumably tasty) resin from hollows in Carapa procora *trees.*

The Mahale chimpanzees employ a technique similar to termite fishing to capture tree-dwelling carpenter ants. A small twig is carefully poked into the narrow entrance of a nest and pushed gently in and out. When the ants swarm out, they are picked off with the lips or mopped up with the back of the wrist. One female was seen sponging up the ants with a handful of leaves — which is what a Gombe female once did to remove bees from the surface of their nest, late in the evening. The Mahale chimpanzees shove twigs into bees' nests in trees to extract honey, and on one occasion chimps in the Cameroons were seen doing the same. Although there are plenty of tree-nesting carpenter ants at Gombe, the chimpanzees there have not been seen to feed on them, with or without the use of tools. Nor have they been seen fishing for honey, though they do use sturdy sticks to enlarge the openings of underground bees' nests. The chimpanzees at Gombe regularly use long sticks from which the bark has been peeled to fish for the vicious biting army, or driver, ants. Plenty of these ants occur at Mahale, a hundred miles to the south, yet the chimpanzees there have not been observed to feed on them. But chimpanzees in Sierra Leone, far to the west, do eat these ants, using a technique similar to that practiced at Gombe. The chimpanzees of the Tai Forest in Ivory Coast, who also eat those ants, use much shorter sticks from which the bark has not been peeled.

Chimpanzee hunting techniques also vary from place to place, once again suggesting the importance of cultural tradition in chimpanzee behavior — although the apes are also, of course, responding to differing environmental challenges. Of particular interest is the difference in the hunting behavior in Gombe and in the Tai Forest. Christophe Boesche, the Swiss ethologist who has spent many years with the Tai chimpanzees, has collected data at Gombe as well.

It seems that wherever chimpanzees have been studied, monkeys of various species are the most commonly selected prey. The Gombe and Tai chimpanzees both hunt red colobus monkeys, but the hunting behaviors are distinctive. The Tai chimpanzees hunt in an organized group, with individuals taking on complementary roles. Some of the hunters act to surprise and drive the monkeys; others block potential escape routes; still others position themselves to capture the fleeing prey. These chimpanzees target adult monkeys, and have no difficulty in killing and tearing apart their prey at the conclusion of a successful hunt. At Gombe, where the forest is very different, where there is *much more tangled undergrowth, hunts seem more disorganized. There is an initial period of confusion as many chimpanzees rush in various directions after different monkeys, and although close cooperation is seen, it is mostly between adult brothers. The Gombe chimpanzees pursue infant and juvenile monkeys. Frequently mothers are captured, but then released after their infants have been seized. Unlike the Tai hunters, the Gombe chimpanzees have great difficulty in killing adult monkeys. The amount of meat acquired in a Tai hunt is therefore usually greater, which may explain why Tai hunters are often more generous in sharing.*

Most striking is the fact that Gombe chimpanzees, adult males included, frequently flee, screaming, when approached by aggressive adult male colobus monkeys. This response is unknown at Tai — Boesch found it hard to believe until he saw it with his own eyes at Gombe. The Gombe chimpanzees' method of hunting, with its initial period of confusion, is thus adaptive, since it often prevents the male colobus from forming a defensive group. When hunting baboons, incidentally, the Gombe chimpanzees show exactly the same kind of close cooperation as observed in the Tai hunters.

Like Caliban, chimpanzees are practical botanists, but once again their botanical knowledge and traditions vary from one community to the next. In Gombe, scientists have found that chimps recognize and eat a minimum of 201 plant types. Chimps in the Mahale Mountains, some 100 miles south of Gombe, contend with a different pattern of vegetation, and their diet includes at least 328 different plant species and subspecies. But the chimpanzees' traditional knowledge extends beyond merely recognizing what is good food and what is not.

Anthropologist Richard Wrangham, while studying the eating habits of chimpanzees at Gombe in the early 1970s, discovered another dimension to chimpanzee tradition that had previously been considered unique to humans. Wrangham's curiosity was aroused when he noticed that some chimps, some times, upon leaving their sleeping nests at dawn, would directly seek out certain plants. The plants were of a single species, *Aspilia pluriseta*, growing in six-foot-high bushes with bristly, spear-shaped leaves and yellow flowers. The chimps almost always sought the bristly leaves of this species at dawn, before 8:15 A.M.

The seeming purposefulness of their pursuit of these plants in itself was unusual. More remarkable was the fashion in which the apes selected and then ingested the bristly leaves of *Aspilia*. With elaborate care they selected only young leaves of a certain length, visually inspecting them and even, on occasion, touching and tasting without finally consuming them. (Wrangham observed chimps closing their lips around a leaf still on the bush, holding leaf in mouth for a few seconds as if tasting it, then sometimes abandoning the leaf without removing it from the plant.) When an *Aspilia* leaf was chosen, the chimpanzee would ingest it, again in remarkable fashion. "They picked each leaf individually," Wrangham told me one rainy afternoon in Uganda, "and took it into the mouth on the tongue, left the jaw slack while the mouth was closed, and then rolled it round and eventually swallowed it. Well, these are hairy leaves, and can you imagine just swallowing them?" Chimpanzees ordinarily eat leaves by chewing them, as one would expect. In this case the apes were not chewing at all — they were swallowing the leaves whole, with some deliberation. Normally, when Gombe chimps eat leaves, they ingest them rapidly (approximately thirty-seven per minute for comparable-sized leaves of another genus), but Wrangham found their ingestion of the *Aspilia* leaves to be remarkably slow (about five per minute). That they were swallowing them whole rather than chewing them became even more apparent when Wrangham examined the apes' dung and found *Aspilia* leaves still intact, even retaining their original color, the surface damaged only slightly by minor folds. Further investigation turned up a total of five *Aspilia* species in the Gombe habitat; the apes seemed to be selecting and ingesting two of the five. (When Wrangham later contacted scientists in the Mahale Mountains of Tanzania, he discovered that the chimpanzees there were also swallowing certain *Aspilia* leaves whole, including those from at least one species not occurring in the Gombe habitat.)

The fact that the leaves were not chewed like ordinary food strongly suggests that their value was not strictly nutritional. That the leaves were folded, a process that ruptured some surface cells sufficiently to release surface chemicals, suggests that the chimps were seeking medicinal or euphoric benefits — to get well or high. We now recognize that many animals in surprising ways take advantage of the nonnutritional chemistry around them. Monarch butterflies eat cardiac glycosides and thus become noxious to potential predators. Starlings weave into their nests green leaves with high concentrations of phenolics, thereby discouraging various pathogens. Yet such activities do not necessarily require reflection, self-awareness, or self-diagnosis. In the cases Wrangham was noticing, it seemed that the few chimpanzees who on rare occasions were forgoing their ordinary routines to seek out an extraordinary leaf and consume it in an extraordinary fashion were doing so very deliberately. They were, it appeared, diagnosing and then treating themselves, doctoring themselves.

Wrangham was unable to find a plant chemist with sufficient expertise to analyze samples of the *Aspilia* leaves until 1985, when he became acquainted with Eloy Rodriguez of the University of California at Davis. Rodriguez found a sulfurous red oil in the leaves; the oil yielded a chemical he identified as *thiarubrine-A*. This chemical had been noted previously to occur in plant roots, but never in leaves; Rodriguez was astonished. "It was like finding water on the moon," he subsequently told a journalist.

He had isolated thiarubrine-A on a Friday, April Fools' Day. That weekend Rodriguez was visited by a colleague and friend, biochemist Neil Towers of the University of British Columbia. In casual conversation Rodriguez asked Towers what he was up to. Towers was sorry, but he couldn't say. His lab had just discovered something so exciting that they were all pledged to secrecy, in writing. But, Towers wanted to know, what was Rodriguez up to? Well, Rodriguez said, this fellow Wrangham has sent some plants. He thinks there's something funny inside. I've just extracted this red oil, and here's the formula for it.

Towers couldn't believe it! Rodriguez' thiarubrine-A was identical to the chemical that Towers' group had just extracted from the roots of a plant, *Chaenactis douglasii*, used as a medicine by native Canadians. The plants were from entirely different genera and families, but the chemical was identical. Towers had begun investigating the pharmacology of this chemical, and he already recognized how important the medicine might prove to be.

The following Monday Rodriguez telephoned Wrangham in Ann Arbor with the news. Within an hour Wrangham was in the library, reexamining the published literature on East African medicinal herbs. As it turned out, seven *Aspilia* species were used by local East Africans as medicine. *Aspilia* was a remarkable medicine in the indigenous pharmacopoeia. It ranked in the top 1 percent for a number of different medicinal uses; altogether, *Aspilia* leaves were included in nineteen different treatments — mostly for topical and stomach ailments (wounds, burns, rashes, ringworm, conjunctivitis, stomach worms, and general stomach pain). *Aspilia* roots were featured in an additional twelve local treatments not associated with topical or stomach ailments (including snakebite, whooping cough, back pain, cystitis, gonorrhea, and inadequate milk flow in nursing mothers). Of the seven *Aspilia* species known to be used by local Tanzanians, Wrangham discovered, four grew in chimpanzee habitats at Gombe and in the Mahale Mountains; at least three of those four were already being swallowed whole — like pills! — by the chimpanzees.*

Rodriguez and Towers went back to their laboratories, this time as collaborators. They have so far found thiarubrine-A to be remarkably effective in killing fungi, nematodes (wormlike parasites), bacteria, and certain viruses, including some related to the AIDS virus. Thiarubrine-A could become a potent anticancer agent.

Wrangham went back to Africa and has discovered, with the collaboration of another anthropologist, Kevin Hunt, that chimpanzees in the Kibale Forest of Uganda swallow whole the leaves from two different plant species unrelated to the medicinal *Aspilia* of Tanzania. Only one of the Ugandan plants has been positively identified so far, *Rubia cordifolia*; its leaves are so valued by the local BaToro people as a cure for stomach ailments that they keep it growing in their gardens in order to have a ready supply. Meanwhile, other researchers in the Mahale Mountains have begun searching for more items in the chimpanzee pharmacy. The results so far are intriguing. Two scientists have described an obviously ill female chimp who began sucking juice from the pith of *Vernonia amygdalina*, a plant not normally eaten by chimps but commonly taken as a medicine by people living in that region. This same chimp was found, another time, to consume *Lippia plicata*, a plant local people often use to treat stomachache.

Only three chimpanzee communities have been studied so far to determine their use of plants as medicines. In each of the three, researchers have found at least two *new* plant species used pharmaceutically. Chimpanzees in Africa are headed for extinction, but

---

* The important action might not be swallowing the leaves whole, but rather moving them around whole in the mouth briefly before swallowing. The chimpanzees could be absorbing active pharmaceuticals buccally, that is, via the mouth and cheeks, before the chemicals could be neutralized by some event or environment in the stomach, such as a low pH. This technique would be identical to a preferred method for administering human medicines such as nitroglycerine and to a common method for administering nicotine (via chewing tobacco).

they still endure in many different areas within vastly different habitats; a very large number of chimpanzee communities have not been studied at all. "Scattered throughout African forests," Wrangham believes, "you may find scores of local chimp medicine cultures."

2

Chimpanzees in West Africa, west of the Sassandra River in Ivory Coast, use pieces of flat stone and wood as anvils. They hammer on these anvils with specially selected, large, often rounded stone hammers and also stick hammers. This stone-tool culture persists among chimpanzee communities from the Sassandra through Liberia and Guinea as far west as the Moa River in Sierra Leone. Yet this tradition varies in detail from one locality to the next. Altogether, the nut-cracking chimps of West Africa use their hammers and anvils to crack hard nuts of six varieties — but in every area where this practice has been studied, the chimps seem to prefer a different menu.* Why? The differences could very well result solely from ecological factors — availability of trees, quality of nuts, and so on. We don't know yet. Nonetheless, the differing nut choices of chimps in different parts of West Africa could be at least partially cultural, artifacts of tradition.

Africans at the edge of the great Tai Forest, near Ivory Coast's border with Liberia, used to claim that a tribe of forest-dwelling pygmies lived there. The pygmies specialized in cracking nuts, they said, and if you went deep into the forest, you might find them. The French colonial government, wishing to leave no rumor uninvestigated and no tribe unsubjugated, sent a military detachment into the forest to "civilize" the nut-cracking pygmies. They found no one.

I went into the Tai Forest, and I lay down one night in the camp of Swiss scientists Christophe and Hedwige Boesch, listening to noises that were mostly rhythmic — ten thousand insects in three dimen-

---

* My comments on chimpanzee stone-tool culture are based on recent work by Paul Marchesi and Christophe Boesch (in press). Chimps in the Tai Forest of Ivory Coast crack and eat *Coula edolis* (African walnut), *Panda oleosa,* and *Parinari* (gray plum) nuts. *Panda* nuts are very hard, harder than any nut currently harvested by human hunter-gatherers; to break them, Tai chimps use only stone hammers, never wood, and the hammers weigh as much as forty-five pounds.

sions — and fell asleep imagining myself in the midst of some great living, breathing body. Every few minutes I was startled awake by a random and mysterious motion in the leaves, or by a call or a series of hoots or shrieks or agonized and strangulated cries.

It was still dark when Christophe Boesch and I left camp in the morning. We walked into a pitch-black forest, blinking our flashlights once in a while to find our way, stumbling along dark trails for perhaps half an hour before we stopped walking and sat down on a log. Chimps were in the trees above us, in their sleeping nests, and we listened to them wake up. They made a few brief, sleepy, half-hearted hoots — uh-hooo, uh-hooo, uh-hooo — and a few low cries and inhale-exhalations. We listened to rainfall noises of these chimps urinating from high in the trees, and then we heard brief splashing in the leaves, as some of them jumped from one tree to another. After a while we heard some real hooting, then a crackling of leaves and branches above us. We sat there on the log as dawn moved into the forest, and we looked up into the trees towering high above us and watched the apes, dark shapes moving, trees and tree branches waving with their weight, while detritus dropped into our faces and hair. We listened to more splashes in the leaves, a coughing, then a mild and brief screaming off to one side: wraaaa wraaaaa wraaaaa! I saw one chimp perhaps eighty feet above us, behind a screen of leaves, squatting on a branch and eating leaves, plucking them with his hands. But mostly I just saw moving leaves high up and once in a while a dark, humanlike shape behind pale green leaves before speckles of a pale white sky.

They began leaving their nests and descending. The dark shape of a female leapt into a tree and climbed down it. A young male climbed into the top of a thin, polelike tree that sank, bent down with his weight — and he rode it down calmly, as if it were his private elevator. I heard some screams, a brief chorusing of calls, some grunts and rustling and falling of debris. High above, I saw a chase: a chimp leapt from one tree to another at sixty feet above the forest floor and clambered down the second tree, and a second chimp chased the first. We heard the thumping of feet and hands on branches as the chase progressed and moved out of our vision. We saw, a few minutes later, two big males sitting side by side on the ground. "It's the alpha male," Boesch said, referring to the larger of the two, and soon this one began swaying, rising slowly, then inhale-exhaling until his voice was rising into hoots. He stood up, smashed through some low vegetation, and dove into a rotten tree that disintegrated and crashed into a hundred flying pieces — but not before this displaying male, without losing balance or pace, had already burst into a green cluster of leaves and vines and then jumped into a tree right above us.

There were other chases, screams and squabbles and noisy displays, even some brief grooming, as the dozen or so chimps I was able to see in our part of the forest gradually began their day. Boesch said that nearly fifty chimps belong to this community, though he has never seen them together at one time. Chimpanzees live in what has been called a *fusion-fission* social structure. With remarkable fluidity, the chimps of any community will gather into large groups or splinter into very small units, one or two or three individuals. In fact, sometimes during this day we followed (so far as I could see) only a couple of apes; other times we followed, indeed became part of, a moving band of perhaps twenty or more.

The disorganized start to this day became even more so when one of the chimps, walking along the ground with several others, suddenly stopped, leapt directly backward, and began crying out strangely. The rest of the group stopped too and began screaming. The chimps seemed to be looking at one particular spot in the underbrush. Some of them climbed trees to get a better look. Eventually they stopped screaming and looking at the spot and began moving again, so Boesch and I, walking a few yards behind the chimps, were able to move up to that spot and see for ourselves. I saw nothing but the olive and tan chaos of dry sticks and grass and dead leaves. For at least thirty seconds that was all I saw, until suddenly the chaos reorganized itself in my vision as pattern: a flattened, dully gleaming weave; a reptilian tessela- tion within leaves and grass. "Rhinoceros viper," Boesch said. Deadly.

As the morning developed, as the forest became warmer and brighter, we progressed from food to food with regular resting and some male displaying and juvenile playing in between. The rests were a pleasure, actually, as we all sat or lay down together, two people and roughly a half-dozen or a dozen chimps. The chimps would sometimes turn to each other and start grooming, one scratching away at the other's back, plucking into the fur, holding up discovered particles to examine them, smacking lips or clacking teeth as if to emphasize the intensity of this procedure. Meanwhile, from other parts of the forest, we would regularly hear the hooting or buttress thumping of other chimps from the same community, moving with different compan- ions.

When our chimps rested, they did so with abandon: I remember watching one lie flat down on the forest floor, both arms thrown behind him, curled back so that his hands met just above the top of his head — it was a dancer's pose. A female near us lay on her back, yawned a huge yawn, flung her arms behind her, and lifted both legs straight up to prop her feet against a branch just above. Farther away, a lying-down male suddenly sat up and looked at us, at Boesch and me, with some intensity. What are *these* apes doing here? he may have been asking himself. Then, having decided not to worry about it further, perhaps, he lay down again. Once one of the males in our group was lying back, arms spread out, as still as sleep — but a single hoot in the distance seemed to startle this guy awake and send him screaming and running on all fours into the bushes. He leapt across a fallen tree, then sat down and scratched himself, slowly, as if in thought.

There were mercurial shifts in mood. It seemed as if some chimp would look at the wrong male with the wrong expression, and then there would be swaying, hair raising, inhale-exhalations, working up to a frenzy, explosions of noise and tearing through the bush, screaming, charging around — but soon enough peace would return.

Sometimes the chimps would take to the trees, very abruptly. A big chimp might ascend a hundred-foot tree in ten or fifteen seconds; another might climb right up a hanging liana for forty feet before leaping over into a tree; we would be left looking up, leaves spinning down and falling into our faces, sometimes big branches crashing down.

Late in the morning I heard a noise, a thumping, a light hammering. I looked down a brief slope to see an adult female squatting at the base of a big tree, hammering with a reddish piece of log, both hands lifting up and dropping down one end of this log. I watched her stop hammering and pick up some white fragments and place them in her mouth and eat them. She was cracking nuts. She put another nut in place, on top of a root, and began hammering again. She was squatting before the root anvil, both hands lifting up one end of a three-foot log, and hammering away. The log worked like a lever, one end resting on the ground, the other moving up and down as the chimp hammered. The sound had a distinct pattern — a series of thunking taps that continued until the nut cracked: thunk thunk thunk thunk thunk thunk crack! Then she would stop, put down the log hammer, pick through the pieces, place the nutmeat in her mouth, put another nut on the anvil, and begin again: thunk thunk thunk thunk thunk thunk crack!

Soon I heard more hammering, and I looked over to see on the other side of the tree another female, this one with an infant clinging to her breast. In a third area, I heard more labor — thunk thunk thunk thunk thunk thunk crack! I heard hammering at a fourth site and saw a big chimp facing away from me, squatting at a root anvil like the others, lifting and dropping one end of a log, bent intently over the work, pausing to pick through and chew nut fragments before resuming work with the same tempo and pattern as the others: thunk thunk thunk thunk thunk thunk crack! Sometimes the chimps would get up from their work, walk around under the tree, gather more nuts, and take the new supply back to the anvil. But eventually they ran out of nuts, and finally Boesch and I were left at the top of the slope by ourselves.

These were *Coula* nuts, Boesch informed me; about 85 percent of the time chimps use wood hammers to break *Coula*. He pulled three green, golfball-sized nuts out of his pocket and handed them to me. "Now it's your turn," he said. We walked down the slope to where the chimps had been, and I squatted beneath a tree and picked up the log hammer. It was an irregular piece of hard wood, perhaps three feet long and quite heavy. I found a root with a worn dent in it, placed a nut in the dent, and with both hands lifted the heavy log on one end, hammering down just as I had seen the chimp do: I went thunk, thunk, and after about the sixth blow, the nut went crack! The nut was broken. I reached down and pulled out a piece of the white meat and ate it. It tasted rather like dry coconut, slightly sweet, tasty and satisfying.

I tried the second nut, but it wouldn't crack. Finally, after several frustrating attempts, I threw it away and placed the third nut down. "Typical infant behavior," Boesch said coolly. "That's just what the chimp infants do when they're first learning. If it doesn't crack, you blame it on the nut and try another. The nut is not the problem. It's your technique. Aiming is very important."

But the chimps were on the move again, so we left the log hammers and anvils and caught up with them; they walked at a steady pace for some time, pausing to climb this tree, eat those leaves, drink that water. When they were tired of moving, they rested. At one of our resting spots, I watched a shaking bush with laughter coming out. The laughter emerged irregular and breathy, infectious; it continued for perhaps twenty minutes. There was a whistling bird here, lots of motion and splashing in the leaves — and two chimps, juveniles I imagined, laughing and laughing and laughing. The laughter was becoming more and more frantic. It sounded like a fast sawing of wood: whuuu, whuuu, whuuu. A whole area of branches and leaves, an entire bush, shook as the laughter coming from inside became frantic. An arm, a head, an ear, a body would appear and disappear into the bush.

We traveled again, juveniles riding piggyback on their mothers. We entered a small swamp where the chimps drank and then ate the pith from the leaf stem of a knee-high plant with oblong green leaves. A male stood upright and gobbled leaves; he was perhaps three and a half feet tall. We watched a brief mating, the female on the ground on all fours, the male behind her, quiet. A bird went valvoline valvoline valvoline. Somewhere a hornbill played a buzzy kazoo, then flew away with noisy feathers.

A male chimpanzee, walking upright on two legs and revealing an urgent erection, chased a female — who fled.

We stopped at a place in the forest where a massive tree had fallen, breaking open the canopy. Sunlight poured through and the fallen trunk provided a pleasant place for several of the chimps to sit, sprawl, loll, nap, groom, and be groomed. Around the fallen tree several more chimps lolled about, some on the forest floor, some in trees. Once I counted ten chimps on the log, and perhaps another ten in the forest around the log. The adults seemed mostly to be napping. Two juveniles were wrestling and tumbling and laughing in an open area near the log; later I watched one big male with a gray splotch on his back play and wrestle and tickle a toddler — a one-year-old. The big male chased him around and around a tree, then tickled and tickled and tickled the toddler, who laughed desperately. Up on the fallen log, one young male was blissfully sacked out, knees up, eyes closed, arms flung back into a remarkable concave fit around the big trunk. The light fell across his body, and he seemed to keep his face pointed toward the sun, as if working on that tan. There was also grooming going on, on the log — one male bent over in a salaam position, head in hands, rump high, being groomed by a neighbor.

After perhaps an hour, the siesta was over — abruptly, it seemed to me — and the group started moving with some unanimity and cohesion. We walked fast, and when we entered parts of the forest where it was relatively open, I was surprised to see how many chimpanzees were in our group. We crossed an invisible border. "They've entered the territory of the neighbors," Boesch commented. Soon we came to a gargantuan tree, towering, with a giant crown high above us and perhaps twenty or thirty great lianas hanging down like cables. The chimps, hooting and screaming, climbed straight up the lianas, which swayed softly, and about eighty feet up entered the crown of the tree and disappeared from sight. All I could see then were old leaves falling down and dust passing through beams of late-afternoon sunlight.

Time passed. We continued moving. It seemed as if at some point we were joined by more members of the group, and finally I felt in the midst of a mass migration — all around us chimpanzees, male and female adults, youngsters, infants, were on the move. We came at last to a big area of several nut trees, and presently half the apes started cracking nuts with wood hammers on wood anvils. Soon there was hammering all around us, a thunk thunk thunking from many directions at once. To the right, thirty-five feet away, one laborer with a short log hammer lifted it wholly into the air before crashing it down on a nut and anvil: both hands in the center of the log hammer, lift and slam, lift and slam. Under the tree right in front of us, three different apes worked at three anvils, hammering away. And to the left, as well. Behind us another used a log hammer, lever style.

A young chimp tried to crack open nuts using a fallen tree as the anvil. He kept knocking the nut off — couldn't quite get the hang of it. A second juvenile came over, pushing the first one away. He couldn't get the hang of it either.

The whole forest was filled with the industrious sound of hammering. By then it was late afternoon and the light was fading. I turned to watch a mother play with her baby, nibbling on his toes, wrestling with him, looking into his little face with a goofy bliss. In another spot three young adult females surrounded and played with an infant, all four of them hanging in a low cluster of vines and branches. One of the adults was below the baby, the other two above it, and all three seemed to be sharing it, tickling and kissing the infant. I saw familiar expressions on their faces, absolutely familiar: human expressions, Madonna-like expressions of pure adoration. It was astonishing!

All my chimpanzee experiences before this moment had been fragmented, I from my world peering briefly into theirs. Now for the briefest time I had been blessed to pass through a door into another universe. Christophe Boesch and I were accepted, tolerated, as a strange and perhaps mildly parasitic species of ape — yet fundamentally harmless, neither predator nor prey — and so we were able momentarily to merge with the coming and going, the fusion and fission, the motion and rest and play and occasional squabbles and struggles that make up the chimpanzee world. It was a richer and more satisfying world than I had imagined.

My co-author could have told me this. I should have understood it from my reading. But perhaps it was necessary to discover it for myself. I suddenly recognized why I or anyone should care about what happens to the African great apes. Not, ultimately, because chimpanzees so resemble us, anatomically, behaviorally. Not because they can solve problems, learn language, recognize themselves as individuals in mirrors. Not because they have their own forest medicines and cultures, nor because they use tools and know how to snare the nimble marmoset. And not because they are intellectual beings. But because they are emotional beings, as we are, and because their emotions are so obviously similar to ours. In the course of the day I had witnessed anger, fear, and irritation — but also, I thought, real comradeship, affection, and love.

Surely some of my reaction had to do with the beauty of the forest itself, but mostly I was moved by the play, the incredible laughter in the bushes, the adult male chasing a toddler round and round a tree, the mother nibbling her baby's toes and looking blissful, the three females playing with and adoring a single infant. These remarkable beings have our emotions. They feel! That was my discovery.

4 • Caliban's Island

CALIBAN:
> This island's mine by Sycorax my mother,
> Which thou tak'st from me . . .
>
> here you sty me
> In this hard rock, whiles you do keep from me
> The rest o' th' island.

The blue-gray waters of the lake settled smoothly under the clear sky, and the little boat made fast progress. We were traveling south from the Burundi border at the north end of Lake Tanganyika, following the eastern shoreline of that great lake to my home at Gombe.

It was the first time I had made the journey by boat in ten years, and I was appalled at the changes that had taken place in such a relatively short time. Where were the lush forests, the deeply wooded slopes descending to the shore? What I saw now were bald and eroding hills, desolate, already collapsed here and there with rusty scars of open soil and gashed with red gullies. Even on the steepest slopes the forests had gone, and in their place farmers were making pitiful attempts to grow crops of cassava and beans. But without the trees the soil was quickly eroding, every heavy rain washing more of the precious topsoil into the lake. I remembered vividly how, when I had last flown over the area, during the height of the rainy season, the lake had been edged with a reddish brown. Soon, if this appalling desecration continues, the hills will rise from the water bare, rocky, and virtually barren. Already the chimpanzees, and most of the other animals too, have gone, apart from a few doomed groups hanging on in the most inaccessible pockets of forest, surrounded by people and cultivation. It is increasingly difficult for the farmers to eke out a livelihood from the degraded land.

On the white beaches along the shore, between the rocky head-

lands, the fishermen were drying the night's silvery catch of dagaa, little sardines, on the sun-warmed gravel — a few shining patches here and there. How different from the huge catches that had silvered the beaches when I first arrived in 1960. In those days the fishermen had used nets on long poles that looked like giant butterfly nets. They fished only during the dry season, from May or June until November, and then only two weeks each month when there was no moon. (They attract fish to the light of their tilley lamps, a technique that is not effective when the moon is shining.) But today the fishermen have been taught to use skein nets, and they go out almost every night, wet or dry, except during the one week a month when the moon is full. Not only is the lake overfished, but the soil washed down in ever increasing amounts from the despoiled hills is rapidly silting up the shallows, so that the remaining fish are finding it harder and harder to breed.

What will become of these people? They cannot move on in search of new land — there is nowhere for them to go. For not only has the local population expanded here, as elsewhere in Africa, but refugees have moved in — from Burundi and from Zaire across the lake. I was filled with pity for them, trying desperately to survive, cutting down the life-sustaining trees in their doomed efforts to provide more food and fuel for themselves and their ever-increasing families. Unless something can be done to halt the erosion, unless some major restoration program can be initiated, there is no hope.

One and a half hours after we had set out from Burundi, the landscape changed. Suddenly our little boat was moving past thick forests. The wild, glorious call of a fish eagle fell toward us from above, and the scent of the trees and soft soil came wafting across the water. Gombe: I was home.

Gombe today is like some enchanted oasis, surrounded on its three landward sides by bleak and virtually treeless hills. Back in the early 1960s the forests and dry woodlands stretched north and south from Gombe, and far inland to the east. Chimpanzees lived there. But burgeoning human populations have surrounded the thirty square miles of Gombe National Park with dwellings and cultivated fields that press right up to the boundaries. Each year, as the forests are cut down, there seems to be less rain and the seasons have become less predictable. There was a time when the heavy rains began in mid-January and lasted until May — in February and March it used to rain, heavily, almost every day. That predictability is a thing of the past. "It

is because the trees are gone that there is less rain," one of my field
staff told me. He was in the process of planting tree seedlings in his
shamba, *his little plot.*

When I arrived thirty years ago, there may have been ten thousand
chimpanzees dwelling in wild habitats across Tanzania. Today perhaps a quarter of that number remain. It saddens me to have witnessed such a loss and to know that the same sudden destruction is
taking place all across Africa. Chimpanzees, already extinguished in
four African nations, may soon disappear from five more. Only four
nations today harbor significant numbers of chimpanzees, and in each
of those four, the wild apes are receding before the relentless advance
of an ever-expanding human presence.

It would be a happy consolation to imagine that such is the price of
"progress," that the human inhabitants of Africa are somehow better
off today than they were not so long ago when chimpanzees were a
common species — but that is not the case. The loss affects us all,
human and animal alike.

1

Displacement is the first problem. "This island's mine," Caliban complains to Prospero, who, empowered by magic, has displaced Caliban
from every portion of the island except "this hard rock." But Prospero
obviously feels that the displacement is a normal manifestation of
order in the universe, an act necessary to transform the island wilderness into a productive garden.

Prospero's hatred of Caliban is partly a hatred of Caliban's island.
For Prospero the island, like Caliban, is nature without nurture. It is a
cursed place where he and his daughter have been banished, a chaos
that must be ordered, a desert needing irrigation, a wilderness requiring gardener, a profane tangle of wasteful growth that must be subdued with the assistance of all the magic he can squeeze out of his
books. Prospero would probably have used the word "jungle" to describe the island, except that the word was invented only when later
British colonialists in India and Persia seized upon a Hindu word for
describing dry and tangled wasteland scrub, *djanghael,* itself derived
from the Sanskrit *jangala,* meaning wasteland or desert. Rudyard Kip-
ling and Edgar Rice Burroughs helped popularize the notion that the

forests of the tropics are wet and tangled wastelands, *jungles*, thick and threatening places that must be subdued with all the magic we can squeeze out of our twentieth-century knowledge — the magic of the bulldozer, chainsaw, and match.

The island would never have been a *jungle* for Caliban, I like to imagine, given that word's colonialist history and connotations. Caliban saw the island more clearly, knew it more intimately. Caliban knew it as a productive wilderness that didn't need to be ordered, irrigated, gardened, or subdued. It was already for him a bountiful land, every inch fertile with berries and fish, crab apples and earth nuts, edible birds and nimble marmosets. Had he been less poetical, Caliban might have preferred the expression "tropical rain forest" to describe his island habitat; had he been more polemical, Caliban might have argued for preserving the island's forest wilderness intact in its primordial state.

We now recognize that Caliban was, in some sense, right. Tropical forests are planetary gardens, not wastelands, full of beauty and extraordinarily rich with diverse and productive life. Aside from providing critical environmental services — averaging extremes of rain and sun and wind in the tempestuous tropics, retaining soil in areas where erosion can be devastating, absorbing carbon from the atmosphere, recycling moisture into the air at twenty times the rate of evaporation over oceans — tropical forests serve as our most significant gene bank, storing within 6 percent of the earth's land surface some 90 percent of the earth's plant and animal species. Yet we have been reacting to these forests in the style of Prospero. When Shakespeare wrote *The Tempest*, forests covered almost ten million square miles of land in the tropics. Today we are left with fewer than four million square miles, roughly a fifth of which are found in Africa. Conservative estimates suggest we are permanently destroying nearly fifty thousand square miles of tropical forest each year and in the process extinguishing countless expressions of life — up to one million species by the end of this century.

A million species, found nowhere else in the universe, permanently dissolved. It is a devastating loss to future generations, a deficit that may not be recovered by natural evolutionary processes for billions of years. In cutting, burning, and paving the tropical forests, moreover, we are destroying not merely species but "the source of species diversity itself, the machine that cranks them out and ultimately protects us from calamity," to quote botanist William Rodriguez of the Institute for Amazonian Research in Brazil. Nineteen million tropical trees are felled daily, the burning continues — and other scientists describe the crisis in equally cataclysmic terms: "the sleeper issue of the twentieth century," "the greatest biological disaster ever perpetrated by man," "a threat to civilization second only to thermonuclear war."

Newspapers in the United States still too often relegate tropical conservation news to the back pages. The crisis is apparently too great for us to think about coherently. But in Africa the effects of deforestation are palpable. You can see the effects, feel them, know them in a generation. "Ten years ago . . ." is the start of many a wistful conversation. Fuelwood, the major source of energy in Africa, is going. In 1980 a total of 180 million Africans met their daily fuelwood needs only with great difficulty, if at all; by the year 2000 that number will reach 464 million, a threefold increase. Timber is going. In 1964 Nigeria, selling some 27.3 million cubic feet of tropical timber, was one of the world's leading exporters. That volume has declined by more than nine-tenths; in 1985 Nigeria earned only $6 million from all forest product exports, yet had to spend $160 million on forest product imports. Nigeria, in short, has become a net timber importer, as will one-third of today's exporting countries by the year 2000. Soils are going. Ethiopia, whose forested area has declined from 50 percent to 3 percent during this century, is today losing an estimated 1.6 billion tons of arable topsoil yearly from erosion on deforested land.

It is indeed difficult to generalize about a continent with 660 million people inhabiting more than fifty modern nations, speaking some eight hundred languages, adhering to the traditions of at least as many ancient ethnicities. But if generalization is necessary, we might begin by acknowledging two basic facts about the human world in Africa: poverty and population. Africa is the poorest continent on this planet, with an annual per capita Gross National Product (GNP) of $600 — one-twentieth that of Europe, one-thirtieth that of North America. Not coincidentally, Africa also includes the fastest-growing populace on earth, currently doubling in numbers every 24 years (compared to a Europe doubling every 266 years and a North America every 93 years). The great wealth of the temperate zone nations, in Europe and North America, induces a kind of zombielike consumerism: our economies are dedicated to expanding the possibilities of appetite. And our slow population growth induces a dreamy complacency. We fail to see the problem. We have the luxury, the time and wealth, to consider the relationship of population growth to the price of copper, to debate the moral niceties of family planning, and so on. In Africa the crushing combination of deep poverty and explosive population growth induces, among other things, political chaos and personal despair.

As we move into the new millennium, the capacity of the planet will be tested not only by an increasing human population but also by increasing needs and expectations. The solution cannot be to leave the people of the developing nations in poverty; neither can it be the headlong and wasteful exploitation of resources. A sustainable global society must be based on both stable population and stable consumption. Nevertheless, no measures will have any lasting or significant effect until population growth is stabilized. In West Africa, where human numbers are doubling every twenty-three years, forests and wildlife are everywhere declining. West Africans depend on bushmeat as a major source of protein; in many areas that will be gone in another generation and West Africans will be even hungrier than they are now. In Rwanda, two-thirds of the world's remaining mountain gorillas endure on a tiny island of volcano and forest surrounded by cultivated farmland that right now supports the 780 people per square mile living there. What will happen in twenty years, when those people are doubled in number? In Madagascar, people doubling their numbers every twenty-two years are halving their stunningly rich rain forests at about the same rate; their per capita income has declined each of the past fifteen years.

Of course, we in the temperate zone have already destroyed our own primary forests. Europeans cut their ancient forests centuries ago, except for some final stands in Poland. In North America, we have chopped up and sawed down nine-tenths of our native forests and are busy figuring out how to finish off the remaining tenth. We have no reason to feel superior. But the past destruction of temperate forests does not excuse the ongoing destruction of tropical forests. Africa is like few other places a cornucopia of life, and the destruction of this wealth must concern us all.

The destruction is all the more painful to witness for its suddenness. This planet has seen mass extinctions in the past — the demise of the dinosaurs, for example. But those changes took place "suddenly" only in the framework of biological time, where "suddenly" might mean a thousand or ten thousand or a million years. In stark contrast, the destruction of the forests and other wild habitats, and the sudden and devastating displacement of wildlife everywhere in the tropics, have taken place over a single generation or a few generations in human time. When Shakespeare envisioned Caliban living on his island, millions of chimpanzees were living unchallenged in a part of Africa larger than Europe and the United States combined. Today, perhaps one or two hundred thousand of these great apes survive in very rapidly disintegrating habitats. Chimpanzees may have begun declining not long after the first Europeans brought their own particular style of exploitation to the African continent, but that decline has surely accelerated precipitously since the middle of this century.

And so it comes to this: Jane Goodall sitting in a boat, looking across the waters of Lake Tanganyika into the final forests of Gombe National Park, recognizing that during the last thirty years the chimpanzee habitat in Tanzania has been decimated — that three-quarters of the chimpanzees there when she came, such a brief moment ago, are now gone.

In one African nation where chimpanzees are disappearing quickly, I followed a rough road through some of the best remaining forest fragments in the region. This "road" was, in fact, more like a double-rutted track, and whenever we came to a "bridge," we had to stop and rebuild it before crossing. But the forest was largely intact, and the people in villages along our track had ample use of the forest's larder.

Suddenly the track opened into a bare red-clay strip ninety feet wide, and all around us were bulldozers and the turpentine smells of oozing sap. The machines were huge orange and yellow monsters, clawing and tearing. They had giant hooks in the back and giant blades in the front. We listened to the squeak and whine and clank of metal on metal and the roar of diesel engine as a bulldozer cleared a route for us through the wreckage of trees. Where did these bulldozers come from? The African Development Bank. Why were they tearing a broad highway through some of the final stands of virgin coastal forest in this part of the world — a forest sacred to the local people, a final refuge for the region's few remaining elephants, pygmy hippos, buffalo, and ten primate species, a forest the World Bank had just sought to protect with an $80 million loan — instead of cutting through already deforested and degraded land five miles north? Why had the

African Development Bank allowed construction to proceed, after
they had formally agreed to wait? Why were they now cutting the road
in apparent secrecy, in apparent haste? "What I'm really afraid," said
my host, "is because of this new road, the rest of the forest will go in
the next few years. There must be development, but we must respect
what is remaining."

We were, in fact, driving through one last remnant of chimpanzee
habitat in that whole region, and the next day we came to the end of it:
a place that looked as if it had been cleared with a bomb. A hot sun
glared across brush, weeds, grass, denuded soil, and massive tree
skeletons, silvered and charred. "Ten years ago," my host said, "this
was primary forest for hundreds of miles. In the north now, people are
actually buying wood."

A week later we drove through extended regions of artificial savannah, twenty years ago primary forest, today colonized by a fast-grow-
ing weed species from Central America. No animal eats this weed, so
far as I was able to learn — not wild elephants, not domestic rabbits — and it forms eight-foot to ten-foot impenetrable walls of vegetation. The thickets produce clusters of small, bluish white flowers and
leaves that are thin, soft, and papery, like wadded tissue paper. Some
of the leaves turn brown in dry weather, giving the full thicket a rather
dirty appearance. It seems to reproduce with runners, making it a
terribly fast and virtually ineradicable encroacher, putting the final
touch on what are now huge tracts of deforested wasteland.

I went also to one of the West African nations where chimpanzees are
now extinct, The Gambia. There *are* chimpanzees in The Gambia,
actually, about forty-four of them living on three of the five Baboon
Islands within the River Gambia National Park. But none of those
chimps originally lived in The Gambia; they have been placed on the
islands as part of a rehabilitation project for chimpanzees that were,
for various reasons, confiscated in neighboring (and in some instances
European) countries. The project is superbly run and a credit to the
nation, an example of African conservation at its best.

I was met at the airport and, a couple of days later, driven east
several hours to the Chimpanzee Rehabilitation Project. We drove
along a straight road through semidesert landscape, past mosques and
square mud-brick huts with conical thatched roofs, past occasional
cotton trees and baobab and woodland, into a haze so strong it created

a false horizon at five hundred yards. I watched cars on the road ahead disappear into the haze, white and ominous, and my escort in this land of the Sahel said: *harmattan.* "Harmattan," she repeated. "The word sometimes refers to the wind that blows from the northeast, across the desert, raising dust storms. But it can also refer to the dust. When I was first here, fifteen years ago, the harmattan lasted only three days a year. Now it's several weeks."

I stayed at a camp across a river from the Baboon Islands chimpanzees and visited with some of the people who manage the rehabilitation project: Janis Carter, the director; Boiro Samba, a conservationist and member of the Fulani tribe; and Jim Zinn, an American Peace Corps worker. One evening Boiro, Jim, and I took a boat upriver for about a half-hour, docked the boat, and walked to a village — carrying slides and a projector, a can of gasoline, a portable generator, and a sheet. We had dinner with the village chief, and after dinner, when it became dark, we tacked the sheet against a wall, fired up the generator, turned on the projector, and began showing slides.

A whole firmament of stars spread silently overhead, and sixty villagers sat or stood around in a rough horseshoe of a crowd as the projector pushed its beam of light onto the sheet on the wall. The light splashed into color and pattern, and Boiro, lanky and fine featured, wearing a leather cap, paced before the crowd and lectured like a professor, speaking in rhythmic bursts of Mandinka, terminating each paragraphic burst with the Mandinka equivalent of "Look" or "You see," speaking over the noise of the putt-putting generator and the complaining of village goats, sheep, and chickens. Jim whispered a translation of the lecture for me. On the sheet appeared images of the biggest and best-known African animals: giraffes, lions, leopards, buffalo — and chimpanzees. "These are animals that used to live in The Gambia but are now gone," Jim said. "Boiro is asking, 'Have you ever seen it in the bush?' " The lecture proceeded. Boiro explained what chimpanzees are and how very much like people they are, how chimpanzees were exterminated in The Gambia, how they are disappearing in Africa, what can be done to reverse the process, and what is going on at the Baboon Islands Chimpanzee Rehabilitation Project.

After the slide show, the village chief apologized for the simplicity of the meal he had given us, and as a parting gift he handed us a chicken. In the dark, we walked through rice fields back to the jetty, a quarter of the village accompanying us, carrying our equipment and just generally keeping us company, and we climbed in the boat and followed the starlit center of the river through dark and bursting forests.

On the way back to camp, Boiro told me that before the Europeans came, Africans traditionally believed that at one time chimps had been human. But then a group of people were cursed by Allah for fishing on a sacred day and banished to the forest — they became chimpanzees. Africans didn't hunt chimps until the Europeans came and taught them that they could make money by killing chimpanzee mothers and selling their babies.

Jim Zinn told me that he and Boiro had been conducting a survey of local attitudes toward wildlife in The Gambia. The older people, Jim said, many of whom remember the days when there were animals other than those now regarded as crop pests, have "a good respect for animals. They'll say things like, 'God works through the animals, and when the animals aren't there, then God can't help us out.' But the younger people, who have never seen any of the now-extinct animals of The Gambia, they think that any animals, if they ever did come back, would be pests. Because the only animals they see left now are baboons, monkeys, bushpigs, and hippos, which are all pests around here."

Giraffe, lion, leopard, buffalo, and chimpanzee. All are gone from this part of Africa. The Gambian government has become fully committed to general principles of conservation; but in the meantime, each year the harmattan lasts longer, the rainy season gets shorter, the supply of fuelwood declines, the nation's central river becomes more saline. The ongoing displacement of chimpanzees in Africa is part of a continental tragedy, a massive and sudden unraveling of ecosystems that until recently protected animal and human alike.

2

Hunting is the second problem. In some parts of French-speaking West Africa, a generic word for wild animal is *viande* — meat. In parts of West Africa where the administrative language or lingua franca is English based, a generic word for wild animal is "beef." French and English are, of course, second or third languages in Africa; and it is not clear to me whether this usage reflects a historical tendency in African languages, simply translated, or some strange inheritance from the

colonialists.* It is not an indication of ignorance. Africans familiar
with the bush have a very sophisticated and detailed knowledge of
individual plants and animals. In any case, when you talk about
animals in Africa you often are talking about viande or beef, and that
quirk occasionally leads to expressions that are mildly comic to the
European ear. "Listen," an African said to a European acquaintance of
mine, regarding a beautifully singing bird, "the meat is singing." It
seems to me an anticipatory way of thinking. Europeans call animals
meat and beef only after they are dead. Africans call them that before.

It also reflects the fact that many African cultures are, by an ancient
tradition that powerfully survives today, hunting cultures. It is quite
true that in several parts of chimpanzee territory where domestic meat
and fish are commonly available, Africans do not eat chimpanzees.
But subsistence hunting is as old as Africa. No one can blame people
for feeding themselves; and the taste for wild-animal meat is a far
older, hence more natural, inclination than any fussy predilection for
domestic meat.† As African human populations have exploded in
numbers during this century, however, hunting has become overhunting. What were a few people hunting animals with simple weapons in
large wilderness areas are now many, many people hunting animals
with sophisticated weapons in diminished and fragmented forests.
Chimpanzees are seriously hunted as meat in several West and Central African nations, including Guinea, Liberia, Ivory Coast, Ghana,
Cameroon, Equatorial Guinea, Gabon, Congo, and Zaire.‡

*

* In Kiswahili the word for animal is *nyama* — meat.

† Just as, in my opinion, subsistence hunting is a more honorable activity than hunting
for sport. Europeans killing orangutans in Borneo and gorillas and chimpanzees in
Africa just for the fun of it have, in a few instances, decimated local populations. An
Englishman, Fred Merfield, killed 115 gorillas for sport (and donated the remains to
European museums). The American explorer and gorilla hunter Paul du Chaillu expressed an interesting ambivalence about this activity: "Fortunately, the gorilla dies as
easily as man; a shot in the breast, if fairly delivered, is sure to bring him down. He falls
forward on his face, his long muscular arms outstretched, and uttering with his last
breath a hideous death-cry, half roar, half shriek, which while it announces to the
hunter his safety, yet tingles his ears with a dreadful note of human agony. It is this
lurking reminiscence of humanity, indeed, which makes one of the chief ingredients of
the hunter's excitement in his attacks on the gorilla."

‡ Although it is convenient to refer to African nations, the reader should remember
that the national boundaries remain an imposed artifact from colonial times. Tribal
variation is the important issue when discussing African traditions, not national
variation. Within each country there is actually a wide variety of attitudes about
bushmeat.

When the German naturalist Johann Büttikofer sailed to Liberia to collect specimens for the Leiden Museum a century ago, he found a wilderness so unbroken he was compelled to restrict his expedition to the coast and navigable rivers, and so rich he was able to find at least 125 mammal, 310 bird, and 74 reptile and amphibian species concentrated in an area smaller than the state of Pennsylvania. Subsistence hunting has fed Liberians for centuries, but the spears, vine snares, fish traps, and nets of tradition have been replaced by shotguns and rifles, steel traps and wire snares, and even (for fishing) dynamite. The great Liberian forests are now fragmented, and all remaining wildlife is disintegrating under an onslaught of hunting. Liberia may have more guns per capita than any other nation in equatorial Africa. Although Liberians have recently turned these guns on one another in a cruel and bloody civil war, we can assume that hunting with shotguns continues, day and night, unregulated, without regard to the rarity of the animal, its age, its sex, or the breeding season. All animals are hunted, including rare coastal manatees, leopards, forest elephants, and chimpanzees.

Liberian wildlife is so overexploited that hunters in the western part of the country prefer to bribe border guards and cross into neighboring Sierra Leone, where they use guns, wire snares, pit and vine and wood traps to clear out selected areas. They specialize in night hunting with carbide headlamps and spotlights. After giving a portion of the meat to local chiefs, Liberians transport the bulk of it by truck across the border, and from there into markets as distant as the capital city of Monrovia. The Liberians prefer primate meat — a dead adult chimpanzee will sell for as much as $60 in Liberia — but they will take anything that moves. No one has estimated how much wildlife is transported across the border, but the amount must be substantial. One to two trucks fully loaded with bushmeat (perhaps two thousand to three thousand smoked monkeys or the equivalent) are said to pass each week through the Sierra Leonean border town of Zimi, bound for Liberia.

In the now-scattered islands of West African forest most wildlife is hunted, frequently including chimpanzees. Forest destruction combined with hunting has already decimated chimpanzee numbers here, reducing what may recently have been a population of eight hundred thousand to today's estimated eighteen thousand to twenty-five thousand West African chimps. It is true that hunting and eating habits vary considerably from locale to locale. In the Ivory Coast village of Yaélé, for example, chimpanzees are a sacred totem for the entire village and therefore never eaten. The story goes something like this: A family in Yaélé was having only male babies. Then they had a daughter. Unhappily, she went into the forest to gather nuts and became lost. But she was seen later in the forest with a group of chimpanzees; she had become half chimp. The chimpanzees saved her life, it was said, and so the chimp became a village totem. Actually, totemic traditions seem to protect many animal species from human predation in small pockets throughout this region. I recall stopping in the village of Zagné, in Ivory Coast, and looking over the edge of a bridge into brown water. I was instructed to drop a piece of bread into the water; when I did, the surface of water swirled and then solidified into a surface of fish — big catfish, gray and whiskered, virtually climbing on top of one another to get the bread. Fish in this section of the river were totemic, a villager told me, as were the monkeys in a stretch of trees on the other side of the road. The government of Ivory Coast would like to conserve its wilderness heritage; nevertheless, the hunting of chimps in many parts of Ivory Coast, according to the zoologist Adriaan Kortlandt, is extinguishing them from their remaining habitat there.

I was fortunate to travel into several forests in West Africa with an African government official interested in conservation. I'll call him Abu. We walked into one national park with the assistance of a compass, a machete, and a local teenager who said he knew his way in the forest. It was, in fact, a very large forest, yet strangely quiet because it was devoid of monkeys. We did find duiker droppings, elephant dung, and chimp nests. We also found plenty of spent shotgun cartridges and snares, which seemed to explain the missing monkeys.

The snares were brilliant constructions, effective and well made, yet simple. They were based on three elements: a spring force (bent sapling), a noose (thin wire cable), and a trigger. The trigger, constructed from carefully positioned twigs, would collapse when touched, thus releasing the force of the spring, closing the noose, and snatching — not killing — the animal. One snare I found used a woven stick and brush barrier with a circular hole in the middle; the barrier was placed on top of a fallen log. Any small animal, a monkey perhaps, scurrying along the log would pass through the hole in the barrier and trigger the snare. I prodded it with a stick. My prodding stick was instantly wrapped in a tight noose and vigorously whipped into the air.

This was a national park, not a hunting forest, so Abu and I felt only mild compunction as we cut the snares, hacked through the saplings with machetes, and threw away the cable nooses. But the villager who was helping us warned: "The hunter will cast a malediction in your direction. Bad luck will come your way." And so I was left with a bad feeling and an unpleasant image lingering in the brain, a fisheye view of a fisherman casting a great circular net.

A couple of days later, we traveled to the northern edge of this same national park, a region where the forests became drier and gave way to savannah. We sat on some rocks atop a small hill, listened to the rattling of a few brown and green leaves on scrub trees nearby, looked across a sweep of savannah and woodland, enjoyed the smell of grass, and absorbed the stark beauty of the grasslands — rippling waves and streaks of olive and pale green, yellow, amber, gold, ochre, and brown colliding into dark greens of the forest to one side and, in the distance, forested hills a pale gray with bluish tint. As we surveyed the grasslands, about two dozen forest buffalo trotted out, so Abu and I went down the hillside to get a closer look. On the level grasslands they were in fact much less visible. We saw mostly brown shapes moving through a brown and rough cover, and sometimes the white flags of cattle egrets that accompanied the buffalo. Then a hartebeest buck came into some brush near where I stood. He halted, raised his head high, looked, looked, looked, looked, then turned and, his head high, his horns a straight black U on top of his head, pranced elegantly away, setting up an alarm for the buffalo, who fled in turn with a low rumbling sound, raising egrets as they moved.

The buffalo were gone, and Abu and I returned to our perch on the rock on the hill. As we were just about to leave, we heard a shotgun fired somewhere over to our right: poachers. "It's by day," Abu said. "They don't care at all."

It was a mistake to chase after them, since they had guns, but luckily we found the poachers before they saw us. Inside a small copse of trees and down a slight incline, I glimpsed a patch of red shirt. It moved. We heard voices. There were at least two of them. "I'm sure that they are professional," Abu whispered. "Come into the park to get food for a local restaurant." We tried to pretend that we knew what we were doing. Slowly and carefully we moved to different sides of the copse. On a signal, Abu whistled in imitation of a police whistle and shouted, "Arrest them! Arrest them! Arrest them!" while I threw stones into the trees and brush and tried to make the noises of several men in hot pursuit. The poachers, surprised, ran as fast as they could. And Abu and I, after listening to their crashing in the brush recede, returned to our spot on the rock.

Within a few minutes, however, we heard shooting to the left: more poachers. Then we heard shooting from another direction, and later, as we moved into a different area of the park, we saw the rising plume of smoke from a poachers' fire, probably smoking meat. This "national park" had no tourists and no rangers. It was filled with hunters, cleaning up.

In fact, Abu and I met hunters nearly everywhere we went — inside protected forests, national parks, reserves. One hunter, known in his village as Peter the Little Hunter, came to dinner one night. He was a young man, born in 1967, spectacularly handsome, small (thus his nickname) but built like Mr. Universe, a superbly athletic man who spoke to us with great poise and self-assurance, gesturing as he spoke with jabs of a finger, flicking his hands to emphasize various things.

Peter told us he is the only hunter in his village, a community of eighteen adults. When he hunts he takes the meat for his family, but he also brings meat to other members of the village. When he has more than enough for the village, he sells meat to people outside the village. He hunts four times a week, and also cultivates a small plantation of rice, cassava, and bananas.

Peter said he hunts duikers and other small mammals at night, using a spotlight. Once he shot a leopard. By day he hunts primates, monkeys and chimps. The first animal he kills (by "first" I think he meant "most frequent") is the monkey — dianas and mangabeys. Red colobus, not so much. They are very rare, he said, because they're so easy to hunt. You just have to go under a tree where they're eating; they don't flee very far away when you kill one, so you can kill several at once. Hunting chimpanzees, though, can be dangerous. Once he shot a mother and infant, who fell, dead, out of a tree, and then a male arrived, screaming, so he had to kill the male too. All told, Peter said, he kills about ten chimps a year. Last year it was seven. On occasion he manages to pull a live baby off its dead mother, and when that happens he tries to sell the baby. Twice he's sold chimp babies to French tourists — but it's not only white people who are taking baby chimps as pets. An African, a garage owner in a nearby city, has two chimps working for him. They carry things, such as tin cans or cans of petrol.

There seem to be three categories of hunter in West Africa. Almost every rural person, I have been told, is a casual hunter, using, for example, simple snares to catch rats or squirrels. And villages usually have their own specialist hunters, one or more people who are good hunters and provide for the village. Peter the Little Hunter belongs to this category. But there are also professional market hunters, who will supply meat for restaurants or for companies that truck bushmeat into the urban areas.

Abu and I stopped at one of the centers for bushmeat traffic. Actually, we were flagged down by a woman who offered to sell us cane rat. We parked our car and entered a warren of small meat markets and restaurants — a series of small porches in long concrete buildings, the porches functioning as restaurants, each with a kitchen in back, and behind the kitchen a long interconnecting corridor with dead animals along it and people sitting, laughing and talking and carving up the animals. Since bushmeat is usually carved up and cooked without disguise — that is, the skin, feet, and head are usually not removed — Abu and I were able to make an informal census of the species available at that moment in that market: two small antelopes, several duikers, several cane rats, some giant rats, one porcupine-like animal, and some monkeys. I'm sure that a Kansas City abattoir is no prettier, but for someone used to the deceits of marketing and packaging, this was starkly realistic: duikers with burst eyes and green cud hanging out of their mouths; antelopes in pieces; a cane rat with its throat slit; a monkey cooking on a grill, stomach and entrails removed, bent backward until the head met the rump, tailstump actually stuffed into his mouth, lips drawn back from his teeth in a rictus of seeming agony.

A woman offered me the monkey for the equivalent of $16. That seemed high to me, but Abu reminded me that it was a starting price.

We asked several people if it was possible to buy chimpanzee meat. One woman told us, "Ah! We don't get them very much. Maybe twice a year." Another woman said, laughing: "We never get chimps. There's no more forest here."

Even in Central Africa, where the forests are still relatively intact, modern excess overtakes traditional restraint. The BaAka pygmies of the Dzanga-Sanga Forest in Central African Republic have long hunted bushmeat with arrows, spears, and nets woven from bark and vine. But after the Yugoslav company Slovenia Bois began logging the forest two decades ago, some fifteen hundred sawmill workers and other outsiders have completely altered the nature of hunting there. Traditional hunting tools are being replaced by guns, snares, and poisons. Heavy steel cables stolen from the logging camps are coiled into elephant traps; villagers use bicycle brake cables to snare meat; wealthy outsiders lend their high-powered rifles to the pygmies, then pay for the meat with a pack of cigarettes, a pint of *bako*, or some used clothing. Similarly, in the Ituri Forest of Zaire, the Mbuti pygmies have lately increased their subsistence hunting to supply meat to commercial traders.

But the BaAka and Mbuti have never specialized in chimpanzee hunting; it is unclear how much the recent increase in hunting in Dzanga-Sanga and the Ituri affects the great apes. In Gabon, however, bushmeat has long been a major source of dietary protein, with chimpanzees and gorillas among the preferred foods. According to a 1980 report, chimps and gorillas are also considered dangerous vermin and destructive crop pests, so they are killed for a variety of reasons. The reliance on bushmeat has seemed enormous — workers in a small exploratory iron mine in Belinga, Gabon, were said to have required twenty-four tons of bushmeat a year. A more recent study of subsistence hunting in particular regions of Gabon noted that even light hunting reduced chimpanzee numbers by a quarter, while heavy hunting cut chimp populations in half. The nation nonetheless remains a great reservoir of biological diversity. Still densely forested and sparsely inhabited, Gabon has been described as a sample of how the rest of Africa used to be fifty years ago. When I visited that part of Central Africa in 1991, chimpanzee expert Caroline Tutin told me that the Gabonese are now self-sufficient in domestic poultry and wealthy enough to import beef; they also prefer domestic meat, so that bushmeat is becoming an exceptional rather than a common addition to their diet. Nevertheless, the completion of the trans-Gabonaise railroad and the concomitant opening of the interior to large-scale commercial logging and other sorts of exploitation continue to threaten the great apes of this Central African nation.

*

Where they are not hunted as meat, chimpanzees may be killed for other reasons. A member of one of the southern tribes in Congo informed me that the southern Congolese do not eat chimpanzee and never would, even if they were hungry. They do eat gorilla. "What's the difference?" I asked. He said he couldn't explain, but it was a big difference, a very big difference. The southerners don't eat domestic dogs or cats either, although people to the north do.

Congo is a sophisticated and comparatively urbanized country, but even in the cities many Congolese still prefer the taste of bushmeat. Thus, hunting in Congo has become highly professionalized — "industrial" is the word one observer used — with daily trucks carrying huge loads of bushmeat from the remaining forests into the major cities of Brazzaville and Pointe Noire. It is true that I found no chimpanzee or gorilla meat in the markets I visited in Brazzaville — not, that is to say, in the bushmeat areas of the markets. But when I wandered over to the vendors of magical objects, of fetishes and potions, it was a different story. One merchant displayed the head of a gorilla, skin and fur still there but starting to rot, lips pulled back, eyes shrunken into the sockets. He also offered a gorilla hand for sale, black furred, thumb and forefinger torn off, and ants crawling in and out of the broken parts. The head I could buy for the equivalent of $40; the full hand would be worth $14, but I could have it for two-thirds that price because someone had already taken some pieces of it. The head and hands give you strength, the merchant said, and are often bought by athletes. You boil the gorilla parts in water until the water is gone, then pulverize the remains, cut an opening in your skin, for instance on the back of your hand, and press the powder into the cut. It will give you strength.

In the next stall over, I found — among dozens and dozens of pelts, heaps of dried snake heads, dried lizards, eagles' and hawks' talons, an elephant's tail, an alligator's head, feathers, fetish dolls, dried black chameleons, and a live green chameleon slowly suffocating to death inside a sealed jar — two chimpanzee hands for sale. These, like the gorilla hands, would impart some of the wild ape's strength to a civilized man, if boiled and pulverized and inserted under the skin. In another stall I found four chimpanzee hands for sale; and the next day, in another market, I located half a dozen gorilla hands, some with fingers missing, all looking very much like big human hands.

Where chimpanzees are displaced and their habitats destroyed by human intrusion, they will sometimes move into agricultural areas and raid crops, so they are also regularly hunted as crop pests. In western Uganda, according to one account, crop-raiding chimpanzees were caught with snares, killed with spears, then butchered and fed to dogs. The chimps' brains were scooped out and likewise given to the dogs, while the skulls were sold to a shaman. The shaman burned and pulverized the skulls, then mixed the powder with other ingredients into a paste that, when rubbed into cuts in a person's skin, would theoretically speed the healing of a broken bone.

Chimpanzees are in many places protected by law, and in some by tradition. But laws not backed by tradition are usually ineffectual, while traditions can themselves produce mixed results. Before inter-tribal warfare drove them out, the Bakonjo and Bamba tribes hunted chimpanzees and other primates for food in the Kibale Forest of Uganda (where hunting is illegal). The two tribes were replaced in 1962 by the Batoro, who not only refuse to eat primate meat but may even refuse to eat from the plate or drink from the cup of anyone who does. The Batoro sometimes hunt with nets. Gangs of up to forty hunters with dogs would regularly drive large animals — bushbuck, duikers, bushpigs, forest hogs, waterbuck, buffalo — into widely stretched nets, where waiting spearsmen would dispatch them with iron-headed spears. When, on occasion, monkeys and chimpanzees became caught in the nets, the Batoro might release them. But Batoro cable snares have been less discriminating. Michael Ghiglieri, who studied chimpanzees at Kibale during the late 1970s, found three of his approximately sixty study animals to be mutilated by snares. When he observed some chimps in a different part of the forest, however, he found that almost a quarter were maimed. The injuries varied from scars and minor deformations to crippled and missing fingers and toes, missing hands, withered legs, and severe festering wounds. In one case Ghiglieri sighted a young female with a cable twisted around her foot and embedded in the flesh. The foot, grotesquely swollen and gangrenous, looked like "a loaf of bread dough constricted in the middle by a tight rubber band." She disappeared soon afterward, and Ghiglieri realized that counting the mutilations of live animals gave a very conservative estimate of snare casualties, since the fatalities were missing.

Ursula Rahm, who during the mid-1960s assisted in capturing chimpanzees in a supposedly remote section of eastern Zaire, found similar effects from snares apparently intended for other species. Of the forty-four captured chimps she examined, more than half showed deformations or old injuries of various sorts. The aim of the capture operation had been to acquire chimps who had never had "direct contact" with humans, so that they could be experimentally infected with hepatitis in French and American laboratories. However, a significant number already showed signs of indirect contact. Six of the forty-four had most clearly been injured by cable snares. One adult male was crippled by a cable grown into the flesh around his right ankle, causing muscular atrophy and threatening gangrene. He was shot. A juvenile male likewise had an ingrown cable around his ankle, already resulting in gangrene up to his knee and a "completely putrefied foot." He was shot.

3

As a child I had dreamed of living in the African forests, silently moving from tree to tree, surrounded by animals — invisible animals, perhaps, but surely ever present. My dreams were realized in the forests of Gombe National Park in Tanzania. But now I was half a continent away from my beloved home in Tanzania, in the Central African nation of Congo.

I moved away from the others, away from the road. The silence of the forest closed around me as I walked deeper into a world that, for me, is more beautiful than all others. I sat under a tree, leaning against its enormous smooth trunk, and looked up, way up, to its branches and leaves in the canopy above. Now that I was quiet, now that the voices of my receding companions were the vaguest blur of sound pushed out to the fringes of my consciousness, I could listen to the music of the forest. A buzzing, soft, louder, soft, as an insect flew by and vanished into the green depths behind the tree. The whispering of leaves, increasing in volume as a breeze gusted among the treetops, setting the foliage astir so that speckles of sunlight danced crazily on the forest floor. The breeze moved on, and the humid air settled more closely. Small scuffling sounds moved rapidly down a neighboring tree trunk; turning my head slowly, I spied a squirrel. Undisturbed, with frequent flicks of a handsome tail, the little rodent moved out of my sight . . . A whir of wings heading directly toward me, a startled cry, an abrupt change of direction, then a burst of avian scolding as the small bird perched, staring at me, and angrily demanded that I be gone. But I stayed, and soon the bird flew off to a less alarming spot . . . Then a haunting song, the liquid notes dropping softly into the heavy air. It sounded like one of the robin chats of the Tanzanian forest I am so familiar with, but I could not see the singer. I turned to investigate rustlings among the fallen leaves, but whoever moved there was out of sight. Another small bird flew by, another breeze sighed in the branches overhead.

Suddenly I heard a gunshot. It was far away — yet near enough to shatter my peace. For a few moments I had allowed myself to forget the reality of the forest around me, but now I was returned to stark knowledge. There are no monkeys anymore, leaping overhead; no shy bushbucks or noisily rooting pigs, moving along the trails. No elephants remain. The chimpanzees are gone, too. No longer do their calls ring out above the trees, nor the screams of their quarrels, the barks and grunts of their pleasures, the spine-chilling wail of their alarms, the hooting chorus of their evening songs. All the large animals and birds are gone from that forest, shot, sold in the village market, and trucked from there to the big town.

The magic gone, I made my way back to the road and my companions. We had been searching for a suitable site to build a sanctuary for orphaned chimpanzees, youngsters confiscated from hunters who had shot their mothers. Continuing the search, we drove our vehicle deeper into the forest. Soon we met a huge truck and so drew to the side of the road. I watched it pass, sick at heart, for it was filled with the enormous trunks of six forest trees. Trees such as the one that had afforded me shade and comfort in the forest. Trees that had taken more than a hundred years to reach that size. We met three such trucks in an hour. Following the rough road, we drove on, moving deeper into the desecrated forest.

5 · What, Ho! Slave!

PROSPERO:
> *We cannot miss him. He does make our fire,*
> *Fetch in our wood, and serves in offices*
> *That profit us. What, ho! Slave! Caliban!*
> *Thou earth, thou! Speak!*

PETER THE LITTLE HUNTER had described an automotive garage in a nearby city where two chimpanzees were made to do work, such as carrying cans of petrol. When I arrived in the city, I saw a man walking down the street wearing the uniform of the forestry department — the bureaucracy charged with enforcing national laws against hunting, capturing, transporting, and selling endangered animals, including chimps. Did he know where the chimps in the mechanic's garage could be found? Oh, yes, he knew about those and two others in town. If I wanted to buy chimps, it would be possible. But I'd have to stay around for a day or two while arrangements were made.

He gave good directions, and soon enough I pulled up in front of a large garage with perhaps two dozen people milling around outside. I entered the crowd and saw a young male chimp chained with a huge iron chain around his neck to the undercarriage of an old truck. This ape, standing upright, acted very feisty, and somehow he had gotten hold of a stick and was brandishing it at the crowd. I took some photos, and while I was doing so the chimp picked up a handful of dirt and threw it at me, much to the amusement of the crowd.

Behind this unfortunate young male, two adult chimps, male and female, stood in the hot sun, both chained with heavy iron chains at their necks to a large piece of rusty scrap metal. They looked absolutely pathetic. The male was big and rather handsome; the female, big as well, had a long, loose lower lip and floppy ears. This area was, in fact, recently deforested, and for a second I imagined those three creatures living in the dim green world of a high forest right there; I imagined the forest destroyed and all the animals in it destroyed as well, save for these three sad survivors, cursed to stand in the searing sun and serve as roadside exhibits.

I found the owner of the chimps. He said he had had them for seven years. There used to be four, but one died. He wanted money because I had taken photographs. When I refused to pay, he offered to sell the chimps for two hundred dollars each . . .

I came to a luxury hotel owned by a Swiss expatriate. Behind it sat two chimps, chained by their necks to a big concrete doghouse with a concrete patio around it, and a picket fence around that. A few banana peels were scattered across the patio. A sign on the doghouse said "Oscar and Judy." Judy, I thought, might have been an adolescent. Oscar seemed fully adult. Judy, very quiet, had a light, freckled face. She walked away from the doghouse, the twelve-foot chain rattling on the concrete as she moved until the chain was tight; then she stood upright and looked at me expectantly — hoping, I thought, for a banana. She turned around, bent forward, and reached back toward me with one foot, as if to say, "Please place a banana here." When that didn't happen, she turned around, picked up one of the banana peels from the patio, and tossed it to me. I caught it and thought I understood the message, but I didn't have any fruit with me. I tossed the peel back at her feet. She picked it up and sniffed it. Meanwhile, Oscar simply sat in the shade of the doghouse, on the doghouse stoop, barely glancing my way, left foot propped up, carefully grooming his toes with a most absorbed expression on his face. An employee of the hotel told me that Oscar and Judy had been there since 1980; she said the female was gentle, but the male threw stones . . .

I met two forestry officers and their families, all living in the government barracks supplied for officials who, among other duties, are responsible for arresting poachers and traffickers in live and dead contraband, including chimps. They had two baby monkeys as pets, one a tiny infant vervet, the other a young diana chained to a post. They also had a baby chimp, a tiny creature with spidery body, cream-colored face, and a dazed look in his light brown eyes. I watched one of the forestry officer's children poke at the infant chimp with a stick. The child's father told me the chimp was a gift from a poacher. The other officer told me they had had another one last year, but he died. "I took him back to the forest," the man said . . .

I walked into an isolated rural village and found, in the middle of the village, a young male chimpanzee hunched over, sitting on top of a rough wooden platform, chained by the neck with several bicycle chains doubled over and padlocked to the platform. The chains were so short and tight that the ape couldn't even sit upright. He was forced into a permanent hunch. All he could do was spin around on the chains, hopping with his feet, spin around and face the crowd of village children who were gathered to tease him, spin around with an unmistakable fury on his face. The chimp's name was Tolbert, I was told.

I was greeted by Tolbert's owner, a middle-aged man who walked up and said what he must have imagined I expected him to say: "These are people of low intelligence! This is cruelty to animals!" Indeed, the children were taunting Tolbert, laughing as he spun around angrily, delighted when he picked up any stones he could reach, hurled them, then threw banana peels, furious, stomping as well as he could in fury. Tolbert's owner said the chain was so short because the ape had gotten dangerous. He said he had killed Tolbert's mother while hunting and brought Tolbert home. Then he said he hadn't killed Tolbert's mother; a hunter did that and gave him the baby. He said he was the owner, but then he said he wasn't the owner. He used to be Tolbert's owner, but he gave the chimp to a cousin who lived in the city. Unfortunately, the cousin neglected to teach Tolbert any tricks, so now nothing could be done with him. He had gotten very strong and dangerous, and that's why it was necessary to keep him on such a short chain, to protect the children. Surely I could see how vicious Tolbert was . . .

1

Orphaned chimpanzee infants in Africa are sometimes kept in villages, the by-product of hunting for the pot. Sometimes hunters will offer them for sale in village and town markets, so the infants occasionally end up in the hands of well-off Africans or European expatriates who can afford the few dollars asked.

I'll never forget my first sight of Little Jay. Exhausted, dehydrated, and utterly depressed, the two-year-old chimpanzee was lying on top of a wire cage at the side of the road in the main tourist market of Kinshasha, Zaire. He was fastened to the cage with a piece of string, looped around his waist. Tied to other cages or the legs of tables were a number of young monkeys, also for sale. And there was a sickening row of African gray parrots — birds whose swift flight through the air is a joy to watch, whose cognitive abilities are astounding — crammed into tiny wire prisons.

I was with Nick Nichols, a photographer on assignment for the National Geographic, *and Chris Bane from the U.S. Embassy in Zaire. When we approached the chimpanzee, he sat up and looked at us with glazed and almost hopeless eyes. But when I crouched beside him and made small sounds of greeting, he put one arm around my neck. A noisy crowd had surrounded the captive, but when Nick began to take pictures they faded away. Only the seller, angry and demanding, remained. When we returned later, the little chimp was lying down again, still tied by his waist. The thin shade of some acacias did little to lessen the scorching midday heat, and his face shone with sweat. Yet when we offered him a drink, he turned his face away. I didn't see how this infant could survive for long.*

What were we to do? To buy him might save his life, but it would also encourage the hunter to capture another infant for the trade. We drove away, unhappy and perplexed.

The market is opposite the American Cultural Center, where I was to give a talk that evening. Nick and I had been invited to stay at the residence of the American ambassador, William C. Harrop, and his wife, Janet. On our way back after the lecture we passed the market. It was dark and almost deserted, most of the people and cages gone. But the little chimp was still there, a tiny and solitary figure in the headlights. He sat up as we slowed down and, as we drove past, reached toward the car with one small arm. That did it! None of us would be able to sleep unless we first worked out some way of rescuing the infant. Later we sat in the Harrops' sitting room, making plans.

That was my first visit to Kinshasha, and I was there for two reasons. First, because I had for several years been receiving letters from one Graziella Cotman, Belgian citizen, begging me to try to do something about the continuing illegal sale of infant chimps in the markets and streets of Kinshasha. She had rescued and raised one unfortunate and was deeply concerned about the trade. Then, five months earlier I had been invited to have lunch with the U.S. secretary of state, James A. Baker III, who, by chance, was about to depart for an official visit to Zaire. I had begged him to discuss the chimpanzee situation with President Mobutu. That discussion took place, and Baker arranged for me to see Mobutu.

Mobutu, however, was unavailable when I finally went to Zaire. He was attempting to deal with one of the many minor eruptions of discontent in his cabinet. But because of the earlier talks with Baker, Ambassador Harrop believed that he could persuade the minister of the environment to confiscate the infant chimpanzee. The following day, just prior to my departure, we collected the minister and drove to the market. We knew Little Jay (who, for some reason, we had believed to be a female and had first christened Little Jane!) was still there, for the minister had sent a gendarme to the market in the morning. I cut the string myself and took the bewildered infant into my arms. It was a very moving moment, and I think we were all close to tears as, for the second time, he put his arms around my neck. We drove to Graziella's house, for she had offered to nurse Little Jay back to health.

This incident was the start of a series of confiscations, orchestrated by the American Embassy, in the market and streets of Kinshasa. During the next several months six more infants were confiscated. The first of these, acknowledging the role of the secretary of state, was named Little Jim B. Another, who really was female, became Little Jane. The older ones went to N'Sele Zoo, to join many others who over the years had been placed there by pet owners when the apes got too big for the house. Graziella's original orphan was there, and, because the zoo's budget was totally inadequate, Graziella had been driving out twice a week for the past several years — with extra food for between fifteen and twenty chimpanzees.

In August of 1991 I visited Zaire for the third time. Things looked better. The Friends of the Chimps group, started the year before, was going strong in the American School in Kinshasa. Some of the pressure was off Graziella, as the children made regular trips to the zoo with food. A strong conservation movement was developing that included a number of enthusiastic Zaireans, and we were making plans to build a sanctuary where all the former pets and confiscated infants could live together. Unhappily, all these plans came, at least temporarily, to an end. On the day I was due to leave, to cross the river to Brazzaville in Congo, rioting broke out in Kinshasa. Part of President Mobutu's army, dissatisfied because they had not received paychecks for two months, started the looting, and presently half the civilian populace had joined in. There was a lot of shooting — most of which, initially, seemed to be into the air. I was staying with Cedric Dumont and his wife, Ruth, who were caring for two of the confiscated infants. Ruth and I watched the looting and rioting in the center of town from the veranda of their apartment. Whenever the shooting got heavy the two chimps, Chris and Calamity, huddled on the floor of their cage and hugged each other for comfort.

Next day a detachment of French paratroopers landed in Congo, then crossed the huge Zaire River that flows between the two capitals, from Brazzaville on the northern shore to Kinshasha on the southern. As the troops took control of the center of town, the shooting, for a while, became much worse. A bullet exploded through the Dumonts' bedroom window with such violence we thought at first it was a bomb. We saw a French soldier hit by gunfire just across the street from the apartment. But on the third day everything in the center of town was quiet. Still, there were many accounts of looting and violence in the outskirts of the city, and it seemed that the trouble was spreading to other parts of the giant country. I was finally able to leave Kinshasha, joining the first ferryload of American evacuees to cross the river to Brazzaville.

What would happen to all our confiscated chimpanzees? Ruth was forced to leave, evacuated with almost everyone else, but Cedric was part of the skeleton staff staying on, so temporarily Chris and Calamity would be well cared for. But what of those in the N'Sele Zoo? Once again Graziella Cotman came to the rescue. She had arrived, distraught, at the Dumonts' on the evening of the first day of the rioting — she had been robbed at gunpoint of all her belongings. Even the lavatories, basins, and electric wiring had been ripped from her apartment. But Graziella is a strong person. When things calmed down, she managed to talk her way through three military roadblocks, got to the zoo, and rescued Little Jay, Little Jim B, Little Jane, and two other newly confiscated infants. Joined by Chris and Calamity, all seven were evacuated across the river to the Brazzaville Zoo. Fortunately,

the American ambassador to Congo, Dan Phillips, and his wife, Lucie,
long-time friends of mine, were there to help organize things. Chester
Zoo in England lent us a chimpanzee keeper, Vince Smith, for a couple
of months. And many other people hastened to help.

Graziella lost her job in Zaire; the entire office was closed down.
She now works for the Jane Goodall Institute (JGI) in Brazzaville,
caring for the chimpanzees in the Brazzaville Zoo — including the
seven newcomers, the refugees she brought from Zaire. At the time of
this writing there are some twenty chimpanzees in her care. She
shares responsibility with Jean Maboto and another Congolese keeper,
and all the young chimps are taken into the forest each day. Cedric
Dumont has been relocated in Brazzaville, joined by Ruth. For now
things are stable. But those chimpanzee infants are getting larger and
stronger, and we need to find a solution to their long-term survival at
the zoo.

It is not surprising that caring and tender-hearted people buy, in order
to rescue, pathetic orphans such as Little Jay. In principle they may
know that such a purchase can only perpetuate the trade: the hunter,
blood money in his pocket, will shoot another mother to get more. But
once you have looked into the eyes of an individual, if you have any
compassion at all, it is impossible not to respond to the appeal for
help. Without the know-how or clout to press for confiscation, these
people have no other alternative — besides theft.

Of course, not all infant chimpanzees are bought for reasons of
compassion. There is a real demand for these pitiful survivors. Some
are bought to lure visitors to a hotel or bar or other place of business,
some to attract attention by proclaiming ownership of an exotic animal, and some simply to fill a need for surrogate human offspring.
While the ultimate fate of all young chimpanzees bought privately in
Africa is similar, their early experiences are vastly different. Those
with caring owners will, for a while, enjoy their lives again, unnatural
though they may be. They can, in many ways, join in the life of the
human family: eating at table, playing with the children, roaming the
house and garden.

But after a while this freedom comes to an end. It is not easy to
discipline chimpanzees without increasingly severe physical punishment. As they get older, they rapidly become stronger and more agile.
They can escape by climbing the drapes or swinging through the

branches. They are inquisitive and intelligent. They can find hidden keys, raid closets and refrigerators. They are hard to toilet train. And they become increasingly resistant to the kind of discipline one applies to human children, ever more liable to throw tantrums — and to bite. And so, when they are between four and six years of age their life of comparative freedom comes to an end. They spend more and more time shut in tiny cages or chained in an outhouse or yard. If, as so often is the case, their owners are expatriates, stationed in Africa for only a few years, what can they do with their "pet" when they leave? Today strict international laws govern the export and import of live animals. It is illegal to import chimpanzees into the United States and most European countries without special permits, impossible to obtain for private owners. So the "pet" must go to another home, or to a local zoo (if there is one). Or be killed.

The problem occurs across the chimpanzee's range in Africa, wherever hunters search them out. That this hunting is illegal, and that the selling is usually illegal, makes little difference, for in many African countries the laws exist on paper only. Most bush hunters, in most Central and West African countries, have absolutely no idea that killing chimpanzees and selling their babies is a violation of the law. Only when local conservation or welfare groups are prepared to work with the government on a program of confiscation and education can we hope to end this heartrending trade. Unless provisions are made for the care of confiscated infants, government officials cannot confiscate. This is why there is an urgent need for orphanages and sanctuaries across Africa.

To date there are two completely successful sanctuaries. The first was set up in The Gambia by Eddie Brewer and his daughter, Stella. This program, now sponsored by the government and known as the Chimpanzee Rehabilitation Project, has been relocated from its original site in Senegal to three of the five Baboon Islands in the River Gambia National Park, and it is well established. So, too, is the Chimfunshi Wildlife Orphanage in Zambia, where over forty chimpanzees from many parts of the world are cared for by a British couple, Dave and Sheila Siddle. But two sanctuaries are nowhere near enough.

Aliette Jamart and an associate have started a sanctuary on an island in Congo close to the Gabon border. In eastern Zaire, a small group of chimpanzees has been established on another small island. A beleaguered woman in Guinea, who took in one chimpanzee out of pity, now has well over twenty youngsters in her back yard and is desperately trying to find somewhere for them to go and obtain some further support. In addition, Peter Jenkins and Liza Gadsby have taken over two youngsters confiscated by the local wildlife authorities in southern Nigeria. I know of at least thirty chimpanzees in Cameroon in need of sanctuary. And so it goes on. Rosalind Alp, initiating a study of chimpanzees in Sierra Leone, told me just yesterday of a young female in that country who has remained in the small cage in which she was confined at age four — three years ago. She cannot stand, nor can she sit upright. Her bed is a two-foot-thick layer of feces.

The Jane Goodall Institute is involved in creating three sanctuaries, one (being built by Conoco, the Texas-based oil company) in Congo, one in Burundi, one in Uganda. Plans to establish a sanctuary in Burundi arose when Dan Phillips, then the American ambassador there, and his wife, Lucie, found that young chimpanzees were being smuggled over the western border from Zaire and sold as pets. Some of these youngsters, having outgrown the cuddly stage, were being held in inappropriate and sometimes cruel conditions by owners who simply did not know what to do with them. Once our plans for the sanctuary progressed, most of these owners were only too glad to place their unruly chimpanzees in a more suitable environment. Two of the owners, though, refused — initially.

One is a Lebanese auto-garage owner. His chimpanzee, Whiskey, once lived in his house with the rest of the family. But when Whiskey became too strong, he was banished to a small dark cell at the rear of the house, adjoining the workshop. This cell, with its concrete floor and brick walls, with a hole in its tin roof, was clearly an unused toilet, a lavatory. In an area six feet wide and seven feet long, Whiskey had been imprisoned for two years, attached to an iron post in the corner by a two-foot chain. I had seen photographs of this chimp, but when I actually met him I was seized by a powerful mixture of emotions: pity brought tears to my eyes and anger set my pulse racing.

"This is Whiskey. He is like a son to me," said his "father," smiling. Could he be serious? I asked myself. A "son" chained in a lavatory? Yet in a peculiar way he was fond of Whiskey — the two embraced. "His chain is lengthened at night," his father assured me. "And sometimes he is taken around the yard in the evenings."

Whiskey held me tight when I made soft chimpanzee greeting sounds in his ear. When I left, he hurled himself about at the end of his chain, hitting the wall with hands and feet. He reached toward me with one hand, then, turning, extended a foot. That gave him a longer reach. When I did not respond, he hurled a banana skin in my direction.

The second reluctant owner was a Belgian, owner of a hotel, the Club de Vacance in Bujumbura. He had a long history of exploiting chimpanzees and other animals to attract tourists and amuse customers. I went to the club for the first time with Geoff Cresswell, our JGI representative in Burundi. I met Safari, a young male chimpanzee living by himself in a ramshackle cage outside. It looked as though any self-respecting chimpanzee could escape through the roof — and, indeed, Safari did sometimes get out. So far that had not mattered, but soon he would reach puberty and become potentially dangerous. We knew chimpanzees at the hotel had, in the past, mysteriously disappeared when they outgrew their cages. There was another infant in the house, I was told. Her name was Akilla. But she was sick, and we could not see her.

A year later I went back to see Safari. By this time the hotelier had acquired yet another chimpanzee, having bought him illegally "to save his life." We followed the Belgian into the house. There we met Akilla. She had been let out of her little cage and seemed quite friendly. Then we went onto a veranda, where a group of people talked and laughed loudly. The new infant, Uruhara (which in Kirundi means "bald"), sat inside a tiny cage littered with bits of food quite inappropriate for his age — raw vegetables and fruit. Only six to nine months old, he needed milk and baby cereal. A servant approached to pick him up, and the infant cowered, terrified. As he was seized and lifted out, he began to scream hysterically. He quieted when the Belgian held him, and we could see that he had lost most of his hair, through malnourishment and stress. His lower back was absolutely bald, and I saw the great raw weal where a leather belt had been cut away from his waist. The thick strap, the Belgian said, hard and caked with blood, had bitten deeply into the chimp's tender flesh.

While the Belgian held him as we talked, Uruhara remained motionless, rigid with fear or despair or both. When it was time for us to go, his owner put down the pitiful orphan, and he began to scream again. Bewildered and terrified, he tried to run after the Belgian. The servant pounced on him and, afraid of being bitten, pressed him to the ground. The liquid feces of fear squirted over the carpet as Uruhara *screamed and screamed. Perhaps he still called for help to the mother whom he would never see again.*

Eventually Whiskey, Safari, Akilla, and Uruhara were all handed over to our new JGI representatives in Burundi, Dean and Susanne Anderson. It had not been easy to persuade their owners, so we felt a great deal of satisfaction when these four chimpanzees joined the other eleven in temporary caging that we call the Halfway House, where all the orphans await the construction of their sanctuary. How tragic that Whiskey, off his chain at last, fell sick of some internal infection from which he never recovered.

2

Keeping primates as pets or servants is at least as old a tradition as, say, keeping wolves and turning them into dogs. Archaeological remains in the Great Caves of Niah, in Borneo, indicate that Borneans thirty-five thousand years ago ate orangutans, and one expert speculates that they might have kept baby orangs as pets. Ancient Egyptians coddled hamadryas baboons in temples, provided them with good meat and wine, and worshipped them as servants of the baboon god, Thoth. Less sacred baboons were taught to climb fig trees and gather their fruits. Malaysians in more recent times have trained pigtailed macaques to climb palm trees and harvest coconuts. South Africans have used thirst-inspired baboons to find water, and, inspired by the truffle-snuffling pigs of France, they have trained other baboons to root for edible tubers.

I was not surprised when Peter the Little Hunter's tale of two chimpanzees laboring in a garage turned out to be in reality three chimps chained to a truck undercarriage and a piece of scrap metal along the roadside. Some wild animals can be trained and forced to carry out routine tasks for a human master; but chimpanzees may be too creative, too strong and volatile, to settle quickly into such a situation. The occasional tale of laboring chimpanzees (for example, an old newspaper report of three chimps working on a furniture assembly line in Texas) often proves to be apocryphal. One must remain skeptical about Olfert Dapper's account, published in 1670, of discovering chimpanzees in Sierra Leone, West Africa, who were raised from infancy and trained well enough that they could "give almost as much service as slaves. Ordinarily they walk quite erect like men. They can grind millet in the mortar, and go to draw water in a pitcher. When they fall down, they show their pain by cries. They know how to turn the spit, and do a thousand clever little tricks which greatly amuse their masters." And the story told by a nineteenth-century American naturalist, R. L. Garner, of finding in a West African village a young chimpanzee who, like Caliban, would obey orders to collect firewood from the edge of the forest likewise warrants skepticism. (Garner wrote that he offered to buy the ape, but "the price asked was nearly twice that of a slave, and I could have bought any child in the town at a smaller cost.")

If chimpanzees would make poor slaves in reality, people still have been moved to fantasize about chimpanzee slaves. Toward the end of the nineteenth century, when individuals and institutions around the world were coming to recognize human slavery as the evil it was, a Frenchman named Victor Meunier wrote *Les Singes Domestiques*, promoting his idea that people should domesticate apes and monkeys and thereby create a new class of slaves — slaves who could be as useful as human slaves but whose exploitation would induce no guilt, since they were animals. Meunier thought that breeding stations could be established in the tropics to breed enslaved primates for improved intelligence, morals, and looks. Looks were important, since many primates "are constructed in a manner to be a formidable trial to our aesthetic senses." Morals would be important, in Meunier's scheme, because he was deeply concerned that these slaves might attack their masters; especially, it seems, he was worried that the male apes and monkeys could present a sexual threat to women. But in case selective breeding and education were insufficient, castrating any nonbreeding males ought to curb their "violence, rudeness and wickedness," and removing their canine teeth would provide a further safeguard. This new class of slave would liberate humankind, since no person would be forced to do offensive, tedious, or dangerous tasks any longer. No longer would the fireman risk his life climbing a ladder and entering a burning building; no longer would the farmhand labor to exhaustion; no longer would the housewife cry tears of boredom. The primate slaves, our "poor relations," would take over: "with the dog we conquered nature, with the ape we will found the happy society."

I too met Whiskey, the chimpanzee chained to the steel post in an old lavatory in East Africa that Jane writes about. Whiskey was curled up in a corner of his cell, asleep perhaps, and he opened his eyes and gazed at me directly. He had, I thought, a sweet, sad face, brown and wide-nosed with a heavy brow ridge. Lethargically he took the banana offered, ate the insides and most of the peel, then threw the remainder at me. Then he wheeled around, pulling against his short chain. Steadying himself with his hands at the steel post, Whiskey reached back with one leg, stretched out an open foot, and looked at me over his shoulder, waiting for a banana to be placed in the foot. The fruit was offered; he grabbed it with his foot, turned around and ate it, and once again threw the final piece of peel back at me.

During my travels in Africa, I saw well over a hundred orphaned chimps, either still in primitive and often abusive conditions of captivity or being cared for in one sanctuary or another. A few of them were, like Whiskey, chained at the neck, and when I came face to face with these pathetic creatures I was compelled to ask myself why the situation seemed so disturbing. We frequently chain domestic dogs by the neck, after all, and why should anyone expect different treatment for another species of animal? Is this an aesthetic problem? Is it a question of differing standards for domestic and wild animals? And if the chaining of Whiskey is mere cruelty, couldn't we lessen the cruelty by lengthening the chain?

Chimpanzees are either blessed or cursed by the honored shape. They can look so human in form that a heavy chain at the neck disturbingly reminds us of what we wish to forget. When I see a chimpanzee in chains, standing in the hot sun along an African roadside — or crouched inside a filthy cage in a dark basement in the United States — I am sometimes jolted to imagine what I am glad never to have witnessed, the evil of human slavery. After overcoming the sober judgment of one's rational censor, perhaps, a thought steals into consciousness: *So this is what it was like.* In chains, or from inside a small wooden box or rusty cage, a woeful face looks at you with an undeniably human expression, while the "owner" blithely discusses price or breeding or personality.

What is a slave? We might say that a slave is someone who works without choice; and we conjure the image of a man in chains engaged in heavy labor. If this man in chains rests, or if he is forced to do nothing but sit beside the road and amuse passersby, is he not just as much a slave? Of course he is. Slavery is not defined by action, but by condition. We know a person to be a slave not by what he does but rather under what conditions he does it. We are also accustomed to recognizing slavery as a uniquely *human* condition. Slavery, in this light, is the treating of a person as if he or she were not a person. The idea, of course, presumes that being human automatically entitles one to certain rights and protections — that by belonging to the human species, or perhaps by possessing a human consciousness, we are automatically (if imperfectly) protected by certain universal moral standards or traditions, what in the last few decades we have begun to call "human rights."

Human slavery is condemned by every religion and every nation on earth; it is universally known as a shameful nightmare from our past. Yet most remarkably, slavery was a common and accepted practice for all of history until the last century. Depending on when you think history began, this makes slavery part of the way people have treated other people for perhaps 98 percent of historical time. What changed our minds? I suspect that human ethics took an abrupt turn in the nineteenth century for several reasons. With the arrival of an effective industrial economy — reasonably functional tools and machines — slavery's economic value to slaveholders declined. That may have been one reason. Another may have been the obvious reality that slaves were human and deserved certain fundamental protections. Although nineteenth-century slaveholders and slavery proponents did sometimes try to justify themselves and their actions by arguing that slaves were not human and therefore were not entitled to human moral protection. It was finally impossible to deny the poignantly obvious humanity of slaves, and thus slavery entered a fierce and unsustainable realm of moral paradox.

Shakespeare's *Tempest* engages more than anything else that paradox. Caliban is a slave. If we feel sympathy for Caliban, we feel it not so much for someone abused as for someone enslaved; we would not lengthen the chain but rather remove the collar. Yet simultaneously we find the slaveholder Prospero to be a powerfully sympathetic character, a nobleman seeking to regain his rightful place, a kind if stern father, a powerful restorer of moral order who speaks with great eloquence and even at times seems to speak for the playwright himself. Prospero has several justifications for treating Caliban as a slave. For one thing, Caliban tried to rape his daughter. But his most consistent justification is that Caliban is hardly human. He is "earth," a fish, a

monster. Prospero denies Caliban's humanness, his *continuity* with
the human moral world.

I recall having an argument, a heated argument it seems to me, with
a friend who is the editor of a journal on comparative religion. We had
been considering whether apes deserved some sort of ethical consideration. "But don't you agree that people are higher?" my friend said.
Higher! That word at that moment seemed peculiar. What did he
mean by "higher"? Not "taller," obviously. Mentally higher? Perhaps.
Morally higher? Possibly. Although if humans are morally higher, I
thought, we are also morally lower. It is true, as Jane Goodall witnessed at Gombe, that chimpanzees are capable of real acts of brutality — intracommunity war, cannibalism, infanticide — but only humans are capable of torturing complete strangers; only humans are
capable of cold genocide or hot slavery; only humans have the capacity
to destroy whatever they touch for the sheer pleasure of it. But my
friend offered as an example of what he meant by "higher" the fact
that only humans could sit around and discuss the very issues we were
discussing. Perhaps. And yet I could imagine a gaggle of serial murder-
ers on death row discussing these very issues. I have not actually
decided whether humans are "higher." Perhaps when I understand the
expression better I will know what I think about it. But if "higher"
means superior to the point of discontinuity, then I don't think we
are.

There are two ways of looking at the human relationship with the
rest of the natural world. Either we stand coldly separate and perfectly
discontinuous from the natural world, or we stand in continuity. If
discontinuous, if the divide between man and beast is an unbridgeable
chasm, if for example only humans have consciousness while all
animals are entirely unconscious machines, then comparing a chimpanzee in chains to a person in chains may seem insensitive (when the
comparison is imagined to deny the bitter humanity of the slave) or
sentimental (when the comparison is imagined to elevate falsely the
status of the chimp). But if humans exist as part of the natural world,
not separate from but continuous with it, then it would seem that the
image is worth considering, and that we must, as a consequence,
reexamine our ethical relationship with those animals enduring just
beyond the edge of our moral island, the great apes — who laugh,
anticipate, learn from one another, recognize each other as individuals, are demonstrably self-aware, and so on.

The day I met Whiskey I also heard about an event that had happened a few miles to the north only two or three weeks previously, that has affected my thinking about chimps. The French director of a tea plantation in Burundi bought two young chimpanzees on separate occasions. The first one, Jolie Coeur, was a male of about four or five years. The second one, whom he named Cleopatra, was approximately two years old. Both were orphans, separated by hunters from their mothers' carcasses, and since chimps up to the age of five desperately need a nurturing parent, these two chimpanzees quickly developed a powerful bond. The older ape, Jolie Coeur, took on the role of mother and "adopted" the two-year-old Cleo. Jolie Coeur used to chew up food and give it to Cleo from his lower lip. He would hold Cleo at night and comfort her. If anyone tried to take Cleo away from him, Jolie Coeur would go absolutely crazy and attack. Retrieving Cleo, he would fiercely clutch her in his arms. One day while the chimpanzees' owner was away, Cleo accidentally disturbed a hive of African bees, which swarmed and attacked the two chimps. Jolie Coeur was chained — he was unable to escape. When the bees began to sting Cleo, Jolie Coeur just wrapped her up in his arms, actually bent double around her, and shielded her from the stinging insects. She survived. Jolie Coeur took more than two hundred fifty excruciatingly painful bee stings before he finally died, still protecting his small friend.

It is not necessary to imagine Jolie Coeur's protection of Cleo as perfectly equivalent to the greatest acts of human heroic behavior. We must remember that in times of stress a chimpanzee will naturally embrace a companion. The story is still a wonderfully moving one, however, and scientists in the field have recorded many instances of similar chimpanzee behavior that might be interpreted as altruism.

My own clearest example of true altruism from thirty years of research at Gombe concerns a twelve-year-old male named Spindle and an orphaned, sickly three-year-old male, Mel. During an epidemic of some pneumonia-like disease, a total of eight chimpanzees died, including Miff, a female I had known since her infancy. When a mother dies, leaving a dependent infant, usually it is an elder sibling who adopts the orphan. But Miff's infant, Mel, had neither elder brother nor elder sister to care for him. He had been very sick a few months earlier and was still, at the time of his mother's death, emaciated and small for his years. We all thought he would die.

For the first few weeks following his mother's death, Mel followed first one adult, then another. Usually he selected one of the males. All tolerated the infant; none showed special concern. And then a strange bond was forged between Mel and the twelve-year-old Spindle. As the weeks went by, the two became inseparable. Spindle waited for Mel during travel; he permitted the infant to ride on his back, even allowed him to cling beneath, as a mother carries her baby, when Mel was frightened or if it was raining. Spindle shared his nest with the infant at night; he shared his food in response to Mel's whimpering and outstretched hand. Most remarkable of all, if Mel got too close to one of the big males during social excitement, when inhibitions are sometimes swept aside, Spindle would hurry to remove his small charge from danger — even though he sometimes was buffeted himself.

For a whole year this close relationship endured, and there can be no doubt that Spindle saved Mel's life. We may never know why, but there is this: Spindle's old mother died in the same epidemic that claimed the life of Mel's mother. Even though a twelve-year-old male is no longer dependent on his mother, he will often spend peaceful times with his family, particularly after traveling with the adult males when tensions have run high. Perhaps the loss of Spindle's mother left a hole in his life, a hole that close contact with the small dependent infant helped to fill.

Toward the end of the year the two males began to drift apart. Mel attached himself to the large sterile female Gigi — "Auntie" Gigi, who has always loved infants and who now travels through the Gombe forests with anywhere from one to four orphans in her wake.

If a "wild animal" possesses such strong bonds of humanlike affection and sometimes exhibits an apparent altruism that will endure danger and pain, can we still regard that being as absolutely beyond the circle of our moral concern? Like the European characters in *The Tempest*, we are perfectly convinced that our little drama is the only one that matters, that our little island has space for only a single species, that our little mental universe contains the sole important reality and ethical significance.

Caliban knows better.

6 • No Doubt Marketable

SEBASTIAN (seeing CALIBAN and two lower-class
characters, drunk and dressed in purloined clothes):
Ha, ha!
What things are these, my Lord Antonio?
Will money buy 'em?

ANTONIO:
Very like. One of them
Is a plain fish and no doubt marketable.

"DO I KNOW YOU?" the tall, one-armed white man asked me curtly, as I walked onto his farm outside the city of Freetown, capital of Sierra Leone.

"I've come with a message for you," I said. "Someone has captured a pygmy hippo up north."

"I'll buy it if that's what he wants," the man said.

At that time, 1987, I was visiting Sierra Leone to look at endangered black-and-white colobus monkeys. While I was in the country, a rare and highly endangered pygmy hippopotamus had been captured in a chiefdom up north. Some people were worried that the animal would die or be killed, and one individual thought it might be possible to transport the hippo and release him in a protected area. That person asked me to inform the one-armed white man, Franz Sitter, of the capture ("even if it means doing a deal with the devil himself"), since he was the only person in the country capable of transporting a hippopotamus.

We were standing at the edge of his patio, next to a modest frame house with a bright sports car parked out back and rock music blasting through an open door. A young European couple, both very blond, had been visiting with Sitter on the patio; they disappeared into the house soon after I appeared. Sitter looked to be in his mid-sixties, with gray hair, a rather long face, a nose like the blade of an oar, pale blue irises; he wore sandals on his feet, which seemed to me curiously pale; and he kindly invited me to sit down. Would I like tea? We had tea and cookies and talked about the pygmy hippo. Sitter spoke with what seemed to be a German accent. "If it's a mother's baby," he said, "it will have milk fat, but only for two or three or maybe four days. It will get thinner and thinner and thinner." He agreed to contact my friend.

Franz Sitter wanted to know what I was doing in Sierra Leone. When I mentioned that I had come to see black-and-white colobus monkeys, he garrulously described how to treat them. You can't put them in a small cage. They need lots of room. You make someone go and chase them — not to hurt them, just enough so that they get their exercise. They must have room! He said that black-and-white colobus monkeys are really harmless animals. They don't eat crops, as some of the other monkeys do; they just go in the trees and eat leaves. But Sierra Leoneans don't distinguish between monkeys. For them, all monkeys are bad. So Sitter thought that the government must teach, or rather that the people must be taught, which monkeys are harmless. The problem is that Sierra Leoneans like to eat black-and-white colobus.

But the real problem is the Liberians who come across the border. These people take a gun and go boom, boom, boom! Ach! He hates killing! (He turned to me with a glare of fierce anger at the thought.) One time he saw some hunters with a high stack of skins from zebra duikers. Ach! Such a beautiful animal! Such a waste! Something must be done about the Liberians. They come into this country and take everything! He has been trying to get people to do something about this smuggling of skins and bushmeat from Sierra Leone into Liberia. Sierra Leoneans get no foreign exchange from it; they lose their monkeys. It would be much better if the government would stop this traffic and then maybe take the most useful animals (here he squinted and drew his fingers close together to indicate how few that would be) that could bring some foreign exchange.

The conversation turned to chimpanzees. A few weeks — no, a few months ago — he sent some chimps, twenty chimpanzees, to Austria. What a commotion! He doesn't mind, of course. People for a long time write many bad things about him, but they are not true. He doesn't care anymore. He's used to it. One Austrian journalist even said he smuggled heroin out with the chimps. Ach! Even his friends believed

that! (Across his face came an expression of great disgust.) And then all
these people, Americans, send printed cards to Sierra Leone to protest.
But what can he do? These chimps are knocked by the falling-down
tree and chased by the running dog. They will die! Africans bring the
apes to him because they know he can take care of them. So he buys
them and feeds them. But can he feed them forever? What will he do
with them? Maybe he lets them go, but they maybe get diseases and
then pass them on to the wild populations. What will he do? It's the
same with that pygmy hippo. He can take care of it, make it healthy,
but then he has a hippo. What can he do with it?

1

This is the story of white people in Africa and their relationship with
chimpanzees through the live-animal trade. It is a complex and convoluted tale, a puzzle of many pieces that pulls us back and pushes us
forward in time, that ultimately takes us out of Africa to America, to
Europe and Japan, then back into Africa.

*The hunting of chimpanzees for food has been going on for count-
less years, perhaps from the time when the first true humans emerged
to share the forests with chimpanzees and gorillas. By and large, true
hunters concentrate on males, for the simple reason that if they kill
mothers wholesale they jeopardize their future supply. Of course, you
can pick up extra money at the market when you bag a mother-infant
pair, disposing of the female for meat and the infant to whoever shows
interest. Even so, the meat will generally yield a better profit.*

*But when the big dealer in live chimpanzees enters the picture,
things suddenly change. The dealer is usually a white man; he is
invariably serving non-African interests. For the African hunter,
though, the big dealer merely represents a new market, a buyer who
pays more than the infant would fetch at the village meat market or
the roadside. The hunter does not realize how absurdly underpaid he
is — for the dealer will turn around and charge many, many times the
original amount to his overseas customers once the infants have been
shipped (these days, mostly smuggled) out of the country to the international pet, entertainment, and biomedical research industries.*

Live chimpanzees have been traded out of Africa from a number of
ports — but most regularly and most heavily from Freetown, Sierra

Leone. In recent decades, most of the Sierra Leone chimpanzees have passed through the hands of a single dealer, Dr. Franz Sitter. Franz Sitter has stood at the very center of the live chimpanzee trade in Africa, in other words. And so this story of white people in Africa becomes predominantly a story of Franz Sitter and his marketing of no doubt marketable chimpanzees. It is also the story of two other men who ultimately came to oppose Sitter's trade, Dr. Jan Moor-Jankowski and Dr. Geza Teleki.

During a 1987 television interview, Franz Sitter suggested that the American people should be very pleased with him, since he has provided between 1,000 and 1,500 live chimpanzee infants for medical research in the United States alone. (He has also marketed somewhere between several dozen and a few hundred baby chimpanzees into Europe and Japan.) Sitter's approximation is accurate, I believe, and interesting for at least two reasons. First, it is roughly estimated that only 1,800 live chimpanzees altogether are held by U.S. biomedical laboratories. Clearly, the American reliance on this one dealer has been enormous. Second, if we accept the estimate that for every infant chimp taken into the trade and surviving the first year at his final destination, an additional ten chimpanzees have been killed, then Sitter's dealings with American laboratories alone may have been responsible for the deaths of between 10,000 and 15,000 chimpanzees. Franz Sitter could have had an enormous impact on wild chimpanzee populations in his little corner of West Africa.*

A background issue here takes us for the moment beyond the story of Franz Sitter. He told me personally that his chimpanzees were unfortunate casualties of the falling-down tree and the chasing dog, and I will not for the moment contest those assertions — except to note that they anticipate and defuse certain critical questions. How damaging has this trade in live chimpanzees actually been? How cruel?

---

* Sitter has been an exporter of live animals since the late 1950s or early 1960s. From 1973 to 1979, according to Sierra Leonean customhouse records, he formally exported at least 824 chimps out of the country; so his own lifetime estimate of 1,000 to 1,500 to the United States alone is reasonable. He was not alone. His principal competitor for a while, Suleiman Mansaray, exported at least 739 additional chimps during that period, but went out of business soon afterward. Generally predating both Sitter and Mansaray, an American importer named Henry Trefflich maintained a "collection" headquarters in Freetown that provided about 4,000 chimpanzees to American consumers. Two independent reports estimated that approximately 2,000 chimps remained in all of Sierra Leone by the late 1970s. Chimpanzees reproduce very slowly in the wild. The trade may well have decimated Sierra Leone's wild chimps.

How much, really, has the trade accounted for the decline of African chimpanzees, now endangered, someday perhaps extinct? Many of the people responsible for taking live chimpanzees out of Africa during the last several decades, dealers there and importers and buyers here, have understood at least intuitively that the trade raises a number of such questions that, from their perspective, might best be avoided.

In America the pattern of avoidance was first established by Robert M. Yerkes. A generation after Victor Meunier proposed in *Les Singes Domestiques* that humans selectively breed apes and monkeys in the tropics so that they might serve us in a variety of trades and occupations, Robert Yerkes, distinguished Yale professor of psychobiology, proposed in an article published by *Science* magazine in 1916 that a primate breeding and research station be established in the subtropics so that apes and monkeys and other "infrahuman organisms" could be made to "contribute importantly to human welfare." These animals, he later wrote, would become "servants of science." Robert Yerkes was an immensely talented and energetic scientist, remembered today as the foremost pioneer in American laboratory primatology, and he pursued his life's vision with an enormously detailed practicality. His original manifesto in *Science* recounted with three sets of numbered lists what might be the five general purposes of such an institute; the four general categories of possible research; the six sorts of trained personnel required. He also listed, without actually numbering them, the sorts of untrained personnel required; the parts of the world where such an institute might be most suitably established; the varied and total projected costs of establishing and running such an operation; and so on. His thoroughness was impressive. Really, it would seem that the only practical problem Yerkes forgot to mention in that 1916 manifesto was this: How does one acquire the primates?

Yerkes' favorite primates were chimpanzees, and in a book published in 1943, he did consider the acquisition problem. Where do you get chimps? You buy them in New York City. During the past half-century, he wrote, hundreds of chimps entered the trade in New York, and it was possible to buy for a mere $100 a chimp "which the dealer knows to be stupid, a bad health risk, or otherwise relatively undesirable"; but the best specimens could cost up to $1,200 (at that time). In the past, the supply of these apes was virtually "unrestricted," Yerkes noted, but during the previous two decades "agitation for wild-life conservation" led the major colonial powers in Africa to limit the ape

trade solely "to the satisfaction of educational and scientific needs."
(This final comment was, at best, only partially true, since in the
United States into the 1970s circuses and entertainers, pet stores and
pet owners, were most certainly buying live chimps taken from Africa.)

Yerkes did acknowledge that the "transition from freedom in Africa
to captive existence in Europe and America" would probably cause
"more or less serious and permanent ill effects from the procedure of
capture, rough, unintelligent, or inhumane handling, parasitic infestation, diseases of the digestive and respiratory tracts resulting from
human contacts, and malnutrition." But when he tried to describe
actual details of chimpanzee capture in Africa, the scientist waxed
uncharacteristically fanciful: "Imagine being captured in the wilds of
Africa by a well-disposed but determined band of apes and held indefinitely at their pleasure! Certainly the adventure would be hazardous. The passage of a chimpanzee from its natural habitat to ours must
be equally exacting."

As for particular techniques of capture, Yerkes did not believe that
any single method could be "described as best or as universally used."
There was the additional problem that "usually hunters are not writ-
ers," and probably many of the best methods remained "trade secrets"
of the collecting profession. Traps and snares might be used, and he
was aware of unconvincing reports that natural chimp foods and
drinks might be spiked with alcohol "to stupefy the apes." Of the
techniques mentioned in the scant "literature" on the subject, Yerkes
could think of only one "worthy of detailed description": using nets
to isolate and capture chimps. He then briefly paraphrased an account
of net capture in West Africa written by the live-animal collector
J. L. Buck and published in *Asia* magazine in 1927. (In those days,
one might imagine, the African and Asian continental plates had not
yet drifted apart.) Here was a hunter who was a writer, or at least
collaborated with one, and who presumably would reveal his trade
secrets.

Buck's tale began in Sierra Leone, where he described meeting
Hector, his "faithful African boy." Hector one day heard news of a
group of chimpanzees "ravaging the groves" to the north; so Buck, his
son Warren, and Hector journeyed for several days until they arrived
at the village of Kamaro, where they were met by the village chief.
Buck persuaded the chief to supply "a hundred boys" to engage in the
hunt. And to work his "hundred boys" into the proper spirit, Buck,
imitating a big chimpanzee, provided an old-fashioned pep talk. "Who

comes tramp, tramp, tramp, into the village, with the howl and the ugly face? Who terrifies the women in the cassava patch? Who, some days, tears the faces of the *pikins* and gobbles up the village rice? Let us catch him, the rascal. Let us rid ourselves of an enemy and earn a good dash, besides." The talk continued in this vein until the collector finally explained in detail how they would take the beast alive using nets woven from vines. "Tangle up their arms in nets. Tangle up their legs. Hold them till massa comes. He brings his medicine. He puts big rascals off to sleep." Medicine? Buck held up a bottle of chloroform in front of the crowd. He promised a prize, a flashlight, for the "boy who does big work in the hunt."

Thus inspired, a group of about a hundred men marched off toward a cotton tree grove that the big rascals were said to frequent. Once there, the men hid their several large nets in the underbrush and then hid themselves, waiting for the chimps to come home in the evening. After a time, a family of perhaps ten apes filed into the grove, following the precise trail Buck had reckoned they would follow, led by an "old, broad-shouldered, hairy, tawny-black male."

Evening came; the chimps moved into the trees. The old leader and one of his younger females, after some negotiation, climbed into the same nest and made love, and then all the apes dozed into oblivion. "Silence fell upon the jungle." At that point, Buck and his son, Hector, and the hundred African assistants stealthily emerged from their hiding places, pulled out the many large nets, and placed them around six trees supporting the sleeping creatures. They all waited, Buck keeping an eye on his trusty bottle of chloroform, his sponges to apply the anesthetic, and his tarpaulin to place over an ape's head while the fumes took effect. Dawn approached. Finally Buck gave the signal. Fifty Africans raised a din of shouting and drum banging, and the rudely awakened chimpanzees clambered out of their nests, only to land in the nets.

It had been Buck's intention to capture only the youngest chimps, but as luck would have it, the biggest adult male became entangled. A young African boy moved too close. "Out tore a pair of arms from the snarl of nets. They flashed up, ugly and vengeful, and had clutched the poor wretch about his spindling body before Hector or I could help." The boy was killed. The Africans flung additional nets over the enraged creature, and Buck ran for his chloroform bottle. As he poured the contents onto a sponge, however, the big chimp happened to roll over onto Buck, who accidentally spilled the anesthetic onto himself and then passed out cold. When he regained consciousness, the melee was over. He saw his son Warren holding a smoking revolver, and quick as a flash realized that Warren unfortunately had been forced to shoot the big male; the ninety-nine Africans in the meanwhile had managed to net two young chimps from the group.

Buck's 1927 account of capturing chimpanzees is one of the most patently fanciful and dishonest pieces of writing I have ever read. (It is also racist, in an antique and unconscious way, reminding us that this indeed was a time when Africa served Americans and European colonialists as a convenient field of dreams, a blank screen to be filled with dramatic and self-elevating products of the imagination.) Yerkes described Buck as "an experienced collector." Buck claimed to have killed several gorillas and captured 127 live chimpanzees, many of whom he sold to Yerkes. We have little reason to doubt those claims about what Buck did. Why should he lie about how he did it?

Perhaps the truth was simply too unpleasant for J. L. Buck's customers to bear. I have lived in Tanzania for more than thirty years. For most of this time there has been almost no trade in chimpanzees, to my knowledge, and they are not eaten. But during the mid-1980s, when a panic was generated in the United States because of a perceived (never actual) shortage of chimpanzees for AIDS research, a number of cases of illegal chimpanzee hunting were reported in the Kigoma region. My Tanzanian field staff described seeing tightly tied sacks obviously containing infant chimpanzees (the men recognized the cries) transported northward along the lake in the local boats that serve the shoreline villages. One poacher was apprehended in Kigoma and put in jail. Unfortunately, his contraband, a small infant chimpanzee, was also put in jail, where he quickly died. If only I had been there at the time to stand bail.

There is one story of an infant who escaped. His mother was shot by two poachers after several days of abortive hunting in the Kabogo region, south of Kigoma. The first female they shot, with their one ancient rifle, was merely wounded. She may well have died later, but far away in the forest where the infant could not be found. Another female was killed, but unfortunately for the hunters, her infant was so badly wounded that it died as well. Finally the hunters were successful. As a mother lay on the ground, dying, the two men put down the gun and approached to take her frantic infant. Suddenly there was a crashing in the undergrowth, and a huge male chimpanzee charged out. The hunters turned to flee, but they were not quick enough. The

chimpanzee seized one and hurled him onto the rocky ground, break-
ing several ribs. With a swiping movement of one powerful arm, he
ripped the hair and skin off the other man's head, half scalping him.
Gathering up the still screaming infant, the male vanished into the
forest.

I heard that story because the two hunters turned up for treatment
in one of the local hospitals. After they had recovered, they were sent
to jail. But it is seldom that the tables are turned. Only too often a
chimpanzee adult who tried to protect a hunter's victim is shot and
wounded or killed. And then the terrified infant must endure a night-
mare journey, feet and hands usually tied with rope or wire, crammed
into a tiny box or basket or a suffocating sack. My own field research
has convinced me that the captive infant suffers the same agony of
fear and pain and despair that a human infant in like circumstances
would. When I described the trafficking in young chimps to the Tan-
zanian field staff at Gombe, one member, a man who knows chimpan-
zees as well as anyone, looking inward to stories remembered from
childhood, said, "It is like it was for us in the days of the slave trade, I
think."

It is not surprising that chimpanzees are marketable. We consider
all animals to be objects, and all objects are no doubt marketable.
What does surprise, in the case of chimpanzees, is the degree to which
certain crucial details of the marketing process are regularly ignored or
denied or finessed or concealed. J. L. Buck, with his wildly improbable
tale of capturing chimpanzees with chloroform and sponge, was a
small-time spinner of yarns, a minor obscurantist. But as we examine
more fully the live-chimpanzee trade as it originates in Africa, we
enter a world not of simple lies but of crafted and convoluted obscuri-
ties, a world (like Shakespeare's tempestuous island) where magic
comes from books and words become weapons, a strange and subtle
world of legal nuance and litigious nunnation, of laced irony and
linguistic prestidigitation.

2

Franz Sitter was born in Malikamen, Yugoslavia, on June 6, 1924.
Some thirty-three or thirty-four years later, he appeared in Sierra Leone
with a Ph.D. in parasitology from the University of Vienna. He pur-

chased a two-hundred-acre chicken farm, married an African, and established a nationwide egg business. He somehow acquired citizenship in Sierra Leone, making him that nation's sole white citizen, and expanded his business activities. The chimpanzee export business may have begun soon after his arrival, but Sitter also exported other species of animals, living and dead, as well as African art and artifacts; he imported animal food and agricultural machinery. At some point, he is said to have shared with Siaka Stevens, then president of Sierra Leone, a nationwide business in medical supplies. He was at one time a majority leaseholder in the Cape Sierra Hotel in Freetown; he managed a crude Wildlife Park for tourists. He was and still is, in short, a successful businessman in a variety of areas; but the chimpanzee business gave him notoriety, and it may have given him the best profits.

One of Franz Sitter's best regular customers during that period was Jan Moor-Jankowski, director of the Laboratory for Experimental Medicine and Surgery in Primates (LEMSIP) of New York University. Dr. Moor-Jankowski, a distinguished professor and scientist and a cosmopolite fluent in five languages, is an approximate contemporary of Sitter. In fact, both men are refugees of a sort from wartime Europe. But while Sitter claims to have fought as a young man under Field Marshal Erwin Rommel in the German Wehrmacht, Moor-Jankowski as a young adolescent was shot by the Nazis and served under various aliases in the Polish underground, gathering intelligence in Berlin during 1944 and 1945. For this service and for his later scientific achievements, Moor-Jankowski was awarded the French National Order of Merit in 1984 by President François Mitterrand.

"In 1968," Moor-Jankowski told me recently, "I did not want to buy chimpanzees from dealers in this country, because the way the animals were arriving showed to me that they were very, very poorly treated and that there must have been some awful things going on with these animals. So I sent two expeditions in the '60s, my own personnel, to Africa, with dart guns, trying to tranquilize and capture the animals. But this was rather naive because you shoot the animals and they run away into the jungle and they disappear, or they climb a tree and they fall off and . . . break their bones. And I think there was one case where the ants got to them before our men got to them. So I realized that this did not work." When they were in West Africa, though, his employees decided to visit the facilities of two major dealers, Suleiman Mansaray and Franz Sitter, both in Sierra Leone. The hygiene of Mansaray's operation was "awful," while Sitter's was "very impressive." Moor-Jankowski started dealing with Sitter.

"And I was very satisfied with the health conditions of the animals that were arriving from Sitter." They weren't malnourished or injured or riddled with shotgun pellets, as Moor-Jankowski had come to expect. In shipments from other dealers, sometimes 30 or 40 percent of the chimps would have shotgun pellets. "There were never shotgun pellets in Sitter's animals." In early 1975 Moor-Jankowski imported seventy-two chimps from Sitter — no shotgun pellets. Whereas normally, in Moor-Jankowski's experience, at least 20 percent of imported chimps would die in the first six months, only two of this group died. They were fundamentally healthy. Perhaps most important, very few of Sitter's chimps tested positive for hepatitis B. Since at that time they were being imported primarily for hepatitis B research, previously infected apes were essentially worthless and had to be returned to the importer and resold to circuses or zoos.

How did Sitter do it? How was he able to provide such consistently sound, undamaged young apes? During an extended correspondence Sitter indicated to Moor-Jankowski that one method was to fill a hut with bananas. Once the chimps went inside, the door was shut. A second method was to chase the apes with dogs. When the mothers got very tired, they would leave their toddlers and infants behind. The young ones could then be scooped up without injury. As Moor-Jankowski now reflects, "He was so believable: a perfect con artist."

The relationship between chimpanzee buyer and chimpanzee seller, between Jan Moor-Jankowski and Franz Sitter, was to be influenced by a third person with roots in wartime Europe, Geza Teleki.

In Geza Teleki's earliest childhood memory, he is playing alone with some toys in a room of one of his family's residences in Budapest when a bomb crashes through the ceiling and lands on a bed, cushioned by the mattress and the collapsing bed and therefore undetonated. The Russians were bombing Budapest. The Nazis were retreating. The Teleki family had already traded the last of their inherited fortune, a knapsack full of Maria Teresa gold coins, in exchange for a midnight truck ride away from the last of their inherited lands in Romania. But during the war Teleki's grandfather, Count Paul Teleki, served as prime minister of Hungary, and his father served as minister of education. Both had acquired reputations as outspoken anticommunists; and as the Soviets consolidated their new East European holdings, they focused on the Teleki family as an appropriate target for retribution. With assistance from the Hungarian underground, the family finally escaped Hungary in 1949.

Nineteen years later Geza Teleki, a naturalized American citizen, arrived in East Africa clutching a B.A. from George Washington University, on his way to Gombe National Park in Tanzania to study chimpanzees as a research assistant to Jane Goodall. When he first met Goodall, the young man expressed some apprehension about what Gombe would be like and what would be expected of him. "I remember almost as if I were there, to this day," he told me, "her getting a bit exasperated trying to answer these questions, and then saying to me that if I'm at Gombe then I'm a guest in an environment where the principal occupants are chimpanzees and other animals." He asked her what she meant by that, and she said, "Well, if you're going down a path and a chimp is coming the other way, you're the one who gets out of the path." That comment impressed him, stayed with him for the next twenty years. "I didn't understand the significance of it at the time, but it became the basis for much of what I did over the next twenty years in terms of conservation with chimps." A second thing happened that would affect Teleki's later direction. It was 1968. Gombe had just been designated a national park, and officials from the government visited the site to meet scientists working there. "It was an extremely embarrassing meeting, because . . . these people kept asking these questions about the park assuming that as scientists we would have the answers. And we didn't have the answers. We could tell them all sorts of detailed information about nursing behavior and mother-infant relationships, family life, and social interactions, but when it came to questions like, 'How many chimps are there in the park?' and 'What kinds of habitat in the park are utilized most frequently?' and so on, we had no answers." It was downright embarrassing. "I thought that part of the reason we do science is to be able to better manage the natural environment and make sure that the subjects we're studying and on which we build our careers, when we go home receive the kind of protection that is warranted; and we failed in doing this because the research at Gombe was so focused on the social aspects of chimpanzee life that from the management point of view we were unable to give any useful advice." Teleki resolved always to keep in mind as a general principle the advice Jane gave him about walking along paths; and he resolved never again to do science without including a utilitarian component that would, in some fashion, pay back his research subjects.

Teleki returned to the United States in 1971 and began a decade of working toward a Ph.D. in anthropology and primatology at Pennsylvania State University. In 1977 two organizations in the United States — a pharmaceutical company known as Merck Sharp and Dohme and Albany Medical College — requested government permits to import chimpanzees from West Africa. The U.S. Fish and Wildlife Service asked Teleki, as a chimp expert, to help evaluate the applications. As Teleki discovered, the two applications were for an importation of almost three hundred young, wild-caught chimpanzees. Both named the same country of origin, Sierra Leone. And both named the same dealer to provide those apes, a certain Dr. Franz Sitter. "At that point," Teleki recalls, "I discovered something else which became a fundamental issue in everything that's happened since then: the people who were filing the applications weren't telling the truth." The Merck application stated that 125 chimpanzees would be used for hepatitis vaccine testing and afterward donated to a captive breeding project in New Mexico for the "enhancement of the propagation of the species." The only problem was that the director of the breeding project in New Mexico knew nothing of this hypothetical donation. Ultimately, the Merck application was denied by U.S. Fish and Wildlife; the Albany Medical College application was allowed to lapse.

Teleki began examining recent import documents in Washington and talking with contacts in various U.S. laboratories, and he soon saw that Sierra Leone was exporting more chimps than all the other African nations put together. It also became apparent that Franz Sitter was Sierra Leone's biggest dealer. How could Sierra Leone, one of the smallest nations in Africa, smaller than the state of South Carolina, export such large numbers of chimpanzees? Information available at the time suggested that comparatively few chimpanzees survived anywhere in that part of West Africa, and that the export trade was contributing to the final destruction of populations yet remaining. A brief survey of Sierra Leone chimpanzees conducted during the mid-1960s by Adriaan Kortlandt of the University of Amsterdam confirmed that "there cannot be any doubt that the present exportation rate is much higher than the wild stock can afford." But a more thorough survey seemed necessary.

Several conservation groups provided funds for a census of the chimpanzee population in Sierra Leone. And so, in November of 1979, Geza Teleki flew to a country that seemed to summarize the problems of West Africa: explosive population growth, massive deforestation, and perpetual overhunting. Some 97 percent of the forests had disappeared since the start of the last century; two-thirds of the final five hundred square miles of forest were either being or about to be logged; fallow periods for slash-and-burn farming had declined from twenty years to three. Where monkeys continued to inhabit recently deforested lands, the government declared them "pests" and offered bounties that led to the killing of a quarter of a million over fifteen years.

In fact, many of Sierra Leone's problems may have begun in the fifteenth century, after Portuguese sailors looked over a spectacularly beautiful mountain range along the Atlantic Coast and decided they were seeing the Lion Mountains, the Serra Lyona. In the eighteenth century, Europeans organized a massive trade in slaves and ivory out of Sierra Leone; by the middle of the nineteenth century, European loggers had begun the wholesale removal of Sierra Leone's rich native forests, and by the end of the nineteenth century, Europeans were mining to depletion the country's gold, chromite, and iron deposits. When Teleki arrived in 1979, most of the large mammals of Sierra Leone were approaching extinction, yet European and American sports hunters were still pointing their high-powered rifles at big targets such as chimpanzees, hippopotamuses, and elephants, pulling triggers without even paying the required hunting fees — $15 per chimp, $20 per hippo, $200 per elephant. Sergio Bonora, an Italian who managed a logging operation in the Gola Forest, once described his prowess in killing three extremely rare golden cats. All by himself, a Lebanese pop singer killed forty elephants for fun; he probably would have killed more except that a herd of elephants trampled him to death one day. American missionaries could be seen hunting elephants and other big game in the Wara Wara Hills, the Loma Mountains, and elsewhere. Missionaries also supplied local hunters with ammunition in return for bushmeat; and, in the Makeni region, missionaries supplied raw ivory to a carver who specialized in creating beautiful figurines of Jesus and the Virgin Mary.

Shortly after arriving in Sierra Leone, Teleki visited Franz Sitter's farm outside Freetown. His stationery represented the place as "Dr. Franz Sitter's Zoological Station," but to Teleki it looked more like a run-down chicken farm, with assorted cages and sheds constructed largely from rough sheet metal and wire mesh, housing a menagerie. (A formal examination of the premises in 1981 would describe twenty-six baby chimps, fifteen rock pythons, fifteen royal pythons, various monkeys and wild cats, a bongo, and numerous smaller antelopes.) Perhaps impressed by meeting an aristocrat with a famous name from the Old Country, Sitter greeted Teleki with the standard Prussian greeting, bending at the waist, shaking a hand formally, clicking his heels in salute. His personal demeanor, his gestures, and his speech habits suggested a military background; and while Sitter claimed Austrian origins, Teleki noted his accent to be High German, not Austrian German at all.

The two sat down and spread out a map. Sitter proceeded to give Teleki a guided tour of the country, pointing out all the wonderful places where, in the dealer's opinion, wildlife existed in large numbers. "His purpose very obviously," Teleki believes, "was to persuade me that there were chimps running around all over the country and that his export business was just a small drop in the bucket." Sitter said that the local farmers were trapping these apes and selling them because they didn't know what else to do, and that chimpanzee females, harassed by dogs, had been dropping their babies and abandoning their youngsters. But Teleki knew that mother chimps don't drop baby chimps; mother chimps don't abandon their young.

Teleki was joined by a second American chimpanzee expert, Lori Baldwin of Penn State. They were formally received by President Stevens and provided with one of his personal vehicles to assist in the survey. They were given full support from the Ministry of Agriculture and Forestry. Accompanied by Ibrahim Bangura and Mohamed Mansaray, both top officials with the ministry's Wildlife Conservation Branch, as well as several game guards and rangers and other ministry employees, Teleki and Baldwin drove 5,600 miles in six months and walked another 800 miles; they examined six areas that were being proposed as potential game reserves or national parks, another six areas managed as forest reserves, and several other regions suggested by local people and by Sitter himself.

The survey indicated that only 2,000 chimpanzees, plus or minus 500, still remained in the entire country — distinctly fewer than the 25,000 to 35,000 chimps Sitter had estimated. The survey also revealed some of the chimpanzee dealer's enormous influence. During their six months of travel around the country, the survey team failed to find a single settlement where "the one-armed white man" was unknown; virtually every hunter they spoke with had at one time or another dealt with Sitter or his agents. And Teleki learned that the dealer was paying hunters only a small fraction of the animals' value on the European and American market. A bare-headed rock fowl, which is "a very ugly little bird endemic to certain parts of Sierra Leone," bought by Sitter for $10 or $15 could be worth $25,000 overseas. A live bongo could be bought for $20 to $30 in the country and sold overseas for $40,000 to $50,000. A leopard might cost $10 to $20 but could be resold for $2,000 to $3,000. Chimpanzees, costing perhaps $30 or $40 in Sierra Leone, were worth up to $5,000 overseas.

Around the campfire at night, hunters who worked for Sitter described to Teleki how they actually acquired live chimpanzees. Sometimes they would kill individual mothers with shotguns and pull off their clinging infants. Sometimes they would use beaters and dogs to drive chimpanzee groups into trees, where the adults could be shot and the babies retrieved. And sometimes they baited known chimpanzee habitats with poisoned fruits, so that adults would be killed and nursing babies who were not yet eating fruit could be collected. Then they sold the chimps to Sitter's agents, Lebanese and Sierra Leoneans living in towns across the country. In addition to the adult casualties, Teleki believed, many of the captured infants probably died before they arrived at Sitter's place in Freetown. Some would have died from accidental wounds received during the original capture; others, bound with rope or wire or forced into small wooden crates for days or even weeks, must have died of starvation, dehydration, or sheer physical abuse.

Sierra Leone by itself did not appear to have enough chimpanzees to satisfy the market, so that many of them were being smuggled across the borders from Guinea to the north and Liberia to the east. Ahmed Haidar, Sitter's agent in Kamakwie town, near Guinea, was regularly buying live chimpanzees and other animals that were carried on footpaths and trucked along the Madina-Dula road from that country. Alhaji Seko, Sitter's agent in Zimi town, near Liberia, would buy chimpanzee babies toted in by hunters crossing the Liberian border. Actually, Seko oversaw a bilateral trade between Sierra Leone and Liberia. Many Liberians eat chimpanzees, whereas Sierra Leoneans for cultural and religious reasons generally do not. Thus, Liberian hunters were shooting adults for food and then selling any surviving babies to

Sitter's agent in Sierra Leone; Sierra Leonean hunters were shooting adults primarily to capture babies for Sitter, but they incidentally relied on Sitter's agent Seko to sell the dead adults as meat to Liberians.

Sitter used purchasing agents in every major town near every protected wildlife area in Sierra Leone. But he focused his activities on one of the country's richest remaining wildlife areas, the Outamba-Kilimi region to the north, which the government was in the process of defining as a protected game reserve. Later, in 1982, Outamba-Kilimi was designated as Sierra Leone's first national park — but Franz Sitter got there first. In the early 1970s he constructed a small tourist lodge on the bank of the Little Scarcies River, at the boundary of the proposed game reserve, and he regularly transported tourists out to the lodge to look at wild animals. For three years this operation was managed by a professional "white hunter" imported from Kenya, David Brooke, who, when he was not coddling tourists, organized hunts and game drives and kept an eye on one hundred to two hundred pit traps. With the assistance of Sitter's local agent, Brooke recruited hunters and distributed ammunition and guns. Brooke and his employees targeted everything, even elephants and leopards. To capture chimpanzees, they organized weekly drives, using as many as two hundred men to isolate small chimpanzee groups. Adult males would be driven away. The cornered mothers would be shot for their infants.

It is, of course, difficult to estimate the full effect of Sitter's operation at Outamba-Kilimi during this period, the early 1970s, but it must have been significant. Local people described seeing several shipments of live and dead animals and animal pieces leave the area each week — shipments of crocodile skins, elephant tusks, pythons, dwarf buffalo, duikers, bushbuck, waterbuck, bongo, leopards, servals, green monkeys, black-and-white colobus monkeys, red colobus monkeys, and chimps — all bound for Dr. Franz Sitter's "zoological station" near Freetown.

3

But the door seemed to be closing.

It seemed to be closing in the United States, first of all. On July 1, 1975, the first international treaty regulating trade in live animals and animal products came into force. The Convention on International Trade in Endangered Species of Wild Fauna and Flora — more conveniently known as CITES — was ratified by ten nations, including the United States. And since the United States had been by far the world's greatest consumer of live primates, this was a major event. Currently, more than 110 nations have ratified the treaty.

CITES assigned chimpanzees and the other three species of great apes the highest status for protection: Appendix I, or "threatened with extinction" status. According to the treaty, no Appendix I species can be traded between member countries if the motive is primarily commercial, or if taking them out of the wild would threaten the survival of the species.

As a treaty, CITES has no real force legally. Member nations agree to establish their own laws to implement the treaty's standards. If they wish for political or public relations reasons to sign, yet for commercial reasons to violate the treaty, members simply write exceptions into their implementing laws. In the United States, the implementing laws for CITES were codified in the Endangered Species Act of 1973. But because the apes were important for the biomedical industry, that 1973 act exempted chimpanzees and bonobos from the fullest possible protection by declaring them "threatened" rather than "endangered." The threatened designation allowed the exploitation of chimpanzees and bonobos to continue more or less unchanged within the United States. Nonetheless, the U.S. Endangered Species Act had just enough force to inhibit the trade in wild-caught apes from Africa into the United States. Importers using federal funds to acquire these "threatened" apes for scientific or educational purposes now needed to demonstrate that their actions were "not likely to jeopardize the continued existence of" the species.*

The door seemed to be closing in Sierra Leone, too. Sierra Leone has never joined CITES, but the country began to develop its own live-animal export laws — and importing nations that were CITES members would be obliged to respect those laws. In 1978, President Stevens banned all chimpanzee exports with a special presidential decree; and in 1982, the export from Sierra Leone of any wildlife or wildlife products was prohibited.

---

* Importation of chimpanzees and other primates into the United States for the pet trade was terminated at this time through a simple alteration in the federal public health code.

Yet even after the presidential decree of 1978, Franz Sitter continued to acquire live chimpanzees, stockpiling them on his chicken farm inside a compound of cages and seven-foot walls. Sitter shipped ten chimps to Europe in December 1978, a few months after the ban was imposed. The apes were probably bound for Professor Witold Brzosko of the Polish Institute of Infectious Diseases, but on the way to Poland the shipment passed through the Netherlands, a signatory of CITES, and the chimps were confiscated by Dutch authorities.

By the early 1980s, Sitter was corresponding with a certain Gerhard Stehlik in Vienna. Austria signed the CITES agreement in April of 1982. But in a March 1982 letter, Sitter informed Stehlik that he had about fifty chimps on hand, including ten he was ready to export to Austria, "but Government Officials delay my export papers from one week to the other week." Stehlik, who represented Immuno A.G., an Austrian-based company specializing in the manufacture of drugs and vaccines from human blood plasma, seemed interested in some arrangement with Sitter. By that time, however, Stehlik of Immuno had also started to correspond with a man who identified himself as the "Austrian consul" in Sierra Leone, Klaus Bieber.

Bieber, writing from Freetown, reported to Stehlik in Vienna that the exportation of chimps from Sierra Leone had become (according to a translation from Bieber's German) "a hot issue." For one thing, he informed Stehlik, neighboring Liberia and Guinea supported the ban on exports, since Sierra Leone had been shipping chimps smuggled from those countries; for another thing, the Sierra Leone Nature Conservation Association had been criticizing the exportation of chimps, so that "large parts of the population became familiar with the subject." Bieber didn't think that even "an official intervention of the Austrian government would have any chance of succeeding" in getting an export permit at that time.

The only possibility, as Bieber saw it, would be to set up a research station right there in Sierra Leone, "as you [Stehlik] proposed." Instead of sending chimps to the Immuno laboratory in Austria, why not send the laboratory to the chimps? French oil money was financing a major chimpanzee and gorilla research laboratory in Gabon; the Americans had since 1975 been acquiring chimps for a laboratory in Liberia, right next door to Sierra Leone, and were creating a research operation there. If the Americans and the French were doing it, why not the Austrians? Why not establish an Immuno research laboratory using chimpanzees in Sierra Leone? Bieber added that Sitter was "probably the only possible supplier of chimps."

Although he sometimes referred to himself as the Austrian consul, Bieber was actually an "honorary" Austrian consul. He was not employed by the Austrian government, but worked independently as an entrepreneur and consultant. He had for many years maintained a partnership with Franz Sitter in the wildlife capture and export business. And by the second half of 1982, Bieber was discussing with Immuno how much it would cost to have him lobby for an Immuno research laboratory in Sierra Leone. Bieber eventually received a few thousand dollars from Immuno and an offer of formal employment.

In a letter of September 15, 1982, Bieber delicately informed Stehlik that (again, in translation of the German original) "you will not be able to avoid certain extraordinary expenses in addition to the formation and establishment of the company." Bieber was "a bit worried about this," he wrote, because "I do not know how far you are willing to go." Nonetheless, it was clear that "some people have certain expectations." Early the next month, Stehlik asked Bieber to "let us know what we are expected to do for the certain extraordinary items to expedite the matter, as you quoted in your letter dated Sept. 15, 1982. Precise information, as for example four tires for Mercedes type XY, mode of shipping, address, status, e.g. 'personal gift' would be appreciated." Four Mercedes tires was not quite in the range of what Bieber was thinking; he replied that it would be "necessary in particular to consider an impressive gift for the president. Frequently new cars, which are not known here, are put 'at his disposal.' " Stehlik replied in November 1982, noting that the appropriate Austrian ministries were drafting a treaty between Sierra Leone and Austria, and giving some suggestions "with regard to the impressive gift to President Stevens." Stehlik thought that Immuno could send Sierra Leone's president a "prestigious crystal chandelier made by Lobmaier," or a piano, or Augarten porcelain, or perhaps a "hunting-gun made by Steyr or Ferlach (beautiful piece of work)."*

During this time Bieber also arranged to meet with Geza Teleki in Freetown. Under the sponsorship of the U.S. World Wildlife Fund, Teleki had returned to help establish Sierra Leone's first national park

* The reader should not imagine this once-secret discussion concerned bribes from a private company to government officials. A representative of Immuno later clarified that at issue were simple and ordinary "gifts," intended to foster general good will.

in Outamba-Kilimi. As temporary director of the park, Teleki had legal access to all documents of the Ministry of Agriculture and Forestry; he was the only white person with the legal authority to put people in jail in Sierra Leone for violating wildlife laws. He was not a peripheral individual, in other words, and Klaus Bieber must have recognized that Teleki's cooperation would be important. Strangely enough, as Teleki recalls the meeting, Bieber never discussed a proposed research station in Sierra Leone. Instead, he seemed interested in discovering what Teleki's reaction would be to the idea of exporting chimps from Sierra Leone to Austria.

Be that as it may, Honorary Consul Bieber's industrious lobbying must have persuaded some Sierra Leonean officials of the legitimacy of Immuno's cause. On April 18, 1983 (one year after Austria had signed the CITES treaty), Bieber and an Immuno executive named Gerald Eder met with several high officials of Sierra Leone, including the minister of agriculture and forestry and acting minister of natural resources, Abass Bundu. In his subsequent report to the secretary of the president, Dr. Bundu wrote that the Austrians were proposing to establish a hepatitis research institute in Sierra Leone, "precisely because they would not otherwise be able to import chimpanzees into Austria." The Austrians were asking the Sierra Leone government to supply their research institute with some sixty to eighty chimpanzees per year, Minister Bundu wrote, but he had "been advised" that taking such a large number from the country each year would "seriously deplete our national stock of wild chimpanzees." Once they had conducted research on those sixty to eighty chimps per year, the Austrians would place them on an uninhabited island somewhere for "rehabilitation purposes." Bundu rejected the last idea for a number of reasons, including the belief that such "rehabilitation" would ultimately result in the death of the apes and the concern that it would risk the "transmission of viruses acquired during the experimentation."

Nonetheless, Bundu finally recommended that His Excellency the President accept Immuno's plans for a research station — with a few changes. To avoid depleting the national stock of wild chimpanzees, Bundu had proposed (and Eder had agreed during the meeting) that instead of actually taking sixty to eighty chimpanzees per year, Immuno should establish a breeding farm to produce that number. Sierra Leone might provide fifty to sixty chimps to start the breeding, "whilst simultaneously" Immuno could immediately benefit by "carrying out experiments on a small scale" on those same apes during the first year.

Within another one or two years, Bundu felt, the breeding farm would be able to supply the research center with all the chimpanzees it needed.

Now, it would require a certain sexual heroism for fifty to sixty chimps to produce sixty to eighty babies per year. Female chimps normally produce only a single infant at a time. Of course, not all the breeding chimps would be female; some males would be required. Moreover, even if babies were to be pulled from their mothers by the age of one year to stimulate breeding, eight additional months would still be required for gestation. Beyond the mathematical problems, it might have proved distracting for these chimpanzees to breed "whilst simultaneously" being experimented on. But, according to formal minutes of that meeting, the Immuno people explained that "breeding and research should proceed simultaneously in order not to render chimpanzees an endangered species in Sierra Leone."

Where would the original breeders come from? Where would the breeding farm be located? Bundu informed the secretary to the president that "my Ministry is of the firm opinion that the centre should be located near Freetown. Dr. Sitter is already engaged in activities involving wildlife, including chimpanzees. Instead of proliferating such activities, with the resultant depletion of the number of chimpanzees in the country, Dr. Sitter could be brought into the arrangement and he has already shown a keen interest in the matter. His farm is located at Rokel, near Freetown. Moreover, by locating the breeding farm and centre near Freetown, we would be providing a facility for tourist attraction."

To my knowledge, a chimpanzee breeding farm and research station were never established in Sierra Leone, although the general concept would be resurrected again and again. While these ideas were being discussed, however, Sitter's long-awaited sale of live baby chimpanzees to Austria appeared on the verge of closure. On the same day as the meeting in Freetown between Gerald Eder and Abass Bundu, April 18, the chief conservator of forests in Sierra Leone, a man named M. B. D. Feika, signed a permit authorizing Franz Sitter to export twenty chimpanzees from the country "on or about" June 1983.*

* Feika, incidentally, was both a direct subordinate of Abass Bundu and the immediate superior of Geza Teleki — who, had he known about it, would have vigorously opposed the signing of that export permit.

Sitter must have received the export papers soon after April 18, 1983, and he must have begun preparing to ship the twenty chimps to Vienna. But a few weeks later, on May 11, Bieber received from Vienna an "urgent message" in English to pass on to Dr. Sitter:

> dear dr. sitter,
>
> we have difficulties to get the import license.
> viennese local authorities take an expertice of dr. teleki
> as bases who stated that there were 2-000 free living chimpanzees
> in sierra leone.
> please send us copies of official report, written by dr. teleki
> as soon as possible.
>
> best regards
> dr. eder
> 134925 imuno a

The quick telegram was followed by a longer letter, from Eder to Sitter, confirming that the importation had been delayed and explaining to the chimpanzee dealer that he "could be very helpful in this matter." Because of the CITES treaty, ratified by Austria the previous year, Austrian authorities needed to clarify whether the importation of chimpanzees was to be a commercial or a scientific transaction and whether it would be detrimental to the species. Gerald Eder of Immuno had been informed by Bieber several months earlier that "mothers have to be killed in order to procure young babies." Yet Eder now urged Sitter to provide a more positive story: "It would be a considerable advantage to us if you could send us an official comment from which it can be seen that the animals you have primarily were not caught for exportation but are young animals which were brought to you by the natives etc."

4

Sitter's star was ascendant. Not only were the Austrians eager to do business, but the Japanese as well. The dealer was just then concluding an arrangement to ship thirty baby chimps to Japan via the Kasho

Company, serving as agent for Toshio Shikata of the Nihon University School of Medicine in Tokyo. This exchange took place well after Sierra Leone's presidential ban on the exportation of chimps, of course, but Sierra Leone was persuaded to ignore its own export controls because the Japanese government sent a boatload of rice. It was, in other words, a government-to-government exchange, a bilateral agreement overriding and temporarily invalidating the CITES treaty, arranged by and profiting a private dealer, Dr. Franz Sitter.

Japan had for several years been a major importer of Sitter's chimps. Between 1973 and 1977 the Japanese had received almost two hundred infant chimpanzees from Sierra Leone; and even during the early period of Sierra Leone's presidential ban on exports, in 1979 and 1980, Japan had taken as many as twenty-five chimpanzees from Franz Sitter. Japan ratified CITES late in 1980. But Japanese customs officers still passed Sitter's shipment of thirty chimpanzees in 1983. As M. B. D. Feika, Sierra Leone's chief conservator of forests, explained in a letter to one critic of the export (the assistant secretary general of the CITES Secretariat), "to every rule their [sic] is an exception." As Shigeo Honjo of the National Institute of Health in Japan explained in a letter answering one critic of the import (Shirley McGreal of the International Primate Protection League in the United States), in spite of the CITES agreement Japan had plenty of good reasons, including impenetrably mystical ones, to import and experiment on chimps: "We, human beings, always want to be healthy and peaceful. Unless we are healthy and peaceful, we can not be considerate for the protection of chimpanzees. And the chimpanzee can contribute to the promotion of human health. This is the way of thinking of us, Japanese scientists. We usually call this style of thinking the circle of transmigration. Don't you agree with this thought?"

The importing agent, the Kasho Company, would cite a more formal justification for this acquisition of thirty endangered animals: "captive breeding to help propagate the species." The apes were to be used in the development of a breeding colony on the southern island of Kyushu. What really happened, however, was that Sitter's apes were dispersed to laboratories around the country. According to later customs records, eleven chimpanzees, including two from that 1983 shipment out of Sierra Leone, were eventually exported from Japan to China; and some of that group went to a Chinese rare-animal breeding center then being sustained with the charitable assistance of an American laboratory that had recently tried to import chimpanzees directly from Franz Sitter and failed.

Does this begin to sound like a circle of transmigration?

5

Sitter's deal with the Austrians would take longer to bear fruit. Three years longer. Finally, at a few minutes before midnight on July 30, 1986, a chartered plane routed through Lagos, Nigeria, originating in Freetown, Sierra Leone, landed at Vienna's Schwechat Airport. The principal cargo on that flight was twenty very young chimpanzees packed in crates. The cargo passed customs, and the caged apes were quickly loaded onto the back of a truck and transported to a fortress of high walls, barbed-wire fences, and armed guards, the headquarters complex of a company with two thousand employees in Austria and subsidiaries in thirty countries around the world, Immuno A.G. That was the shipment that Franz Sitter told me about when I visited him in Sierra Leone. To repeat his description of the events it inspired, "What a commotion!"

The twenty chimpanzees arrived at the end of July 1986. In early August the World Wildlife Fund of Austria alleged that Immuno had illegally imported the chimpanzees and demanded that they be confiscated. Immuno insisted that the importation had been perfectly legal and requested a formal meeting with responsible Austrian authorities to discuss the matter. On August 21 that meeting was held at the Vienna Town Hall. For years Immuno had postulated a pressing need to acquire chimpanzees for hepatitis research or to test hepatitis vaccines; suddenly at this Town Hall meeting Immuno representatives began to speak of the importance of acquiring chimpanzees in the battle against the AIDS epidemic. The meeting was chaired by Helmut Braun and stabilized by the gravitas of such important Immuno officials as Dr. Johann Eibl and Dr. Gerald Eder. But Immuno's principal supporting expert was an American, Dr. Robert Gallo, from the U.S. National Institutes of Health. According to a paraphrase later written by Geza Teleki, who attended the meeting, Gallo stated that "chimpanzees can be justifiably obtained by his laboratory at any time for the purpose of AIDS research, regardless [of] what import limitations had been set until now by the U.S. Government, as no agency in Washington was likely to oppose such a demand given the prevailing public concern about AIDS, and that Immuno should be granted the same recognition by the Austrian Government in its efforts to obtain chimpanzees for the same purposes."

Geza Teleki had been on vacation in Budapest when Immuno first requested the Vienna meeting. He was suffering from the effects of river blindness, a debilitating parasitic disease he had acquired while surveying the chimpanzees of Sierra Leone seven years earlier; but when someone from the Austrian World Wildlife Fund telephoned him about the Town Hall meeting, he was easily persuaded to make the short trip to Vienna. Just before the August 21 conference, Teleki was unofficially shown the export papers from Sierra Leone. Were they legal? He thought not. The Sierra Leonean export permit was signed by the wrong person, he noted. Moreover, the accompanying "CITES equivalency form" (to supplement the export permit from a non-CITES nation such as Sierra Leone) was printed in German, whereas English is the language required. Additionally, Teleki recognized, the Sierra Leonean who had affixed his signature to that German-language document understood not a word of German.

If the export papers were inappropriate, at least from one person's perspective, the Austrian import papers were evocative. In Austria, the Ministry of Trade and Commerce is responsible for ensuring compliance with CITES. To justify granting an import permit in the case of chimpanzees, that ministry would normally consult an expert, who would then assess whether the treaty's restrictions were being respected. In the city of Vienna, the formal scientific authority for CITES on all primate trade, Dr. Ulrike Goldschmid, learned of the importation into Vienna only after it happened. The opinion cited on the import papers had been written, instead, by the CITES scientific authority for the state of Lower Austria (but distinctly *not* for Vienna), Dr. M. Schweiger, a beetle expert.

Further information about this mysterious beetle expert of Lower Austria was to appear quite fortuitously. In the last two weeks of September, Geza Teleki and individuals from the Austrian World Wildlife Fund and the government examined approximately three thousand pages of documents on the subject of Immuno's importation of chimpanzees, preparing for a press conference on October 2. "It was a real undercover operation," Teleki told me. "We were so afraid of leakages, so afraid of potential lawsuits, that we worked in a private home with locked doors; and every copy of every paper that anybody wrote by hand was burned in the oven before we left the premises in the evening, and the only thing that came out of that room was the material that was put together to officially serve as the press release."

During weekends and some evenings, Teleki took a few trips within Austria for, to use his expression, "relaxation purposes." Once, he drove to the village of Bad Deutsch-Altenburg in Lower Austria, where he had heard there was an African museum. It was a small museum, privately owned. When Teleki walked inside, he was amazed to discover a collection of hundreds of cultural artifacts and antiquities, leopard skins, elephant tusks, stuffed animals including an elephant, a pygmy hippo, even a stuffed chimpanzee — many from Sierra Leone with the name Franz Sitter on their identifying labels. Making casual inquiries, Teleki discovered that the museum director had been a school chum of Sitter directly after the war, that he had been a business partner of Sitter for the past couple of decades (importing, among other things, African antiquities), and that he frequently visited Sierra Leone as Sitter's guest. In Europe, or in Austria, or at least in Lower Austria, he had established his scientific reputation as a beetle expert. His name was Dr. M. Schweiger.

The Austrian World Wildlife Fund held its press conference on October 2, 1986. On October 7, the Austrian Ministry of Trade and Commerce declared that the import and export papers were valid. By January of 1987, a high official in the Austrian government was describing the investigation as finished and the case as closed. Immuno kept its twenty chimpanzees.

6

In the meantime, Jan Moor-Jankowski, the Polish-born professor of medical research at New York University Medical School and director of the Laboratory for Experimental Medicine and Surgery in Primates (LEMSIP), had come to Vienna. Moor-Jankowski, the reader will remember, was for many years one of Franz Sitter's best customers in the United States, purchasing in 1975 alone more than seventy young chimpanzees from the dealer. Moor-Jankowski also enthusiastically endorsed Sitter to other laboratory directors, thereby helping to extend Sitter's business connections into Japan and Europe.

By the early 1980s, though, the laboratory director had begun to have doubts about the chimpanzee dealer and his methods. For one thing, Geza Teleki had written to the LEMSIP director. "And I liked Teleki," Moor-Jankowski recalls now, "not so much because of chimpanzees, but because you know I am from Eastern Europe. His father and grandfather were very famous anticommunist politicians, so I knew that a Geza Teleki would not lie. But he was telling me bad things about Sitter, and I was telling him that he was wrong, because I had quite a correspondence and telephone calls by that time with Sitter." Moor-Jankowski finally changed his mind after examining Teleki's detailed and thoroughly documented report on his 1979 survey of the chimpanzees of Sierra Leone, which described Sitter's methods.

By 1983 Moor-Jankowski was also questioning Immuno's attempts to establish a laboratory in Sierra Leone and to import chimps from that nation. Because he was an internationally recognized expert on the use of primates in research, his occasionally frank opposition may have helped to account for the long delay Immuno experienced in getting Austrian import papers. In any event, Dr. Moor-Jankowski came to Vienna during the second half of 1986, that explosive time of accusations and counteraccusations, partly because his name was appearing in print. The chief of Immuno's legal department had complained about a "dishonest" campaign to sully the firm's clean image, an attempted "murder of reputation," much of which seemed to be coming from the United States in general and New York City in particular. One publication likened the criticisms of Immuno to recent criticisms of the newly elected Austrian president, Kurt Waldheim, who was found to have concealed a Nazi past: "Certain voices from the so very much democratic America attempted with unimaginable but still not sufficient or factual means to destroy totally the future victor of the murderous election fight for the Presidency of the Federal Republic. The results are well known! And now again shrill shouts emanate from that example of liberal economics. J. Moor-Jankowski, Head of a chimpanzee center in New York — and on the side recipient of contracts from the pharmaceutical industry which works on similar products as the Austrian Immuno A.G. — threatens with a chimpanzee theft the 'bad boys' of our nationally competing enterprise . . .

This is reason enough for many gullible opponents of animal experimentation to send to hell the Austrian model enterprise which exports 80 percent of its products."

In addition to such public comments, an irritating nuisance perhaps, the Polish-American scientist and laboratory director had been given something more particular to focus his mind: Immuno A.G. was suing him for $4 million. Actually, Immuno was suing a lot of people. Its lawyers were busy filing suits against some four dozen individuals and organizations in Europe: journalists and politicians, newspapers and newspaper editors, most of the firm's significant critics, it would seem, up to and including the secretary general of the Austrian World Wildlife Fund and the director of Austria's TRAFFIC (an organization that monitors international trade in wildlife). Prince Philip and Prince Sadruddin Aga Khan, president and vice president respectively of the World Wildlife Fund International, wielded their considerable influence during this time to protest the original export of chimpanzees from Sierra Leone and then to encourage the leashing of Immuno's unleashed legal staff. But the litigation proceeded in Europe.

In the United States, Immuno's biggest target was Jan Moor-Jankowski. To understand his legal troubles, let us return to April 18, 1983, when Klaus Bieber and Gerald Eder sat down with Abass Bundu and other government officials in Freetown. Immuno submitted a proposal to the Sierra Leone government for its hepatitis research station during that meeting — but almost a year previously Bieber had circulated a draft of the plan. A copy of that early draft had, by late 1982, fallen into the hands of a woman living in South Carolina, Shirley McGreal, chairwoman of the International Primate Protection League (IPPL).

Mostly, the draft plan stated what we already know from having considered Abass Bundu's April 1983 report to His Excellency the President: that Immuno wished to establish a chimpanzee research institute in Sierra Leone, seemingly to overcome the problem of CITES restrictions on trade in endangered species, and that Immuno wished to acquire sixty to eighty chimpanzees per year for research or testing.

Shirley McGreal knew nothing about Bundu's report, for the simple reason that in late 1982 it had not yet been written, but her understanding of Immuno's proposal almost exactly parallels Bundu's understanding. She believed that the proposal could be criticized from several perspectives. Early in 1983 she mailed a letter incorporating her comments to the *Journal of Medical Primatology*, a specialized publication with a total circulation of approximately three hundred, edited by Jan Moor-Jankowski. Because the letter criticized Immuno, before printing it Moor-Jankowski sent a copy to Dr. Johann Eibl of Immuno, soliciting his rebuttal. Eibl's reply was simple: he turned the letter over to the firm's lawyers in New York. The New York lawyers demanded access to the documents in McGreal's possession and threatened to sue if the letter was published before they could formulate an appropriate response. Moor-Jankowski didn't believe that Immuno needed him to retrieve their own documents for them, but as a courtesy, he delayed publication by several months and extended his deadline for a rebuttal. Finally, in December 1983, he published Shirley McGreal's letter to the editor. Immuno sued for libel.

Immuno sued Shirley McGreal for $4 million. Immuno sued Jan Moor-Jankowski for $4 million. Immuno sued the publisher and the distributor of the *Journal of Medical Primatology* for $4 million each. Because Moor-Jankowski at about the same time had voiced brief criticisms of Immuno's chimpanzee plans, and because those criticisms were quoted by a journalist writing for *New Scientist* magazine, Immuno also sued the author of that article and the publisher of that magazine for $4 million each. Just in case its message wasn't getting across, Immuno sued the distributor of *New Scientist* for $4 million. Here is the infamous letter:

Letter to the Editor

A Project With Potential to Spread Non-A, Non-B Hepatitis in West Africa

The International Primate Protection League has learned with some concern of proposals submitted by the IMMUNO AG Company of Austria to the Government of Sierra Leone, West Africa, regarding the company's plans to establish a chimpanzee research facility in Sierra Leone, West Africa.

According to a statement dated August 23, 1982, submitted to the Government of Sierra Leone by Klaus Bieber, Austrian Consul in Sierra Leone, the animals would be used in hepatitis non-A, non-B research and testing of hepatitis B vaccine. The purpose of establishing the facility in Africa was stated to be "to avoid the problems involved with the importation of live chimpanzees." Presumably, these "problems" include national and international laws and treaties regarding the movement of live animals belonging to endangered species. The chimpanzee *Pan troglodytes* is listed in Appendix 1 of the Convention on International Trade in Endangered Species.

Besides getting round restrictions on the international movement of chimpanzees, cheapness of wild-caught chimpanzees appears to be a motivating factor for the IMMUNO Company. According to the Austrian newspaper *Presse* (February 3, 1983), Immuno official Johann Eibl stated that captive breeding of chimpanzees was not an economically viable proposition.

The proposed facility would procure 60–80 chimpanzees per year, to be obtained from the wild. However, according to Bieber's statement, "it must be emphasized that the research will not bring about a decimation of chimpanzees: on the contrary, their numbers would remain stable." Readers familiar with the destructive method by which chimpanzees are caught (killing of mothers in most cases) may be surprised at this statement. However, Bieber cheerfully explains the nondetriment theme by saying, "Because, after going through a research circle of about 3 years, the animals will be in perfect condition and ready for rehabilitation into the wild."

The International Primate Protection League is concerned over IMMUNO's plans on many grounds; to cite just a few of them:

1. Release of chimpanzee "veterans" of hepatitis non-A, non-B research would be hazardous to wild populations, as there is no way to determine that an animal is definitely not a carrier of the disease. Should release of the carrier animals occur, hepatitis could well spread among wild chimpanzees over large parts of Africa. Thus chimpanzees could well become a reservoir for hepatitis just as bats are a reservoir for rabies. The result might be increased human persecution of chimpanzees.

2. Although chimpanzee rehabilitation has acquired a certain "chic," it is known that wild chimpanzees attack introduced newcomers. For this reason, chimpanzees in the Mount Asserik project in Senegal directed by Stella Brewer had to be recaptured and released on islands in the River Gambia with no resident chimpanzees. As yet, no permanent home has been located for these animals. The rehabilitation procedures take many years per animal and are extremely costly and hence not feasible on the scale that would be required to start 60–80 animals per year on rehabilitation. Assuming a 5-year training per animal, there could be up to 400 animals undergoing rehabilitation at any given time, at the cost of millions of dollars annually. It is questionable whether, in spite of the most

dedicated efforts, any rehabilitated chimpanzees will become totally normal, since they are usually removed from the wild at 1–2 years of age and thus miss the most critical years of their social development.

3. Capture of wild chimpanzees for research is in clear violation of the World Health Organization's 1982 statement on the procurement of primates for biomedical research. Chimpanzees are listed in the Red Data Book of the International Union for the Conservation of Nature as "vulnerable." The WHO statement "strongly recommends" that

> endangered, vulnerable, and rare species be considered for use in biomedical research projects only if they are obtained from *existing* [emphasis added] self-sustaining captive breeding colonies (i.e., captive-breeding all animals required to at least the F-2 generation).

4. Currently, there are over 1,000 chimpanzees in US laboratories, as well as large numbers in the Netherlands, Poland, Liberia, etc. These animals should be enough to supply any legitimate requirements for chimpanzees.

The International Primate Protection League shares the scientific community's concern over hepatitis. However, we feel that a way can and must be found to solve this problem without recourse to the dwindling populations of wild chimpanzees. Therefore, we appreciate the opportunity to draw this situation to the attention of interested parties.

Shirley McGreal, MD
Chairwoman
International Primate Protection League
P. O. Draw H
Summerville, S.C. 29483

Compared to most letters to the editor, McGreal's $16-million composition is carefully written. It makes no extravagant claims, indulges in no patently loose or figurative or hyperbolic language, and it identifies no individual company officers. In approximately five hundred words, it analyzes a specific document, the original Immuno proposal written on a certain date in 1982, and it methodically raises what seem to be reasonable concerns — the same concerns that Abass Bundu raised when he was shown the proposal in Freetown. We have seen that Bundu was concerned that taking sixty to eighty chimps per year would "seriously deplete our national stock of wild chimpanzees," and he was concerned about the spread of viruses from "rehabilitated" chimps. (Later Dr. Alfred Prince, discoverer of the hepatitis non-A non-B virus, would express in his own letter to the editor substantially similar opinions about the Immuno proposal.) The only outright error I have been able to find in this letter is the positioning of an "MD" after Shirley McGreal's name. She has a doctorate in education. As I understand it, later arguments in court would point to this error as evidence of a deliberate attempt, even a conspiracy, to deceive the journal's three hundred readers concerning Shirley McGreal's authority. So far as I have been able to determine, the error appeared because McGreal originally signed her name without any indication of degree. That sort of titular nakedness in a journal read by those with M.D.'s and Ph.D.'s perhaps caused a nervous typesetter to add "MD."

The letter was printed in December 1983. Immuno's top attorney in New York, Raymond S. Fersko, filed a complaint in December 1984. The case moved into pretrial "discovery" proceedings before the Honorable Beatrice Shainswit of the lowest civil court in the New York City area, called (confusingly, I think) the Supreme Court of the State of New York, New York County. But unhappily, even the preliminary, pretrial *discovery* phase of this case became very expensive. It also became aggressively personal and nasty: Immuno's lawyer Raymond S. Fersko would describe Moor-Jankowski as a "liar" and a "vain and venal" man; McGreal was a "crazy woman" and a "nut case"; and so on. Even Judge Shainswit joined in, at one point referring to McGreal as "that silly woman." Eventually, Fersko began to express interest in Shirley McGreal's sex life — and asked her whether she ever engaged in sexual intercourse to promote her interests and beliefs. Thousands of pages of documents were produced, petitions were filed, fines were levied, depositions were taken, and after about a year of discovery, costs had mounted to the point where everyone but Moor-Jankowski gave up and settled with Immuno. Actually, McGreal herself never settled, but her insurance company, having paid $250,000 in legal bills, settled over her protest for $100,000.

That left only Jan Moor-Jankowski, defended by his attorney, Philip Byler. Judge Shainswit at one point told Byler to negotiate a settlement with Immuno; Byler refused. By September 1986, after more than a year and a half of pretrial discovery, Byler submitted a petition for *summary judgment* — asking that the judge end the prolonged and expensive proceedings and make a decision on the case. An opposition brief was filed, then a reply, then a sur reply, then a supplementary reply, then a sur sur reply . . . By April Fools' Day 1987, after nearly two and a half years of discovery, Justice Beatrice Shainswit decided that Immuno and Jan Moor-Jankowski were ready for an actual trial. She denied the motion for summary judgment.

Philip Byler appealed her denial, however, and the case of Immuno versus Jan Moor-Jankowski went before the Appellate Division of the Supreme Court of New York, with the Honorable Francis T. Murphy presiding. After examining a court record that by then had grown to over four thousand pages, the appellate court in January 1989 unanimously reversed the lower court's decision and dismissed the case. That decision included a stinging criticism of Judge Shainswit's analysis, describing it as "flawed in several respects." Although McGreal's letter to the editor might well have been damaging to Immuno, the facts she stated were "evidently true." The firm was damaged by a truthful description of the reality of its own behavior. That problem did not justify a libel suit. The appellate court also emphasized the importance of summary judgment in libel cases, since they are "notoriously expensive to defend," so that to "unnecessarily delay the disposition of a libel action is . . . to enhance the value of such actions as instruments of harassment and coercion." The appellate justices, moreover, found it "disturbing" that Immuno "had, by threatening legal action, managed to delay publication of the McGreal letter for almost a year, and that it succeeded in coercing . . . 'substantial settlements' from all but one of the original defendants for the obvious reason that the costs of continuing to defend the action were prohibitive."

More than four years had passed since the case over a letter he didn't write began, and Dr. Moor-Jankowski was overjoyed by the appellate division's unanimous and unambiguous decision. The *New York Law Journal*, in a lengthy commentary, hailed it as the "decision of the day." Immuno appealed, however, and the case was taken on by the New York Court of Appeals in Albany. By this time, various *amici curiae* — literally, "friends of the court," which is to say, organizations wishing to interject their opinions into a case — had begun appearing. Moor-Jankowski and his attorney were ultimately assisted by thirty-four friends of the court, primarily groups concerned about conservation and First Amendment matters. As Immuno moved to bring the suit to the New York Court of Appeals in late 1989, an entity known as the National Association for Biomedical Research (NABR) moved to present its *amicus curiae* brief in support of Immuno.

The brief provided by the NABR is perhaps a digression — but it is also Exhibit A in the discussion of just how far from reality *Immuno* v. *Moor-Jankowski* had traveled by that time. The NABR describes itself as a nonprofit organization representing more than three hundred institutions "intimately involved" in biomedical research, education, testing, and so on. The organization, we are assured in this brief, "steadfastly supports a broad construction of the First Amendment to preserve our nation's treasured freedoms of the speech and of the press." The NABR is additionally "committed to returning civility, morality and, above all, truthfulness to the presentation of and reporting upon the research activities of its membership."

The NABR brief focuses the court's attention on the red-flag threat of antivivisectionists — crazy animal-rights activists — engaging in "arson, death threats, bomb threats, vandalism, theft, break-ins, obscene phone calls, intrusive picketing, and abusive harassment of individual scientists." These animal-rights terrorists have additionally "waged a vicious guerrilla campaign that consistently includes resorting to the deliberate dissemination of whole lies, half-truths, and innuendo." Therefore (to boil this implied syllogism down to the paste of its absurd logic), Dr. Jan Moor-Jankowski (professor of medical research at the New York University Medical School and director of the Laboratory for Experimental Medicine and Surgery in Primates, which houses one of the world's largest colonies of research chimpanzees) must be punished. But to suggest that Dr. Moor-Jankowski was in some fashion colluding with animal-rights "terrorists," as the NABR did at that point, simply violates ordinary common sense. Furthermore, the brief got some of its alleged facts wrong — and it repeated Immuno's regular defense that no chimpanzees in Sierra Leone would ever be hurt because "an experienced and respected zoologist who did not capture chimpanzees by killing the mothers" would be in charge of capture operations (referring, of course, to Dr. Franz Sitter).

Anyway, the New York State Court of Appeals, the highest court in the state, threw out the case on December 14, 1989, pointing to it as an example of the "chilling effect" of libel litigation on free speech in America. By then Moor-Jankowski had been traveling from one court to another for five full years, pleading for freedom from attack over a letter he had not written.

What else could happen?

What happened was the United States Supreme Court took on a libel case known as *Milkovitch* v. *Lorain Journal.* Under the leadership of Chief Justice William Rehnquist, the Court ruled on that case in a fashion that more narrowly defined the kinds of speech protected by the First Amendment. Immuno's lawyers, having noted the outcome of *Milkovitch,* petitioned the U.S. Supreme Court for a new trial and, indeed, the U.S. Supreme Court instructed the New York State Court of Appeals to reconsider *Immuno* v. *Moor-Jankowski* in light of the *Milkovitch* decision. Thus, Jan Moor-Jankowski found himself back in court once again, and the case of the letter he had not written was reviewed once again in the New York State Court of Appeals — which, after a careful look at the *Milkovitch* decision, began to express concern about "core constitutional values." The court finally decided that letters to the editor are a legitimate means for people to air their grievances, that letters to the editor are generally recognized as opinion, that opinions on the humane treatment of animals and international treaties protecting endangered animals are matters of legitimate public concern, and so on. Once again the New York Court of Appeals decided unanimously in favor of Moor-Jankowski. Immuno's lawyers mailed a 190-page petition for *certiorari* protesting the Court of Appeals' decision to the U.S. Supreme Court, but finally, on June 3, 1991, their petition was denied without comment.

7

Geza Teleki remains one of the few major critics of Immuno who has not yet been sued. It is clear in any event that Teleki is conceptualized as an adversary. In a January 1987 letter to the late Sir Walter Salomon (a major Immuno shareholder in Britain), Immuno's attorney Raymond S. Fersko complained about Teleki. Fersko wrote that he did not intend to "knock" Teleki — but the man was a "fanatic" who had "made false statements which can be documented as false." Very generously, Fersko imagined that Geza Teleki — like those representatives of the World Wildlife Fund in Austria who had falsified Sierra Leonean laws in order to smear Immuno — meant well. However, he continued, "history has taught us that the ends do not always justify the means."

The term "fanatic" has been frequently applied to isolated individuals who oppose the vision of chimpanzees as a marketable resource. But by the end of 1986, Teleki was no longer working in isolation. In November of that year, the Chicago Academy of Sciences sponsored the first international symposium on "Understanding Chimpanzees." Most of the participants were thoroughly alarmed by the devastation of wild chimp populations in Africa, and Geza Teleki was joined by Jane Goodall and other prominent chimpanzee researchers — including Roger Fouts, William McGrew, Toshisada Nishida, Yukimaru Sugiyama, Frans de Waal, and Richard Wrangham — to form an organization that would work on behalf of the apes. A group called, in deference to someone's taste for alliteration, the Committee for Conservation and Care of Chimpanzees, was thus established. Originally sponsored by a total of thirty professionals studying or working with chimpanzees on four continents, the CCCC today consists of about one hundred fifty members, all recognized chimp experts, from approximately twenty-five countries. Teleki was elected chairman.

The attempts to discredit Geza Teleki continued. But after November 1986, chimpanzee scientists promoting conservation issues could no longer be so easily dismissed, one by one, as fanatics. "November of 1986 was a milestone," Teleki declares. "It was a milestone that totally changed the entire scenario in terms of what was going on with chimps: what the concerns were, what the attitudes were, where the fights were. And it changed for the very simple reason that people who could not be disposed of as a bunch of 'animal fetishists' suddenly became concerned."

The reader will recall that when representatives of Immuno held their formal meeting with government officials at the Vienna Town Hall during the summer of 1986, Dr. Robert Gallo from the National Institutes of Health in the United States had contributed his credibility as a biomedical research scientist and argued on behalf of Immuno's right to take wild chimps from Africa. Although it was denied at the time, the NIH had signed a collaboration agreement with Immuno in Austria one week before the importation of the twenty chimps. The NIH was soon to sign another collaboration agreement with Immuno of Austria's affiliate in the United States, known as Immuno-U.S. The full story of the United States NIH involvement with Immuno is too complicated to consider at length in this chapter. But that strange business with Dr. Robert Gallo in Vienna during the summer of 1986 may have been the most immediately alarming sign that a perceived or real laboratory demand for chimpanzees, emanating most significantly from the powerful American biomedical research industry, was on the verge of overwhelming whatever weak barriers against the live-animal trade CITES and the U.S. Endangered Species Act had erected.

Thus, the first business of the Committee for Conservation and Care of Chimpanzees was to petition for a formal strengthening of American laws to protect wild chimps in Africa. With the collaboration of dozens of field scientists who had worked or were still working in chimpanzee habitats throughout Africa, the CCCC assembled an extensive report on the recent collapse of wild chimpanzee populations and passed that report, along with a petition (formally submitted by three other conservation groups), to the U.S. Fish and Wildlife Service. The petition requested simply that U.S. Fish and Wildlife upgrade the legal status of chimpanzees as defined in the 1973 Endangered Species Act from "threatened" to "endangered." Since the act serves as the legal mechanism for U.S. compliance with CITES, a declaration that chimpanzees were "endangered" would more fully confirm the CITES agreement and in the process terminate any U.S. participation, direct or indirect, in the live-chimpanzee trade out of Africa.

Fish and Wildlife received the petition and documentation on November 4, 1987, and solicited comments until a deadline of July 21, 1988. By the time of the deadline, the agency had received forty letters of support from major authorities or organizations and from the governments of African nations with wild chimpanzee populations; seventeen of those letters were written by scientists who had actually studied chimpanzees in the field. The agency received, in addition, 54,212 letters and postcards from the general public in favor of formally reclassifying chimps as endangered.

Six comments opposed to the reclassification also slid through the Fish and Wildlife letter slot during this period. Although the six experts who opposed the reclassification generally presented brief yet dignified arguments, their identity is interesting. Two of the experts were important officials at NIH. Two were associated with the Robert M. Yerkes Primate Research Center in Georgia. The fifth worked for a three-ring circus. The sixth worked for Immuno-U.S., Inc. (This final letter described Immuno-U.S. as a "newly established small business" that, because of its affiliation with an Austrian big sister, might promise "enormous health benefits" to the American people.)

It was 54,252 to 6, but in the end, U.S. Fish and Wildlife chose with all the wisdom of Solomon to cut this baby in half. United States law now describes chimpanzees as "endangered" if they are wild or otherwise live in Africa and "threatened" if they happen to exist inside a cage outside Africa.

Every two years, nations that are signatories to the CITES treaty send delegates to a Conference of the Parties to review new developments, patterns of evasion, and so on. Nongovernmental organizations are allowed to attend and can take part in most proceedings, provided they are "technically qualified in wildlife conservation."

Geza Teleki of the Committee for Conservation and Care of Chimpanzees lacked funds to attend the July 1987 CITES conference, held in Ottawa, so the CCCC was not represented there. Immuno's importation of twenty chimpanzees from Franz Sitter was still a fiercely controversial topic, however, and at the conference a member of the Austrian delegation defended Immuno's point of view. According to the Austrian delegation: "Dr. Franz Sitter, a member of the technical committee charged with finding means of preserving wildlife, describes . . . how trapping and hunting are part of the traditional native law, and how farmers seek to protect their crops by setting traps that surround the ground used for agriculture. If Dr. Sitter or someone in his position does not happen to buy the animals that fall into the traps, the animals end up in Liberia, where they are eaten and their hides are worked into shoes." The Liberian delegation to the conference reacted with outrage: "There is no tannery in Liberia and we have never heard of or seen 'chimpanzee shoes' on sale in Liberia." But most peculiar of all was the behavior of an organization called the Committee for the Conservation of Chimpanzees, which was attending the conference and handing out a press release that said, among other things: "Conservation of chimpanzees is vital for mankind. We must have healthy populations of chimpanzees in the wild not only because they are an irreplaceable part of the natural systems of the earth but because of their ever-growing value for scientific purposes in urgent medical research."

Many delegates at the conference were utterly confused by the miraculous manifestation of the Committee for the Conservation of

Chimpanzees (3 Cs). Since Jane Goodall was a member and supporter of the Committee for Conservation and Care of Chimpanzees (4 Cs), the Jane Goodall Institute was compelled to deny at the CITES conference that Dr. Goodall supported the Committee for the Conservation of Chimpanzees (3 Cs). The CCC in turn issued a formal denial that it had ever said she was a supporter.

By June 2, 1989, a certificate of incorporation was filed in New York for the Committee for the Conservation of Chimpanzees (3 Cs), naming the not-for-profit organization's temporary directors to be Immuno's top New York lawyer, Raymond S. Fersko, and two others who shared his law firm's address in New York. At approximately the same time, a proposal from the CCC landed on the desk of the minister of forestry, agriculture, and natural resources of Sierra Leone.

According to my copy of the proposal, the Committee for the Conservation of Chimpanzees exists as an "international charitable foundation" and "a non-profit foundation dedicated to insuring the conservation of Chimpanzees (Pan Troglodytes) [sic] to insure their survival as a specie [sic] because, inter alia, their continued utilisation is absolutely necessary for Biomedical Research, safety, efficacy and potency testing for certain biological products in compliance with various governmental requirements throughout the world." The CCC proposed to establish, cooperatively with the government of Sierra Leone, "a national wildlife conservation area" to be located in the Loma Mountains region.

The Committee for the Conservation of Chimpanzees wished to see that poachers are controlled and that the various national laws are respected in this region, in order to "help promote interested tourists, naturalists and conservationists in making camp within the area so as to observe the natural fauna and flora." True, this wildlife conservation area cannot be expected "to immediately attract hoards [sic] of people," since "To spend time there, will be a rugged experience." But by supporting such a conservation-minded project, the nation of Sierra Leone would surely "enhance" its presumably already excellent "international reputation relating to conservation and responsible utilisation of its wildlife." In short, the wildlife conservation area would become a "symbolic focal point" for Sierra Leone, at the same time providing for tourism and all kinds of other very good if somewhat abstract objectives, such as "the growth of our ken of understanding of animal life in their [sic] natural habitat."

The proposal contained what it called a "second prong," which poked forth by the middle of page three. The Committee for the Conservation of Chimpanzees was also interested in breeding chimpanzees in Sierra Leone. In fact, the committee was currently negotiating land rights in the Freetown area in order to create a breeding facility and expected to begin construction soon. The proposal promised that all chimps for the facility would be "acquired legally and responsibly" and "in full compliance with all applicable law, regulations or pertinent government requirements." Still, the proposal did not state precisely how these chimps would be acquired, or (if they were to be captured) from what region of the country. Perhaps the isolated Loma Mountains wildlife conservation area was regarded as a potential source.

Strangely enough, this proposal by a "charitable foundation" discussed "investing" money in Sierra Leone. Yes, the Committee for the Conservation of Chimpanzees would be "investing" some hundreds of thousands of dollars. Among the anticipated costs "being budgeted" would be a "substantial" level of "Indirect expenses." These might include "consulting fees to contribute to the . . . understanding and compliance with local conditions, law, etc." But just in case this nonprofit charity should nevertheless run into opposition of, say, a legal or political nature, it was establishing "permanent legal representation" in Sierra Leone "to stay abreast of all legal and political developments."

The proposal was brief and apparently a rough draft. It did not identify its author. It did name the founder of the Committee for the Conservation of Chimpanzees: Dr. Gerald Eder of Immuno A.G. in Vienna.

According to one of the temporary directors of the CCC, Immuno recently acquired all requisite permits from the Sierra Leone government and purchased land for a "facility." This temporary director stated to a journalist in 1991 that the facility would neither take chimps from the wild nor reintroduce them into the wild after they had contributed to whatever sort of human health benefits Immuno wants them to contribute to. Where would the chimpanzees come from? The facility would coordinate its activities with an animal dealer in Sierra Leone who operates his own chimpanzee colony, who was recommended to Immuno years ago by Dr. Jan Moor-Jankowski himself, a dealer who buys chimpanzees, seemingly as a kind of eccentric charitable activity, to save them from the violence of hostile

African farmers: a distinguished zoologist and live-animal dealer named Dr. Franz Sitter.

Such was the situation in 1991. More recently, I understand, Immuno's charitable plans for Sierra Leone have changed and perhaps even been suspended, at least temporarily.

8

What I find remarkable about this whole story is how little some of the principal characters know or even seem to care to know about Africa, how quickly they have dismissed anything that challenges their particular vision, and how readily they have relied on the good character of a man who stands to benefit so handsomely from that reliance on his good character.

It is true that Dr. Gerald Eder of Immuno went to Africa — long enough to discuss a potential transaction with government officials in a capital city. It is true that Raymond S. Fersko went to Africa — long enough to interview a few people in and around Freetown. But neither of them, nor any of the other individuals involved in Immuno's conservation charity can claim any formal expertise on wild animals, and to the best of my knowledge none has traveled more than approximately eight miles outside the city limits of Freetown. Geza Teleki is by formal training a chimpanzee expert and has traveled very widely indeed in rural Sierra Leone. Yet he has been quickly dismissed as a "fanatic." His survey with Lori Baldwin of the chimpanzees of Sierra Leone was conducted during a six-month, 6,400-mile journey, which crisscrossed that small country numerous times. It was conducted with the assistance of numerous field workers from Sierra Leone and the support of top government officials including the president himself. It remains the single most authoritative survey of Sierra Leonean chimpanzees. Yet it too was expeditiously dismissed.

Perhaps most astonishing was the attempted entry on behalf of Immuno into the lawsuit against the scientist Jan Moor-Jankowski by an organization in the United States that claims to represent science and scientists and that lobbies on behalf of biomedical research interests — the National Association for Biomedical Research. No one from that organization, to my knowledge, has been anywhere near

Africa. Yet that group too, in its special version of the spirit of scientific inquiry, felt compelled to ignore the Teleki survey and to testify on behalf of the very, very good character of Dr. Franz Sitter.

Sitter's actual character remains a mystery of considerable murk. I believe it was not until the mid-1980s, when he visited Vienna, that Jan Moor-Jankowski heard a rumor concerning Franz Sitter's past association with the Nazis. Moor-Jankowski has never fully recovered from Nazi gunshot wounds he received as a teenager. I think he was shocked to hear the tale. But the Nazis had many talents, including an impressive efficiency at keeping records. Many of their old records are still intact and preserved in Berlin and Washington, D.C. These papers are not generally available to the public, but Moor-Jankowski was able to penetrate the Berlin Archives and retrieve one document with the name Franz Sitter on it.

Sitter had claimed to Teleki that he lost his arm in North Africa, while serving in the Wehrmacht under Rommel. He also claimed that he was born in Austria. But the autobiographical sketch Sitter wrote for his doctoral degree at the University of Vienna states that he was born in Yugoslavia, in a certain town on a certain day in 1924. The document Moor-Jankowski acquired, officially stamped with the old eagle and swastika, signed with an enthusiastic "Heil Hitler!" and dated October 13, 1941, tells of a Yugoslav from the same town, of the same birth date and the same name, one Franz Sitter, who served as an officer of the Hitler Youth in occupied Czechoslovakia. The document states that Franz Sitter was convicted of stealing money from the Hitler Youth in Czechoslovakia and sentenced to prison for one year.

Now, a generous interpretation of that document might hold that no one should be held accountable for deeds done during adolescence. A generous interpretation might ask whether stealing from the Hitler Youth is, after all, such a bad thing. And any interpretation at all should point out that belonging to the Hitler Youth does not automatically make one a Nazi war criminal, and that millions of relatively innocent young men survived or tried to survive Hitler's war by serving in the Wehrmacht.

But Moor-Jankowski is not inclined to read that document in such a generous fashion. In Germany, he notes, young people had to belong to the Hitler Youth; but in occupied countries, such as Czechoslovakia, no one had to join. And no one became an officer of the Hitler Youth in an occupied country, he believes, unless that person was "a rabid Nazi." The Hitler Youth in Germany were not armed. They wore long knives, but the knives were meant as decoration, not weapons. In occupied territories, though, the Hitler Youth were armed with real firearms and "were used as hooligans, and mainly to attack Jews in the ghettos and so on." So, Dr. Moor-Jankowski believes, Franz Sitter has been suffering from the "Waldheim disease." Worse, he was expelled from the Hitler Youth and impelled into prison for stealing from his colleagues. "So he was not only a Nazi, he was just a criminal." As for Sitter's claimed service in the Wehrmacht in North Africa under Field Marshal Rommel, Moor-Jankowski notes that the regular German army, the Wehrmacht, did not accept convicted criminals. Other, more specialized organizations did.

7 ◆ The Stuff of Dreams

PROSPERO:
We are such stuff
As dreams are made on, and our little life
Is rounded with a sleep.

IT'S THE DAVID LETTERMAN SHOW! Three million Americans are staying up late tonight to watch this show! And tonight, folks, we have the ever-tiny sex therapist, Dr. Ruth — not to mention Zippy and the late-night monkey cam.

Dr. Ruth is already sitting on the couch. David Letterman is at his desk, and now he calls in the trained ape. "Zippy, come out here, buddy!" But, whoa! Something's wrong with the picture. No, wait! It's not the picture! Don't adjust your TV, folks! It's absolutely crazy out here! I mean, crazy! This is the late-night monkey cam!

In runs Zippy the Chimp, wearing sneakers on his feet, wearing a small boy's pants and shirt, suspenders holding up the pants, a small portable television camera strapped to his back, trotting, circling, running around the couch, spinning, bursting with energy, never still for a second, looking for all the world like a mischievous Boy Scout on the loose or a hyperactive kid who has just filched all the Ritalin. The strapped-on camera is turned to peer over his shoulder, so that whenever the studio engineer flips the switch — zap! — we get a Zippy-eye view of things. Hey, it sure is crazy down here! Letterman: "Whatever you do, Zippy, it's fine with me. Have you seen Dr. Ruth? What do you think of Dr. Ruth?"

We see Zippy's face: cream colored, dark freckled, boylike, glowing with an angelic intensity. Dr. Ruth laughs her maniacal laugh and returns to her scientific discussion of sex that is simultaneously fun and serious. But Zippy is stealing the show. He won't sit still! Now he's swinging on a rope, back and forth just above Letterman's desk — and that absurd Dr. Ruth begins talking about Zippy as a "she." Dr. Ruth says "she" several times, even after Letterman corrects her. So Letterman corrects her again, with a bemused and histrionic exasperation: "It's a boy! It's a boy! This is a boy monkey! You ought to know this!" Dr. Ruth laughs her laugh and continues chattering about sex; but as the engineer flips the switch back to a late-night monkey-cam view of the world, once again the conversation drifts back to Zippy, and once again Dr. Ruth repeats her error — calling Zippy a "she." Letterman blows up (but always, really, in good fun): "Zippy! It's a he! It's a he! It's a male monkey! No, it's a male monkey! I'd think you would know!"

Yes indeed, as three million viewers of David Letterman can now tell you: Monkeys are funny! Boy monkeys are very funny! Especially that Zippy! You remember Zippy — didn't we see him down at the shopping center five years ago? Gosh, he does look a lot like people, especially when he's dressed up like that. I'm sure it must be just great to be a boy monkey and get to appear on the Dave Letterman show!

That's the art, the stuff of dreams to tickle us when we say *tickle*. The reality behind this stuff of dreams is the following. First, Dr. Ruth was right. This particular chimpanzee was a female. In fact, of the approximately thirty young chimps who have played the Zippy character for the Zippy business during three and a half decades, about twenty of them were female. Zippy was a stage name for a fictional character — like Mickey Mouse or Big Bird. The actual pet name, for this chimpanzee, was Jade. Second, Jade was not a funny monkey, but a highly intelligent and sensitive ape — an individual of an endangered species being used as a toy. Third, in spite of the intense pressure of that situation, Jade may have been enjoying herself. But just in case her enjoyment declined before David Letterman and three million American viewers were ready, Jade's trainer stood right behind the cameras and lights with a radio transmitter in her pocket and a wire antenna taped to her leg, finger twitching over the button that could transmit a signal to the shocker mounted at the solar plexus beneath Jade's little-boy clothes. Fourth, just to make sure Jade didn't in a moment of passion bite off a finger of David Letterman or Dr. Ruth or any of the dozens of other people in the studio waiting and waiting for something very funny to happen, all of this chimpanzee's teeth had already been removed (as had all the teeth of all the other Zippy chimps). She would never be able to eat normally or to defend herself if she ever had to live with other chimps. Fifth, her face had been shaved to make her look more like a prepubescent human male. Sixth, she had been taken from her mother at an unnaturally early age and raised by humans; she probably would never herself have developed into a normal enough chimpanzee adult to reproduce. Seventh, we'll never know what kind of adult she might have become. Like all of the other Zippy chimps, Jade was removed from the entertainment business near the end of her childhood, for entirely sensible reasons, by the trainers whom she regarded as her parents and who loved her as if she were their child. Jade was a child actor reaching retirement age. Nearly all of her predecessors in the Zippy business had already disappeared into private and public hands, and, in at least one case, I believe, into a laboratory doing AIDS research. I don't know what happened to most of them; I do know what happened to Jade.

By the time she was eight years old, Jade's owners had decided to deliver their foster daughter to Primarily Primates, an amazing sanctuary in San Antonio, Texas, for abused or unwanted primates. But an animal-rights organization stepped in and persuaded them to keep Jade in her unnatural life, her unnatural clothes, for a while longer. Why? So she could contribute to that organization's particular stuff of dreams. So they could use her as an "ambassador" for chimpanzees. So they could take her to Washington, to lobby senators and congressmen on behalf of chimpanzees and other animals. Jade appeared at fundraising luncheons and dinners, and her chance to become a chimpanzee again was delayed. A little campaign started to set Jade once more on her way to Primarily Primates. She was even given a new set of teeth.

Jade came at last to Primarily Primates, and I visited her inside a big cage with soft straw on the ground, filled with toys and enrichment devices. It was early morning, and the sunlight filtered through the vegetation around us. I had already spent an hour with the chimpanzees Willy and Henry (who played Virgil and Ginger in the movie Project X). The slide door opened, and in came Jade. Not the pathetic pseudohuman actor, wearing clothes over fur, who used to be known as Zippy. It was a real chimpanzee who came through that door. And after politely greeting me, she proceeded to show, quite clearly, that she would tolerate no nonsense from either of the two young males.

Thanks to Wally Swett, the director of Primarily Primates, Jade was given a chance for a good life, a chance to become a chimpanzee among chimpanzees. That she fell sick was a tragedy — and no one could have fought harder to save her than the team that gathered at Primarily Primates. Not only Wally and his staff, but Jade's owners and, touchingly, the veterinarians from the primate research facility nearby. While she was providing the stuff of dreams for the animal-rights organization, Jade had been given hormone therapy to prevent the development of any distracting signs of approaching sexual maturity. It is possible that the physiological results of withdrawing this therapy weakened her and made her more susceptible to the bacteria that finally killed her.

Although chimpanzees have a normal life expectancy of several decades, up to fifty-five years in captivity, Jade lived to be about ten years old before she died of an infection. In essence, she gave her life so that millions of Americans could swim in the stuff of dreams and imagine they were seeing a funny "boy monkey" who acted like a cute kid, or an absurdly dressed-up "ambassador" for animals.

The treatment of Caliban in *The Tempest* combines humor with punishment and discipline. "I shall laugh myself to death at this puppy-headed monster," Trinculo the jester says at one point, commencing a declaration that concludes with, "I could find in my heart to beat him." Caliban serves the European characters in this play as a receptacle for some mixture of derision and aggression.

An audience, disturbed, might conclude that Caliban is an object of clinical sadism. Yet the audience doesn't. The audience is actually amused, right along with most of the characters in the play, amused partly because the play's music and special effects, its contrived and dreamlike atmosphere, generate a pleasant sense of unreality. *The Tempest* includes a play within the play, which in this case is sup-posedly performed by spirit actors who exit, as Prospero puts it, "into air, into thin air." After the actors have vanished into thin air, Pros-pero informs us that their play is as fleeting and ephemeral as "our little life" itself: the "stuff as dreams are made on." Of course, Pros-pero himself is a character in a play, and so "our little life" in one sense refers to the reality of the larger play. But we also recognize that the reality of our own little lives, our own play outside the play, is also rounded with a sleep, is also the stuff of dreams.

A good deal of the discipline Caliban endures or worries about enduring at the hands of Prospero appears to be necessary (if we accept the ethical context of the play, which only lightly questions the appropriateness of enslaving Caliban). Caliban needs to be disciplined because he is powerful, intelligent, and not naturally submissive. Caliban makes a good slave, in other words, only when his own desires and impulses are continuously checked and controlled. Otherwise, he is dangerous. Prospero disciplines Caliban with every means available, ranging from vocal instruction and reason to a number of imaginative physical punishments — magical techniques that produce unpleasant aches, pinches, stitches, and so on. And although we (the audience) are allowed to observe Prospero verbally instruct and threaten Caliban, we never actually observe the physical discipline, which might disturb the otherwise delightful lightness of the play.

Prospero's controlling, manipulative power extends far beyond Caliban. At one point or another he controls and manipulates every other character in the play. And when at the end he steps out of the play's fictional frame — walks out to the very edge of the stage and directly addresses the real audience — we begin to realize that he controls and manipulates us, that he is in some partial and no doubt whimsical sense identified with the creator of the fiction himself — William Shakespeare, playwright. Prospero is the prototype for a long tradition of dynamic and domineering stage entertainers to come: the stage hypnotist, the stage magician, that tuxedoed fellow who stands out there and manipulates for us, as an act of entertainment, our entire sense of reality as it unfolds on the glittering, glowing stage. Prospero is, as a matter of fact, a master hypnotist, capable of inducing in the other characters a host of standard hypnotic phenomena: drowsiness, hypnagogic "sleep," hallucinations, hypnotic paralysis, muscle weakness, amnesia, posthypnotic suggestion. (The term "hypnotism" didn't exist in Shakespeare's time, having been invented in the nineteenth century to replace what must have seemed by then an antique term, "mesmerism." Anton Mesmer invented mesmerism at the end of the eighteenth century. But Mesmer was merely refurbishing with pseudoscientific terminology, in response to intellectual fashions of the European Enlightenment, already well-established techniques of dynamic, authoritarian suggestion.)

It should be obvious that Prospero is not a villain. Rather, he is a complex character whose actions can be examined from more than one ethical perspective. And I must emphasize that this chapter does not serve the pursuit of villains, nor is it intended to attack any particular individual. Rather, it would examine dispassionately the larger ethical issue of how humans deal with their biological siblings, the great apes, within the stuff of dreams.

1

Perhaps all trained-animal shows are minitheater, plays within plays, developing themes that create a distorted vision of the actual animals. Big-cat shows are little plays about courage — not of the animal but rather of the trainer. Horse shows dramatize love and control — largely the trainer's love and control of the animal. Great-ape shows could dramatize the courage of a trainer, since apes can be as danger-ous as lions and tigers. Great-ape shows could dramatize control; they could dramatize affection; they could dramatize athletic prowess. In fact, a few do emphasize one or another of these themes.* But by and large, great-ape theater dramatizes the theme of kinship.

Caliban is special not because he is different, but because he is the same; he is very much like the other characters of the play. Whether he is an animal-like human or a humanlike animal we can never be sure; the play is ultimately ambiguous on that point. But we do recognize that he profoundly resembles a human. In spite of Prospero's protestations to the contrary, Caliban seems to think and even feel quite like the other humans in the play. This astonishing similarity, this kinship between servant and master, is perhaps the quintessential element of their relationship. Apes share the honored shape, and many ape shows emphasize this fact, squeezing it to the point of comic exaggeration — in the process producing clowns, comically inferior reproductions of the human form. I know a few trainers who will

_____

* Bob and Mae Noell's Gorilla Show, an itinerant carnival-style act that toured the southern United States between 1940 and 1971, featured boxing chimpanzees. Wear-ing boxer shorts and padded leather gloves, also leather muzzles, the chimps were ready to challenge with cash bets any person in the audience confused enough to imagine he or she could outfight chimpanzees (described as "gorillas" to avoid challeng-ing the intelligence of the audience). Certainly, the boxing gloves were not in this case mere humanizing decoration; they, and the leather muzzles, prevented the chimps from tearing their usually bewildered opponents to pieces. All the surviving Gorilla Show apes and their progeny are now retired and living in a roadside zoo in Florida called the Noell's Ark Chimp Farm.

protest: their characters are not "comically inferior" but "charming and cute," meant to appeal to the strongest human instincts of affection. Be that as it may, the ape character actors — Bonzo and Zippy and J. Fred Muggs and Mr. Jiggs and Mr. Stubbs and so on — express not so much the reality of a kinship between two species, human and chimp, as a human fantasy about that kinship. Before our very eyes these creatures become tame and virtually civilized, loved and loving, cute and compelling, clothed beings with all the appeal, and all the reality, of Mickey Mouse himself.

Even at the most fundamental level — that of personal identity — the great-ape character actors reside within the stuff of dreams. This fact became clear to me one day while visiting a man and his ape in their kitchen in northern New Jersey. Ron Winters has owned the performing character chimpanzee named Mr. Jiggs ("World's Smartest Chimp") for nearly thirty years. Jiggs is one of the biggest chimps I've ever seen, weighing some 190 pounds. I confess that I was mildly alarmed to be sitting in a kitchen with a wandering ape slightly larger than I am, who as a friendly grooming activity began prodding at my fingers, chewing busily on the hair of my arm, and then, when I was least expecting it, approaching from behind and plucking and eating hairs from my head. But I got used to it, and Mr. Jiggs after a while became bored with eating my hair and so retired into the next room and lay down on a bed, while Winters continued to narrate the story of his performing chimpanzee.

Ron Winters taught water skiing in Florida in the late 1950s and early 1960s; during the same period, he sold South American woolly monkeys to tourists on the beaches. Then, in 1964, a Miami-based animal dealer offered him a year-old chimpanzee just shipped in from Africa for about a thousand dollars, so Winters bought the chimp and began his new career. Mr. Jiggs was small enough at that time to hold in one hand, yet "he was such a healthy specimen when he was little he looked like a little gorilla, so I figured . . . he'd be smart." Mr. Jiggs turned out to be smart indeed, and Ron Winters started renting out his chimp for children's birthday parties. Mr. Jiggs would arrive at the party wearing baby clothes, then amuse everyone by eating ice cream with a spoon.

Mr. Jiggs was toilet trained at an early age. Winters says he used "the reward system," giving the chimpanzee a spoonful of ice cream for appropriate behavior. Mr. Jiggs learned to smile. Mr. Jiggs learned to roller-skate. Mr. Jiggs learned to ride a motorcycle. "First I taught him on a tricycle," Winters explains, "then a bicycle." Eventually, Winters "built a little motorcycle for him special — because they have to have a very low seat, because their legs are so short. So I got him this little motorcycle. He starts it up, runs the siren, circles around, turns the ignition off and parks it, and puts it on the kickstand, all in the proper sequence." In addition to riding the motorcycle, Mr. Jiggs has learned to flick on a lighter and to light and then smoke a cigarette. ("When he smokes in his act, he never inhales. He's smart, because he knows that it makes him cough. Accidentally, he will inhale and cough like anything.") Jiggs has learned to mix cocktails and sneak a drink when Winters isn't looking; to take good photographs with an instant camera; to fire toy pistols like a Wild West character; to bring in a fake fish with an actual rod and reel.

In addition to these routines, the ape responds to hundreds of verbal commands, Winters says, some of which were demonstrated to me that day in the kitchen: "Give him a smile." (Smiles.) "Give him a raspberry." (Makes raspberry sound.) "What do you do when they call you a monkey?" (Extends middle finger.) "Say yes." (Nods head.) "Say no." (Shakes head.) "Show how sexy you are when you're on a date." (Shimmies.) "Make fat lips." (Flips lip down.) "Play gorilla." (Slaps chest.) "See no evil." (Hands over eyes.) "Hear no evil." (Hands over ears.) "Speak no evil." (Hands over mouth.) Mr. Jiggs is truly an extraordinary being, a trained ape who has, during a long and brilliant career, roller-skated and motorcycled and smoked cigarettes on the Ed Sullivan show, the Johnny Carson show, the Mike Douglas show, *That's Incredible, What's My Line?* and so on. In 1975 the Mr. Jiggs performance was voted "Animal Act of the Year" by the American Guild of Variety Artists and was featured on a ninety-minute CBS special filmed in Las Vegas.

When Ron Winters' son was born, in 1975, Mr. Jiggs would hold him and feed him with a bottle. The only problem was that as the baby grew into a boy, Jiggs wouldn't let anyone spank him. Mr. Winters is divorced now; he and Mr. Jiggs live together in a state of semiretirement, doing little more than a couple of bar mitzvahs and birthday parties every week, the rest of the time staying at home or traveling around in Winters' motor home.

Parties are generally just fun for Mr. Jiggs, Winters says. As their advertising literature puts it, "He's happy, he loves the ladies, and to him your party is his party, because he gets cocktails and ice cream that he never gets at home." Mr. Jiggs arrives at a party dressed in black pants, white shirt and tuxedo dickey, wearing custom-made roller skates. After the various elements of his usual act are performed, this chimpanzee can sit down and relax with the rest of the celebrants, tasting a Coke or ice cream if it's a children's party, or downing as many as ten alcoholic drinks with impunity if it's a cocktail party.

I was impressed with the intelligence of Mr. Jiggs and the patience and talent of Mr. Winters. I was impressed by the apparent fact that Mr. Winters loves Mr. Jiggs as a father might love a son. But I was surprised to discover that Mr. Jiggs is a female. In the act, of course, Mr. Jiggs is dressed as a male and presented as a male — a male character. But no chimpanzee really wants to wear clothes at home, and in the privacy of their kitchen Mr. Jiggs was naked enough that I couldn't help noticing that this "he" was very much a "she." The situation might not have been so confusing, except that Ron Winters himself kept referring to his ape as "he" and "him." Over the course of our extended conversation, therefore, a certain verbal struggle broke out: I would ask questions about a "she," while Winters forthrightly answered my questions by referring to a "he." Clearly, this was not deceit but habit. Winters apparently has become so accustomed to the fictional character he created that the character is as real to him as the beloved ape who plays the part.

The fact is that very few people can distinguish between a male and a female chimpanzee once that creature is dressed in clothes, and so the gender of a performing ape often has no relation to the gender of the character played. More fundamentally, since few people can distinguish between one chimpanzee and another (even though they are as individually distinctive, in appearance and character, as people), the same character may be played by more than one chimp. Mr. Jiggs has always been one individual, a female. But the famous performing chimp known as Zippy was in fact about thirty chimpanzees, the majority of them female. Cheeta, the chimpanzee who played alongside Tarzan in dozens of movies, was several chimpanzees; there are still a few Cheetas living in various places in the United States. The Marquis Chimps, who used to be a family act — father, mother, children — were a large number of chimps, male and female, chosen to play the roles of parent or child entirely on the basis of size.

Clothes make the ape. Rita Mae in a skirt becomes Mr. Smith with suspenders. Gender, number, name — the clothes worn by ape character actors disguise all of these aspects of identity and more. (Just as we wear clothes partly to disguise and control the sexual aspect of our nature, so clothes on a performing great ape both remind us of their similarity to humans in certain dimensions and simultaneously allow us to forget their similarity in others.) But clothes are only part of the disguise. Ape character actors learn to "smile" as a trained reaction to the smile cue. (Wild chimpanzees show their teeth and lips in a fear grimace, not as a signal of friendly intentions.) They learn to sit at a table, eat with utensils, ride a bicycle, shoot a gun, and so on. The whole point of their training, in short, is to develop an anthropomorphizing repertoire, to exaggerate their honored shape.

While live character acts tend to stress the physical kinship between ape and human, cinematic magic enables filmmakers to stress, sometimes to exaggerate, psychological and intellectual kinship. *Gorillas in the Mist*, the 1988 Universal/Warner Brothers film starring Sigourney Weaver as Dian Fossey, showed the psychological continuity between humans and wild gorillas. Some of the big gorillas in that movie are wild gorillas filmed in Rwanda; in other sequences the gorillas are played by five human actors dressed in ape suits; and when Weaver cuddles a tiny "gorilla" snatched from poachers, she is really cuddling a baby chimpanzee, provided by a Hollywood animal supplier and plastered with enough makeup and false fur to play the role.

Another reasonably realistic film about apes, *Greystoke: The Legend of Tarzan, Lord of the Apes* (Warner Brothers, 1984), partially filmed in Africa (Cameroon), also emphasizes psychological continuity and raises the image of interspecies communion, in a modern reinterpretation of the classic Tarzan fantasy. Adult chimpanzees are dangerous and don't work according to union rules, so most of the *Greystoke* apes were actually humans in multimillion-dollar sculpted outfits that included mechanized and sometimes remote-controlled parts (eyes, for example). But no human could be as convincing as those baby chimpanzees who mingled with the costumed people.

Cinematic comedies that feature performing apes have less respect for reality. In ape comedies often no one bothers to make the critical distinction between apes and monkeys, for instance. And often the apes are humanized to such an exaggerated and surprising degree that they become central characters in what would otherwise be purely human drama. *Bedtime for Bonzo*, a 1951 Universal International film, is generally recognized as a classic of this genre, if only because one of the actors eventually graduated into better roles on a bigger stage. Peter Boyd, played by the young Ronald Reagan, is a handsome and charming psychology professor who happens to be slightly vague and emotionally remote. He is engaged to marry Valerie Tillinghast, daughter of the dean at the university where he teaches. But when Dean Tillinghast discovers that Professor Boyd is the son of a criminal, he insists that the engagement be broken, fearful that Boyd may have inherited some of the criminal tendencies of his father. Of course, this leads to a nature versus nurture debate between the dean and the psychology professor.

After this distressing encounter with the dean, Professor Boyd retreats to the laboratory of a colleague, a Germanic sort named Hans Neumann. A chimpanzee, Bonzo, inhabits a cage in Neumann's lab, and after a while Boyd and Neumann notice that the diapered chimp appears to be upset.

"What do you suppose is wrong with him?"

"I don't know. He's very young. Only a month ago he came from Africa. Maybe he misses his mama."

Boyd decides to give Bonzo his baby bottle. "Hans, bring me the bottle," he says. "I want to try something." The cage is opened. Bonzo scrambles out and then climbs into Boyd's arms with a calmness and affection that surprises Professor Neumann.

"That's amazing! Maybe he thinks you're his papa," Neumann says, inspiring Boyd with an idea.

"His papa! Hans, you hit it!"

"What? What did I hit?" Neumann wants to know.

Boyd explains, "I want to see if he'll accept a human environment."

"You'll teach him to sleep in a bed, to eat with a spoon, and . . . make pattycakes? What will that prove?"

"If I could teach this monkey the difference between right and wrong . . . by getting him to do right without hope of reward, to avoid wrong without fear of punishment. Something my father never had a chance to learn. Don't you see, Hans? If it works, Dean Tillinghast will have to admit that environment is all important, that heredity counts for very little."

In the end, as we might have guessed, instead of Professor Boyd's teaching Bonzo to be more human, Bonzo teaches Boyd to be more human — to descend slightly from his professorial remoteness and to recognize that he really loves the beautiful woman he hired to help him play "father" to Bonzo, rather than the spoiled and manipulative woman he thought he loved, Valerie Tillinghast.

Every Which Way But Loose (Warner Brothers, 1978), starring Clint Eastwood and an orangutan identified in the credits as Manis, is another ape comedy classic. Unabashed barfighter and bare-knuckled prizefighter Philo Beddoe beats and bashes several dozen other guys who used to think they were tough until they met Philo Beddoe. Clint Eastwood plays this part with his usual minimalist intensity, covering almost an entire range of apparent feeling with two facial expressions: one expression says, "Ouch! That smarts!"; the second says, "That don't smart at all!" Beddoe actually speaks, too, on occasion, and eventually we recognize that beneath his chiseled Ice Age exterior churns a New Age male sensitivity: he has feelings to express.

Unfortunately, Beddoe can find no one else in the movie with whom he can express his feelings. The girl of his dreams, a Country and Western singer played by Sondra Locke, is constantly betraying him in order to extend the plot. His best buddy, Orville, is too bluff and besotted. Beddoe might have a lot of deep things to say to the other men in the film, but they are too busy being beaten up. This is where the orangutan comes in. Philo Beddoe needs to talk to someone, after all, so Clyde serves as the barfighter's confidant and foil — at once pet, pal, and sidekick. Late one night Beddoe and Clyde sit together under the stars; the barfighter, utilizing facial expression number one, unburdens himself to the ape: "I suppose you think I'm crazy, traipsin' across the country after a girl I hardly even know. Hell, I'm not like Orville. Takes me a long time to get to know a girl. Even longer to let her know me. Know what I mean? I'm not afraid of any man, but when it comes to sharin' my feelings with a woman, my stomach just turns to Royal gelatin." Beddoe even takes Clyde to bars for a drink once in a while, and in a moment of enormous inspiration decides that Clyde needs a positive sexual experience ("to get laid"), just like any other normal guy, so they break into a zoo and find a female orang for Clyde. Discreetly, we are shown Clyde entering a cage occupied by the female of his choice and then the door slowly closing. Clyde has found his own stuff of dreams.

2

If the exaggerated anthropomorphism — the creation of humanlike characters out of captive great apes — is itself the material of illusion, it leads us yet into deeper and deeper levels of illusion. Once people look at a Clyde, a Bonzo, or a Mr. Jiggs, and believe they are seeing something or someone profoundly humanlike and ultimately fragile, they are in danger of asking the following provocative question: If this animal is so much like a person, why is he being treated so much like an animal? In order to avoid answering that question too many times in too many unpleasant situations, the treatment of the ape becomes to some degree a trade secret, itself the stuff of dreams.

Trade secrets run deepest on the issue of control. Adult chimpanzees and other great apes are several times more powerful than adult humans. They are faster, far more agile, and emotionally less predictable. Wild chimps are not especially dangerous, incidentally. I have moved very closely among African chimps who, habituated to people, mostly ignored my boring presence. Wild chimps not habituated to people I have occasionally heard and not seen as they fled, or in one instance seen only for several seconds — a mother carrying her infant fled high through the trees with such frantic desperation that she broke a branch and fell twenty feet before catching herself in a lower tree. In thirty years of research in Africa involving over a hundred people, with hundreds of thousands of hours spent in close proximity to chimps, no human being has ever been seriously hurt by a wild chimp. But under the unnatural circumstances of captivity, chimpanzees are often transformed into dangerous beasts, paradoxically closer to our usual image of "wild animal." I could name some ape trainers with missing fingers, a torn forehead, and deep scars who will testify to that fact. Having placed chimpanzees in a highly abnormal confinement, in short, we discover that they resist confinement. They become dangerous, and we suddenly realize we must protect ourselves from the monsters we ourselves have created.

The first aspect of control is protection: self-protection and protection of the public. Jan Wright, who with her late husband, Jean de Troy, owned and managed the Marquis Chimps for many years, says: "With one another, they're very aggressive, so you must not fall into the trap of thinking that they are poodles. They're not. They are an inherently aggressive animal with one another, and they will do that with you. They're not aggressive all the time. They're extremely affectionate most of the time. But you have to be prepared for it. You have to think. You just have to watch. You never really stop moving your eyes. And you must keep other people away from them, to quite a large degree."

All chimpanzees in captivity, not merely the performing ones, are powerfully controlled by rough actions and a refined technology designed for human protection, for setting limits. One chimpanzee owner, David McKenna, who until recently kept a male chimpanzee named Herbie in a small, family-run zoo in Maine, described for me his experience of setting limits for Herbie. "It used to take two of us, my brother and I, to go in and clean him in the morning," McKenna told me, "because we didn't have a divided cage for him, so we had to go right in with him." One morning Herbie was his usual aggressive self. "And he was hitting my brother and trying to open the door . . . so I slapped him and told him to stop. Well, when I did, he turned around and he came after me. Just when he got within leg's distance of me, I let him have it — I kicked him right underneath the chin. Well, that drove him backward. He got back up again, and he started at me again, and I had the shovel in my hand, and I let him have the shovel right over his back. Well, he stopped right in his tracks. Ever since that day, he never came back after me. But . . . this is what the males do to the females. They show them who is boss right off and pretty near kill the female at first, so it was just about the same thing. But he never bothered me again after that. We were real good friends."

For performing apes, however, control has a second aspect: manipulation. The trainer must somehow persuade an ape to do something he or she would not ordinarily do. If the act is a simple one, not requiring a significant change from the ape's usual actions or orientation, the problem of manipulation may be comparatively simple and perhaps need some simple inducement: the carrot. If the act is demanding or pressured, requiring difficult and precise behaviors regularly repeated, the manipulation becomes complex indeed and will probably require some complex inducement: carrot plus stick.

Many great-ape trainers do not distinguish between *protection* and *manipulation*. Whatever method they use to control their apes becomes justified under the rubric of *protection*. And some great-ape trainers are not inclined to reveal their specific hard technology of control. Instead, they prefer to talk about a soft technology, the rather abstract, emotional element of control: "I love my animals. My animals love me. I'm just the big father (or mother) ape in their family. They do it because they love me, and they love to perform." There is no question that many ape trainers do form powerful emotional ties with their apes. But emotion by itself is not necessarily enough; and love backed by muscle can become abuse. Unlike our favored domestic animals, great apes are not easy to dominate and manipulate. They resemble humans in that regard and, like humans, even after they have been dominated they may nevertheless challenge future attempts to dominate or manipulate them.

They are powerful. They are intelligent and capable of deceit. And they don't particularly like to be dominated or manipulated. This combination of factors can provoke an extreme technology of control. Thus, although we may be heartily amused by Zippy and Bonzo and Clyde and the rest, our dreamy amusement is sometimes purchased with a real price, paid by the actor. The orangutan who played Clyde alongside Clint Eastwood's Philo Beddoe in the original beat-em-up fantasy, *Every Which Way But Loose* (1978), may be one of the orangutans currently laboring under significant discipline in a nightclub slapstick comedy act in Las Vegas. The orangutan who played Clyde alongside Beddoe in the 1981 sequel, *Every Which Way You Can*, was apparently clubbed to death at the end of that movie.

This might explain why the starring orangutan is not identified in the credits for *Every Which Way You Can*, except to note that he or she was supplied by Gentle Jungle, a Hollywood purveyor of live exotic animals for entertainment. In fact, the orangutan was originally named Ichibad and then renamed Buddha before he finally became Clyde. According to one observer, Buddha was trained at Gentle Jungle with the encouragement of a can of Mace and a pipe wrapped in newspaper. According to another observer — Kenneth DeCroo, assistant animal trainer on the set — Buddha's head trainer, Boone Narr, thrashed this young male the day before filming began, to make him more docile. "He made [Buddha] sit and started making him do part of his tricks." But when the orangutan became momentarily inattentive, Narr "beat" him with a cane and then an ax handle. Buddha was "protecting himself with his arms . . . moving and rolling in a circle." That was before the filming began. According to a third observer, Robert Porec, a trainer formerly with Gentle Jungle, near the end of the filming of *Every Which Way You Can*, in May of 1980, the orangutan was caught stealing doughnuts on the set and had otherwise been "a discipline problem." He was brought back to Gentle Jungle and led into a barn by his trainers, who carried with them a three-and-a-half-foot ax handle informally known as "the Buddha club." "For the next twenty minutes," Porec stated, "I could hear a great deal of hitting and pounding. I could hear Buddha vocalizing, a low grunt. It appeared that a fight was going on. I was later told that Buddha fought back." Buddha may have fought back, but he didn't have an ax handle; he was injured badly enough that for the next several days the orangutan refused to emerge from a steel drum inside his cage. In early August, Buddha was found dead in his cage, blood seeping out of his mouth; an autopsy was said to indicate cerebral hemorrhage. The movie had just been completed, and so, not to disturb that particular stuff of dreams, another orangutan named Dallas, renamed Clyde, Jr., or C.J., was hauled out to promote the film.

Theoretically, animal actors have been shielded for fifty years from the excesses of Hollywood animal trainers. Protection for animals in the film industry began in 1939, after people expressed displeasure that a perfectly good horse was forced to jump off a seventy-foot cliff during the filming of *Jesse James*. As a result of that scandal, the Hays Office on Censorship established standards for the treatment of animal actors as part of its general code of mandatory censorship. Censorship was censored in the 1960s, however, and the Hays Office was abolished.

But a private organization known as the American Humane Association has, since the 1930s, reviewed any movie scripts sent voluntarily. The AHA also sends its own observers onto movie sets, when they are invited, to keep an eye out for animal abuse. The AHA regularly screens films to determine whether they are "acceptable" or "unacceptable" according to its own code; during the past decade, the group has rated some sixty films as unacceptable because animals were killed or injured or otherwise mistreated during filming. Unfortunately, AHA officers do not seem to visit animal-training compounds away from or even adjacent to a movie set, and, remarkably, the Hollywood office of this organization has not filed a single formal complaint of abuse in twenty years. This state of affairs, along with the suggestion that the AHA Hollywood office "serves as a job referral service for animal trainers," has led some people to accuse the organization of establishing too cozy a relationship with the industry it purports to monitor.

In any case, the American Humane Association claims that one of its trained observers from the Hollywood office was on the Twentieth Century–Fox set for all eighty-one days of the filming of a movie called

Project X, during late 1985 and early 1986. *Project X* might be described as an animal-rights fantasy based on a true story. The true story is this: The United States Air Force subjected approximately three thousand rhesus monkeys imported from India to blasts of radiation up to two hundred times the standard lethal dose (the dose known to kill half the monkeys in sixty days) and then observed how well and how long they could perform various tasks while they were dying of radiation sickness. The idea was that these dying monkeys would show the Air Force how efficiently dying American pilots would bomb the Russians once the Russians had bombed us. In spite of the fact that monkeys are distinctly imperfect models of human physiology, and in spite of the problem that the monkeys didn't know why they were suffering and dying, whereas humans would know and might be expected to react to that knowledge, these experiments continued for years — until Shirley McGreal of the International Primate Protection League pointed out to several Indian journalists that the United States (which during one period was importing up to two hundred thousand rhesus monkeys annually from India) acquired them in violation of a formal agreement that guaranteed their use for the batch testing of polio vaccines or for significant medical research.

Project X, produced by Walter Parkes and Lawrence Lasker, took that basic story but substituted chimpanzees for monkeys, recognizing that apes would much more fully communicate their own personalities and potential for suffering. "This is a film about people coming to grips with the fact that nonhumans have emotions and intelligence, and that therefore we have a responsibility toward them," said Parkes. The central chimpanzee character is a charming young individual, named Virgil in the movie. He has been taught sign language by a beautiful woman scientist (played by Helen Hunt) before winding up in an Air Force laboratory cage that is opened and closed by a handsome young pilot on probation for being too much of a hotdog (Matthew Broderick). That a caged chimpanzee can communicate with sign language leads the hotdog pilot to wonder where he came from, which leads boy to meet girl and a mutual love interest to develop, which leads the Broderick character to begin "coming to grips with the fact that nonhumans have emotions and intelligence, and that therefore we have a responsibility toward them."

Fifteen chimpanzees were used in the filming of *Project X.* The producers asked Roger Fouts, an expert on chimpanzee sign language acquisition, to consult on matters of chimpanzee realism. He declined after Parkes and Lasker informed him that they had hired a Hollywood trainer, Ron Oxley, who believed it would be necessary, as the producers expressed it, to "knock the chimpanzees around." It is not clear that Oxley himself actually knocked the chimps around on the set (in any case, he died of a heart attack during the filming and was replaced by trainer Hubert Wells); but according to Karl Mitchell, himself an animal trainer for fifteen years and the owner of a Hollywood dog and cat rental company, when he visited Ron Oxley's private compound one day, he watched Oxley train a five-year-old chimpanzee for his part in the film by beating him "repeatedly with a rubber hose filled with sand and rocks. Oxley beat the chimpanzee so violently that the animal defecated and urinated." And according to Paul Mueller, an employee in the special effects department for *Project X* who ran a mock Air Force flight simulator in a special "training room" for the chimps on stage 16 at Fox studios, "every day . . . I saw trainers beat the chimpanzees with clubs, blackjacks, and their fists . . . The trainers struck the chimpanzees across the back, shoulder area, and chest area with clubs and blackjacks. On several occasions one trainer hammered away repeatedly at his chimp in the chest and rib area with his closed fists. On one particular day this trainer became so infuriated with his chimp that he appeared to have gone berserk. He beat the animal with his fists so severely that I stopped the motion of the [mock flight simulator] machine." At least two other people who had been on the set at other times in other places made similar comments, but withdrew them while simultaneously expressing concern about their future employment in the film industry.

When five of the chimpanzees from this film were eventually retired to Primarily Primates, a sanctuary in San Antonio, Texas, sanctuary director Wally Swett had the opportunity to talk with Mark Hardin and Julian Sylvester, two assistant trainers for *Project X.* Swett says the trainers spoke of "knock-down, drag-out fights" with the apes. When Swett expressed surprise that the newly arrived chimpanzees, let loose on the sanctuary grounds, made no effort to run away, Sylvester explained that he had trained them not to run away by chasing and kicking them whenever they tried. Swett noted that two of the apes were extremely afraid of black rubber boots; that the adult teeth of one had been completely removed — possibly knocked out — on the left side of his upper and lower jaw; and that all five of them flinched and cowered whenever any nearby person moved too quickly.

These and other reports seemed to indicate abuse, at least to television game-show host and animal-welfare activist Bob Barker. In June of 1987 Barker publicized what he had learned and soon provoked the Los Angeles Department of Animal Regulation to investigate. Officers of the department investigated for three months, and — after extensive interviews and an examination of photographs showing, among other things, trainers on the set carrying blackjacks, sawed-off pool cues, revolvers, a cattle prod — felt there was enough evidence to warrant filing criminal complaints on eighteen felony counts of cruelty to animals against six animal trainers involved in *Project X*. The Los Angeles district attorney's office decided not to prosecute the criminal charges, however, apparently since the felony statute for cruelty to animals applies only when a person is cruel to an animal owned by someone else. Twentieth Century–Fox owned most of the chimps, so how could Twentieth Century–Fox or its direct employees be guilty of cruelty to animals it owned and therefore had a legal right to be cruel to?

Be that as it may, the allegations of abuse hurt many people's feelings. Twentieth Century–Fox was hurt. Producers Parkes and Lasker were hurt — "shocked" is how they described it. The trainers were hurt. But no one had more hurt feelings than the people of the American Humane Association, whose Hollywood representatives had monitored the filming of *Project X* and who, after Bob Barker made his opinions public, conducted their own retrospective "in-depth investigation" and found "not a single instance of abuse that can be substantiated."

Many ape trainers love their apes, I am sure, although what they mean by "love" may not be what I mean. Some apes probably love some of the attention and the exercise they get while performing. Still, few great apes would voluntarily submit to a life that consists of imprisonment alternating with forced exercise according to some other ape's routine, even when people describe that forced exercise as "family entertainment." It is not surprising, therefore, that every ape trainer I have met or spoken with finds control to be a problem.

Some assert that the problem is minor and that their animals can usually be manipulated with the psychological approach. According to

Lima Hussey, head trainer for an act using young chimpanzees at Marine World/Africa U.S.A. in northern California: "All the training for the chimps is basically positive food rewards . . . Most of the punishment you can use with the chimp is time-outs, which is basically ignoring them. You can take away some of their favorite foods from them." Physical discipline does occasionally become necessary, Hussey says. "The only time we use physical discipline is if the animals are physically aggressive to a trainer or to the public." What sort of physical discipline? "Oh, you bonk them. There are a number of ways of doing it." With a hand? "Yeah, that's why my knuckles are so sore." I will speculate here that "bonking" means knuckle rapping on the head, an unexceptional technique of punishment I've seen applied on two different occasions — with a young chimpanzee and a very young gorilla.

For other trainers, particularly those working with adolescent or adult apes, control usually requires a more substantive approach. One person I know occasionally uses a cattle prod. ("You've simply got to have something to intimidate them.") A trainer who worked until recently for a chimpanzee show in Florida regularly made his opinions known with a wooden club. Others I've met and heard about sometimes fasten remote-controlled shock devices onto their actors. ("We have one. We don't use it at all. The only time we use it is when we're in a high-risk situation.") Another trainer, I am told, uses a split leather strap to discipline and control the apes she has raised as part of her family, including one she breastfed while he was an infant.

One chimpanzee character was sometimes disciplined with a baseball bat, it has been asserted. Three chimpanzees once featured on a popular television show were beaten by their trainers, according to a witness. Mickey Antalek, who for years thrilled circus audiences with his four performing chimpanzees at Ringling Brothers, Barnum and Bailey, was said to club his apes; they were also castrated. According to Nick Connell, a trainer at Ringling: "I first witnessed the training of four chimps in winter quarters in Venice, Florida. They were on a long, multiseated bicycle on which three of the large chimps rode as passengers while the largest chimp, Louie, steered and pedaled. The vehicle was difficult for even a human to ride under those conditions, and Louie had a hard time of it, spilling the ensemble repeatedly. And, repeatedly, he was struck with a sturdy club. The thumps could be heard outside the arena building, and the screams went farther than that. My blood boiled. I'm ashamed to say I did nothing!" After Antalek died in 1984, incidentally, his four performing chimpanzees were sent off to the White Sands Research Center in New Mexico, where they would have been given numbers and presumably placed on the assembly line for testing insecticides, cosmetics, and drugs had not a few sentimentalists, including Shirley McGreal, interceded. The chimpanzees were finally sent to the Wild Animal Retirement Village of Waldo, Florida, an excellent private sanctuary and small zoo run by two former circus people, Gene and Rusty Schuler.

As many as one hundred fifty very young chimpanzees currently serve as photographic props to amuse tourists on the beaches of Spain. The apes are dressed in little suits, of course, and drugged to ensure their docility. Their teeth have been removed. They are beaten; and, at least on occasion, the tip of a burning cigarette has served as an obedience reinforcer. (Unlike chimpanzee entertainers in the United States, moreover, the Spanish beach chimps are still acquired in Africa, mostly Equatorial Guinea, and smuggled to their destination. Since the apes' careers begin in infancy and end at the age of four, when they are disposed of — killed or, conceivably, marketed elsewhere — the beach photographers need to be continually resupplied with fresh baby apes from Africa. The drain on wild chimp populations could be enormous, but Spanish authorities continue to express wry amusement at widespread concern elsewhere in Europe over the situation.)

I will imagine that some trainers use attractive "soft" methods only. But what I have seen directly and otherwise learned during my own research into the subject indicates something different: regular and common reliance, backstage, on an unattractive hard technology of control. If the performance of apes is to conform to what the public wants to see and to know and to imagine, then the technology of control must remain covert and concealed, eternally one more ingredient in the stuff of dreams.

3

Where does legitimate control end and abuse begin? Most of us would base our ideas of "abuse" in the treatment of great apes on our experiences and observations of the treatment of dogs and cats and children. We might consider that striking a dog or a child hard with a stick is abusive, whereas we might believe that a spank or a single slap to some part of the body other than the face, or (at the canine level) a whack with a rolled-up newspaper, is not abusive. We seldom stop to imagine that powerful, intelligent, psychologically complex wild animals are very different from small, comparatively simple domestic animals. But the idea of *abuse,* in the great-ape entertainment business, suggests that there exists a regular state of *nonabuse* — that abuse is simply a temporary violation of the norm, an unhappy aberration from an otherwise happy and acceptable situation. I believe we have to examine the norm itself.

I began to think this way after some enlightening conversations with Ron Winters, the owner and trainer of Mr. Jiggs. The relationship between Mr. Winters and Mr. Jiggs is certainly one based on affection and the sort of bond that can exist between parent and child, even though in this case the "child" could tear apart the parent in a few seconds. And I believe Winters when he argues that things have worked out so well with Mr. Jiggs mainly because they love each other and because Mr. Jiggs is fundamentally a good-natured and happy ape. But just in case this 190-pound chimpanzee should have a momentary lapse in basic etiquette, God forbid, during a birthday party or bar mitzvah, her front teeth have been removed and her mouth is tied shut, with nylon string wrapped around special dental fittings in the molars, during any party or performance. She can still drink things and eat anything soft, such as ice cream; she just cannot bite.

Aside from love, and aside from the jaws wired shut, as an added precaution Winters relies on a device he calls "the radio unit." During the day Mr. Winters always wears attached to his belt a small radio transmitter with a two-button control. During the day Mr. Jiggs always wears a radio receiver and a large battery pack cabled and padlocked to her back, with a stainless steel collar mostly insulated with neoprene running around her neck. Should Jiggs begin to get out of line, well, Winters can press that first button. It activates a mild shock at the collar, a "tickle" of warning at the chimpanzee's neck. If, however, Mr. Jiggs is moving toward trouble of a more serious nature, Mr. Winters can press the second button. A shock from that: "My chimp can't move. It stops him. Period."

Winters doesn't use the radio unit as a training device, I believe. Mr.

Jiggs enjoys doing a show. In fact, Winters seldom has to press the button at all these days, so happy and well behaved is his chimpanzee. Winters also doesn't recommend a radio unit for every ape owner, since the batteries need to be recharged every few days — which means that someone has to be able to take off and put on the device. "If the chimp is totally mean or if he's been abused or whatever," then the system won't work. But if your chimpanzee is nice enough to allow you to put the shocker and battery pack on, with the stainless steel collar around the neck and the padlocked nylon waist cord, then the radio unit is excellent. "A couple of zaps from that, he'll be a different chimp," Winters says. "It's like night and day."

Of course, no one sees this electronic system during a show, since Mr. Jiggs wears a tuxedo-style costume over everything, and the whole unit is removed at night. After a big evening snack — cabbage and lettuce and tomatoes and so on — and a final trip to the bathroom and a toothbrushing, Mr. Jiggs is ready for bed. Winters unlocks the padlock, removes the battery pack and radio receiver and shocker, and attaches Mr. Jiggs to a simple rope attached to a steel cable, so that she can sleep in her own bed in peace. In case of fire, this chimpanzee knows how to unbolt a window and climb down the permanently fixed ladder; the steel cable runs outside, so that she can escape from the house and still remain attached to the rope and cable. Other potential necessities are also anticipated. "At night, if he has to tinkle or anything, he has a little potty alongside his bed," Winters explains, "and then he knows never to do number two because that's for the morning when he gets up and can go to the toilet and flush."

It is true that the large battery pack and the rest of this apparatus look mildly bizarre when you first see them, but Ron Winters carefully explained to me the logic of the radio unit, why he built it for his chimpanzee, why he has sold units to other chimpanzee owners and might be willing to custom build another radio unit for anyone else in his situation — for about $3,500. In terms of using an adult ape in entertainment, the radio unit is important, Winters says, because "it makes me the dominant male." And continual dominance is absolutely necessary. "A chimp is not like a dog. A dog is submissive. They follow the leader. A chimp is an independent creature. He's saying, 'Oh, you're in another room. What's to stop me from going over and getting the booze?' You know what I mean?" But more significantly, because of the radio unit Ron Winters never has to put Mr. Jiggs in a

cage. No other adult chimpanzee in the United States, Winters believes, has the luxury of living entirely outside a cage. "The rest of
them . . . in cages . . . you don't go near them, because after they've
been in a cage all their life they hate everybody. A lion can take a cage
because they're stupid. You know, if they're well fed, they go to sleep.
But a chimp is smart. He knows he's not supposed to be in a cage.
They hate that because their mind is so intelligent. They're bored to
death."

To learn more about cages, after I visited Ron Winters and Mr. Jiggs in
New Jersey I booked passage on a transcontinental air ship to Hollywood, California. Imagining that to know the stuff of dreams you
sometimes have to enter it, I went to Hollywood in disguise. I knotted
a tie around my neck and thereby magically transformed myself into
the executive vice president of a major East Coast advertising firm,
looking to hire performing chimpanzees for a series of "Discovery of
Fire" commercials promoting Sugiyama 5.6 stovepipes on Japanese
television.

In this fashion I visited some people in the Los Angeles area who
specialize in renting animals — dogs, cats, horses, camels, lions, tigers, chimpanzees — to the movie and television industry. I met Greg
Lille, who seems to own the second-largest group of mostly performing
chimpanzees in the western United States. Lille is actually from northern California; his chimpanzees regularly strike poses for Hallmark
greeting cards.

I went to a television studio and endured the pilot presentation for
CBS-Television of a comedy game-show concept that included double
entendres and male strippers, a sweating comedian who asked me in
front of the television cameras if I liked being an advertising executive, and a two- or three-year-old chimp who was supposed to leap into
the arms of the master of ceremonies but became confused at the
critical moment.

I toured an exotic animal ranch and there met a couple of young
chimpanzees available for rent. The cages at this ranch were new and
clean — concrete floors, wire sides, tin roofs — laid out in regular
rows with their bestial contents randomly distributed within: dog
here, chimp there, lion over there. But the cages seemed built for
storage, and I am still disturbed by the memory of that huge, bemaned
African lion lying inside a kennel with a concrete floor that looked no
bigger than my desktop.

By far the largest private collection of chimpanzees in the Holly-wood area is owned by a man named Bob Dunn. When I visited him, Dunn had twenty-two chimpanzees, all kept in cages in a backyard that didn't seem much bigger than mine. Michael Jackson's former surrogate baby, Bubbles, was there, incidentally, having inconve-niently outgrown malleable babyhood. ("He thought Bubbles would always stay small and adorable and be his playmate forever," a close associate of Jackson's has blabbed to the tabloids. But one day the growing chimp grabbed Michael by the arm and dragged him down to the floor, so eventually Bubbles was taken away. "Michael is broken up about the situation. He loved Bubbles like a son.") Bubbles was perhaps seven or eight years old when I was there, and Dunn took him out of his cage and had him sit on a table, next to the rifle and the can of Mace, to do a few tricks.

Some of Dunn's other chimps were also youngsters, also available for rent and capable of giving some level of performance. But most of his apes seemed to be retired adults, and although Dunn and I dis-cussed how we might use an adult or two for the Sugiyama stovepipe commercials (they could hover in the background, restrained with cables wrapped about their waists and staked into the ground or tied to rocks), in general those big chimpanzees were serving humanity and the entertainment industry as breeders, producing more and more baby chimpanzees for any carefully selected customer who could come up with perhaps $20,000 to $30,000. But Dunn's cages looked home-made to me, and I found the ones with the painted cinderblock walls dark and depressing. The big creatures inside acted aggressive, perhaps frustrated. It was very hot that day, and Dunn regretted that it had been too hot to exercise the older chimps outside their cages, implying that they were regularly released and exercised, although I couldn't figure out how or where. Still, the cages were close together, some-times stacked on top of each other, and I imagined that that arrange-ment might actually be superior to the evenly distributed storage kennels of the other exotic-animal rental operation, since chimpan-zees are such deeply social beings.

Dunn has argued that his apes, at least the ones still young enough to perform, are much better off than chimpanzees in zoos. "In zoos, animals get bored to death," he once told a journalist for the Los Angeles Times. "But these guys love working — it makes them twice as smart. They get to go places and see things."

In the end, I had to shake my head and recognize this fact: we are all so used to seeing animals in cages everywhere, all the time, that we don't even think twice about their situation. Young chimpanzees, so cute and personable on stage, may spend most of their offstage careers in a cage. Chimpanzees are child actors; and by the time they reach late childhood, with a few exceptions they will be permanently retired to a cage. If they are unfortunate enough to have exploitative owners, their cages may be used as one more form of deprivation, one more aspect of control and manipulation. If they are fortunate enough to have ethical owners, their cages will be larger and more fun.

Lee Ecuyer, the creator and owner of Zippy the Chimp, once told me he thought putting Zippy in a cage was cruel. "You couldn't just put Zippy up. It was like putting a child away in a cage, really." Of course, when the thirty chimps who were known as Zippy became older, they did go into cages before they were sold — "but a great big cage, and then he had another chimp with him, and he seemed to be very happy." But after visiting with Mr. Jiggs and speaking to Ron Winters that one morning in a kitchen in New Jersey, and then flying out West and touring the chimpanzee rental operations in southern California, I began to appreciate Winters' point of view. Indeed, I personally would rather walk around with a radio unit attached to my back and neck than live in a cage approximately as spacious as the inside of a small truck.

Too bad one or another seems absolutely necessary, as we happily if dreamily watch all those endangered animals dressed up in tutus and tuxedos, turned into children and clowns, so that we may continue to linger for just a little while longer in our own stuff of dreams.

8 ⬩ To Laugh, to Beat

TRINCULO:
I shall laugh myself to death at this puppy-headed monster. A most scurvy monster! I could find in my heart to beat him.

DRIVING IN from the great American desert, I see his image expanded into mythic proportions, the top of his head actually rising above the billboard frame: dark curly hair, neatly trimmed mustache, long jaw, his head cocked with a bemused expression, eyebrows arched ironically. His right hand lifts and points with a forefinger across to his left. On his right shoulder rests a hairy hand. The source of that hand stands to the man's left, where he points — a broadly grinning creature, an orangutan, who grins and bares a white fence of teeth surrounded by a field of gums. Man and orangutan stand side by side, arms across shoulders, primate pals posing chummily across half of the billboard. The other half features a painted spread of stars and a reminder that the Stardust Hotel's *Lido de Paris* nightclub show features, as its starring attraction, Bobby Berosini and his orangutans. Welcome to Las Vegas!

I came to Las Vegas pursuing the story of chimpanzees in entertainment, planning to interview the manager of the mailroom of a large hotel, a woman who formerly shared a famous chimpanzee act with her late husband. I imagined I might incidentally meet with Bobby Berosini to discuss the two chimpanzees who once performed an acrobatic finale to his orangutan show a few years ago in the MGM Grand's *Hallelujah Hollywood!* It took me a while to recognize that the town's real story, at that moment, had to do with Berosini's orangutans — and that, in spite of temperamental differences between the two great ape species (chimpanzees are more volatile), Berosini's trained orangutans might reveal some general realities about great apes in entertainment.

So I went to the *Lido de Paris* show at the Stardust Hotel. The full show was not, from my own meager observations, atypical of Las Vegas productions: feathers and huge hats, bare breasts and buttocks, enormous and complicated dance spectaculars that seamlessly combine bland respectability with tartly turpitude. I enjoyed parts of the show — the dancers coming out of the ceiling, for instance, the flying saucer, the ice rink rolled onto the stage, the roaring waterfall pouring out thousands of gallons of real water somehow right there onto the stage. There was a dance routine with an African theme. Two white hunters, male and female, dressed in safari outfits, arrive in the jungle and begin thinking about sex. They tear off their safari outfits. Then a whole bunch of African warriors arrive, and they begin thinking about sex, too, so they chase the white woman and tie her up on top of an Easter Island idol with smoke coming out of its eyes.

Introducing the show's featured act, the band revs up, hot and brassy, and then five orangutans appear on stage. The orangutans just appear — as if by magic — and they're wearing shorts, bright skirt-flaps above the shorts, and funny hats. Bobby Berosini appears too, wearing a black tuxedo and white shirt, bathed in spotlight, showered with applause, accompanied by a blue-garbed female assistant who does almost nothing and a darkly-dressed male assistant who stands, arms crossed behind his back, for the entire show. But Berosini is there, electric, tense, pacing, with an Edgar Allan Poe forehead and a Charlie Chaplin mustache. Dressed like Houdini, he commands and dominates and manipulates this luminous, glittering little island of a stage with all the power and finesse of Prospero himself. The orangs are standing now on five metallic, drum-shaped stools, their arms raised like champs. As Berosini moves to center stage in front of the five standing orangutans, one jumps off a stool and laboriously walks over to kiss him, then a second does the same. The female assistant hands Berosini a microphone, and he says: "Good evening, ladies and gentlemen! My name is Bobby Berosini — and this is a high-class monkey show!"

He introduces the apes. First the one on his far left. "To my left is Lady Orangutan Tiga! Take a bow, Tiga!" She takes a bow. *Taaaa!* goes the band. "To my right is Lady Orangutan Rusty. Take a bow,

Rusty!" Rusty takes a bow. *Taaaa!* goes the band. He introduces the two apes on his near left and near right, and is about to introduce the one in the middle — when that one grabs Berosini forcibly by the shoulder, brings his own face up close, and elongates his lips into a sloppy trumpet kiss. The audience laughs. "Folks, you saw him in Clint Eastwood's *Every Which Way But Loose!* You like it, eh? Take a bow, Popi!" But Popi gives Berosini the finger instead, then sits down. The audience laughs and applauds, and Berosini looks miffed. Popi hides with a hand over his face — *it wasn't me!* — and then, just as Berosini turns away, Popi gives him the finger again. *Taaaa!* goes the band, and the audience laughs.

"Let's go with the monkey show! Here we go!" By now the orangs are all seated on their stools, legs hanging down, and Berosini wants a volunteer. The apes all shake their heads, put their hands over their ears. "You fat monkey!" he says to one. "Don't get smart with me! Raise your hand!" Still no ape volunteers. The orang to the far left even shakes her head so hard her lips flap. At last Popi leaves his stool, comes up. He'll volunteer. Berosini puts his arm around Popi's head; Popi grins a huge, toothy grin; and Berosini says, "Jimmy Carter!" The audience breaks into gleeful laughter, applause, whistles.

About halfway through the show, Berosini pauses to introduce one serious moment. "Ladies and gentlemen, the orangutan — man's closest relative." Orangutans, he tells us, are an endangered species. They come from the "jungles" of Borneo and Sumatra, where fewer than five thousand are left. Luckily, captive breeding has been very successful. "It will enable us to conserve these marvelous animals for the benefit of future generations!" At this point, one of the apes raises his arms in a champeen's triumphal gesture — and the remainder of the show demonstrates for us what sorts of benefits might accrue to future generations: slapstick comedy. Accompanied by noises from the band — strike of the drum, crash of the cymbals, honk of the ooga horn, glissando of the pennywhistle — the orangs slap Berosini and he slaps them. They kiss him, grab him in the ass, goose him, give him the finger, give him the Bronx cheer, make funny faces. He, in turn, shouts "silly jackass" and "smartass" and "damn monkey." "I'm the boss," he says. "This monkey better jump!" "Cut it out, kid!" he says. "You have the monkey suit; I got the high-class Hollywood tuxedo!" And, in a moment of mock exasperation, Berosini pulls out a wooden gun, goes *Bang! Bang!* and one of the apes falls down. The audience loves it! They shriek, whistle, applaud like crazy, and then the band begins playing boogie-woogie, and the orangs and Berosini join in a wild and crazy boogie-woogieing.

We are treated as well to genital humor. An orang keeps lifting her skirt, showing her shorts underneath, pulling the skirt down again whenever Berosini looks in her direction. Finally, her extraordinarily long arm reaches around her back and she places her hand between her legs; she leaves it there, flapping like a butterfly at her crotch. "I bet Tom Jones can't do that!" Berosini comments. "He try, he'd break his ass!" The audience roars with approval.

"Lot of people ask me how I train my orangutans," Berosini declares, nearing the end of his show. "Well, I train them by hypnotizing them." He will demonstrate. He turns to Popi, who purses his lips way out; Berosini grabs those lips and massages them. "First of all, folks, you've got to squeeze the lips." Certain hypnotic juices will flow from the lips to the brain as a result of this squeezing, Berosini explains, and . . . but just at this point, he appears to become distracted by the enormous size of Popi's lips. He pauses. Finally he says, "I don't know if you noticed it, folks, but this orang has very big lips. This is a special breed of orangutan called Big Lips Orangutan. You know about Bigfoot? This is Biglip." The audience laughs, and Berosini continues on this theme. "He's got big lips, big brain," he says, pointing to the lips, then the head. Then he pauses, picks up and holds a loose flap of flesh hanging at this ape's chin (a laryngeal sac). Berosini looks momentarily puzzled. "And here is something hanging down here. I don't know what the hell it is. Something fell down from his face." And then the entertainer begins to laugh. He laughs and laughs, and then he leans back and laughs some more. When the people in the audience see Popi look up at Berosini with an exaggerated, pouty, hurt expression, they roar with laughter. Berosini retracts the insult: "Hey, don't worry. You're beautiful! I was just kidding! We'll fix it after the show — a little Crazy Glue! Don't worry!" Then the entertainer remembers he was talking about bigness, so he returns to his theme. "Big lips, big brain, big stomach, big feet. Did I forget something?" he asks, at which point the orangutan waves that skirt up and down over his crotch. The crowd can't stand it! They laugh, scream, whistle, cry in delight! They love the show! They love Bobby Berosini and his orangutans!

After the show, Bobby Berosini sat down for a chat in the Stardust snack bar. He looked smaller in real life, less formal (with his black bow tie loosened), slightly more relaxed, perhaps more in the character of his real self, Czechoslovakian-born Bohumil Berousek. "What can I do for you?" he wanted to know.

I was curious about the chimpanzees who had done acrobatics in his show at the MGM Grand years earlier. He said he had retired them when he decided to create a comedy routine. "Chimpanzees are incapable of comedy," he said, "because they have no sense of limits. They always go all out." He still keeps the chimps at his place, though, and he assured me that they were well taken care of. "They live in a large cage, and I play with them every day and let them play with the orangs every day." But Berosini seemed uninterested in talking any further about the retired chimpanzees. He was too preoccupied, I believe, with a scandal that had recently broken in Las Vegas. Someone had secretly videotaped him backstage, purportedly beating his orangutans. The videotape had been mailed to local television stations by two animal-rights organizations.

He began talking about the videotape, which was about to become the focus of his several-million-dollar lawsuit against a few people and the two organizations. "When I first saw that videotape," he told me, "my response was, 'Who is that person? That isn't me!' The people who made the videotape doctored it." It had been sound enhanced, light enhanced, possibly even altered by computer, he declared. The people who made it were a bunch of cocaine-addicted dancers with a personal grudge against him. The animal-rights people publicizing the videotape and picketing his show were primarily interested in raising money for themselves — and with that videotape they had raised millions. The strange thing was that they didn't like either people or animals, he felt. One animal-rights woman even caused a dozen hamsters to be euthanized. These people were fanatics, and America has always had problems dealing with fanatics. Hitler, for example.

He had been set up. Dancers had been making noises behind the curtains to distract his orangutans, forcing him to discipline them. "Yes, of course, I discipline my orangutans. I'm a father to them, and I discipline them just as you would a child. You have to mix love and discipline. Too much love makes the child a brat, and too much discipline makes the child fearful. I do discipline them — as a last resort. But I use a forceful tone of voice more than anything else." He loves his animals. Moreover, they love him, and they love to do the show. They are much better off than other captive apes, zoo apes for instance, who have to sit in a cage all day long and be bored. Orangutans are very intelligent animals, and they need the stimulation his act provides. "Everything needs something to do, a purpose in life, from worms to humans — everything — and that includes primates. My orangutans are happy because performing gives them a purpose." His animals love doing the show, and so does he. In fact, even if he made no money from the act, he would still do it, just for the sheer joy of being onstage with his orangutans.

He expressed alarm, dismay, and deep anger at the criticisms of the so-called experts. "I'm the world expert on orangutans," he concluded at last. "You can learn more from working with captive animals than you can from chasing them about in the wild, as Dian Fossey and Jane Goodall have done." He's worked with animals since he was three years old. His father owned a circus in Czechoslovakia, with horses, cats, bears, birds, an ape. They left in 1956, came to the States, and soon started working with several apes. During the 1960s it was easy to buy orangutans in Holland for about a thousand dollars each. "Now, of course, they're endangered in the wild — but that's not my fault. Indonesia is cutting down all the trees. In captivity, there are actually too many orangutans. My orangutans haven't bred yet, but maybe that's because orangs are so much like people: The smarter they are, the less they are interested in sex."

The day after my talk with Bobby Berosini at the Stardust Hotel, I met the person who had hidden the video camera and set the controls on automatic "record" before several shows at the Stardust during a week in July 1989. Ottavio Gesmundo did not strike me as one of the "cocaine-addicted dancers" that Berosini had described, but rather a somewhat ordinary young man dressed casually in tennis shoes, jeans, and sweatshirt, who, incidentally, had been born into a circus family and could not be considered naive about trained-animal acts.

His grandfather, Ottavio Canestrelli, emigrated from Italy to the United States sometime after World War II, carrying on the ship a massive python that later bit him during his first performance at Madison Square Garden. Grandfather Canestrelli continued with his animal acts at the Ringling Brothers' circus and eventually wound up with a chimpanzee act at the Circus Circus casino in Las Vegas during the 1960s. His daughter, Ottavio Gesmundo's mother, performed with Ringling Brothers on the bounding rope, a long rope with elastic at both ends. The act is a difficult one, and Gesmundo believes his mother was the only woman ever to perform a double somersault on the bounding rope. She met his father in South America, where he had a circus trapeze act. Gesmundo's uncle and cousins used to perform in a circus trampoline act, and his cousin Marco Canestrelli is listed in the *Guinness Book of Records* as establishing two separate world records for twisting back somersaults on a trampoline. At Ringling Brothers, Marco's most dramatic act may have been the elephant jump. He would put on a Superman suit, run and spring off a trampoline, then leap over a group of standing elephants in a somersaulting dive. Gesmundo's sister, Elisa, used to hang by her teeth and spin on a trapeze. The trapeze was itself attached to a high monorail, and it slowly circled an entire casino at Circus Circus, high above the gamblers and the game tables and slot machines. She can be seen hanging by her teeth and spinning in the James Bond movie *Diamonds Are Forever*, which includes scenes filmed at that casino.

When he was a young boy, Ottavio Gesmundo used to watch his grandfather's chimpanzee act. Grandfather Ottavio had three or four chimps that he dressed up to look like soldiers. They would march out wearing helmets and uniforms, carrying rifles on their shoulders, then halt, put down their rifles, salute, and do acrobatic tricks. One time, the grandson remembers, his grandfather saw a child running up a ramp toward the stage and tried to stop the child before he came too near the chimpanzees. The old man slipped, hit his head, and was knocked unconscious. No one was able to assist him because the chimpanzees positioned themselves around their prostrate leader and wouldn't allow anyone to approach. He suffered a fatal stroke soon afterward.

A few years later Gesmundo himself worked briefly with a performing ape act. His mother's sister, Chi Chi, married into a Mexican family that owned a circus, so he went to Mexico when he was thirteen to help his uncle, who trained chimps, camels, horses, and a hippopotamus. His uncle had little luck training the hippo, who was permanently locked in a cage on wheels with water on one half of the floor and dirt on the other half. Sometimes the hippo would lounge around in the water, and sometimes he would move back to the dirt. ("To this day," Gesmundo reflects, "I think, 'Well, that was probably cruelty right there in itself.' I don't know how aware of it we were back then.") The camels used to spit at him, he remembers, and the three chimps were chained and locked in cages and only taken out for shows. They were very difficult to handle. His job was simply to care for the apes, to assist his uncle in dressing them before and undressing them after a performance, then to take them away afterward.

After a year in Mexico he drifted back to Nevada — this time to Reno, where he became a stagehand. When he was nineteen, his girlfriend convinced him that he was a good dancer, and so he took dance classes and eventually was hired to dance in *The Chorus Line* in Reno. In the summer of 1987 he was chosen for a part in the *Lido de Paris* show in Las Vegas.

After dancing in the *Lido* show for about eight months, he began noticing a thumping sound coming from behind a curtain at the end of the African number. The African number precedes the waterfall display, where some dancers carrying torches climb to the top of the sixty-thousand-gallon-a-minute waterfall, after which Berosini comes onstage with his orangutans. While the waterfall was being assembled, Gesmundo and the other dancers would be standing, stage right, on one side of a curtain. On the other side of the curtain was a backstage area, the "prop room," where Berosini and his assistants and orangutans would wait for their entrance cue. The waterfall would be ready; Gesmundo and the other dancers would be holding their torches, waiting for a stagehand named Woody to light them. "When he lights our torch, that's the time Mr. Berosini comes down with the animals, and you know you hear the . . . pitter-pattering of their feet, and whatnot, and you can hear it: *dum! dum!* And you can hear it! I didn't know what it was." Gesmundo estimates that he heard the thumping at least six times a week. (He danced twelve of the nightclub's fourteen weekly shows.)

One night, for some reason, the orangutan Popi was replaced by a younger and less well trained orangutan, Bo. Popi had been trained to smile on cue, but Bo apparently hadn't mastered that response. Gesmundo hypothesizes this because, he says, he watched Berosini violently poking Bo, jabbing Bo in the face, trying forcibly to push his lips open into a smile. "And he repeated this, like every night, until this orangutan got it right. And at points . . . he was like shaking it, and just, 'Come on! Come on!' And he was just poking it in the face to get it to smile, and after a while I guess after doing that violently he would just have to tap it now and then, and he [the orang] would remember about the violent jabs and smile. And that disturbed me. That's when I realized, 'Well, wait a minute. Something is really not right here.' "

Gesmundo had recently purchased a small, inexpensive video camera. He took it to work one day in July, and then he cut a hole in the side of a costume box. During a costume change late in the African number, he told me, he would open the box, place the camera inside, turn the camera on, press "record" and the date, take the lens cap off, close the box, tape it shut, and carry the box to the prop room where he would place it on a shelf and angle it just so, to record Berosini and his entourage while they paused there. After the first or second night, some of the other male dancers figured out what was going on, and they began to help Gesmundo, keeping people occupied, for example, while he carefully positioned the costume box and the camera. They would perform in their segment of the African number and then return to their position beside the prop room curtain, stage right, waiting for Woody to light their torches for the waterfall sequence.

Berosini has claimed that during this time the dancers made noises from their side of the curtain as part of a deliberate effort to disturb his apes so that they would misbehave and require discipline. Gesmundo had a different story. "If anything," he told me, "we would be very quiet to hear if he was hitting the animals. And sure enough: *dum! dum! dum!*" Then Woody would light their torches, and they would climb on top of the waterfall. After the show was over, he and several of the male dancers would take the camera to a room in the hotel where there was a playback machine and watch the video. "We watched it, I mean immediately afterward. And everybody was just like, 'My God! He's hitting those animals! Look at that! Why is he doing it?'"

Ottavio Gesmundo sent the videotape to a Las Vegas chapter of PETA, the People for the Ethical Treatment of Animals. PETA and a second organization called the Performing Animals Welfare Society, or PAWS, began to publicize the tapes. At that time, he told me, Gesmundo didn't actually know anyone associated with PETA or PAWS. Fearing retribution, he had sent the tapes anonymously. But when Berosini's lawyer, Harold Gewerter, referred to the entertainer's anonymous critics as "cowards," Gesmundo gave his name. Soon after he made his identity public, he received an anonymous phone call late at night: "You better watch your back, you motherfucker."

While I talked with him in his apartment, Gesmundo placed a copy of the videotape into his video machine. The show I had seen the night before at the Stardust Hotel was very simple: five orangutans,

dressed like humans and acting remarkably like humans, smiled and
acted and made faces with some apparent spontaneity, danced and
cavorted with some apparent pleasure, and — within the slapstick
tradition — slapped, slugged, poked, and in various other exaggerated
ways tormented and humiliated their stuffed-shirt host in a tuxedo.
The backstage version of the show, if I can believe that videotape,
existed in some bizarrely precise opposition to the frontstage show:
the host in a tuxedo slapped, slugged, poked, and in various other
ways tormented his five orangutans. Although I didn't know it, just
about then a copy of the videotape was traveling through the mails to
my co-author who, asked to comment as an expert on apes, viewed it
several times.

*In this video I saw the following sequence of events. A door opened
and three men leading five young orangutans walked along a bare
passage toward the (presumably concealed) camera. With these eight
primates was a fourth man, wearing a bow tie. At the end of the
passage the whole group stopped. The orangs, still standing upright,
appeared quiet and well-behaved. I saw no signs of disobedience in
any of them at any time. Yet as they stood there — apparently waiting
to go onstage for a performance — the man in the bow tie began to
abuse the orangs. Suddenly he would seize one of them by its hair and
pull and push it toward and away from him with violent movements.
He would slap one of them, or punch it with his fists. Most of the abuse
was directed at the larger orangs. Once he pulled one around to face
him, then slapped it hard over the muzzle. Occasionally he hit one of
them over the shoulders with an implement shaped like a conductor's
baton. During these entirely unprovoked assaults the handlers restrained the orangs by both arms, holding them upright. The men gave
the impression that they were expecting the abuse and were position-
ing their charges to receive it. Presently, perhaps in response to some
cue from onstage, the nine primates moved out of frame.*

*The whole sequence, or a sequence similar to the one I've just
described, was repeated several times. Apparently it was filmed on
several different days, as clarified by the automatic dating notation at
the bottom of the video frame. The repetition — door opens; orangs
and handlers walk toward the camera; all stop; man in bow tie hits,
slaps, punches, shakes, and otherwise terrorizes orangs; group moves
away — made the video particularly distressing to watch. I was
shocked, sickened, and saddened by the actions of the humans shown*

in this footage. According to an article in the *Las Vegas Sun* printed before the videotape appeared, Bobby Berosini never uses force or physical punishment in training his apes. "It would never work," Berosini said. "Orangutans are introverts. Using force with them would only make them more introverted. It takes love, kindness and lots of patience to help them come out of themselves." After the videotape appeared, another article in the *Las Vegas Sun* noted that Bobby Berosini does use force or physical punishment — as an occasional act of discipline. "Where does discipline stop and cruelty begin?" the entertainer asked rhetorically. "It looks bad," he admitted, referring to the scenes on the videotape, "but it's really absolutely nothing. It's [blows] over the shoulder blades two or three times." Berosini appealed to the experts: "If you show that tape to anyone who knows something about these animals, they would know what's going on."

By that time, in fact, PETA was following Berosini's advice and sending copies of the videotape to experts who did know something about the animals. These individuals returned written opinions during the summer and early fall, and the opinions seemed overwhelmingly to conclude that substantial abuse had taken place. Roger Fouts, a top expert on chimpanzee language acquisition, saw "obvious suffering and anguish" and "cruel and abusive treatment." Robert Schumaker, an animal caretaker at the National Zoo in Washington, D.C., who had by then worked directly with orangutans for seven years, referred to scenes of striking, beating, kicking, kneeing, and noted that all of the attacks were "unprovoked" and "not in response to any aggression or uncontrollable behaviors exhibited by the animals." H. Lyn Miles of the University of Tennessee, an anthropologist and expert on sign-language acquisition by chimpanzees and orangutans, analyzed the eight different backstage scenes shown in the videotape and noted that, during the fewer than seven minutes shown altogether, Berosini grabs nineteen times, slaps seven times, strikes with his hand seven times, and hits with the rod thirteen times; according to this analysis, Berosini hits an orangutan with his hand or with the rod an average of once every twenty seconds. Professor Miles stated as her "overall impression" that she had seen "an edgy and nervous trainer [who] is randomly striking out at his animals and beating them without cause as a reminder that he is in control." Dr. Michael Pereira, a biologist and primatologist at Duke University, wrote as his "professional opinion" that "the severity of the physical aggression" was "unquestionably excessive, unwarranted, and morally objectionable." Stuart Altmann of the University of Chicago, an animal behaviorist specializing in primates, concluded from seeing the videotape that Berosini's orangutans were "apparently being repeatedly subjected to cruel treatment that is an unacceptable violation of any reasonable standards of animal welfare." Anthropologist Jeffrey Schwartz, an expert on orangutans, said that the orangs on the videotape were "beaten and abused" in a manner he considered "appalling and reprehensible." Dr. Biruté Galdikas, who had by then spent eighteen years studying and working with orangutans in Borneo and who is unquestionably the world's foremost authority on wild orangutans, saw Berosini's apes "trembling and shaking in fear." She heard "howls of protest from one of the orangutans being hit" and recognized that the animals' faces were expressing fear.

In addition to collecting expert testimony concerning the videotape, PETA solicited affidavits from dancers and other workers at the Stardust and elsewhere who claimed they had actually seen Berosini beat and otherwise abuse his apes. Dancer Robin Finn claimed she had seen Berosini "physically punch [one] orangutan in the face" and threaten and strike another orangutan with the back of his hand. Dancer Dean Stewart stated that he had seen Berosini "strike the orangutans across the chest, with the back of his hand, in a very violent manner." Dancer Christopher Snow, in his sworn affidavit, declared that he saw "Mr. Berosini repeatedly poke and hit the orangutan in the face," a treatment he had in fact "observed . . . on many occasions." Dancer Bernadette Bransch affirmed that she "personally observed Mr. Berosini repeatedly punching the orangutan with both fists" at one time. Dancer Deidre Cline-DeAndrea declared in her affidavit that she had been present one time when Berosini "punched the orangutan in the face with his right fist." Dancer Jane Rawson declared that she saw Berosini "viciously grab the orangutan under the neck in a pinching manner which appeared to force the animal to lift his head in an upward fashion. It appeared that Mr. Berosini was actually choking the animal." Stagehand and propman Paul Faulkner (who had worked at the MGM Grand and so witnessed Berosini's show during that earlier period) stated in his sworn affidavit that he had on "several occasions . . . personally observed Mr. Berosini strike the animals." He had seen Berosini strike them in the face with his hands, choke them, and strike them with a black baton. Faulkner reported that a couple of times he had actually examined the baton and determined it to be "a heavy-duty welding rod approximately sixteen inches long." John Geremia, having responded to an advertisement for animal trainer while Berosini worked at the MGM Grand, watched the showman bring one of his apes into a private area and "without explanation, beat it indiscriminately with a large lead pipe," while an assistant held the creature. Three orangutans, observing the beating, "cowered horribly" and "looked terrified and started to cry." Geremia also noted that the teeth of the orangs had been wired shut, with wire passing through holes drilled into the teeth, so that they were unable to open their mouths; the apes were fed by pouring a semiliquid gruel through their lips. PETA also acquired the very damaging affidavit of a woman who had herself been an animal trainer for many years. She described Berosini's methods as "intimidation training."

In addition to the documented experts' opinions and the statements of many people under oath that they had personally seen Berosini beat his apes, PETA with the authority of a court order sent its own team of three experts into the Berosini compound to examine the orangutans directly for signs of abuse. The three experts, two veterinarians (Michael Wolff and Robert Stone) and one animal caretaker (Robert Shumaker from the National Zoo), entered Berosini's compound on September 12, 1989, and examined seven orangs. They found two lesions on the back of an adult female orangutan named Tiga, which indicated "swelling and inflammation consistent with traumatic blows." Tiga looked "nervously" over her shoulder and cried as if in distress and urinated immediately when Berosini approached. The experts noted that gently touching the shoulder of an adult female named Popi "elicited wincing, guttural stress vocalizations and postural shifting, indicative of tenderness and apprehension"; all four of Popi's canine teeth had been surgically removed, and she urinated immediately when Berosini approached. The experts found an oval-shaped skin lesion on the back of an adolescent male named Rusty, which was "consistent with lesions produced from chronic blunt trauma." All four of Rusty's canines had been removed, and the minute Berosini approached, Rusty uttered cries of apparent distress and urinated. Examining a ten-year-old male orangutan named Benny, the experts found lesions around his cheekbones "indicative of healing soft tissue lesions consistent with . . . facial blows"; when Berosini approached

Benny, the orangutan immediately urinated, defecated, and made "submissive/distress vocalizations." The experts also found, over the right eyelid of a five-year-old female named Nikki, signs of a "traumatic skin lesion" of "indeterminate cause."

It might seem, from this brief summary of the evidence PETA gathered in support of the videotape, that the organization had established overwhelming support for its version of reality. Why, then, did a Las Vegas jury during the summer of 1990 decide that Berosini's version was the true reality and that the entertainer could properly claim from his critics more than $4 million? I cannot second-guess those Las Vegas jurors. What I offer as explanation for their decision must remain based mostly on newspaper reports, court documents, and a few interviews.

A year elapsed from the time the videotape was released before the trial actually began. During that year many, perhaps all, of the jurors must have depended on the local print media for continuing information on the Berosini story. Yet to a significant degree, I believe, the two major local newspapers and other media printed superficial or biased reports on the story and even, on occasion, served as community cheerleaders for a local hero. Berosini is a family man, it would be stated and implied with some regularity, who loves children and will do anything to help children, whose orangutans are part of his family, and who incidentally loves and is economically important to the good people of Las Vegas. Soon after the videotapes were broadcast on television, for example, Dick Maurice, entertainment editor for the *Las Vegas Sun*, leapt to Berosini's defense: "There's no doubt that the orangutans love Bobby as much as he loves them. They see him as their father and Bobby often refers to them as his kids." Most important, the entertainment editor worried, without Berosini's orangutan show "what about the children who would be deprived of seeing great family entertainment?" Two weeks later Maurice would announce in his "Show Biz Today" column that Bobby Berosini, that "Vegas animal lover," had been "forced to sue to protect his name." Berosini was quoted: "I can't let this go by. These orangutans are like my children."

An adulatory article that appeared a few months later in *Showbiz* magazine would "set the record straight" for Berosini, mentioning that approximately six and a half million people had been entertained by Berosini and his trained orangutans, and reminding readers that the man and his apes had regularly appeared on many charity shows, including the Saint Jude's *Night of the Stars* for homeless and abused children. Father Ward of Saint Jude's Ranch for Children testified on the entertainer's behalf: "Bobby is awfully good to the city of Las Vegas." Berosini and his "family" (wife, son, and three orangutans) embraced one another for a photographic Christmas card in December of 1989, a paid advertisement printed by the *Las Vegas Sun*, declaring thank you and "God bless" for the "heartwarming" support from the people of Las Vegas during this time of "malicious attacks" on himself, his family, and the "integrity" of his work. Berosini brought one of his orangutans to local schools, and a few months before the trial the *Sun* featured interviews accompanied by portrait photographs of some twenty local elementary-school children praising the entertainer. "Thanks to Bobby Berosini," said one charming young girl, "orangutans are going to live." "Thanks to Bobby," declared another, "the orangutans won't become extinct so fast."

It is natural that entertainment editors in an entertainment city should write warmly about entertainers. But the allegations of abuse raised serious issues that to my mind were seldom if ever given full consideration in the newspapers during the pretrial year. So far as I have been able to discover, the actual videotape was never described or analyzed in detail in the print media. Berosini's critics were never given more than a couple of inches of column space to discuss their complaints. With the exception of Ottavio Gesmundo, who was quoted a few times, I don't believe that even one of the several dancers and backstage employees claiming to have witnessed the entertainer beating his apes was ever interviewed or quoted. In the newspapers, Berosini's critics remained primarily anonymous, obscure figures who were at best described as "activists" and "protesters" and at worst referred to (directly or indirectly, within quotes) as "militant" and "radical," "cowards," "kooks," and "fanatics." By the time of the trial, Berosini himself would be comparing them to communists, while one of his attorneys, Harold Gewerter, would petition the judge for permission to refer to them in front of the jury as "terrorists." As an article in the *Las Vegas Review-Journal* described the situation at the time of the trial, the people of Las Vegas had "generally rallied behind" the entertainer. "Berosini has already won one victory in the case — the battle of publicity," the reporter stated. Then he referred to three seemingly official examinations of the orangutans that "found no signs of abuse."

No signs of abuse?

The first exam to find "no signs of abuse" was conducted by Greg Wallen, an inspector for the U.S. Department of Agriculture (USDA), who visited the Berosini compound in late July of 1989. Wallen was not a veterinarian and seems to have concerned himself primarily with husbandry rather than veterinary issues. In any event, someone from the USDA stated at about this time that the ongoing investigation had so far uncovered "no apparent signs of injury or physical abuse." The inspection in July of 1989 did reveal that Berosini had been storing his orangutans individually — in apparent isolation — inside ventilated stainless steel boxes in a bus for an uncertain amount of time, possibly up to twenty hours a day while they were not performing. The boxes were solid steel on all four sides with air holes around the top, holes big enough for the apes to stick fingers through so that they could pull themselves up to peek out whenever they wanted to see what the interior of the bus looked like, or whenever they wanted to look for the fingers and possibly the peering eye of another orangutan. Berosini was later to describe the boxes as "nests," yet those nests were not even large enough for the apes to stretch out while lying down. Berosini was later to clarify that orangutans don't need to stretch out when they lie down. "They have very short legs. They put their legs on their stomachs and hold them with their hands. They are very comfortable," he said. In any event, USDA inspector Wallen finally determined that the boxes were approximately one-third the minimum legal size. The entertainer was given until February 28, 1990, to build full-sized cages for the apes he had often described as his children. The reality of that first inspection and investigation was complex, in summary, but only mildly so to a reporter for the *Review-Journal*, who briefly considered PETA's reservations in the article entitled "USDA: No Sign of Orang-utan Abuse."

The second official examination to find "no abuse" was conducted by Dart Anthony and Keith Brink, president and vice president respectively of the Humane Society of Southern Nevada. President Dart Anthony declared in July of 1989 that his well-known animal-welfare organization was conducting a serious investigation and had already examined all the apes used in the act. "We could not find any signs of any physical abuse to these orangutans at all." Vice president Keith Brink was to echo those sentiments, stating that his organization's official examination found no outward signs of abuse at all, no marks whatsoever — "just freckles." This early effort by the Humane Society of Southern Nevada was to become one more prop for the Berosini version of reality. Yet most later printed references to the vindication would neglect to mention that Dart Anthony's "animal-welfare" organization simultaneously offered animals for rent to the entertainment industry, and that Anthony's qualifications as an animal-abuse investigator, by his own admission, consisted of two things, only one of them easily verifiable: that he was "over 21 years of age and intelligent." Later references to the vindication would usually neglect to mention that Dart Anthony had honed his animal-abuse investigative skills during earlier employment as a liquor salesman, a dancer, and a keno runner. Later references to the vindication would neglect to mention that, according to an affidavit signed by Berosini's wife, Joan, for an unrelated lawsuit, Anthony was never paid directly for becoming a witness for Bobby Berosini; rather, as Mrs. Berosini stated in the affidavit, she did "intend to help Dart Anthony raise money by attempting to obtain entertainers to work his telethon that he intends to run on June of 1991."

The third and to my mind only reasonably compelling investigation on Berosini's behalf occurred on September 12, 1989. While three PETA experts examined the orangutans on that day and found several signs of apparent abuse, two specialists brought in by Berosini almost simultaneously examined the same apes and found no signs of abuse. Although clearly sustaining an ideological predisposition different from that of the PETA examiners, Berosini's examiners were indeed legitimate experts. The first was Dr. Kenneth Gould, a veterinarian for the Yerkes Primate Research Center. The second was Dr. Richard Simmons, a veterinarian for the Laboratory of Animal Medicine at the University of Nevada in Reno. Where the PETA experts had noted somewhat subtle occurrences, such as several of the apes urinating, in one case defecating, and making distress or submission cries whenever the entertainer approached, Berosini's two experts saw nothing. Where the PETA experts complained of the routine surgical extraction of canines, Berosini's experts were unconcerned. Where the PETA experts described "lesions" and areas of inflammation and apparent discomfort, Berosini's experts found a single "callus" on the back of one ape, tentatively attributed to "breakdancing" on the floor during Berosini's nightclub act. (The orangutans never breakdance during the show.) All five authorities did agree that a young female orang had a

scratch on her eyelid, but while the PETA experts declined to hypothe-
size on the origin of the scratch, Berosini's vets imagined that it might
be the result of "roughhousing" with her peers. Berosini himself declared with pleasure on that day that this third inspection had proved
once more that he did not abuse his orangutans. And while PETA's
three qualified and legitimate experts — two of them licensed
veterinarians — left the Berosini compound to write up their report
documenting several instances of apparent physical and psychological
damage possibly resulting from abuse, a reporter for the *Las Vegas
Review-Journal* left the compound and returned to his keyboard to
punch out an article entitled "Berosini's Orangutans Get Clean Bill of
Health after Inspection by Vets."

It is important to remember that Berosini was not on trial. His critics
were on trial. No one had charged him with a crime; no one was suing
him. Even if he had been beating his orangutans, "physical abuse" of
performing animals was not illegal at the time it allegedly occurred.
Moreover, the lawsuit focused on several charges — not only malicious slander, but trespassing, violation of privacy, and so on.

Bobby Berosini's complaint against his critics was multiple. But
central to the litigation, it seems to me, was a theory that Ottavio
Gesmundo and the people of PETA and PAWS had conspired in the
style and manner of animal-rights terrorists. This was the same hypothesis that the National Association for Biomedical Research had
tried to establish in *Immuno v. Moor-Jankowski*, of course, but while
it might only clatter cacophonously when applied to Dr. Moor-Jankowski, once applied to PETA, the theory acquired a ringing resonance.
After all, PETA was an animal-rights organization. After all, it was
PETA people who had silently distributed a clandestinely taken and
anonymously acquired videotape. And — most damaging of all — this
same PETA had been described in a February 1990 article in *Washingtonian* magazine as caring more for laboratory cats and rats than for
dying children; the very PETA that, according to the article, served as
the "above-ground ally" to an underground group of laboratory wreck-
ers and bombers known as the Animal Liberation Front (ALF).* If his
critics were "terrorists," then, logically, Berosini would be the victim
rather than the victimizer.

* PETA sued the author of that article and the *Washingtonian*, and in 1991 won an
out-of-court settlement that included a very extensive "correction and clarification."
There is no evidence of an alliance with ALF or of illegal activities by PETA.

A few days after the release of the videotape, Bobby Berosini began complaining about "death threats." These threats appear to have continued, on and off, and at one point they climaxed in an actual shooting. The person or persons foolish enough to shoot at Berosini in daylight missed completely. I don't believe the bullets were ever recovered, and apparently Berosini did not have enough presence of mind to write down the license number of the car carrying his assailants — but, as I understand it, he or someone close to him did haul out a video camera, pull off the lens cap, hold the camera in position, and record the image of a car speeding away, just in case videotaped evidence would be regarded with any credibility in a courtroom. Berosini's lawyer Harold Gewerter also complained of flying bullets, and even dead birds on his doorstep. Ultimately, this sort of terrorism led to Bobby Berosini's bursting into tears on the witness stand, complaining of people driving across his front lawn, masked people on his rooftop, and telephoned threats "from people saying they were going to put a knife in my gut, blow my head off, ship the orangutans back to Borneo, poison the orangutans . . . put a bomb in my house."

At about the same time that certain terrorists were inflating Berosini's version of reality, other terrorists were busy deflating PETA's version of reality. Aside from the single telephoned threat to Ottavio Gesmundo, the regular telephoned threats to Linda Levine of PETA in Las Vegas, and the scratched message in the paint of Levine's new car, there was a phone call to one of PETA's best potential witnesses — an older, recently divorced woman who had herself been an animal trainer, who knew Berosini well and had worked with him in the past, and who could have provided some very compelling testimony. But she decided to withdraw from the controversy altogether after someone telephoned her one night and carefully explained that her barn would be burned down and all her animals killed if she testified against Bobby Berosini.

By the time of the actual trial, the theory of motivation was oscillating between terrorism and capitalism. During the early days in court, Berosini's lawyer Harold Gewerter was to repeat the entertainer's regular contention that the videotapes had been altered. After Berosini's own video expert declared that the tapes in fact had not been altered, that assertion was quietly dropped. But whether or not the videotapes had been altered was no longer the point. The stated issue by then was that the animal-rights organizations PETA and PAWS had been using the videotape of Berosini to raise money for their own greedy purposes. As Gewerter was to phrase this theory somewhat poetically, they were "dashing for cash"; as he was to note with some emphasis, PETA had raised $8.3 million from contributions during the previous year.

Since this is partly a story about Las Vegas, a city sustained by the casual and constant circulation of very large sums of money, perhaps it is worth devoting one or two paragraphs at this point to the subject of money before returning to the less exciting subject of justice. The city's gross income from gambling during 1989 amounted to $2.8 billion — largely taken in by twelve major casinos. The Boyd Group, an organization described to me, possibly with some exaggeration, as "the second most powerful organization in Nevada," owns five hotels and casinos in Las Vegas, including (via a subsidiary known as California Hotel and Casino) the Stardust Hotel and Casino, where Berosini was paid $500,000 each year to keep his orangutans going through their comedy routine twice a night, seven nights a week, and thereby attracting what was once estimated as $20,000 worth of business nightly (or approximately $7 million each year). The Stardust Hotel formally declared itself to be an "interested party" to the lawsuit on August 17, 1989. One might well imagine that the ultimate owner of the Stardust Hotel, the Boyd Group, also held a significant stake in the outcome of Berosini's lawsuit.

It was common knowledge that the judge in Berosini's lawsuit, Myron Leavitt, had for about ten years been a law partner of Bill Boyd of the Boyd Group. Judge Leavitt, in a laudable attempt to avoid the appearance of impropriety, revealed that fact not long after he took on the case, well before the start of the trial. Did anyone have a problem with that? he asked. No one had a problem with that. After the trial began, however, PETA's lawyers found they did have a problem with their sudden discovery that Judge Leavitt about two years previously had received a $25,000 campaign contribution from various Boyd Group members toward his unsuccessful run for a seat on the Nevada Supreme Court. When this issue was aired, Judge Leavitt noted that the campaign contribution was a matter of public record, so how could anyone object? An editorial writer for the *Las Vegas Review-Journal* was more direct: those PETA people, in raising this "mindless" complaint, were "beginning to sound like spoiled children sensing an impending spanking." Of course Judge Leavitt had received a $25,000 campaign contribution — but, the editorialist noted, "there's probably not a District Court judge in town who hasn't accepted a campaign contribution from the Boyd Group."

As the trial progressed, though, it began to appear that Judge Myron Leavitt had an even closer relationship with certain principals of the Boyd Group. The judge had forgotten to mention until the trial was under way that he had been a college roommate of Bill Boyd. Judge Leavitt also neglected to mention at any point before or during the trial that he had engaged in real estate and financial transactions involving principals of the Boyd Group. Among other real estate and investment documents naming in tandem Judge Leavitt and his wife and Bill Boyd and Charles L. Ruthe (president of the Boyd Group), it is possible to find a "Substitution of Trustee" instrument signed by Boyd and Judge Leavitt and his wife. This paper names those three individuals as beneficiaries on a Deed of Trust securing a promissory note of $586,000 from California Hotel and Casino — which owns the Stardust Hotel and is owned, in turn, by the Boyd group. The document is dated July 6, 1990, three days before the Berosini trial began.

In his own defense, Judge Leavitt has now declared that the real estate transactions took place years ago, while he was a law partner with Bill Boyd; that he had received his share of the $586,000 property as cash in 1983 and only signed the 1990 document at the request of a title company; and that he had during the summer of 1990 "no actual bias against" anyone involved in the litigation. Of course, that post-trial defense fails to address the question of why Judge Myron Leavitt did not himself voluntarily reveal the depth and complexity of his relationship with Bill Boyd and the Boyd Group before he became involved in the case.

We may never fully know what went on during the trial, partly because Judge Leavitt forbade the recording of bench conversations. It is clear, nevertheless, that PETA's attorneys were unable to call all of the witnesses they had hoped to call, partly because Leavitt ruled against consideration of particular events that might have happened more than five years previously. Thus, although Berosini was able to declare before the jury that he was the proud inheritor of several generations' worth of animal-training expertise, PETA was unable to call on witnesses ready to testify about what they had seen during Berosini's earlier stint at the MGM Grand. Moreover, various reasons and technicalities, and at least in one case anxiety about future lawsuits, prevented all of PETA's impressive stable of expert witnesses from testifying except for one veterinarian, Robert Stone. Dr. Stone's testimony was countered by the testimonies of Berosini's two distinguished experts, Kenneth Gould of the Yerkes Primate Center and Richard Simmons of the University of Nevada at Reno. Dr. Simmons, who admitted on the stand that he had never actually examined an orangutan before he inspected Berosini's, was able to describe "marvelously cared for animals."

A number of the dancers and stage personnel who had signed affidavits a year previously did come into the dock and testify. Other witnesses appeared. A former stage manager, Michael Bradshaw, stated that he had once picked up the black baton Berosini used to "discipline" his apes and determined it to be metal wrapped in tape — not spray-painted wood, as Berosini had claimed. Bradshaw's testimony, however, was to appear tainted; he had previously filed assault charges against the entertainer, claiming Berosini had attempted to strangle him during an altercation that occurred some time before the videotape scandal began. (Although many people had witnessed the dispute, "widely contrasting versions" of what actually happened led to a dismissal of the assault charges.) A former costume handler from the *Lido de Paris* show, Jill Milane, also stood up to testify that she had once watched while Berosini "slugged" an orangutan "over and over again . . . with his fist." The creature, she said, "grunted . . . like someone having the wind knocked out of them." Milane's sworn testimony was countered by the contention that she was a friend of Michael Bradshaw.

During the course of the trial, I have been informed, five former stage personnel approached the PETA defense attorneys. These were people who, at one time or another over a period of five years, had formal reasons to be standing five to ten feet away from Berosini and his apes in a dark wing of the stage (much more isolated than the backstage area where the videotape was made), night after night after night. Two of them signed affidavits; all five said they were ready to testify that Berosini beat his apes severely almost every night during their final pause in the dark wing area. At first Judge Leavitt said that these five new witnesses could testify. Then, one morning, citing a technicality, he said they couldn't. The judge did not want, as he put it, a "trial by ambush."

In the end, Berosini won his suit. He was fully vindicated. I understand he was mobbed and congratulated by the jury for their decision.

The *Las Vegas Sun* tells us, "Tears welled up in Bobby Berosini's eyes and his lower lip quivered" as the jury declared his damages to be worth $4.2 million. Berosini and his wife, Joan, hugged each other. Joan Berosini declared that she didn't care about the money. It was the principle: "I just want to pound them into the ground." She also promised new lawsuits against all those experts who were vicious enough to comment professionally on their impressions of the video-tape. And the entertainer walked out of the courtroom soliloquizing, within earshot of a reporter from the *Review-Journal*, "Thank you, God. Thank you, America." Bohumil Berousek, who calls himself "Bobby Berosini," doesn't beat but rather "corrects" the apes he calls "monkeys," and the baton he used when he wasn't beating but rather correcting them was not hard metal but soft wood, and the videotape taken of what he wasn't doing but was doing with that baton doesn't really show the reality it might have seemed to show when we imagined we were seeing what we thought we saw.

For promoting a different idea, Jeanne Roush, an investigator for PETA, was directed to pay Bobby Berosini $1 million. Pat Derby, director of PAWS, was directed to pay Bobby Berosini $100,000. PETA and PAWS were directed to pay Bobby Berosini $2.1 million. Linda Levine had not said anything strong enough to be responsible for damages at all; she could go home and peacefully polish those insults scratched into the paint of her car. But the dancer Ottavio Gesmundo, for placing his video camera inside a costume box with a hole in it and for speaking publicly about why he had done so and what he thought the images on the videotape meant, was himself directed to pay Bobby Berosini $1 million.

I am left wondering which is worse, to beat or to laugh. At the Stardust Hotel in Las Vegas, I saw five endangered apes, by all accounts among the most sensitive and intelligent beings on the planet, brought on a stage, dressed in clothes, made to behave in absurdly, awkwardly abnormal ways, and ridiculed. Most people, I believe, would be horrified to see their favorite breed of dog subjected to this sort of treatment. So why should a Las Vegas audience express only the highest delight when watching that crude spectacle with great apes?

I believe that most people in the audience imagine they are watching animals having fun, rather than being made fun of. After all, Berosini seems to be having fun. The band seems to be having fun.

The dancers seem to be having fun. The rest of the audience seems to be having fun. Indeed, Las Vegas is a place where people come to have fun. And those apes smile and cavort and dance around — they must be having fun, too.

But I also believe that the audience shares with the rest of us an ordinary human tendency toward obliviousness. We are oblivious to the other forms of awareness or sentience around us. We take it as a given that the human drama is the only important one, and that animals are significant only to the degree that they contribute to human welfare or amusement. If any animals have feelings, they are the domestic animals we know intimately: dogs, cats, and horses. All other animals are only unfortunate demicreatures inhabiting a flickering world of dulled consciousness and automated desire. So it is that an editorial writer for the *Las Vegas Review-Journal*, having decided that Berosini's orangutans showed no evidence of physical abuse, could scoff: "If there are no physical signs of abuse, what's left. Psychological abuse? Of an animal? To assume psychological abuse one must first assume that orangutans *have* psyches." So it is that another editorialist for the *Review-Journal* could attack Berosini's critics by arguing that "to anthropomorphize nonsentient creatures is absurd," an odd way of defending a nightclub act in which animals are clothed and made to walk upright, mimic human expressions and gestures on cue, dance and mug and fall dead when someone says *bang.*

This kind of ordinary obliviousness about animals in general, once it is applied to monkeys and apes, sees mostly humor. The humor becomes reflexive, automatic, unconscious. An exhausted intellect claws the bottom of the cliché box and retrieves a series of fossilized phrases to express how terribly funny we find our similarity with these creatures to be — "monkey business," "monkey shines," "make a monkey out of me," "going ape," "going bananas," and so on. The fact is that monkeys and apes make us nervous, and they sometimes make us laugh, because in looking at them we see ourselves. They share, to one degree or another, a shape we regard as the honored shape. Their faces and bodies mirror our faces and bodies. But what we fail to see — or what we see only imperfectly and with some anxiety — is that their minds mirror our minds, as well.

The final irony of people laughing at a group of endangered great apes is that great apes are the only animals in the world sophisticated enough, sentient enough, to laugh back. The ethologist Konrad Lor-

We look into eyes that look back with a steady and inquisitive gaze. (*B. Keating*)   BELOW: In different parts of Africa chimpanzees show various tool-using traditions that are passed from generation to generation through observational learning. Gremlin is one of the most skillful of Gombe's termite fishers. (*Jane Goodall Institute*)

Fifi, most prolific of Gombe mothers, grooms her infant daughter.
(*Gerry Ellis*)

OPPOSITE, ABOVE: We listened to the whine and clank of metal on metal
and the roar of the diesel engine as a bulldozer cleared a route through the
wreckage of trees. (*Dale Peterson*)   OPPOSITE, BELOW: Two adult chimps,
male and female, stand in the hot sun, chained to a huge piece of rusty
scrap metal. (*Dale Peterson*)

Socrates, once part of a human family, was banished to a tiny cage when, at five years old, he became potentially dangerous. (*Jane Goodall Institute*)

For every infant chimpanzee taken from the dead body of his or her mother and arriving alive at his or her destination, we estimate that at least ten die. BELOW: Whiskey was introduced to us, by his owner, as "my son." A son? In a disused bathroom on a two-foot chain?

Ron Winters has owned the performing chimpanzee named Mr. Jiggs ("World's Smartest Ape") for nearly thirty years. Mr. Jiggs is actually a female.

BELOW: Ai is one of the most intelligent captive chimps I have ever met. She can beat high school students in many of the complicated tasks she performs at her computer. (*Jane Goodall Institute*)

We happily, if dreamily, watch all those endangered animals dressed up in tutus and tuxedos, turned into children and clowns, so that we may continue to linger for a little while longer in our stuff of dreams.

The encounter with Grégoire was perhaps our most disturbing experience with a chimpanzee in Africa. Above his cage was the sign "Chimpanzee. Grégoire. 1944." (*Jane Goodall Institute*)

The bonds between mothers and children are so strong that youngsters may pine away and die if they lose their mothers. Little Robin, about four years old when his mother died, showed many behaviors that are reminiscent of socially deprived human children. He lived only nine months after his mother died. (*E. Koning*)

Chimpanzees in West Africa use pieces of flat stone and wood as anvils. They hammer on these anvils with specially selected, large, often rounded stone hammers. This stone-tool culture varies in detail from one locality to the next. Here an adult female cracks *Panda* nuts with a rock hammer while an adult male, watched closely by an infant, uses a twig tool to extract the meat from a cracked nut. (*Christophe and Hedwige Boesch*)

Franz Sitter has stood at the center of the live chimpanzee trade in Africa. (*Dick van den Hoorn*)

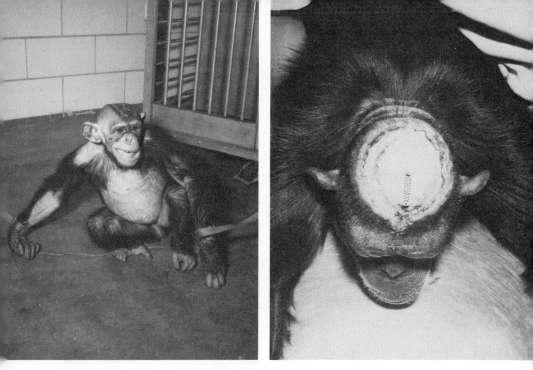

We use them because they are so close to human; it serves our convenience to treat them as animals. The grin on this chimpanzee's face is a fear grimace. (*Jane Goodall Institute*) BELOW: Animal rights activists broke into an anonymous-looking building in Rockville, Maryland, and found five hundred caged apes and monkeys being used in biomedical research. (© *1986* PETA)

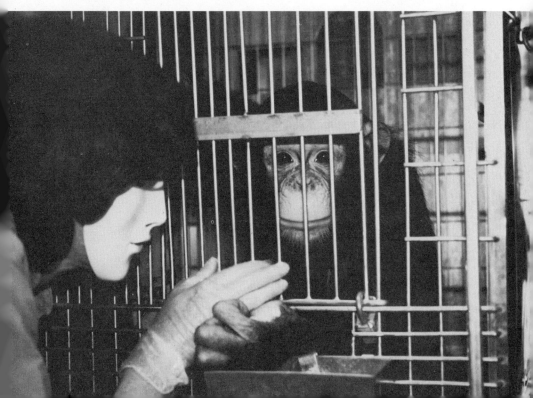

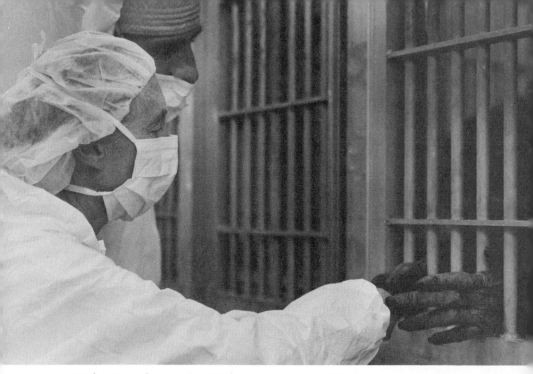

With JoJo and Dr. James Mahoney at LIMSIP. JoJo is trying to groom my wrist. (*Susan Farley*) BELOW: In Point Noire, Congo, chimps rescued from a so-called zoo were cared for in a home while we tried to build a sanctuary for them. (*Steve Matthews*)

enz once described a dog's facial expression of pleasure as a sort of "laughter." But I'm not referring to a mere facial upturn in response to pleasure. And I'm not referring to a sort of pinched vocalization that might be roughly compared with human laughter, as in the "laughter" of a hyena. I'm referring to real laughter, fully recognizable laughter, the kind where you lie down on the ground and shake in a paroxysm of clear amusement and simple pleasure. I have seen wild chimpanzees in an African forest laugh; I have seen a wild-born, orphaned gorilla laugh; once I watched a wild-born, orphaned bonobo laugh. I am told by an expert from the San Diego Zoo that orangutans laugh, too, in quite the same way. And I have come to believe that humans share with only four other animal species the astonishing ability to be overtly amused and to express that amusement with semivocalized convulsions.

People who are aware of ape laughter sometimes imagine it to be a simple response to a simple stimulation, such as tickling, but never a response to the sorts of sophisticated situations that can make people laugh. In actuality, even removed and comparatively complex events can induce chimpanzee laughter. At Gombe, chimpanzees most frequently laugh when they're involved in a chase and tickle game. If, for example, one chimp is chasing another round and round a bush, even though there's no physical contact they may laugh. That may be laughter in anticipation of a tickle, but I also have witnessed chimpanzees laughing at the more complicated circumstance of other chimpanzees' discomfort. Sometimes an older sibling will use something like a twig in playing with a younger sibling. The two will have little tugs of war, where the older chimp will repeatedly pull the twig away from the younger. I can remember the siblings Michaelmas and Moeza playing this sort of game. Moeza, the elder, would often test Michaelmas by rushing off with a play twig into a higher branch where her younger brother was afraid to follow. He would then begin to scream in frustration, at which point Moeza sometimes gave soft chuckles as she watched his fury.

Apes are extraordinary beings that, above all, deserve our respect. Because they have become endangered at our hands, they deserve our care. They exist as individuals capable of physical and psychological suffering; they inhabit an intellectual and emotional universe contiguous with ours — and a performance that asks only the most superficial possible response to an ape's appearance, the response of derision, is one that finally degrades us all, audience as well as actors.

9 ◆ In Mine Own Cell

PROSPERO (to CALIBAN):
> I have used thee
> (Filth as thou art) with humane care, and lodged
>   thee
> In mine own cell till thou didst seek to violate
> The honor of my child.

THE WOMAN THOUGHT he would speak to me, and she gave me directions to his place. He will have a gun, she said, but he's actually very nice and he loves chimpanzees. "Just tell him I sent you." Did I know about the way he dressed? His . . . costume? Well, I should just go out there and walk through the gate. There will be a dog, a big dog, a Doberman or something like that, she thought, but I shouldn't worry. The dog is actually friendly. That is, she thought it was. At least the dog never attacked her and her husband when they went out there. Of course, the dog knows them. Anyway, she believed I could just pass through the gate and walk up to the house, where he and the chimps were. If the dog did attack, did I know enough to protect my throat? I should put my hands up and protect my throat. At least she thought that was how to do it. She turned to her husband. Isn't that the way you do it? she asked him. Put up your hands and protect your throat? Yes, he reckoned that would be the right way.

I drove out to the chimpanzee owner's place in northern Louisiana, under a late-afternoon sky blossoming with bruised clouds, and I came to a long fence and big gate. On the other side of the fence, across an expanse of well-mowed lawn, I could see the skeleton of a half-built mansion, and at the base of this skeleton some large, black, beautifully constructed cages. Big chimps moved inside the cages, I could see. I watched them look at me and listened to them drum on the bars of their cages. The gate was high and ornate, and I paused a moment to read the signs fixed to it. One sign said: "Warning: Trespassing Is a Felony. Survivors Will Be Shot." Another more simply announced: "Warning: Private Property. Do Not Enter." Beneath the text, this sign displayed the black and white icon of a dog's head with red blood dripping from its fangs. A third sign referred to the icon of the second: "Never Mind the Dog. Beware of Owner." That text was illustrated with a victim's view of a six-shooter with smoke coming out of the barrel and five bullets left.

Other signs repeated the same general theme, and I finally got the message. I decided not to pass through the gate but to wait right there, theorizing that sooner or later the man would come out to determine who was standing on the other side of his fence. After about an hour, in fact, he did come out. He drove across his lawn on something that looked like a motorized tricycle, parked it, and walked over.

He had a grizzled beard and glittering dark eyes. He wore a small black cap on his head and big black boots on his feet. Between the cap and boots, he wore nothing at all, other than white underpants and a very large, police-style revolver suspended at his hip with a web belt and holster.

"Hi," he said.

"Hi," I said. I introduced myself. I explained that I had been given directions to his place by our mutual friend, that I was writing a book, and that I would like to meet him and his chimpanzees because I wanted to learn something about owning chimpanzees as pets. I said that our mutual friend thought he would be willing to talk to me. "Well, if you talked to her, she must have told you I wasn't interested." "No, she said you were a nice guy." "I am a nice guy, but I'm not interested in books and that kind of stuff," he said. He turned away, mounted his three-wheeler, and drove back across the lawn to his half-built mansion and his pet chimpanzees living inside beautiful cages.

1

Owning a chimpanzee as a pet is very different from owning a dog or cat as a pet.

For one thing, private chimpanzee owners often use their apes to help sustain personal themes or fantasies, whereas people keep domestic animals primarily for companionship and affection. It is true, of course, that individual chimpanzee owners often insist that they love their chimps and that they receive companionship and affection from them. It is also true that many domestic animal owners fantasize about their dogs and cats. But a baby chimpanzee will cost some $20,000 to $30,000 more than a puppy or a kitten, and my belief is that the price differential reflects not the greater amount of affection expected from a creature who will probably spend four-fifths of his or her life on the other side of steel bars but the greater potential for fantasy anticipated by owning a very large animal of the honored shape. Chimpanzee babies are expensive, rare, and, depending on a variety of state and local laws, legally difficult for private individuals to obtain and keep. Those who do own chimpanzees as pets spend their money and comply with laws as they need to, largely because they are propelled by powerful psychological themes. In some sense, then, chimpanzees serving humanity in the pet industry fulfill much the same function as chimpanzees employed in the entertainment industry, although in the pet industry their audience is smaller and more exclusive.

Themes and fantasies vary. Sometimes they can be simple: I am an interesting and exotic person because I own an interesting and exotic animal. I might speculate that singer Michael Jackson, former owner of Bubbles the Chimp, engaged in this line of reasoning.

Typically, the themes and fantasies are more complex. Russ Cochran of West Plains, Missouri, the owner of two very young chimpanzees named Sammy and Sally, told me that his apes are "just for my own entertainment, my own interaction with them, and because I really respect them as an animal and I want to learn as much about them as I can." But his driving fantasy is the Tarzan fantasy. "My first clear memory," he has written in an autobiographical article for a collectors' magazine, "is that of hearing Johnny Weissmuller's wonderful 'Tarzan yell' while *in utero*, which must have caused my lifelong fascination with Tarzan of the Apes." His own research indicates that his father and pregnant mother went to see *Tarzan Escapes* at the Davis Theatre in West Plains some time in December 1936, while he was a fetus, and he hypothesizes that he must have heard the yell then. More seriously, Cochran notes that as a young boy he went to see at least once, often several times, every Tarzan movie that came to town. For days afterward he would run around his neighborhood dressed in a chamois loincloth, climbing trees and swinging on ropes. He pored over the Tarzan comic strip in the Sunday newspaper during the 1940s and read all the Tarzan books he could find at the local library. He grew up, married, attended college and then graduate school, and one day while discussing a theoretical problem in the physics of liquid structure with his professor, Louis Lund, Cochran discovered that Lund had also been a Tarzan fan as a boy. Cochran's old fantasy — Tarzan of the Apes — was rekindled. Professor Lund lent his student a number of Tarzan books Cochran had never found in the West Plains library; and Cochran now imagines that without the encouragement and escape provided by the Tarzan fantasy he might never have finished his dissertation. "When I would approach burnout on the theoretical physics problem, I would take a Tarzan book and go off into the woods with my bow and arrow and my bulldog, Ginger, and immerse myself in Tarzan long enough to recover my mental faculties so I could return to the physics problem."

Russ Cochran became a professor of physics at Drake University in Des Moines, Iowa, in 1964. Eleven years later he moved back to his boyhood town, West Plains, and back to his boyhood dreams. He purchased an old commercial building and established himself as a publisher of collectors' editions of cartoon and comic-book art. He also dealt in comic-art originals and over time acquired for his personal collection some of Hal Foster's original Tarzans and Prince Valiants; some of Alex Raymond's Flash Gordons, a small collection of original Disney artwork ("mostly centered around my favorite Disney film, *Snow White and the Seven Dwarfs*"), Frank Frazetta's original cover painting for the book *Tarzan and the Jewels of Opar*, a Bob Kane oil of Batman, and over a hundred Dick Tracy illustrations by Chester Gould. He collected original movie posters of the Tarzan series, and has one for the first 1918 production of *Tarzan of the Apes*, as well as all but one of the Johnny Weissmuller Tarzan posters. He has managed to acquire "thousands and thousands" of Sunday newspaper comic sections from 1920 to 1950, including the *Tarzan* series; and he currently possesses a Martin D-45 flattop guitar, Benny Goodman's grand piano, a large bronze statue of Superman, two life-size Superman figures from a carousel — not to mention the ornate black-oak desk on which J. Allen St. John created his superb illustrations for many of the old *Tarzan* books.

Russ Cochran is a collector, in short, and it must have seemed perfectly natural to him to direct this acquisitive energy into the realm of living objects. He already owned two rare African bulldogs; owning a chimpanzee had been, he writes in the collectors' magazine article, "a lifelong dream," arising from the enduring image of Tarzan and his pal, Cheeta. "I always thought it would be really wonderful to have a little companion like Tarzan had in the movies," he told me, "and of course . . . the chimp named Cheeta was the hero of most of the movies because Tarzan would get his tail in a sling somehow and get in a pickle, and it would be Cheeta that would have to bail him out."

When in 1989 Cochran happened to see a newspaper article about Connie Braun, a chimpanzee breeder living in Festus, Missouri, only two hundred miles away, he resolved to visit her and inquire about buying a chimp. Braun is "such a protective foster mother," according to Cochran, "that the big job you have with her is convincing her that you're going to be a good foster parent for the chimp." Braun happened to have a baby available, and Cochran persuaded her that he would be a worthy father. Although wild chimpanzees will nurse until they are two years old and stay very closely attached to their mothers for approximately the first five years of life, one of Braun's baby chimps had become an object of contention between two adult females inhabiting the same cage, so Cochran was able to buy Sammy when he was two months old. Half a year later, searching for a companion for Sammy, Cochran visited trainer and breeder Bob Dunn in southern California and ultimately purchased a one-day-old female chimp, whom he named Sally. Dunn told him Sally had been rejected by her mother. (I don't know that it is relevant to the case at hand, but inasmuch as chimps are worth up to $30,000 as infants and since adult chimpanzee females are ready to reproduce again only after they stop nursing, some chimp breeders deliberately pull babies away from nursing mothers soon after birth. Their story, that the mothers rejected the babies, remains hard to challenge, for under the abnormal circumstances of captivity it is sometimes true.)

Cochran has considered some of the ethical issues regarding the human relationship with this sibling species. He feels strongly that laboratories should not have chimpanzees. To give an endangered ape some fatal disease in order to find a cure for humans is wrong, he believes. "It's possible that . . . a hundred years from now there won't be any chimps." He considers it a sad prospect that chimpanzees and gorillas and the other great apes could disappear from the face of the earth, and perhaps for that reason he has little sympathy for laboratories using them to cure human diseases. But Cochran doesn't object to chimpanzees in zoos, circuses, or as privately owned pets. To him the important consideration is how the ape is treated. "My chimps," he insists, "have a father and a mother and siblings. They're taken care of. They're protected. Their needs are met."

Other owners of individual chimpanzees have told me they hope to help save an endangered species. A woman in Texas who cares well for approximately a dozen chimpanzees, as well as numerous monkeys and other animals, describes her passion for the apes as having begun with a pet monkey. Her husband decided that "if I loved that little monkey so much, maybe I'd like a chimp. So he bought me a chimpanzee." She loved that chimpanzee very much indeed, and began collecting more monkeys and more apes in order to experience more love. A small zoo near Austin, Texas, went bankrupt; when the zoo director refused to sell the woman his primates, she and her husband bought the entire zoo. "We bought alligators and cougars and lions and leopards and coyotes and wolves and foxes and snakes and monkeys and chimpanzees and — we bought the whole little zoo." They resold many of the animals, but kept the monkeys and apes, which the woman now breeds. "I do believe in selling baby monkeys," she told me. "I believe in trying to place them in good homes with monkey mamas." It meant so much for her to have her own baby monkeys and apes, she would hate to cheat someone else out of the experience. "And," she adds with strong emphasis, "extinction is forever. And if somebody like us don't raise a few, some day there's not going to be any . . . If it weren't for the Texas rancher, there wouldn't be any buffalo or elk, you know. The Texas rancher put that back on the face of the map."

To save an endangered species is a laudable goal, and no doubt captive breeding could, as Bobby Berosini has said, "enable us to conserve these marvelous animals for the benefit of future generations." The question is, which future generations and what benefit? Future generations of wild apes will never benefit from the breeding of future generations of captive apes, I believe, simply because it is so extraordinarily difficult to reintroduce captive-born apes into the wild. Captive-bred birds sometimes have been reintroduced; but eggs are easy to move around and can be sneaked into the nests of foster

parents. A few captive-bred hoofed mammal species have been successfully reintroduced into the wild; but their reintroduction essentially consisted of movement from fenced fields to open fields. Captive-bred individuals of a single monkey species, the golden lion
tamarin, have been reintroduced into the tiny fragment of their remaining habitat in Brazil; but golden lion tamarins breed rapidly,
typically producing a set of twins annually — and they do not approach the social and psychological complexity of apes. Does breeding
dogs produce wolves? Obviously not, and breeding captive chimps will
not produce wild chimps. The captive breeding of great apes will
primarily benefit future generations of humans, enabling us to use
them in the future quite as we use them now: as entertainers, pets,
and experimental subjects in laboratories. In fact, laboratories in the
United States and elsewhere are already successfully breeding more
great apes for the benefit of more generations of humans.

By far the most typical theme or fantasy of chimpanzee owners is
that of kinship. Chimpanzees *are* a sibling species, and chimpanzee
owners weave this fact into the tapestry of their lives. Russ Cochran
doesn't really consider his two baby chimpanzees to be pets. "We
think of the chimps as being our kids . . . we really do." Three of four
of the Cochrans' human children have already grown up and left
home, so "when we started running out of kids we moved into
chimps." It is true that many dog and cat owners think of their pets as
children, but Mrs. Cochran insists on the difference between chimpanzees and domestic pets. "Some people say, 'Well, you know, it's like a
dog that you're real fond of.' " She disagrees. "It's nothing like that at
all. I think of them as being like little humans except that they look
different. That's the only thing. My care for them is the same. They
love me, they kiss me every day."

Another chimpanzee owner in the southeastern United States described for me this vision more succinctly and spontaneously: "He's
adorable! He's my boy! What a baby! What a baby!"

2

This, of course, is precisely the vision of chimps that the entertainment industry seeks to develop, and with good reason. Chimpanzees
do profoundly resemble humans. Chimpanzee babies do very much

resemble human babies. The kinship is real. It becomes a fantasy only as we, according to our own tastes and needs, twist it into something it is not. I recall meeting a very young chimp in Hollywood — a child actor — who instantly climbed up my arm onto my shoulder, wrapped her little arms around my head, leaned forward, gently kissed me on the forehead, and looked adoringly right into my eyes. I fully recognize that chimpanzee babies can stir the human maternal and paternal response. Human mothers and fathers do bond with baby great apes as if the babies were human. Baby chimps — and gorillas and orangutans — need and depend on their mothers for many years; they will adopt a human mother as if she were a chimpanzee mother.

But they are not human babies. They are chimpanzee babies, and well-meaning people who adopt them as some combination of "pet" and "child" typically encounter several difficulties as the apes begin to mature. One obvious problem, the new owner quickly discovers, is control. While I spoke with Russ Cochran about his chimpanzees, fourteen-month-old Sammy had gone into the kitchen, where he began opening cabinet doors and tossing out pots and pans. Cochran commented: "Well, that was Sammy, and now he's waiting for my wife to come in and put them back. And . . . this is a game that they play. Of course, he knows it's a game, but my wife doesn't know it's a game yet. She thinks that he's just being a little dickens, you know." When I later spoke with Mrs. Cochran, she too was enthusiastic about Sammy and Sally, but her feelings were a little more ambivalent. "In a word . . . I think that they are great, but they're a lot of work. I in all honesty have to say I'm looking forward to the time when I will have a cage, a big holding cage, to put them in when I'm doing my work, because they help me so much!"

Russ Cochran sleeps with Sammy at night. He is a big man, but he remains concerned that within five to six years his chimpanzees will have, as he puts it, "the potential to become unmanageable." Mrs. Cochran is more immediately worried. She had a confrontation with Sammy the day before I spoke with her. For the first time he didn't want his diaper. Her usual technique for getting Sammy to hold still during a diaper change is to distract him. "I have little games that I play with him. As I've noticed, when he gets older, things like holding a rattle doesn't do it for him anymore. So now I give him a box of wipes to wipe his bottom off, and I let him open it up . . . and get it for me." Yesterday, however, Sammy wasn't distracted even by the box of wipes. He resisted; she insisted. "Well, I really had to win that battle. I had to let him know that he had to lay there and get this done, and it was very evident to me that in a short time I'm not going to be able to control him physically. So I have to do it by intimidation with him. I don't know how much longer it will be, but . . . in six months' time I know there's no way I'm going to be able to physically handle him if he wants to be resistant to me. So I have to work extra hard, and he's been smart and I have to be smarter. I have to work extra hard and make him know that I'm his mother and his boss."

What will the Cochrans do as their chimpanzees grow into powerful and probably thwarted adolescents and adults? Cochran believes he will have to build a large cage. He imagines he might convert one of the spare bedrooms into what he calls a "chimp-proof room," a cage with bars or metal grillwork. Perhaps he will put in a skylight to allow for more natural light, and improve the cage with ropes and toys. In the meantime, there are the control problems with Sammy. "You can't hit him," Cochran told me. "Well, you can hit him, but you'll hurt your hand more than you'll hurt him." A chimp's head is "like a little coconut, and their bodies are so strong." For now, Cochran disciplines Sammy by picking him up by his shirt and yelling at him, or putting him in a chair and forcing him to stay there. But he has also started to learn about other chimpanzee owners' methods of control. He met a woman who uses a small cattle prod, which Cochran understands to be "harmless but makes them behave." He's met a couple who have a remote-controlled shocker for their chimp. He's heard about Mr. Jiggs in New Jersey, and he has been told that the shocker for Mr. Jiggs is so effective it rarely needs to be used. He recognizes that a chimp's threshold of pain is different from a human's, so he would like to learn more about the shock devices available.

Most private chimpanzee owners I've met believe they offer the best of all possible worlds for an ape already in captivity — certainly better than a caged life in a research laboratory, they tell me. Most express a lifelong commitment to their apes, the honorable intention to care for this baby as he or she matures into an adult with a potential lifespan of more than fifty years. But most of them own preadolescent chimps. Somehow, it seems, the bigger ones tend to disappear.

The few people who do possess fully grown apes find they are caring for them in constrained and imperfect conditions — I'm thinking here of the beloved pet named Denyse, bought in 1969 by Gloria and Allen Painten of Jacksonville, Florida, from Mae Noell of Noell's Ark Chimp

Farm. "She traveled with us," Gloria Painten recalls of Denyse. "She ate in the finest restaurants and slept in the best hotels and the whole bit, when she was little." She was toilet trained, wore clothes, learned to eat with a fork and spoon, had good table manners. Denyse knows some sign language, responds well to spoken directions, and is by all other measures an intelligent and well-behaved adult chimpanzee. But the last time Denyse went out on a leash, she dragged Gloria across the street; Gloria wrapped the long leash around a tree, but Denyse simply ran around the tree the other way and unwrapped it. One time a two-hundred-fifty-pound man grabbed her foot, so Denyse pulled him down on his face and dragged him across his front lawn. After Allen returned from a short trip to Massachusetts, the chimp "tore me up pretty bad a couple times." When a woman across the street spoke to Denyse sternly, the chimp ripped off the back of the woman's hand.

One day Denyse was out of her cage, visiting the Paintens in their house, and when the visit was over she didn't want to go back into her cage. After three days the Paintens called their veterinarian and asked for a tranquilizer. They didn't want to shoot or dart Denyse, so they asked for an oral tranquilizer, which the vet gave them, disguised inside candied capsules. But Denyse simply licked the outside of the capsules, then put them back in the bottle. At the end of the third day the chimp, perhaps sensing an increased tension in the household, voluntarily returned to her cage. She hasn't been let out since. Her cage is very nice, I should mention. It consists of a large outdoor section, steel bars and a concrete floor, and an interior cinderblock shed decorated to look (except for the bars on one side and the grillwork on the windows) like a young girl's bedroom: rugs, a clock on the wall, a couch, curtains on the windows, a bed, a table, a lamp, and, on the other side of some bars, a big color television set. Both Allen and Gloria will go into the cage to visit Denyse from time to time, and Gloria sometimes sleeps with her at night to keep the chimp from becoming too lonely.

Other chimpanzees raised as children are less fortunate. Prospero kept Caliban in his hut, "mine own cell," until the day Caliban attacked and tried to rape Prospero's daughter, Miranda. Many pet chimps, kept comfortably in private homes while they are very young, grow up acting as if they believe themselves to be the hairy offspring of hairless parents and develop into psychologically abnormal and sexually frustrated adolescents. Finally, for a variety of understandable reasons, they are given up. What happens to them?

During the 1970s several pet chimpanzees who outgrew their youthful cuteness and docility were donated to a sanctuary, the Primate Foundation of Arizona, run by Jo Fritz and her husband, Paul. By 1975 the Primate Foundation was caring for thirty-two chimpanzees, plus two babies already born to the colony, Geronimo and Cochise. "Every chimp arrived with a heartbreaking story," Jo Fritz wrote then, in a newsletter published by a society of monkey and ape owners. "The one that came in totally bald because she had nothing to do all day but pull out her own hair; the one that had become completely humanized with her own bed, her own room, and her own clothes. She now lived in a cage because she was jealous of her human brother and severely bit him. The male that had spent eight of his nine years in a laboratory and now does nothing but sit in a corner and rock. There are thirty-two similar stories in the colony." Fritz reminded her readers that chimpanzee owners didn't care that their "babies" might have been acquired in Africa when the mothers were shot; they only cared "when that little chimp starts to destroy their home or begins to bite . . . Then the people frantically try to find another home for their chimpanzee. They contact zoos, try to sell it to other unsuspecting people or even try to give it to a laboratory." Some of these people were fortunate enough to find the Primate Foundation of Arizona, Fritz wrote, a refuge for chimpanzee pets who had become uncontrollable. At the time, Jo Fritz was soliciting donations from animal lovers for this nonprofit, tax-exempt sanctuary: "Wouldn't you like to join us in creating the very best place for a captive chimp to live out his life?"

That was in 1975. By the mid-1980s writer Emily Hahn was chummily commiserating with Jo Fritz about "the so-called animal lovers who can see only the sentimental side of conservation," those sullen people who were complaining that the Primate Foundation of Arizona supplies chimpanzees to laboratories. According to Hahn's book, *Eve and the Apes*, she and Fritz discussed how chimps who once served humankind as imitation children would now have the honor of serving womankind by testing intrauterine devices.*

*

---

* Some people in the monkey and ape pet community remain disturbed at this transformation of the Arizona Primate Foundation, but in defense of Jo and Paul Fritz I should say that they turned to laboratory contractual work at first from simple economic necessity. The people who gave up their maturing pets to this sanctuary were not so generous with their financial support.

Mr. C, an adult male chimpanzee now held in a private sanctuary in southern California, was raised as a child in a home. For the first thirteen years of his life he never saw a cage or, so far as I know, another chimpanzee. He learned to dress himself, to button his shirt and lace and tie his shoes, to brush his teeth, to use the toilet, to sleep in a bed, to relax by watching television. But as he grew, he became more difficult, more demanding, more powerful. His owners had him castrated, hoping thereby to improve his manners, but the alteration did not make him more manageable. Finally his owners passed Mr. C to a chimpanzee ranch in the southwestern United States where, it was imagined, he might be rehabilitated and turned back into a chimpanzee. But the new situation must have terrified Mr. C, who had gone from a private home with his own bedroom, television, and loving parents, to an isolation cage next to several other chimps. One day some of the other male chimps broke into his cage and nearly killed him. He became depressed. He lost weight; after a year and a half at the ranch, Mr. C weighed a mere sixty pounds. The owner of the ranch finally decided this chimp was not going to make it, so he gave the unfortunate creature to the woman running the California sanctuary. "He looked like an absolutely starving child — or, not 'child' — because he was too large to be a child," she recalls.

He still lives in a cage but is now, I understand, a happy ape. He has visitors, toys, his own television. He loves being read to. He has learned some sign language and enjoys signing now and then. The castration, incidentally, did not remove Mr. C's libido, which remains fixed on the human female form. He is "quite lecherous," I am told. He gets "so excited," particularly when a young female volunteer comes to the sanctuary wearing shorts or a bathing suit during the summer. One "very attractive volunteer" once got too close while she was handing Mr. C his morning cup of orange juice, and he ripped off her shorts. "He lets you know . . . he still has a libido."

Gus and Gabbie were raised as beloved children by a truck-driving couple, Ernst and Cheryle Berryman, in the midwestern United States. Before he was a year old, Gus would travel from coast to coast in the cab of the Berrymans' truck. "No matter where we go," the Berrymans once wrote proudly, "Gus seems to be the center of attention. There is no end to the questions people come up with! Everywhere we go (and that's a lot of places), everyone seems to love Gus." They "adopted"

Gabbie to be a sister to Gus. In late 1977 Ernst Berryman went to the hospital for open-heart surgery and thus was absent from his "kids" for two months. During that time, the Berrymans recalled, "Gus kind of withdrew to himself, because he was always a 'daddy's boy,' and he just couldn't understand why daddy wasn't coming home. He would peek around the corners, always looking for him." When Berryman finally came back, "the homecoming he got was truly unbelievable! Gus stood and screamed for a solid 5 minutes, and Gabbie just kind of grinned and smiled. Of course, they were a little too strong for him to handle, so all he could do was go down by the cage and feed them. But, little by little, he's getting stronger, and Gus and Gabbie get to go more places now."

Unfortunately, ill health and dwindling finances finally forced the couple to give up their two chimp children. The Berrymans passed them on to a woman they knew they could trust to keep this step-brother and stepsister together — Connie Braun, the chimpanzee breeder in Festus, Missouri. Gabbie still lives in Braun's breeding group — four females and one male — who inhabit interconnected cages in the dark and barely ventilated basement of her house, a converted barn. Gabbie had already produced five babies by the age of fifteen when I visited her in Festus in 1990. (One of Gabbie's five babies was Sammy, the chimpanzee purchased when he was two months old by Russ Cochran. Braun told Cochran that the baby had to be taken prematurely because of an unfortunate conflict between two females. I will presume that Gabbie's other four babies likewise had to be taken prematurely for other very good reasons, since chimpanzee mothers normally would be hard pressed to produce that many infants in a breeding lifetime.) But Gus didn't fit in with the breeding group, and perhaps for that reason Braun has leased him for what I understand to be $5,000 per year, along with some of her other chimpanzees, to an East Coast research laboratory. I am told the chimps are used for breeding only.

Rachel and Aaron were raised as human children in southeastern Florida by a woman who thought she was fully prepared to care for two growing apes, and who considers herself a lover of chimpanzees and a conservationist. Cherie Gray is, in fact, a poised and obviously intelligent young woman, studying to be a medical assistant, who grew up loving primates. She owned monkeys as a girl, but chimpanzees were always at the top of her list of desirable possessions. She read everything she could about chimpanzees, moved from Michigan to Florida to be in a more hospitable climate for the apes, and with her husband purchased a five-acre lot in southeastern Florida that was to be her "pet farm." She acquired the necessary permits to own a chimpanzee, and in 1983 purchased for $10,000 her first baby chimp from Dr. William Lemmon of the Institute for Primate Studies in Norman, Oklahoma. The baby was a female named Rachel, and Gray loved her as she would a child. "Chimpanzees are so close to human children — it's hard to explain. I got Rachel when she was only five weeks old, weighed about five pounds, and you bond with them . . . like a human child."

Gray recognized what many of the problems would be. "I think a lot of people, they see them on TV, they see them in a zoo, they say, 'Oh, how cute! I want one!' They don't understand the strength of these animals and actually the type of facilities you need just to keep them." She felt she did understand; and she had set up her facilities even before purchasing Rachel.

The facilities included a cage, of course. But Rachel never went inside the cage. "I couldn't put her in a cage. She would scream and cry, and I didn't want her to be neurotic." Instead, Gray kept her chimpanzee in the house. "She was raised more like a person than a chimpanzee." The little chimp had a crib, but she slept at night with her human foster mother. She wore diapers and baby clothes including, at times, booties. She had a toy rabbit and a security blanket. She was very clean, accustomed to having a bath daily and brushing her teeth morning and night. The veterinarian gave her all the standard human baby shots; she was disciplined as a child would be, only more firmly. "And she was very, very, very well behaved." In the end, Gray says, it felt as if she had adopted a human baby, except that Rachel was "probably a little . . . slower, maybe like a retarded child. And a lot stronger than a human child."

Cherie Gray had bought Rachel with the idea that she could learn a lot about chimpanzees and, in her words, "love them." She also imagined that breeding chimpanzees might contribute to their survival. Partly for that purpose, about a year after she acquired Rachel, for another $10,000 Gray purchased from Dr. Lemmon a young male named Aaron. "He had a real pretty face," she says. He sucked his thumb, just like a human baby. To transport Aaron from Oklahoma to

Florida, she dressed him in baby clothes, wrapped him in a baby
blanket, fed him enough formula to put him to sleep, and passed him
off as a human infant on a domestic airlines flight. Back home, she
raised Aaron much as Rachel was being raised — "with the intention
of possibly breeding them at some point when they got too big for me
to control. They would have their own facilities, and they wouldn't be
lonesome."

Unfortunately, none of Gray's careful plans came to fruition. Her
marriage came undone. Without her husband's financial support, she
could no longer afford the five-acre pet farm. With the encouragement
of a divorce-court judge, she gave up the apes. Heartbroken, she sold
Aaron to a friend and fellow chimpanzee owner in St. Petersburg,
Florida. But Aaron soon turned on her friend's four-year-old daughter.
"He attacked her every chance he got," the friend told me when I
visited. "He'd cross the room to bite her. The third time he bit her, it
was in the stomach, and my husband was in the room when it happened. He gave me a choice." Aaron "was beautiful," the friend
recalls, "and we bonded real well. Broke my heart to give him up. I
cried two weeks after he left." Nonetheless, the young male was sold
to animal trainers Boone Narr and Sled Reynolds in southern California. I saw Aaron, by that time named A.J., looking rather bored inside
a cage when I visited the Hollywood area. I have been told he is
approaching a chimpanzee actor's retirement age and is probably going
to be taken by yet another private owner in Florida.

As for Rachel, Cherie Gray can barely describe what happened
without bursting into tears. "She was adorable. And there's just no
words to explain how much I do love her — and I still do." Partly
because of what had happened to Aaron, she was reluctant to sell
Rachel to a private owner. A couple of individuals had seemed interested in taking Rachel as a pet, but Gray was not certain that these
people could have cared for the chimp properly; she was afraid her
lovely daughter might wind up in the worst of all possible worlds, a
laboratory doing experimental surgery or AIDS studies on chimpanzees. Thus, ultimately, she sold Rachel to a lab she thought was well
run and would have room for a growing female chimp who might only
breed. She visited the lab. "And I really did feel comfortable. I went
through every part of that place there is to go. There were no locked
doors anywhere. And I know they do certain studies, but they . . .
assured me that Rachel would not be used for anything like that."

Cherie Gray insists adamantly that the people at the laboratory told her that Rachel would only be used for breeding, never for research. There must have been some miscommunication. When I visited the lab, the same person with whom Gray had dealt assured me that he had never agreed that Rachel wouldn't be used in experiments. Rachel arrived at the lab a healthy young chimpanzee, actually suntanned from many trips to the beach with her human mother. Inside an isolation cage she lost her suntan. She went through an extended period of depression and very slowly adjusted to the reality of being a laboratory chimp inside a cage rather than a human child in her mother's arms. And she became a research subject, among other things undergoing surgery for the computerized testing of new artificial sweeteners for NutraSweet. The chances are good that she will contribute to human welfare as an experimental subject in hepatitis and AIDS research.

Chuck, a young chimpanzee, was dressed in clothes, given Winstons to smoke and whiskey to drink, fed steak at the dinner table, and allowed to hang out during the day at the Bel-Aire Coiffures Beauty Shop in Norfolk, Virginia. But by the time he was six years old, Chuck had become too strong to love anymore, so he was donated to the Lafayette Zoo in Norfolk. Chuck had been a pampered human child. Now he was expected to become an ordinary zoo animal, exposed to the gawking public, sharing his crude, jail-cell-style outdoor enclosure and a smaller indoor enclosure with a female chimp named Judy. Chuck never did adjust to the change in circumstances, however, particularly the teasing of a few zoo visitors who, according to one witness, "took great joy in tormenting these unfortunate creatures by yelling at them, shaking their cage, and even throwing things until the chimps were furious." Chuck would throw his own dung at the visitors, and then, in a rage, attack his cagemate, Judy. As a former Bel-Aire Coiffures employee said, "It was like putting a kid in a zoo."

The Lafayette Zoo superintendent, Gary Ochsenbein, eventually recognized the cruelty of the situation and the inadequacy of the zoo's facilities. After Chuck had been an exhibit for about fifteen years, Ochsenbein placed an ad in a laboratory animal supply bulletin, offering to give Chuck and Judy away, free, for "noninvasive, nonterminal research." Local animal lovers were incensed, and Ochsenbein eventually met with a group of them and explained that building proper facilities for the chimps would cost about $1.25 million. These apes, Ochsenbein assured the crowd of critics, were "like adopted children.

We do everything we can to assure that they are placed in good facilities." Ultimately, a suitable destination was found for Chuck and Judy, the sanctuary for abused or unwanted monkeys and apes called Primarily Primates. Wally Swett, the director, was willing to take Chuck and Judy, but he noted that to transport them from Norfolk to San Antonio and then to construct an appropriate cage at the sanctuary would cost some $50,000. The cost of perhaps another thirty years of feeding and caring for the two would be borne by Primarily Primates.

The money was raised, half paid by private groups and individuals and half paid by the city of Norfolk. Chuck and Judy were sent to Primarily Primates — but not before someone, recognizing that Chuck was psychologically twisted from being raised as a child and then being exhibited in a jail-like cell for fifteen years, breathed the word "rehabilitation." In a couple of articles written by Lawrence Maddry for a local newspaper, the *Virginian-Pilot*, "rehabilitation" became "therapy" for animals gone "bonkers." And the city of Norfolk's contribution to the cost of transporting and housing these apes became, according to another writer for the *Virginian-Pilot*, money for "psychiatric help." By the time the story reached the nation's capital, readers of the *Washington Post* were being informed that two chimpanzees in Virginia were destined for a "psychiatric facility" because "they simply can't cope with life behind bars." And by the time it had reached advice-giving columnist Ann Landers, it became the story of deranged people in Norfolk, whose city council was going to spend $25,000 on "psychiatric care for two crazed chimpanzees in the city zoo." Landers pounced on this opportunity to imagine that the city of Norfolk had "gone a little ape."

We are confused about these beings. They serve us as surrogate babies, beloved children, when that vision suits us. When it does no longer, they become animals again, living property with little value other than whatever humor we can extract from the rough details of their existence.

3

If some individual chimpanzee owners ultimately treat their charges excessively like children, a few others seem to treat their chimps more crudely than they would treat a dog. I suspect that the young adult male, apparently underweight, lately seen living by himself in a cage 6 by 8 by 6 feet with no furniture, no toys, no food or water dishes in sight, in a dark corner of a Texas pawnshop, hasn't been out of his cage or received much attention or affection for some time now. And I'm not convinced that the two chimpanzees named Daphney and Sam, not long ago observed at a tourist stopover in the northwestern United States, are well cared for either. According to a woman who visited that operation in 1989: "While their cage was clean, it was very obvious that both chimps were depressed. Daphney was covered with dried, caked on feces and lay on her side. She blankly stared at the ground with glassy eyes for the entire two plus hours we watched. Sam listlessly sat on a large tire, just scratching and picking his nose. His hair was dull looking and he appeared very down."

In the late 1970s chimp brothers Sam and Rudy were abandoned on a farm in Boone County, Kentucky, by a carnival that went out of business. Eventually the two adolescent chimps were kept in the back of a truck in the Cincinnati area and exhibited to people who paid money to feed them candy and sodas. Then Rudy was sold to a young welder, who welded a cage but after a couple of weeks decided he was unable to care for the ape; he considered having Rudy euthanized. Animal lovers Jeremie and Jo Folger offered to rescue Rudy. They called every major zoo in the United States and found that none wanted an adolescent male chimp. The Folgers finally built a large cage in a downstairs room of their house, which Rudy inhabited for a year and a half. The chimp was able to reach out of the top of his cage, however, and he tore down the ceiling of the room. Rudy was also able to move his cage around by shifting his weight, so he broke more than one television set during the excitement generated by televised football games. In 1987 the Folgers sent the chimpanzee to Primarily Primates.

Around the time Rudy was sold to the welder, his brother, Sam, was sold to the owner of a canoe rental business in Loveland, Ohio. The owner used to take Sam out for walks on a leash, perhaps imagining himself to be Clint Eastwood with an every-which-way-but-loose orangutan. After Sam one day bit his owner's hand, he was sold to Ken Harris, owner of the Train Stop Inn, a bar in Foster, Ohio, north of Cincinnati. Harris didn't have a permanent cage for Sam, but in front of the Train Stop Inn was an old concrete pit — an abandoned cistern or perhaps an old foundation. It was converted into rough quarters for Sam, and when in early 1987 Tina Nelson, an investigator for the Humane Society of the United States, responded to complaints about the chimpanzee kept in a cistern, she discovered a concrete-walled hole in the ground that was, she recalls, "so dark that when the door opened the first thing you saw was the chimp trying to focus and see what was going on." Sam's owner, Ken Harris, proceeded to give his chimpanzee a cigarette, while Nelson stood there reeling from the smell of the place — with no windows, no water supply, no ventilation, littered with cans, beer cups, cigarette butts, food wrappers, and chimp dung.

Tina Nelson and the Humane Society were able to have Sam confiscated on April 15, 1987, and taken to temporary quarters at Ohio State University in Columbus. Ken Harris was charged with cruelty to animals and a trial date was set. In response, apparently, Harris had the cistern cleaned, repaired, painted, and otherwise improved. He brought in a television and radio and refrigerator. He had an outdoor enclosure built on top, so that Sam could climb through a hatch and get fresh air and see the outdoors.

Harris's lawyer entered a plea of not guilty and asked for a jury trial. The lawyer noted to reporters that Sam's cage was large, some 15 by 18 feet, furnished with a television, radio, and refrigerator. He had the new cage approved by the U.S. Department of Agriculture. And he began to worry out loud about what would happen to poor Sam at Ohio State University, "locked in a stainless steel cage somewhere without his friends and the sustenance he's used to." To counter the idea that Sam might become lonely in his new, USDA-approved quarters out in front of the bar, the lawyer and Harris found a female chimpanzee named Susie and arranged a well-publicized "wedding" that would occur just as soon as Sam was returned to the Train Stop Inn. The Humane Society people had noted that, along with being kept in a dark pit, Sam was regularly being given cigarettes and beer — and the lawyer astutely joked to reporters, "I'm afraid Sam's in the hands of well-intended yuppies and will be returned to us accustomed to a diet of quiche and chablis instead of beer, potato chips, and cigarettes." The journalists apparently enjoyed the joke and produced quasi-humorous articles entitled "Owner Fears Good Habits for His Chimp," "Was Life Too Wild for Sam?" "Monkeyshines Rile Animal Lovers," and "Sam the Chimp to Leave Vices Behind in Six-Week Quarantine."

The lawyer bought an inflatable rubber ape that he lashed to the back of his motorcycle, on which he regularly roared around town. A *Save Sam the Chimp* fund was started, and jars for contributions were distributed to a number of bars in the area. On each jar was the photograph of a voluptuous, bare-breasted woman and the caption "Don't Mess with My Monkey."

In the end, a jury of his peers seem to have agreed with Harris and his lawyer that the whole situation was a joke. Ken Harris was acquitted of cruelty to animals, and Sam was returned to his improved quarters in front of the Train Stop Inn.

One night in the middle of a thunderstorm I drove out to the Train Stop Inn. The bar is situated on the first floor of a two-story, stone-and-brick building at the edge of a noisy highway and beside a quiet, pale green river. I parked the car in a dirt lot at one side of the building. I could see Sam's outdoor cage from where I was sitting in the parked car. When the rain eased up a little, I saw Sam emerge from his underground quarters and into his outdoor cage, hunched over, looking out of his cage, while great bolts of lightning split the dark sky behind him and thunder crashed through the air. I left the car and walked up to the cage, built over a concrete slab and a hatchway entrance to his underground quarters beneath. Sam sat quietly. Traffic ripped past on the highway. There was a second cage, a wire-mesh enclosure, around the steel-barred cage, obviously to keep visitors at a distance. Nevertheless, I could see the evidence of visitors' generosity to Sam: two dozen cigarette butts and shards of a couple of torn beer cans on the floor of the cage. I could hear the television turned up loud inside his bunker, the sound rising through the hatch.

I entered the Train Stop Inn — a small, smoky place with a pool table, a deer's head on the wall, and a card game going on at one of the tables — and sat down at the bar. Ordering a drink, I asked the woman behind the counter if Ken Harris was around. She said she was his wife and he would be in soon. She seemed perfectly nice, and while tending bar and cooking dinner in an electric skillet, she answered some of my questions about Sam. She said that the Girl Scouts come out to sing to Sam. Sam loves it. Sam loves children. Having a chimpanzee, she said, is like having a retarded child. When they want Sam to get a bit of fresh air, they back their cage-on-a-trailer up to Sam's cage. Sam climbs in, and they take him for a drive. People come to see Sam and offer him beer and cigarettes. They lift the chain-link fence and pass beers to him. She doesn't like that because she has to clean up the mess. She also takes about six or seven cigarette lighters away from Sam every week, because people give him cigarettes and then let him take a lighter, and he doesn't give the lighter back. Sam is a pet, she said; he isn't out there for the amusement of customers. She often thought that a lot of the people who came to see Sam belonged inside the cage, and he belonged on the outside.

After a half-hour had passed, Ken Harris came in, soaking wet, wearing a dented camouflage hat over close-cropped gray hair, barely looking at me through thick glasses as he shook my hand with a single, perfunctory motion. He sat next to me at the bar and talked briefly about Sam. Sam is eighteen years old now. He likes to watch soap operas on television. He eats Monkey Chow and fruit — bananas, apples, grapes. They had a girlfriend, Susie, lined up for Sam and were hoping to mate the couple, but she "got burned up" in a fire earlier in the year.

Harris was polite but not very talkative. As I left the bar, I said goodbye to the ape sitting out front, sitting beneath a sky still split with lightning and rolled under thunder, sitting there alone and looking forlorn, I thought, in his own cell.

10 ◆ Endowed with Words, Confined in Rock

MIRANDA (to CALIBAN):
> When thou didst not, savage,
> Know thine own meaning, but wouldst gabble like
> A thing most brutish, I endowed thy purposes
> With words that made them known. But thy vile
> race,
> Though thou didst learn, had that in't which good
> natures
> Could not abide to be with. Therefore wast thou
> Deservedly confined into this rock.

I sat on the couch, and a young female chimpanzee was brought into the room. Her human surrogate parents, Jane and Maurice Temerlin, stood by to see what would happen. Lucy came and sat close beside me on the sofa, and simply stared into my eyes for a long, long time. It gave me a strange feeling. I had to wonder: "What is she thinking? Is she looking for something to do with my character? Is she wondering who I am? Why I'm here? What is she getting from this deep, searching gaze?" Staring directly into the eyes is not a common behavior of animals. Most animals won't. But chimpanzees permit you to gaze into their eyes, and they will return the scrutiny. On that day, when Lucy looked into mine, I was somewhat unnerved. I knew little about captive chimpanzees, and I had never sat next to an almost-mature chimpanzee on a sofa. (She was about eight years old, as big as a ten-year-old in the wild.) What, I kept wondering, was she thinking about me? Apparently the results of her inspection reassured her, for suddenly she pressed her lips over the lower half of my face in a large wet chimpanzee kiss.

Lucy then went into the kitchen. She opened two cupboards, taking a glass from one and a bottle of gin from the other. She opened the refrigerator, extracted a bottle of tonic, then closed the door with a careful and deliberate action as though it were a pleasurable thing to do. After neatly taking the cap from the tonic with her teeth, she mixed herself a strong drink. She came back into the living room, drink in hand, and turned on the television. After scanning through the channels and finding nothing that suited her taste, she turned it off and then lounged in an easy chair with a magazine and her gin and tonic. It was remarkable.

I had come to speak at the University of Oklahoma. Later on that evening I went to give my lecture, and since Lucy's human parents came with me, the chimpanzee had to be shut up in her apartment. The apartment was very nice, of course, but she was still being shut in. When we came back, I remember vividly how angry Lucy seemed. Like a child who feels let down by her parents, Lucy refused to "speak" to the Temerlins. Of course I was fine, and she made much of me. But "mom" and "dad" who had shut her up in her room were bad people, and for about thirty minutes she ignored them. I was struck by this behavior because a young chimp in the wild sometimes acts in a very similar way when she (or he) is accidentally separated from her mother. As long as they are apart she shows a good deal of distress, crying, even screaming, loudly. But once she sees her mother again, there is none of the frenzied greeting, none of the hugging and kissing, that one would expect. Instead, the child wanders nonchalantly toward the mother, and may even ignore her. She seems to be conveying a message, "You're bad. You shouldn't have left me."

In fact, Lucy might actually have said — or at least signed — something to that effect, for she was being taught ASL (American Sign Language) at the time. On another occasion when she had been left locked up in her room, she signed "Lucy sad cry" to a visitor.

While I was there I watched as Lucy, looking through her magazine, repeatedly signed to herself as she turned the pages. Jane Temerlin translated for me. "Blue" signed Lucy, gazing at a picture of a woman in a blue dress; "that dog" she proclaimed, turning to a picture of a toy poodle. And so on, until she reached the end. She made no mistakes, she only signed about things on some of the pages, and she was utterly absorbed, paying absolutely no attention to either Jane or me. At the end Jane signed "Whose magazine?" and Lucy replied "Mine, Lucy's."

1

Lucy was born in 1964, into the colony of carnival chimpanzees owned by Bob and Mae Noell of Tarpon Springs, Florida. When she was two days old, her mother was tranquilized with a spiked Coca-Cola, and the infant was pulled off. Wrapped in a baby blanket and placed in a bassinet, she was taken disguised as a human infant on a commercial flight to Oklahoma. Mae Noell, always very protective of the ape babies bred in her colony, told me Lucy was sold to William Lemmon of the Institute for Primate Studies in Norman, Oklahoma, with a written stipulation that the chimp be used for noninvasive, behavioral research only — "nice" research — and returned to the Tarpon Springs colony once the experiment was finished. She was never returned.

Lucy's new owner, William Lemmon, turned Lucy over to his secretary, Jane Temerlin, and her husband, Maurice, a clinical psychologist and psychotherapist. The Temerlins' plan was simple: Lucy would be raised in complete isolation from other members of her own species and, as much as possible, treated quite as a human child. She would be forced to grow up human.

The ape was nursed with a baby bottle and cuddled at her adoptive mother's breast. She was dressed in diapers, fed at a high chair, gradually weaned onto baby foods. She was treated for and inoculated against the usual human childhood diseases by a pediatrician, not a veterinarian. She slept in a crib in the Temerlin bedroom; after she learned to climb out of the crib, she slept right in bed between Maurice and Jane. She also had a playroom of her own, toys, books, magazines, television, and frequent access to the rest of the house — to the refrigerator, for example, from which she would extract her favorite tasty treats. The Temerlins' biological son, Steve, became a brother to Lucy; their dog, a chow named Nanuq, became Lucy's pet and companion. Lucy once had her own pet kitten.

After she was too old for the high chair, she learned to sit at a regular table with the rest of the family during meals; to eat with a knife, fork, and spoon; to drink liquids from a glass or cup. When she wanted tea, Lucy knew how to fill the kettle from a spigot, turn on the stove burner, fetch the cup and tea bag, and more or less make her own tea. She learned to use a screwdriver in the appropriate fashion, as well as pliers, wrench, and a host of other common household tools and implements: pencil, crayon, mirror, comb, brush, wastebasket, light switch, vacuum cleaner, matches, lighter, ashtray, rake, shovel, bucket, hose, key. Once she opened the kitchen door by unbolting the hinges. More than once, she let herself out of a locked room by secreting the key in her mouth and then unlocking a door while the Temerlins were gone. With some apparent deliberation, she once closed and locked the door behind Maurice Temerlin when he momentarily stepped onto the front porch, naked. He had to break a window to get back in.

But the chimpanzee saved her "most ingenious use of tools," Temerlin writes in *Lucy: Growing up Human,* for self-exploration and masturbation. She used a hand mirror to examine the inside of her mouth and vagina, the handles of pliers to pull her labia apart for examination, a pencil to stroke her clitoris. She would pull a vacuum cleaner out of the closet, plug it in, remove the brush from the tube, turn the machine on, and sensuously run the suctioning tube all over her body, eventually concentrating on her genitals. By adolescence Lucy had developed a taste for the photographs of nude men in *Playgirl* magazine, particularly their penises. (The nude women in *Playboy* left her cold.) Temerlin describes Lucy's leafing through a copy of *Playgirl,* enthusiastically stroking the penises in the photographs with her forefinger, sometimes rubbing them with a fingernail eagerly enough to scratch and even mutilate them, finally unfolding the centerfold of a male nude onto the floor, squatting over it, and rhythmically rubbing her genitals against the model's penis.

Lucy proved to be deeply sensitive and emotionally complex. At one point Temerlin discovered he could make the chimpanzee eat meals she found unappetizing by playing a role he described as Jewish mother. "For God's sake, Lucy, think of the poor starving chimps in Africa!" he would intone — and Lucy would slowly begin eating. Then he might whine, "Take at least three more bites for your poor suffering father who loves you" — and Lucy would eat more diligently. He would implore histrionically, "How could you do this to me?" — and she would clean her plate. "The emotions she exhibits most clearly," Temerlin concluded, "are affection, anger, fear, joy, tenderness, greed, jealousy, anxiety, concern, protectiveness, and many others." The affection she displayed toward members of her immediate human family was "sufficiently intense I would not hesitate to call it love."

Lucy learned to talk. Chimpanzees lack voice boxes but are highly dexterous, so that "talking" is necessarily carried out with sign language. Graduate students from the Institute for Primate Studies, who had already been teaching sign language to chimpanzees at the institute, regularly visited the Temerlins' house and gave Lucy lessons. She eventually acquired a vocabulary of more than a hundred signs, including nouns, pronouns, verbs, modifiers, and emphasizers. With that basic vocabulary she asked questions, made direct statements, invented entirely new signs, and spontaneously combined some of her old signs to create new ones. After biting into a radish, for example, she combined signs she already knew to call it "cry hurt food." An onion became for Lucy "cry fruit." Citrus fruits were "smell fruits." A watermelon she called "candy fruit." Lucy was obviously capable of deceit — the Temerlins came to recognize her guilty, secretive expression when she was hiding a contraband key or a screwdriver — but once she learned sign language, Lucy was able to deceive with symbols. One time she defecated on the floor. Her teacher, Roger Fouts, turned to the evidence and asked her, in sign language, "What's that?"

Lucy feigned innocence: "Lucy not know."
Roger insisted: "You do know. What's that?"
Lucy yielded: "Dirty, dirty."
Roger continued: "Whose dirty, dirty?"
Lucy, referring to another teacher, lied: "Sue's."
Roger persisted: "It's not Sue's. Whose is it?"
Lucy retreated into a deeper lie: "Roger's."
Roger persevered: "No! It's not Roger's. Whose is it?"
Lucy, at last, submitted: "Lucy dirty, dirty. Sorry Lucy."

If the point of the experiment was to humanize Lucy, it succeeded at least in humanizing Maurice Temerlin's feelings and attitudes about Lucy. Temerlin's book, he informs us, tells "my daughter's story." The attachment began early: "Shortly after we adopted Lucy I began to love her without reservation. I do not remember how long it took — I would guess not more than a week or so — before I failed to make human-animal distinctions with Lucy. She was my daughter and that was that!" This chimpanzee became not Lucy the Chimp, but Lucy Temerlin the daughter, as Maurice Temerlin suggests several times in the book, as he would indicate, again and again, to various people — to the manager who objected to his taking her into a shopping market, to a ticket collector when he took Lucy to see *Planet of the Apes.*

If Lucy quickly became a daughter, however, she always remained a special daughter. For one thing, as Temerlin fully recognized, she was much stronger and probably less predictable than a person. Thus, he constructed for her a lockable playroom with reinforced-concrete walls and steel doors. Lucy exhibited an early fondness for alcohol; and although Temerlin was reluctant to give his teenage son, Steve, alcoholic drinks out of concern for the boy's liver and the neighbors' opinions, he had no such reluctance about providing alcohol to his three-year-old chimpanzee daughter. From the age of three, Lucy took cocktails with her mom and dad nightly and wine with her dinner. She was an "ideal drinking companion," Temerlin thought, one who "never gets obnoxious, even when smashed to the brink of unconsciousness." Although he confessed to the usual paternal inhibitions about discussing sex with his son, Temerlin seemed to have few such concerns about his adopted daughter. In the interests of science, or as her human father more candidly phrased it, "to see what would happen," several times he masturbated in front of her. Lucy ignored him. Once he asked his wife to masturbate in front of Lucy. Lucy ignored her. However, when mom and dad began masturbating each other, Lucy "immediately became very excited, grabbed our hands, and attempted to stop the genital contact."

Temerlin believed that Lucy's intelligence, emotional awareness, and sensitivity elevated her far beyond the status of an owned, living object — a pet or an experimental animal. "The thought of owning Lucy, even as a beloved dog is owned," he wrote at one point, "is to me like owning another human being, and that cannot be done, and could not be done even when the institution of slavery flourished. Minds and hearts have a way of remaining free, if they work and wish, even on the rack." Yet if Lucy was not an owned object, what was she? Born an ape, she was purchased and then, just as an experiment, just to see what would happen, patiently and lovingly transformed into something not an ape — something not quite human either, but perhaps more human than ape. Finally one day, after she had been so transformed, her human parents discovered they wanted "to live normal lives now" and decided to terminate the experiment. As humanized as she undoubtedly was, Lucy remained a powerful and sometimes unpredictable being who had already bitten several people during moments of anger or ardor. Lucy had to be sold . . . or at least provided for.

Surely, making such a change was not easy for the Temerlins. They considered various options: a private breeding colony, a zoo, a research project. But Lucy, at age ten, had never seen another chimpanzee. To Temerlin placing her in a private colony would be like placing some great intellectual in a concentration camp; he worried about producing "chimpanzee madness." A zoo, he thought, would be sterile and boring. Although he insisted that his "daughter's welfare" was far more important than "contributing to science," Temerlin could imagine certain research projects that might not be harmful — research on mothering, for example, so that Lucy might, to recall his rather blissful jargon, "actualize her potential for motherhood." Nevertheless, any male chimp who mated with Lucy would have to contend with a very particular father-in-law. "Indeed, I have strong feelings about the qualifications which must be possessed by the future husband of my darling virginal daughter."

In the end, the Temerlins decided that their ape turned into a human might best be turned back into an ape. She was sent to Africa with the idea that she would be returned to the wild. By then Lucy was famous as a near-person, a rather spoiled one at that, who ate with people, who drank, slept, and conversed in sign language with people. She had appeared on television several times, had become a familiar subject for readers of *Life, Psychology Today, Parade, Science Digest,* the *Los Angeles Times,* the *New York Times.* And so to send her into an African forest with the instruction, *Become a wild animal now,* aroused some criticism.

Among the critics was Mae Noell, owner of the colony of retired carnival chimps into which Lucy was born. Noell (and her late husband, Bob) kept and bred and raised and lived with chimpanzees for fifty years; she currently maintains one of the largest privately owned groups of captive apes in the world, almost thirty altogether, including chimps, gorillas, and orangutans. She knows chimps — at least, captive chimps.

Over breakfast one morning at a Florida coffee shop, Mae Noell gave me her forthright opinion about the Temerlins' disposition of Lucy. She began by explaining that even though she is a Christian fundamentalist, a Baptist, her lifelong intimacy with chimps has taught her something other Baptists might not understand: that "this critter is a very close cousin, *very* close cousin. He is a human being except for his ability to talk and understand morals. He can't understand morals and the Bible . . . but he is a very close cousin. The truth is, he's got the same number and type of teeth that we've got, same muscles, same bones, and they've recently found that they've got the same blood types. How much closer can you get?" Chimpanzees, she continued, are "always distressed about the fact that you don't have a big thumb on your foot. They just cannot *stand* it that you don't have a thumb on your foot. But I really feel that they are people — of a lower grade. And I've been criticized for that. Now the way I answer some of these Bible people: We know that the Lord made two people, a man and a woman. They had two children, two sons. One of them killed the other. The murderer, according to the Bible, was sent out into the wilderness and found himself a wife! Think about it! That's all I'm going to say. It's something to think about, you know. It ties in with evolution."

But Lucy, Noell insisted, was rightfully hers. She still has somewhere Dr. Lemmon's formal statement, scrawled on stationery of the Institute for Primate Studies, that Lucy would be returned once the Temerlins' experiment was over. As for sending this young ape to West Africa, "Most cruel damn thing that could have been done to anything!" Why? Noell explained. "You're sitting here now, at a table. And she sat at a table. You're wearing clothes. She wore clothes. You're drinking warm coffee; you're eating hot food already prepared for you. How would it be to take all your clothes off and go out into that tree" — she nodded toward a tree we could see through the coffee shop window — "and say, 'There's nothing but trees around here, and I've got to figure out what I can eat and how I can cover my body so I don't freeze to death or get rained on'?"

The North African desert sweeps southward, year by year expanding farther south toward the desiccating and recently deforested lands of West Africa. On the way, it enters a purgatory of red dust and scrub, of dry savannah and bottle-shaped baobab trees. In the dry season, a dry wind insinuates a fine dust everywhere, and baboons bark through a puzzle of scattered scrub and brittle grass. This dry land recalls a moonscape, its earth a hard floor of dark cinder and pitted laterite — until the land splits open suddenly into a steep escarpment, and so you plummet into green: down to an olive green river with dark green forests along the edge, a pale mist rising from the river's surface in the morning, and, in the middle of the river, long islands dense with trees and vines and fanning fronds.

You hear a tooting and hooting of birds down on the islands, calls and cries of some five hundred species taking refuge from the desert and the dry land, permanently here or pausing temporarily on their long migration from there to there. You listen to the mooing and snorting and belching of hippopotamuses in water. In the shadows of trees at an island's edge, you see the backs of hippos slowly rising, slowly lowering — dark, glistening, round, like overturned ceramic bowls.

These are the Baboon Islands. This is the River Gambia, cutting west to the Atlantic — cutting through Senegal essentially, but insulated by the sleeve of its own small riverine nation, The Gambia.

Here is where Lucy went, endowed with words.

The Temerlins sent Lucy to The Gambia because they had become enthusiastic about a project there attempting to habituate formerly captive chimps to the wilderness. That project began during the mid-1960s after a Guinean trader arrived in Banjul, capital city of The Gambia, carrying a tiny wooden box with a two-year-old male chimpanzee inside. The baby chimp was folded over, face to knees, and tied with an old piece of electrical cord so that he couldn't move. The trader, eager to unload this pathetic being before he died, offered to sell him to The Gambia's director of wildlife conservation, Eddie Brewer, and his young daughter, Stella. Out of pity, the Brewers bought the baby for a few shillings, then soon realized that a local market for baby chimps, captured after their mothers were shot, was developing. Gambian authorities challenged the trade by confiscating all baby chimps brought into the country, and the Brewers established an orphanage to care for them. By the time they were six or seven years old, however, these orphans had become far too strong and vigorous for the orphanage facilities, so Stella Brewer started the rehabilitation project, trying to return several young chimps to a wild existence in a forest of Niokolo Koba National Park, Senegal.

Most of the chimpanzees involved in this early project had been born in the wild and experienced a comparatively brief period in captivity. Their mothers were shot; they were transported from one African country to another; they were confiscated. A few other chimps had been born in British zoos; none of that group survived. Eight other chimpanzees in the project may have been illegally exported from Sierra Leone to the Netherlands by the notorious Franz Sitter; they were confiscated in Holland and sent to The Gambia. Still others had been smuggled into Spain, where they were dressed in clothes, fed tranquilizers, and forced to endure fourteen-hour days as props for beach photographers. They too were confiscated and sent to The Gambia. But none grew up as a psychotherapist's daughter in a posh American suburb; and none could talk to humans. Lucy was a long shot for this project.

In the summer of 1977 the Brewers agreed that Lucy and a second captive-born chimp from America could enter the rehabilitation project. That September, Maurice and Jane Temerlin — and a young woman named Janis Carter — arrived in The Gambia with two chimps inside wooden crates. One of the chimps was Lucy, eleven years old by then; the second was Marianne, a younger female from the Yerkes Primate Center in Atlanta, Georgia, who had recently become a playmate of Lucy's.

While she was a graduate student at the University of Oklahoma, Janis Carter had earned spending money by working for the Temerlins as a babysitter and cage cleaner. She learned to communicate with Lucy using ASL, American Sign Language. But she had never been one of Lucy's teachers, and she never became as fluent a signer as Lucy. The young woman did establish a good relationship with the chimpanzee, however, and the Temerlins hired her to help in what they apparently imagined would be a brief transfer. Carter anticipated being in Africa for three weeks, during which time Lucy was supposed to become acclimated to her new surroundings and greater freedom. Then, it was imagined, the Brewers would take over and eventually return Lucy to a semiwild existence in Senegal.

The adjustment was not so easy. Lucy and Marianne were given temporary quarters inside a large cage within a tiny forested reserve on the edges of the city of Banjul. The Temerlins left. Despite the spaciousness of her new cage, Lucy became depressed and seriously ill. Meanwhile, although Stella Brewer's rehabilitating chimps in Senegal were doing well, she became concerned that wild chimpanzees in the same forest, naturally territorial, would attack the newcomers. Janis Carter, unwilling to abandon Lucy under such circumstances, extended her initial three weeks to three months.

Three months turned into three years. As the Brewers decided in the spring of 1979 to move their rehabilitation project out of Senegal, Janis Carter oversaw the transfer of Lucy, Marianne, and seven other chimpanzees from their cages in the small reserve near Banjul two hundred miles upriver to one of the five Baboon Islands on the River Gambia. All of the seven other chimpanzees had been born in the wild. Some of them clearly remembered skills they had acquired early in life — how to climb a tree, what foods to eat. None was fully prepared for survival in a forest, however, so when Janis Carter moved these nine apes to the Baboon Islands in 1979, she moved herself as well. British commandos with time to spare built a big cage on the island, and Carter moved her few possessions into the cage. She herself sometimes went inside the cage and later began sleeping there, but at first Janis Carter slept outside on a platform in the trees, thus encouraging Lucy, Marianne, and the seven other chimps to build their own nests and also sleep in the trees at night. "We shared the island," she recalls in an article for *Smithsonian*, "with baboons, vervet monkeys, red colobus monkeys, hippos, spitting cobras, vipers, hyenas and a variety of antelope, cats and birds." Even though the island was "ideal for chimps, my living conditions were primitive. We had no electricity or running water; heat, mosquitoes and tsetse flies we did have."

Living, she has written, "more as a chimpanzee than as a human," Carter explored and climbed and foraged; she consumed unripe figs and ripe ants; she went to sleep at night and woke up in the morning — all with the companionship of Lucy, Marianne, and seven other chimpanzees. Lucy was the least prepared of the nine for life in a forest, and in normal circumstances she might have been the least dominant, most trampled-upon member of her social group. Lucy's large size and her special relationship with the one human made her, instead, the highest-ranking chimpanzee on the island. Yet her special relationship with humans was precisely the problem now. Lucy refused to drink from the river as the other chimps did, for example. She wanted to drink from a bottle, as she saw the only human on the island doing. The other chimps readily climbed up broad-trunked baobab trees on the island, pursuing edible leaves, flowers, fruits, and bark — but Lucy either didn't know how or chose not to climb baobab trees. While other chimps of the group were climbing, she would sit at the base of the tree and wait for pieces of food to fall. On one occasion, apparently frustrated because the other chimps were up there in a baobab tree getting the best food, Lucy turned to her human companion and asked, in sign language, for help. Carter showed her an easier route into the baobab from a neighboring tree. But Lucy would have none of that. She pulled Carter by the hand up to the tree, placed the woman's hands onto the trunk, and pleaded, in sign language: "More food. Janis go." Carter finally gave in, to the extent that she returned to camp with Lucy, and together they brought back a long plank of construction lumber, which was then propped up against the tree and served as a ladder for Lucy.

The human had stopped talking to the chimpanzee when they first moved to the island, and eventually Carter ceased helping Lucy find food. "I felt there was no way that Lucy could survive if she had a special interaction," Janis Carter told me when I visited the Baboon Islands in 1991. But the sudden change precipitated a crisis. Lucy became emaciated and pathetic. She would hang out near her human friend's cage and sign: "Food . . . drink . . . Janis come out . . . Lucy's hurt." She would find a minor sore on her body and sign: "Hurt! Hurt! Hurt!" She whined and pulled her hair out and sat abjectly within Carter's view. Carter would tell Lucy to get out of sight, so she would move away and then slowly creep back. This sort of behavior continued for about three months. "Then one day," Carter told a journalist, "she just broke. I was at my absolute wits' end. I didn't think she was going to eat a leaf. I didn't think she was going to do anything, and we had fight after fight after fight. We fell asleep on the ground next to each other — we weren't having contact with each other — and when I woke up, it was as though she had decided during the nap that she was going to start trying. She sat up and picked a leaf within arm's reach and handed it to me to eat it, and I ate it and then shared it with her. After that she started trying. I don't know how much longer she could have gone on, or myself, either. I was to my absolute limit."

Lucy survived. She regained her health and strength. She adopted an orphaned baby male chimpanzee. In 1983 her adopted son died of a stomach parasite, and Lucy herself nearly died of a hookworm infestation. But chimpanzee blood was hand delivered by James Mahoney, a veterinarian from LEMSIP in New York, and frequent transfusions saved Lucy's life. Janis Carter moved off the island in 1985 and took up residence in the base camp downriver, but she regularly came by in a boat to check on the apes. One day, six months after leaving the island, Carter returned for a visit. Lucy greeted her with a mouth-to-mouth kiss, wrapped her arms around her old friend, and nestled her head at her friend's breast. Carter had brought some items Lucy once valued: some books, paper and pens, a hat, a doll, a mirror. But after that brief meeting and a quick examination of the artifacts from another life and another world, Lucy walked away. In some sense, she had become a chimpanzee again.

Although she was in excellent health and beginning to develop sound social and sexual interests in the other chimpanzees on the island, Lucy died suddenly at the age of twenty-two. Her entire skeleton, minus hands and feet, was found intact near Janis Carter's old campsite on the island. There was no evidence of injury from a fall, no signs of an attack by other animals. Death by snakebite or a sudden viral illness seemed unlikely: Lucy would have possessed the strength to return to a provisioning area where project workers regularly checked on the apes. Perhaps, it was thought, Lucy had been shot by human intruders. She was always the first chimpanzee to approach people coming to the island. She was unafraid of people. After all, she had been raised as a person herself. She was even endowed with words.

2

Nearly thirty other chimpanzees were kept at the Institute for Primate Studies in Norman, Oklahoma, during the time Lucy lived with the Temerlins, on loan from the institute. To one degree or other, all of these other chimps were also trained in sign language as youngsters — all endowed with words — and nearly all of them grew up to find that humans had lost interest in communicating with them. Unlike Lucy, who ultimately experienced some measure of freedom, these apes grew into adult lives of total confinement. For most wild animals, of course, captivity is identical to total confinement. Yet these captive creatures had a special relationship with humans, based at some level on respect, affection, and communication. Many had experienced some freedom as youngsters — and as adults, in some sense and to some degree, they all had the capacity to *ask* for their freedom. In the end, however, sign language work at the institute terminated not long after Lucy left for Africa, in the late 1970s, and the great majority of Oklahoma's language-using chimps were trucked out to New York State, where they became research subjects at LEMSIP, the New York

University Medical Center laboratory directed by Dr. Jan Moor-Jankowski.

The story of the Oklahoma language chimps and their diaspora has
been told by Eugene Linden in *Silent Partners* (1986). In that book
Linden suggests that sign-language work at the Institute for Primate
Studies ended in the late 1970s due to unfortunate declines in two
commodities: funding and fingers.

The decline in funding had to do mostly with two chimps, one a
success, the other a failure. The successful chimp was Washoe — who
was, in fact, one of the world's first successful language-using apes.
Born in West Africa in 1965, originally taught sign language by scientists R. Allen and Beatrix T. Gardner during the latter half of the 1960s
at the University of Nevada, Washoe early in life learned to indicate
"dog" by slapping her thighs; "clothes" by brushing her fingers down
her chest; "flower" by touching one of her nostrils with an index
finger; "fruit" by placing a closed fist beside her mouth; "baby" by
making a cradling gesture; "drink" by creating a bottle shape with
closed fist and outstretched thumb, then placing thumb to mouth; and
so on. She learned to combine individual signs into meaningful combinations — for example, "Hurry give me toothbrush" and "Baby in my
drink" (the latter in response to seeing a small doll inside a drinking
mug). And she learned to generalize and transfer meaning — "dirty,"
which at first referred to her feces, was generalized into a swear word,
a way of describing things or people she didn't like.

The Gardners eventually passed Washoe on to their best graduate
student, Roger Fouts, who in 1970 accompanied the chimpanzee during her transfer from the University of Nevada to the Institute for
Primate Studies in Oklahoma. (Washoe, who had never seen other
chimps before moving to Oklahoma, must have been disturbed on
encountering these aggressive, hairy creatures for the first time; her
early invented term for chimpanzee was "black bug.") Fouts and his
wife, Deborah, remained at the institute for nearly a decade until a
$300,000 National Science Foundation grant enabled them to move,
with Washoe and her one-year-old adopted baby, Loulis, to a better
situation at Central Washington University in Ellensburg, Washington. The director of the Institute for Primate Studies in Oklahoma,
William Lemmon, by then had begun claiming ownership of Washoe.
Fouts, fearful that Lemmon would keep Washoe, snuck away with his

chimp prodigy and her adopted son in the middle of the night on August 25, 1979. The Institute for Primate Studies thus lost its best-known scientist and language-using chimpanzee.

The National Science Foundation grant enabled Roger and Deborah Fouts to continue their excellent work with Washoe and (currently) half a dozen other signing chimpanzees at Central Washington University. For the remaining language-using chimps at the Institute for Primate Studies in Oklahoma, however, government funding pretty much disappeared during the late 1970s. Linden, in *Silent Partners*, attributes this decline at least partly to a climate of opinion created by the failure of a second chimpanzee from the institute, a young male named Nim Chimpsky.

Nim, born at the institute in 1973, was two weeks old in December of that year when Dr. Lemmon sent him to New York City so that he could become the central experimental subject in a study run by a Columbia University psychology professor, Herbert Terrace. Trained as a behaviorist (he had studied under the founder and chief proponent of behaviorism, B. F. Skinner), Terrace hoped to duplicate some of the language work being done with Washoe, Lucy, and a number of other apes at the Oklahoma institute and elsewhere. Behaviorism is a branch of psychology that, in imitation of the successful physical sciences, avoids traditional psychology's inclination to speculate creatively about nonobservable concepts — thinking, for example. As an alternative, behaviorism emphasizes rigorous experimental design by asking small questions and looking at observable results — behaviors. Terrace had already investigated the trained behaviors of rats and pigeons. In acquiring Nim, he hoped to be able to study a chimpanzee who learned language, as the Gardners had done, as Roger Fouts and several others were doing, but perhaps with a more rigorous experimental design.

The theoretical approach itself was not so important. Professor Terrace, in fact, has gone to some pains to deny that he was limited by a rigidly behaviorist orientation. But the psychologist's approach was fundamentally different from the other experiments in a more practical sense. Virtually every previous ape language experiment had presumed that chimpanzees would acquire language just as human children do, by maturing within some version of a stable family where the human experimenters become substitute parents or siblings, in which the ape learns to use language not solely in response to simple rewards but as a more global response to the language of others within an emotionally compelling context. Even before Allen and Beatrix Gardner began their pioneering sign-language work with Washoe (and David and Ann Premack with Sarah), psychologists Keith and Catherine Hayes raised a baby chimp, Viki, in their household as part of their family and tried to teach her spoken language. (Sign language for apes hadn't been thought of yet, and young Viki, gesturing expressively, learned to articulate four words: "mama," "papa," "up," and "cup.") Roger Fouts' work with Washoe in Oklahoma and then Washington State was always sustained and supported by Deborah Fouts. In California, Francine Patterson and her partner, Ron Cohen, worked closely together to teach sign language to the gorilla named Koko. And, of course, Lucy acquired sign language in the home of Jane and Maurice Temerlin.

I certainly do not mean to suggest that Herbert Terrace's bachelor status doomed his experiment to failure. Indeed, the most exciting ape language project outside the United States today seems to work largely because one person, Tetsuro Matsuzawa, has developed a powerful emotional bond with a chimpanzee named Ai at the Kyoto Primate Center in Japan. But I will assert that Terrace resisted the parenthood model altogether, and that he did so to the detriment of his experiment. He later insisted that "Nim was socialized as much as possible like a human infant," but during the three years that Nim served as the subject in this experiment, he had to adjust to the comings and goings, the demands and temperaments, the tensions and techniques of more than sixty different teachers, many of whom were volunteers suffering from, as Terrace describes it, a "nonprofessional attitude." Nim also lived in three different places, commuted to a fourth place that served as his schoolroom, put up with several babysitters, and clearly developed strong bonds with two or three human surrogate mothers; those mothers all withdrew from the project after various periods, each time apparently leaving the surrogate child depressed. Professor Terrace himself insisted on maintaining a rather lofty attitude toward his subject. He, of course, "felt more affection for Nim than for the pigeons and rats with whom I had worked"; nonetheless, the scientist always regarded the chimp "as the subject of an experimental study." Terrace was typically so busy with other duties at Columbia — teaching, administering, running his pigeon laboratory — that he was able to spend only, as he wrote, a "meager amount of time," merely "a few hours a week," with the chimpanzee. Most of the teaching and experimental work with Nim was done by assistants, an extended parade of them.

The bulk of Terrace's book about this experiment, *Nim*, was written while the author believed his ape was successfully acquiring sign language. Thus, we read enthusiastic reports: Nim learned to express 125 different symbolic signs during the first forty-four months, mainly in response to his teachers' approval and the very pleasure of communication; Nim creatively combined signs ("more drink" and "more eat," for example) nearly twenty thousand times during the experiment, and some of the sign combinations involved as many as sixteen different words; Nim creatively used at least two signs ("bite" and "angry") as substitutes for physical actions — when it seemed apparent that Nim was about to bite, he paused and signed the word "bite" instead; Nim used signs to misrepresent situations or needs; Nim creatively invented his own original signs for symbolizing two different things or concepts (for "hand cream" and "play"); even very early in the experiment, Nim began making "many spontaneous signs."

At the end of three and a half years, in September 1977 (as Lucy was being flown to West Africa), Nim was sent back to the Oklahoma institute. The experiment was over, and Terrace began his final scientific analysis of the data by reviewing videotapes of the chimp. In doing so, the professor made the "dramatic and unexpected discovery" that his teachers had "prompted" most of Nim's signing and that it was "largely imitative" of what had just been signed to him. As Terrace finally wrote, Nim's "unspontaneous and imitative" signing occurred in marked contrast to the "largely spontaneous and creative" linguistic behavior of human children.

Terrace reversed himself entirely. In the 1987 edition of *Nim*, written mostly before but partly after Terrace's change of mind, he forcibly argues both sides of the debate. In one section, he describes in considerable detail several instances of Nim's seemingly creative signing; in another, the professor deplores its "imitative" nature. In one place, Terrace tells us that Nim began making "many spontaneous signs"; in another, he complains about the "unspontaneous" nature of the signing. In one part, he states that "Nim's main reward for learning to sign was our approval and being able to sign about something that was important to him"; in another, Terrace insists that the chimp was merely signing as "a last resort" when he had been unable "to obtain his reward by direct physical means."

Which parts of the book should we believe? More to the point, why did Terrace so completely change his mind? Terrace himself attributes his reversal to the wonders of videotape technology: the truth about Nim's signing "could be seen only by painstaking, frame-by-frame playbacks of videotapes." But one also is drawn to imagine that Professor Terrace, vexed by other pressing commitments, left too much in the hands of volunteers afflicted with "a nonprofessional attitude" and never entirely knew what was going on in his own research project.

Nim was returned to the Institute for Primate Studies, and Terrace published his book, confessing the failure of his experiment. But of course it was a failure in one sense only. It failed to demonstrate that one chimpanzee could "talk" — that is, engage in linguistic behavior. On the other hand, it seemed to succeed in demonstrating that one chimpanzee really did not "talk." And if it helped to demonstrate the more general proposition that no chimpanzee could talk, then the Nim experiment would turn out to be a significant success indeed. Terrace soon became a professional critic of all the other ape language studies. He reviewed videotapes of other studies and regularly pointed out that researchers were cuing and prodding their subjects, that chimpanzees were merely imitating researchers, and so on. He joined forces with a linguist named Thomas Seboek and, on at least one notable occasion, a magician named Amazing Randi, and together the three of them were able to present some very convincing arguments that all the ape language experiments were failing to prove their claims.

Skepticism is an extremely important arrow in the scientific quiver, but Terrace's criticisms typically rest on an analysis of brief segments of videotape — an hour, a few or several hours — when the actual data produced by these projects are massive. Patterson and Cohen have been working several hours a day for twenty years with their signing female gorilla, Koko. The Foutses could call upon thirty years' worth of data for their chimp, Washoe, and at least a decade's worth of data on each of Washoe's half-dozen chimpanzee companions. Moreover, Terrace has never really explained how Koko could be imitating humans when she signs to herself, alone, as she plays with dolls or leafs through a magazine — videotaped with a hidden camera. Nor has Terrace ever satisfactorily described what human language user has been prodding the chimpanzee Loulis, Washoe's adopted son. Between March 1979, when Loulis was adopted at the age of ten months, and June 1984, human researchers were careful to use in the presence of Loulis only seven signs: "who," "what," "where," "which," "name," "sign," and "want." Yet during that period Loulis learned to express himself with a total of fifty-five signs beyond these seven. It would seem that Loulis acquired his vocabulary from the other chimps sharing cages with him, most particularly from his mother. In some instances Washoe was observed actually teaching Loulis signs. Terrace has lately associated himself with Sue Savage-Rumbaugh's careful studies of symbol-manipulating chimpanzees and bonobos at the Yerkes Primate Center in Atlanta. Savage-Rumbaugh, he concedes, at least has demonstrated that a chimp "can use a symbol to initiate a conversation and thereby announce what game he wants to play without any prompting from the teacher." As for all the other projects, Terrace is still waiting for the videotapes that will prove him wrong.

The vigorous and partly reasonable criticisms of Herb Terrace, as well as of Thomas Seboek and Amazing Randi, and the well-publicized "failure" of Nim, probably influenced the level of funding available for ape language studies throughout the country.* At the Institute for Primate Studies, funding had disappeared by the end of the 1970s. A single large grant, that $300,000 from the National Science Foundation, migrated along with Roger and Deborah Fouts, Washoe and Loulis, north to Central Washington University.

So a loss of funding was the first problem in Oklahoma, a complicated one. The second problem was a loss of fingers. Lost fingers had long been a theme at the institute. Free chimpanzees in the wild very rarely attack humans. It is certainly a measure of their limited options that caged chimps do attack and bite people with some regularity. The most famous language-using chimpanzee of the Oklahoma institute, Washoe, had bitten several people, as had Lucy, as had other apes owned by or associated with the institute — Eugene Linden places the damaged digit score at eleven fingers and one thumb.

William Lemmon, director of the institute, added to the bitten

---

* At least in Eugene Linden's opinion. An alternative view was expressed in a 1983 letter to the editor by psychologist Mark Seidenberg: "There is no conspiracy to repress ape language studies, only the recognition that more than ten years of this research has demonstrated very little about linguistic capacities in nonhuman species or about the nature of language."

finger imagery with a dramatic story. He occasionally sold chimps to
private individuals who wished to acquire pets. (An earlier chapter
describes the fate of two babies who came from the Oklahoma colony
and served as pets for a brief time before moving into laboratory work
and show business.) He also bought chimps. And in this role as dealer,
buying and selling, lending and leasing, Dr. Lemmon came to know
some people in show business, including Bob and Mae Noell, who had
provided Lemmon with Lucy when she was two days old. In 1953 one
of the chimpanzees in the Noells' carnival show damaged two fingers
on Bob Noell's left hand and entirely bit off two fingers on his right
hand. Noell, who had been a skilled juggler and magician as well as an
ape handler, was thus handicapped for the rest of his life. Lemmon,
who apparently treasured the drama of rubbing elbows with circus and
carnival people, liked to tell the story of the lost fingers and embellish
it by declaring that Noell stored his severed appendages in a leather
pouch attached to his belt.

But the theme of lost fingers at the Institute for Primate Studies
reached a tragic climax the day a scientist from Stanford University,
Karl Pribram, came to see the famous Washoe. For unclear reasons,
Washoe bit and damaged Pribram's finger; it had to be amputated. It
has been said that Washoe was very upset after she bit Pribram's finger
and that she signed, "Sorry, sorry, sorry." But Pribram, feeling he
should have been warned that the caged ape was a dangerous animal,
hired a lawyer and initiated a multimillion-dollar lawsuit against William Lemmon, Roger Fouts, and the University of Oklahoma, which to
that point had provided the institute with prestige and academic
legitimacy. Pribram claimed that the termination of his finger terminated his ability to practice neurosurgery; Fouts declared that Pribram hadn't actually practiced neurosurgery on any person in thirty
years. (Since the 1950s, apparently, Pribram had experimented on
monkeys. In one project, he experimentally excised parts of their
brains and then observed how the mutilated monkeys responded to
various "noxious stimuli," such as sharp objects, burning paper and
matches, and bitter food.) Karl Pribram ultimately withdrew his threatened suit, but not before the University of Oklahoma recognized what
a liability those talking chimps at the Institute for Primate Studies
might be.

The university decided to terminate its association with the institute. And so, finally, Dr. Lemmon decided to terminate his association

with all those chimpanzees. Thus, approximately thirty chimpanzees were put on the auction block in 1979, all of them to various degrees still endowed with words.

3

Before Europeans came to the island, Caliban was mute — capable merely of "gabbling" like an animal or, to recall the words of Prospero's daughter, Miranda, "a thing most brutish." Out of pity Miranda taught him language, and Caliban became one of the most eloquent characters in the drama. (He is also the only character who speaks both verse and prose. The Europeans are limited by class: aristocratic characters speak only in verse, while lower-class characters express themselves entirely in prose.) It would seem that language elevates Caliban to the moral level of the Europeans. He can apologize, argue, plead, express pain and despair. He can speak of justice and injustice. Language articulates his individuality and his consciousness; it informs his existence as a serious and suffering creature. Language endows Caliban with great dramatic power. And it emphasizes for us the paradox of his treatment by the Europeans. He talks entirely like a person, like an intelligent and refined fellow European; but the Europeans continue to regard him as a slave or animal, an irritatingly contentious piece of property that can be bought and sold and owned and used, a strange and deformed brute who by his very nature is "deservedly confined into this rock."

Here is the fundamental paradox of our treatment of the great apes in general and of chimpanzees in particular. We use them because they are so close to human; it serves our convenience to treat them as so close to animal. Nowhere has the paradox been starker than inside many research laboratories. Even if we regard the most dramatically destructive laboratory experiments on chimpanzees — the head-bashing and heart-snatching sort — as unfortunate aberrations, minor and unrepresentative, the fact remains that chimpanzees inhabit approximately the same legal world as laboratory mice. Endowed with words, they seem to achieve an elevated, almost magical status for us. Confined in rock, they have almost no status whatsoever.

Scientific researchers understand better than most of us how different chimpanzees and the other great apes are from the most common laboratory animals — mice and rats. Robert Yerkes once argued that chimpanzees were important to research precisely because they possess such a rich range of humanlike emotions. "Many, if not all, the chief categories of human emotional expression are represented in chimpanzee behavior," the scientist wrote in 1943. "Chimpanzee emotional expression is fascinating and at the same time baffling in its complexity and variability. It may give a rich reward of sympathetic insight and understanding to the lover of pets, and it is important as material for the investigator. Long and intimate acquaintance with the animals enables one to recognize and distinguish expressions of shyness, timidity, fear, terror; of suspicion, distrust, resentment, antagonism, anger, rage; of interest, curiosity, excitement, elation, contentment, pleasure; of confidence, friendliness, familiarity, sympathy, affection; of disappointment, discouragement, lonesomeness, melancholy, depression." Two decades before the ape language studies began, Yerkes clearly recognized that chimpanzees live in an emotional and perceptual and psychological universe similar to our own. When it came to their importance to research, few people understood better the unique value of chimpanzees. But when it came to their legal or ethical status inside the cage, chimpanzees were for Yerkes, as it appears they have been for the biomedical research industry in general, fundamentally indistinguishable from rodents. They were all experimental subjects, all confined to provide, as Yerkes said of his chimpanzees, "material for the investigator."

When journalist Eugene Linden visited the Institute for Primate Studies in April 1982, just after the contract for sale had been signed with LEMSIP and just before the apes had actually been shipped to that laboratory, he met chimpanzees who had not been spoken to by humans for many months. He approached the cage of one big male, Ally. Linden was accompanied by an employee of the institute, who used sign language to ask the chimpanzee, "Who is he?" Ally had seen Linden before, but he gave no answer. The employee then asked the chimp, "What do you want?" Ally signed, "Key."

Linden went into another building to visit another male chimpanzee, Herbert Terrace's former subject, Nim. As the two humans approached, Nim was sitting hunched over in a corner of his cage. Asked what he wanted, Nim signed "food" and then "drink" and then "key."

The next day Linden returned to the institute to visit some of the other chimps who were no longer being spoken to by people. A female named Jezzabel, during an extended exchange with a human signer, made the signs for "eat" and "drink" and "berry" and "hat" and "key." Another chimpanzee in the same cage — his name was Mac-Arthur — entered the conversation and signed "eat" and "key."

Why were these caged apes apparently so preoccupied with the sign for "key"?

When Dr. James Mahoney, the LEMSIP veterinarian, visited the institute at about this time to examine the apes his laboratory had just acquired, he was amazed at their behavior. Mahoney, born and raised in Ireland, told me the following story with a gentle Irish lilt: "The first time I met the chimp Booee, he was in one of the large indoor cages. It was very large, and there were several chimpanzees, and they had huge tractor-trailer tires to sit on and manipulate. They had a young man, who I guess was a student, feeding the chimps . . . I had a camera on my neck, and I was leaning up against the wall, maybe four or five feet between my wall and the wire of the cage. I'm leaning up against the wall, watching, and finally the young guy gives all the food, and then he leaves. I'm left on my own. And Booee is sitting on this bloody great tractor tire, upright, and he starts making signs to me. And he's pointing about me. I look down, and I thought . . . first of all that he was asking for more food, so I said to him, in [spoken] English, 'I don't have any more.' And he kept on and on, making those signs, and getting quite agitated. So finally I looked down, and I realized I had a camera around my neck. So I said to him, 'Is this what you want?' And he just lost his temper! He jumped off the tire. This huge tire. He just picked it up and threw it! Well, I didn't know. He kept on and on [making signs], and I looked down again, and I realized I've got cigarettes sticking out [of my pocket]. And I said, 'Is this what you want?' And he just became like a lamb! Shaking his head. I took out a cigarette, gave it to him, and I lit it for him, and he puffed it, and he gave it to me, and I puffed it. We went back and forth, sharing the cigarette. And at the end of it, I went in and said to Lemmon, I said, 'You know, I just had the most amazing experience,' and I described it all. He said, 'Well, the only thing that was amazing about it was that he shared his cigarette, because he's one of the meanest buggers we have.' And he did, he shared it with me. But he got so angry, it was amazing. He truly lost his temper. I couldn't understand what he was saying."

It must have seemed peculiar, even mildly paradoxical, to share a cigarette with a being you will soon inject with harmful viruses. In fact, Dr. Mahoney remains quite aware of the ethical dilemma of chimpanzee research: when creatures who share 98 percent of their genetic code with humans are used in experiments that ethically cannot be performed on 100 percent humans. He describes himself as deeply conflicted over his role as a veterinarian in a chimpanzee research laboratory, professionally ensuring the health of sentient beings so that their health can be experimentally challenged; but he has decided that the research advantages to humanity outweigh the health disadvantages to chimps. In any case, not long after Jim Mahoney's brief examination of that colony, a specially equipped tractor-trailer rig pulled up at the gates of the Institute for Primate Studies and took on the first of several live cargo loads, well over two dozen chimpanzees, destined for their new home two thousand miles to the east, the Laboratory for Experimental Medicine and Surgery in Primates: LEMSIP.

The transfer might have taken place smoothly had not CBS-Television briefly featured it as a newsworthy event. That short piece led to further reports — in the *New York Times*, the *Washington Post*, the *Village Voice*. Thus an animal-loving public was alerted to the fact that language-using apes were going to a research laboratory. Concerned individuals and animal-welfare groups began writing letters, sending telegrams, making phone calls, standing in picket lines. Professor Herbert Terrace of Columbia University lent his authority to the protest. Both Dr. Moor-Jankowski and Dr. Mahoney of LEMSIP have insisted to me that Terrace was fully aware of Nim's pending sale to the laboratory months before it was completed and publicized, but the psychology professor has insisted that the news shattered his peaceful sleep one night in May 1982, when a television correspondent delivered it by telephone. Terrace soon placed himself in front of several television cameras, protesting the morally outrageous treatment of his famous chimpanzee, and threatened litigation against various responsible parties. The full brouhaha ultimately led LEMSIP and the Institute for Primate Studies to reverse their transaction for the two best-known chimpanzees, Nim and Ally, who accordingly were taken from cages in New York and returned to cages in Oklahoma.

Nim ultimately was retired to a spacious cage at the Black Beauty horse ranch in Texas, owned by the animal-welfare advocate Cleveland Amory. Ally was less fortunate. He had been one of the most successful of the signing chimps at the institute; as a juvenile, Ally was a "scholarly-looking, freckle-faced chimp" with a winning personality and the strange habit of making the sign of the cross (before coming to Oklahoma at the age of four, he may have been raised in a religious household). Now, having been rescued from the perceived terrors of LEMSIP in New York, Ally was taken from the Oklahoma institute to join seventy other chimpanzees and five hundred monkeys at the White Sands Research Center in Alamogordo, New Mexico, a private laboratory specializing, as its advertising has explained, in the "development of new drugs, insecticides, cosmetics, medical devices, etc."

At least it *appears* that Ally was sent to White Sands. No one seems to know for certain. No one at White Sands acknowledges the existence of a signing ape; and the two male chimpanzees who arrived at White Sands from the Institute for Primate Studies on November 19, 1982, were shipped without names. They have since been named Harry and Midge.

I think I understand why Dr. Lemmon chose to sell the Oklahoma chimpanzees to LEMSIP. The laboratory has always maintained an open-door policy. There is little sense of secrecy at LEMSIP, and the director, Dr. Jan Moor-Jankowski, resists terminal research on chimps. He has avoided some of the more intrusive experimentation that others have failed to avoid.

Moor-Jankowski at one point in his career pursued research on cross-species organ transplants, or xenografting. Xenografting is an interesting and potentially valuable medical tool, since human-to-human organ transplants are limited by an imbalance of supply and demand — that is to say, more people want new organs than are willing to give them. Xenografting remains experimental at this point, largely because the human immune system normally rejects tissue from other species. In 1964 Dr. James Hardy of the University of Mississippi's Medical Center actually grafted a chimpanzee heart into the body of a sixty-four-year-old man; the heart beat for about ninety minutes before its new owner died. But the discovery in 1972 of cyclosporin-A, which neutralizes the usual rejection of tissue inserted from one human into another, foreshadowed the successful transplant of organs between species: from animal to human. As the nonhuman species closest to humans, chimpanzees are obvious candidates to supply organs for future xenografting needs. Indeed, Dr. Keith Reemtsma at New York's Columbia–Presbyterian Medical Center recently transplanted a chimpanzee kidney into the body of a human who had been dying of kidney failure, prolonging the person's life by nine months. At the Milwaukee County Medical Complex in Wauwatosa, Wisconsin, Robert McManus has been studying the transfer of rhesus monkey hearts into baboons. By September of 1988, he had done ten such transplants, and one of the hearts continued to beat for fifty-eight days. Dr. McManus considers that his ultimate goal is to learn how to transfer hearts from living chimpanzees into dying people. "It would be unethical today to do it," he has declared. "We don't know enough about it." But someday he believes the technique will be perfected to the point where it would then become ethical: "We are involved in this research so that someday we can solve the donor crisis and we don't have to watch people die unnecessarily."

Of course, it might be possible to solve the donor crisis by asking for more human donors, but in case not enough humans sign up, their nearest biological relatives could be drafted. Thus, the U.S. National Institutes of Health (NIH) recently agreed to contribute $3.36 million toward research on implanting chimpanzee hearts in human bodies at the Columbia–Presbyterian Medical Center in New York. Dr. Moor-Jankowski, whose chimpanzees at LEMSIP are only a bus ride away from the center, believes people could breed chimps, quite like farm animals, specifically to supply hearts and livers and other spare parts for the benefit of humanity. But, for ethical reasons, he has decided not to become involved in xenografting and its attendant reliance on chimps.*

Those language-using chimpanzees transferred from the Institute

---

* I would hope that no chimps in U.S. laboratories have contributed to head transplantation research. Work in this field of endeavor began as early as 1887, when a French scientist tried attaching the heads of guillotined prisoners to the bodies of very big dogs; in 1912, Russian scientists demonstrated that it was possible to keep severed dogs' heads alive for several hours with the help of an artificial circulation machine. More recently, Robert White of Case Western Reserve University School of Medicine in Cleveland, Ohio, experimentally severed the heads of a half-dozen monkeys and kept the heads alive by piping in blood from whole monkeys. "The monkey [head] became awake and acted like a monkey," Dr. White recalled for a reporter from the *Washington Post*. "They followed you around the room [with their eyes]. They'd try to bite your finger off. There was every indication that the brain was functioning as it was when it was on its own body."

for Primate Studies to LEMSIP in the spring and early summer of 1982 were drafted to serve humanity in a different way. They became subjects in the batch testing of a hepatitis B vaccine. Since chimpanzees are susceptible to hepatitis B in the sense that they develop antibodies but unlike humans never come down with any overt symptoms, LEMSIP's chimpanzees were not even made very uncomfortable by the research. At most, they had to endure the occasional injection and blood sampling. Later, a few of those same apes became subjects in AIDS research and vaccine testing; once again, although their blood recorded the presence of the AIDS-causing virus, their bodies never developed the full-blown disease.

Of course, HIV-infected chimpanzees at LEMSIP and elsewhere are often quarantined from one another and will probably be permanently quarantined from close contact with people. They will not be allowed to reproduce. And once they have finished contributing to medical research and still have a significant portion of their fifty-five-year life span to experience, what will happen to them? Dr. Moor-Jankowski and Dr. Mahoney have considered purchasing an island near Puerto Rico as a refuge for any chimpanzees retired from LEMSIP, but for the present the language chimpanzees remain at the laboratory, a decade now since their purchase from the Oklahoma institute, and they are still doing their level best to help solve various human medical crises. They see people coming and going, people dressed now in sterile paper — puffy paper gowns and booties and masks and hats — people anxious about touching or even lingering too closely near creatures infected with the virus that causes AIDS. The chimps have not seen daylight or the outdoors for the last ten years, I believe, since the hangar-style buildings containing their cages have no windows or outdoor runs. Nor, I think, have any of these apes touched the floor for ten years — since, for what Dr. Moor-Jankowski fervently argues are compelling sanitary reasons, their big cages are hung from the ceiling, suspended a few feet above the floor.

11 ◆ I Acknowledge Mine

PROSPERO:
These three have robbed me, and this demi-devil
(For he's a bastard one) had plotted with them
To take my life. Two of these fellows you
Must know and own; this thing of darkness I
Acknowledge mine.

To LEARN MORE about "head impact tolerance," Doctors Ayub Ommaya, Paul Corrao, and Frank Letcher of the U.S. National Institutes
of Health (NIH) immobilized eleven chimpanzees by taping and plas-
tering casts around their limbs and affixing the casts to racks constructed from steel pipe. Then the scientists banged ten of the unanesthetized apes in the head with a compressed-air-driven piston capable
of delivering "impact forces of up to 4,000 lbs . . . with satisfactory
reliability." Two of the unanesthetized chimps were killed outright.
Five were rendered unconscious for various periods after one or more
blows of the piston. Two others were "stunned." And, at intervals
between two and a half hours and three days after their injuries, all the
experimental subjects were "sacrificed" for further examination.

Chimpanzees were chosen for this study because of their large
brains. The researchers had already conducted similar studies on monkeys, but felt they now needed a species with brain intermediate in
size between that of rhesus macaques and humans.

When this 1970s NIH study inspired a 1990s script for the American
television series *Quantum Leap* — in which a human inhabiting the
body of a chimpanzee discovers his head ready to be smashed by a
piston for research purposes — some research-industry spokespeople
leapt into action, eager to deny any image that so powerfully compared
the suffering of humans to the suffering of chimps. Dr. Kenneth
Gould, chief of reproductive biology at the Yerkes Regional Primate

Center (and one of the two bona fide research professionals who testified on Bobby Berosini's behalf during his Las Vegas lawsuit against
PETA), charged, though he had not actually seen the script, that it
was "evident" that animal-rights groups were "deliberately setting
up" the story. Another researcher who had not seen the script, James
Parker, declared to the show's producer that the story was "a piece
of propaganda for a small and fanatical group of people who are opposed to animal research." Frankie Trull, executive director of the National Association for Biomedical Research, also complained to the producer. As Trull wrote elsewhere, having a person enter a chimpanzee's
body in a piece of fiction on television might "reinforce the idea that
at least some animals are morally equal to humans."

Laboratory research scientists are heroes, both in the eyes of the
general public and in reality, I think. But, like Prospero, they are
heroes expected to perform perfectly on an imperfect island, to act
insightfully in an eternally expanding universe. Some biomedical research scientists acknowledge the ethical complexity of using highly
sentient and emotional beings as human substitutes in laboratories.
But other representatives of that community seem to deny that using
chimpanzees as human substitutes in laboratories raises any compelling ethical issue whatsoever.

1

Shakespeare's *Tempest* is about revolutions and reversals. Prospero
was wrongfully separated from his dukedom; during the process of the
play he reverses that early revolution. That is the major plot. Of
course, it can be said that Prospero, in turn, displaced Caliban from his
rightful rule of the island. In a minor, comical subplot Caliban allies
himself with two lower-class characters, a jester and a butler, riffraff
who have stumbled out of the shipwreck. The three of them, drunk
and bumbling, foment their own revolt against Prospero's rule of the
island. By act 5 that revolt has collapsed, and Prospero introduces to a
gathered assemblage of aristocrats from the shipwreck the three chas-
tened, abecedarian revolutionaries. Two are from the shipwrecked
party, he notes. The third, "this thing of darkness," as Prospero calls
Caliban, "I acknowledge mine."

In referring to Caliban as "this thing of darkness," rather than, say, "this dark thing," Prospero is describing Caliban not so much by complexion as by identity. Caliban, regularly identified with images of animals and earth, is also (according to Prospero) the son of a devil, and if Prospero calls his slave on occasion a "thing of darkness," it may be that our protagonist recalls with those words the Prince of Darkness. To a modern sensibility, "this thing of darkness" can also evoke the idea, best expressed by psychoanalytical theorist Carl Jung, that people harbor a hidden aspect to their personalities, a "shadow" side. And so I like to imagine that, in "acknowledging" Caliban, this thing of darkness, in the final act of the play, Prospero is also expressing a final gesture of healthy insight, in some sense embracing the dark side of his own personality.

Certainly, by stating the idea so grandly — "I acknowledge mine" — Prospero moves beyond, for example, "consider" or "recognize" or even "admit." With "I acknowledge mine" he engages the more formal language of confession and perhaps of reconciliation and resolution. Prospero verbally embraces Caliban; we might even imagine a brief gesture on stage, perhaps hand touching shoulder.

If act 5 provides a bright and satisfying resolution to the play's major plot — Prospero has regained his rightful position as the Duke of Milan — it also implies a deeper, echoing resolution to some of the moral and psychological issues suggested by the subplot with Caliban. If *The Tempest* dramatizes revolution and reversal, in other words, it also galvanizes the natural tension between acknowledgment and denial. Prospero declares before everyone that Caliban is his own slave, yes, but he also acknowledges more deeply what he had so fervently denied during the first four acts of the play: a primordial feeling of kinship with Caliban and some responsibility for Caliban's misery. "This thing of darkness I acknowledge mine."

We share a close kinship with chimpanzees, and we are at least partly responsible for what happens to them. We can acknowledge or we can deny that kinship and that responsibility. This chapter will describe a tension between acknowledgment and denial, a conflict between forces that would save and forces that would consume chimpanzees, a battle between scientists who would study chimpanzees in order to understand them and scientists who would use chimps to understand us and to solve our problems. To some degree, this chapter will examine a historical divergence in attitude and vision among scientists.

The split between scientists who study chimpanzees and scientists who use them can be fundamental, extending beyond intellectual debate into the realm of assumption, ultimately entering and informing the very structure and texture of language itself. The 1970s NIH head-smashing research studied a living object, an abstract "animal." Field scientists would agree with biomedical research scientists that chimpanzees are "animals" — but field scientists would put people in that category, too. Biomedical research scientists, in my experience, rely on the word "animal" and the language of animal husbandry far more frequently than anyone else who works with great apes, and what they appear to mean by the word is something different from what field scientists mean. For laboratory scientists "animal" seems to mean not human. Then it becomes possible to regard all "animals" as ethically equal: a cat is a mouse is a rat is a chimpanzee. That idea is common among those of us outside the biomedical research community, of course, and the fact that all "animals" are bought and sold and owned, restrained with chains and ropes, imprisoned in cages, treated by veterinarians, and experimented upon for scientific purposes, simply solidifies the presumption.

But if a laboratory rat in a laboratory cage one day began looking her scientist in the eye. If the rat developed an interest in smoking cigarettes, then in sharing cigarettes occasionally with the scientist on the other side of the cage door. If the rat suddenly could laugh, truly and unmistakably laugh, when tickled, even laugh on occasion at funny or provocative events outside her cage. If the rat learned to communicate with sign language and seemed to understand a good deal of spoken language. If the rat picked up her infants and stared devotedly into their eyes, tickled their feet, even when necessary defended their welfare with her life. If the rat made funny faces at herself in a mirror, preened herself in the mirror. If the rat threw tantrums. If the rat seemed emotional in intuitively obvious ways to a person. If the rat had hands. If the rat sometimes stood upright, like a person. If the rat shared with people the honored shape! Would the scientist then decide that this rat was not a rat? Would the scientist consider opening the cage? Would the scientist reexamine the research being done and the necessity for doing it? I believe so. Yet laboratory chimpanzees, who do exhibit all of the above qualities and behaviors, are for us in some fundamental ways still rats in cages.

Perhaps our society will decide that human welfare "necessitates" that we experiment on those "animals." We may deny that chimpanzees deserve any special position within the hierarchy of laboratory subjects. But if so, we ought at least to acknowledge what we are doing to them, in the name of "science" and "progress" and "health" and "need."

2

Well over two dozen laboratories in the world use approximately three thousand chimpanzees to study human diseases and problems.* Some of those uses are more critical to human welfare than others, obviously, but while all those chimps have been sitting inside laboratory cages and helping solve human problems, human expansion in Africa has turned their species from a common to an endangered one.

Most biomedical scientists now acknowledge that chimpanzees are endangered in the wild; but some members of the biomedical research community would deny that using chimpanzees in laboratories has ever contributed to the conservation problem in Africa. The biomedical research industry has acquired its usual expertise on wild chimpanzees at a luxurious remove, however. Until the mid-1970s, when wild-born chimpanzees stopped coming to North America at all because of the CITES treaty and the U.S. Endangered Species Act, chimpanzees often arrived at American laboratories in a box. What part of Africa they came from, how they were acquired, how they were placed in the box, how many died in other boxes that didn't arrive — no one knew, and few asked.

People curious about such matters might think to address their questions to the middleman, the live-animal importer in New York or Miami or some other port of entry. Perhaps the biggest of the old-time live-animal importers, Henry Trefflich, brought into the United States

---

* Some estimates of the total number of animals in U.S. laboratories run as high as 100 million. A more standard but probably inappropriately low estimate cites around 20 million. Of those 20 million, the vast majority are rodents; perhaps 60,000 of the total, about 0.3 percent, are primates — monkeys and apes. Estimates of the number of chimpanzees in U.S. labs can run as low as 1,200. That number is certainly far below the actual figure; I suggest the number 1,800 in the United States plus another 500 in European and Japanese labs, some 500 in African labs, and roughly 200 in East European and Asian (non-Japanese) labs. My total estimate for world labs, incidentally — 3,000 chimpanzees — is more than most African countries have in the wild.

between 1928 and the 1960s a million and a quarter monkeys (mostly rhesus), nearly two hundred gorillas, some two hundred fifty orangutans, and four thousand chimpanzees. Yet in his 1967 autobiography, *Jungle for Sale*, Trefflich never explained how those monkeys and apes were caught — even though the dealer himself had occasionally visited Africa, not too long after the days when, as he put it fondly, "the lion was still a major African problem." In describing how two gorillas were taken, to be awarded as joke prizes in a Green Stamps contest in New York, the dealer did mention that those "rarest of animals" were "captured in West Africa by a group of native trappers that my African headquarters has long done business with," certainly implying that they were trapped. But gorillas are not found in what is usually called West Africa, and they have never inhabited any part of the continent within a thousand miles of the Trefflich African collection headquarters in Freetown, Sierra Leone.

Robert Yerkes deserves much credit for wondering out loud, at one point in his career, how chimps were acquired in Africa. Perhaps he half believed one of his suppliers, J. L. Buck, the man who wrote in 1927 of capturing chimps with the help of a hundred local people, some very large nets, a sponge, and a bottle of chloroform. But that story wouldn't pass for decent fiction today, and it strayed far enough from the known reality of Africa then to find publication in a magazine called *Asia*.

The live-animal collector Phil Carroll had another angle on the subject. Carroll used to express anguish over the cruel irony that while gorillas were brutally slaughtered by Central Africans, he still had trouble obtaining export permits in order to save baby gorillas by sending them to North American zoos. This argument contains a pip of truth, and people have retold it to justify importing gorillas and chimpanzees. Africans eat gorillas and chimpanzees, it is argued, and the babies we buy are merely a by-product of that terrible appetite. Indeed, the one hunter I met in Africa who was willing to talk about killing chimps indicated that he would sell babies when he could. And so it has sometimes been suggested that importing baby chimps into the United States and elsewhere is equivalent to saving them. But the fact is that buying even one baby chimp in Africa creates a small market and encourages the hunter to go out, shoot another mother, and acquire another baby. When a real market appears in Africa, based for example on steady laboratory demand from the United States and

financed with American dollars, the normal backwoods subsistence
hunting quickly becomes a secondary enterprise.* Acquiring more and
more babies becomes the primary goal, and adults, typically breeding-
age females, who get in the way are blasted out of the way. In Sierra
Leone, moreover — export point for Henry Trefflich's four thousand
chimps and an additional thousand to fifteen hundred chimps later
sent out by Franz Sitter, plus another seven hundred fifty exported by
Sitter's occasional competitor, Suleiman Mansaray — the local people
generally don't eat these apes at all.

Everyone acknowledges that habitat loss and subsistence hunting
are the two major causes of the sudden decline of wild chimpanzees.
But there surely has been a third cause: the live-animal trade. During
this century three people alone, Trefflich, Sitter, and Mansaray, have
exported approximately six thousand live chimpanzees from a single
point in West Africa, primarily into the American market. A significant portion of the chimps sent to America went into U.S. laboratories. If the trade required only a few losses beyond those numbers
among the African chimpanzee population, then its conservation impact might be thought comparatively minor.† But if, as field scientists
believe and have been able to document reasonably well, the trade has
left as many as ten chimpanzees dead for every one successfully

* A slight variation on this story will describe "surplus" or "urban" chimps made that
way by logging or slash-and-burn farming; the laboratory "saves" the young chimps by
purchasing them at prices low enough to "discourage" any deliberate traffic in the apes.
It is true that paying low prices allows the laboratory supplier to save money and
therefore make a better profit, but even $50 — the price I have sometimes heard —
represents anywhere from a month's to a year's earning power for the rural African
hunter. A market has been created.

† That these six thousand were taken over a period of several decades would appear to
support even further the attractive image of a sustained "culling" from a "renewable
natural resource." Even in the best of circumstances, however, wild chimpanzees
reproduce very slowly. Females mature and begin reproducing at around twelve years of
age; they normally produce single infants, not twins; and they don't wean their
offspring for five to six years. The average female can be expected to produce not more
than five live births in her lifetime, perhaps only two of those maturing into full
adulthood, so that six thousand infants taken even from a much larger population over
several decades would have significant impact. This trade undoubtedly concentrates
its effects on the most important members of a breeding population, fertile females and
healthy infants, so that the actual numbers taken only begin to suggest the long-term
damage. The fact that West African chimpanzees are already fragmented into geographic, and hence genetic, islands means that even comparatively large (but isolated)
populations could be headed for extinction once their sex ratios have been skewed
because of the "collecting." A computer simulation of the likely progression is provided
by Oldfield, Folse, and German (1992).

brought alive and well into an American cage, then its impact in places may have been severe indeed.* And the American biomedical research industry might actually wish to acknowledge some role in the decline of wild chimpanzees in Africa.

There has been little urge to acknowledge any such thing. "The allegations are absolutely untrue," is how Dr. George Galasso, head of the NIH AIDS Animal Model Committee, once angrily denied the concept. "Making them endangered would endanger our research."

This intellectual debate turned into a legal one once the United States signed the Convention on International Trade in Endangered Species (CITES) in 1975 and moved to enforce that treaty with the U.S. Endangered Species Act. As I mentioned in an earlier chapter, the CITES international treaty provides its highest category of protection (Appendix 1) to a number of primate species, including all the great apes. According to CITES, chimpanzees cannot be exported from Africa unless a scientific authority in the country of origin certifies that the apes were captured legally and that their export will not be detrimental to the survival of the species, and they cannot be imported unless the scientific authority in the country of destination certifies that the imported apes will not be used for "primarily commercial purposes" or in a manner that further threatens the survival of the species.

The treaty, designed to protect endangered species from the destructive impact of international trade, has a number of weaknesses. For one thing, the language is open to interpretation. What does "primarily commercial purposes" mean? When a large commercial enterprise

---

* The live-animal trade is a brutal business in general. The collector Jean-Yves Domalain speculated that he was killing 80 percent of the animals he hoped to bring back alive. During the middle decades of this century, some seven hundred chimpanzees were exported from the Pasteur Institute research station in Guinea to Europe. The ratio of deaths to successful exports then was estimated at approximately five to one; and, at least during one period, some one-third of the exports died before reaching their destinations. Barcelona zoologist Jorge Sabater Pi observed members of the Fang tribe in Equatorial Guinea use snares, dogs, firearms, and poisoned arrows to acquire young chimps for the live-animal trade; Sabater Pi estimated a total loss of some two hundred chimpanzees for the procurement of sixty-six young apes who were still alive after a week in captivity, a ratio of loss that would certainly expand markedly after that first week, since wild chimpanzee babies are extremely dependent, physically and psychologically, on their mothers. Teleki's 1979 survey in Sierra Leone confirmed high ratios of loss during actual capture; he noted that those high ratios should be multiplied by additional ratios of loss during transport to the point of holding and then export. What we know of the capture of gorillas suggests similar devastating losses.

that manufactures pharmaceuticals for profit uses chimpanzees for vaccine testing, for instance, does that use fall under the rubric of "research" or "commerce"? But by far the most serious problems emerge because power resides in national, not international, law. The CITES management authorities cannot enforce this international treaty; they must depend on member nations to do so.

In the case of chimpanzees, CITES enforcement in the United States is critical, since this country has long been the world's greatest consumer of these apes. Yet the United States chose from the start to enforce CITES in a way that was supposed to do two inherently contradictory things: discourage the harmful international trade in chimps but encourage all kinds of "legitimate" domestic access to them. Thus, while the CITES treaty would have given chimpanzees the highest protection as an Appendix 1 species, the U.S. mechanism for enforcing that treaty (the Endangered Species Act) gave chimpanzees only the second-highest level of protection: declaring the species "threatened" rather than "endangered." The law is mildly complicated, but in its simplest reading, an *endangered* status would have prohibited all domestic and international trade and transportation of chimpanzees with some formal exceptions: permits would have been given for trade "for scientific purposes" and "to enhance propagation or survival" of the species. An *endangered* status probably would have shut down chimpanzee shows in circuses and nightclubs, and I expect it would have doomed keeping chimps as pets. Most significant for our story, an *endangered* status might also have narrowed the access of the biomedical research industry because it would have required laboratories purchasing or transporting chimps, domestically or internationally, to obtain permits declaring their purposes to be "scientific" or "to enhance propagation or survival."

The *threatened* status finally given to chimps by the U.S. Endangered Species Act of 1973 allowed zoos, private owners, circuses, carnival and stage acts, and laboratories to continue using and selling and trading and transporting chimps pretty much as they had always done — with the single important exception that federal agencies had to ensure that their actions, or actions they funded, were "not likely to jeopardize the continued existence" of the species.

In the mid-1970s some $9 billion was spent every year for biomedical research in the United States, and more than a third of that consisted of tax money parceled out to various institutions by a single federal bureaucracy, the National Institutes of Health. Chimpanzees were held in several major laboratories in the United States at that time, all of which received or hoped to receive substantial funding from the NIH. Federal funds bought African chimps, in other words. So, as I say, the debate about whether or not acquiring wild-born chimps from Africa was a conservation issue suddenly moved from an intellectual to a legal realm.*

The problem was that no one had bothered to breed laboratory chimpanzees. The American research industry had long treated its chimpanzees as a "valuable renewable resource," to quote one laboratory director. Before CITES and the Endangered Species Act, this resource was simply plucked from the forests and woodlands of Africa rather than bred in captivity. Laboratory managers had no particular reason to imagine they were in the breeding business and, in fact, breeding certainly would have cost far more than continuing to consume baby chimpanzees from Africa. Moreover, many of the chimps already held in U.S. laboratories were experimentally infected with various diseases and nearly all of them were socially and psychologically abnormal enough that they might not be inclined to reproduce even if they had the chance.

Jan Moor-Jankowski of LEMSIP was the last person representing an American laboratory to import chimpanzees from Africa when (with NIH funding) he acquired seventy-two of them from Franz Sitter in 1975. But after October 1976, when the machinery of the Endangered Species Act had been properly oiled, any federally funded laboratory hoping to acquire chimps from Africa needed to deny formally, before the U.S. Fish and Wildlife Service, that getting chimps from Africa might "jeopardize the continued existence" of the species.

Thus, when in 1977 officials of Merck Sharpe and Dohme and the Albany Medical College applied for permits to buy chimps from Sitter,

---

* The statement that federal funds could only be used in a fashion "not likely to jeopardize the continued existence" of the species was, as far as I can tell, the sole significant aspect of the law really protecting African chimps from American market forces. The *threatened* category in U.S. law was, moreover, particularly weakened by a special "exemption" clause stating that the usual "prohibitions" meant to protect even threatened species in the U.S. would not apply to chimpanzees (or bonobos) held in captivity by or before October 1976, or their progeny, or the progeny of any chimps or bonobos legally imported after that date. This stipulation, intended to allow business to continue as usual for research, zoos, and entertainment, diminished even further the law's protection.

the applicants stated that they intended some of those apes to join breeding groups in the United States (this may have been partly true), and Alan Creamer from Merck dutifully explained to Fred Bolwahnn of the Federal Wildlife Permit Office why the capture of chimps in Africa would not adversely affect the species. Bolwahnn wrote down the story for his files: "Dr. Creamer said that capturing of chimps was accomplished . . . generally by locating a group of chimps, surrounding them with a number of people and chasing them. The juveniles would usually tire first and these were captured by hand. Females carrying young get away. Females that are nursing young are released. Occasionally chimps are shot by the natives for food or because they are damaging crops etc. When a female that has a young has been shot, the infant is taken and sold to a dealer . . . This information was obtained from Franz Sitter of Sierra Leone."

When the United States signed CITES and moved to enforce it with a federal law, that law was already weakened with specific exemptions for chimpanzees and bonobos. But for perhaps a decade and a half after the CITES treaty was signed and a federal law created to enforce it, the world's largest biomedical research bureaucracy, the U.S. National Institutes of Health, moved in both official and unofficial ways to challenge even that weakened version of the treaty and its enforcing law.

The challenge began with exaggerations of need. At approximately the same time that the applications for import permits submitted by Merck Sharpe and Dohme and the Albany Medical College failed in 1977, the NIH created an Interagency Primate Steering Committee. This steering committee, instructed to think about ways "to assure both short-term and long-term supplies of nonhuman primates for bioscientific purposes," steered itself into a special task force that asked reputable scientists what their future "needs" for more chimpanzees might be. The task force felt that in some areas of endeavor "the actual utility of the chimpanzee as a model" had not yet been fully appreciated, but by 1978 it had concluded that a total of 735 chimpanzees would be required to meet all research and testing needs in the United States. To maintain that supply over time, the United States would need somehow to replenish the basic stock with 300 to 350 new chimpanzees every year.

Those numbers may have been a deliberate exaggeration. One scientist who served on that task force now recollects, "We had several sessions, and we discussed the need for chimpanzees, and we came to the conclusion that there was a yearly need for . . . little more than 100 chimpanzees." But the members of the task force were directed to destroy their notes and turn over their conclusions to a single individual who solemnly and officially described the need for 300 to 350 new chimpanzees every year. That official projection seemed to buttress NIH's double-edged intent: first, to spend millions of dollars on a major chimpanzee breeding operation ("a chimpanzee production program") in the United States, and second, to take more chimpanzees out of Africa. Each aspect of the plan would reinforce the other — more chimpanzees from Africa should buttress the breeding population, and the breeding project should justify overcoming CITES and the U.S. Endangered Species Act in order to take more chimpanzees from Africa. The task force's report noted that "it is reasonable to expect that a limited number could be imported if they were to be used in the establishment of breeding colonies."

In that same year, 1978, the NIH promulgated its formal plan for chimpanzee breeding, the National Primate Plan, confirming in print its own belief that the chimpanzee was an "irreplaceable model" for certain diseases and projecting a "need" for 180 new chimpanzees per year — about half the number of new chimps per year that had just been projected by the NIH task force, but still a substantial enough need to justify, beginning in 1986, the expenditure of several million dollars in AIDS research money to breed chimpanzees at five different NIH-supported institutions in the United States: the Yerkes Primate Center in Atlanta, New Mexico State University in Alamogordo, the University of Southwestern Louisiana in New Iberia, the University of Texas at Bastrop, and the Arizona Primate Center in Tempe. This five-institution breeding project gathered together some 350 chimpanzees not irreparably damaged or infected by captivity and research, healthy enough that they could still reproduce, and moved to create a younger generation of seminormal chimps, also capable of breeding, by eschewing the usual damages inflicted on very young chimps in laboratories. Producing seminormal chimpanzees would require, among other things, not pulling babies from their mothers and not placing "yearling animals in socially depriving or infectious research."

The five-institution breeding project was indeed a success. Between 1986 and 1992, the project was producing approximately 50 new baby

chimpanzees per year (with about 25 placed into the research group
and 25 kept in the breeding group), thus significantly stabilizing the
U.S. laboratory population of chimpanzees. But by 1991 there were
signs that even 25 chimpanzees added per year to the research group
were too many. The NIH AIDS Animal Model Committee noted in an
internal report that "chimpanzees are readily available" and expressed
concern that "some reviewers [of chimpanzee research proposals]
might be getting too involved in the science and might recommend
disapproval based on disagreements with the science." In 1992 Dr.
Milton April, then director of the NIH AIDS Animal Model Program,
informed me that there was a "real good reserve" of chimps, enough
that the NIH had run out of space for more apes so that the breeding
project was "restricted to maintenance level only."

In sum, a projected "shortage" of chimps for urgent research purposes "requiring" some 300 to 350 new chimps per year in 1978,
turned out by 1992 to be a surplus when 25 new chimps per year were
added to the research population for a few years. And while the NIH
was struggling during those years with the externally publicized problem of "too few chimps," it recognized, internally, an opposite problem: too many chimps.* According to the 1990 report of the NIH
Working Group on Chimpanzees: "Chimpanzees generate a tremendous cost for competitive research dollars. This is primarily due to the
high cost for proper care and housing. There are also immediate
concerns about the direction needed to be taken for immediate upkeep
of chimpanzees after their utility for breeding or research has ceased."
In other words, after the chimps had been infected with all the diseases possible, what was to be done with them?

One apparent solution was to kill them. A 1984 draft of the NIH
breeding plan had called for "euthanizing" surplus chimps. This early
idea provoked enough public controversy, however, that the NIH soon
announced a changed mind. A representative declared that while
"euthanasia may be financially advantageous," it was nonetheless not
"tenable" for public relations reasons — because of "the intense public interest in the fate of these animals." As an NIH official, Dr.
Thomas Wolfle, summarized so vividly to a reporter at the time, "The
euthanasia issue is dead." The head of the NIH AIDS Animal Model
Committee, Dr. George Galasso, further confirmed to a journalist in

* Of course, a shortage and a surplus are not necessarily contradictory. There could be a
shortage of usable chimps and a surplus of used-up chimps.

1988 that "we would never support research that was a terminal experiment — in which a chimpanzee would be injured in some fashion." Euthanasia didn't stay dead for very long, however, and terminal experimentation experienced a miraculous revival. The 1990 internal report of the NIH Working Group on Chimpanzees introduced "euthanasia" and expressed "continued support" for "terminal experimentation," this time in carefully refined terms: euthanasia was recommended for a chimp who is "terminally ill or in serious pain"; terminal experimentation was recommended "when, for scientific reasons, this is the sole means for obtaining the requisite information for a study."*

When the breeding project was first proposed in the late 1970s, the laboratory chimpanzee population in the United States, suddenly cut off from further imports from Africa, was threatened as a result of laboratory conditions and policies. Laboratory chimps were psychologically and socially abnormal and thus not reproducing; many were already infected with various contagious diseases; and the chimps were aging. They were not a self-sustaining population. The multimillion-dollar breeding project successfully reversed that situation. It may have been a sound and reasonable plan.

But while some people had created on paper, in 1978, an alarming shortage of chimpanzees that eventually turned out to be not quite so alarming, other people during the subsequent decade reinforced again and again, for public consumption, the message that a dire shortage still existed, a shortage that seemed to threaten our national capacity to fight a most serious war against a terrible and very frightening

---

* The 1990 report also introduced an alternative option for chimpanzees who had outlived their experimental usefulness: "long-term care" supported by "retirement funds" established during research. The Southwest Foundation for Biomedical Research in San Antonio, Texas, pioneered the creation of retirement funds as a way of assuring lifetime support for laboratory chimps; that laboratory and its former director, Dr. Jorg Eichberg, deserve credit for this humane approach. But the lifetime care of chimpanzees can be very expensive indeed, and the "financial advantage" of euthanasia and terminal experimentation is still potentially huge. Care of a single chimpanzee costs at least $5,000 per year, according to NIH estimates. NIH records also note a "very limited 1–2 research period of utility for the chimpanzee." That very significantly underestimates the true "research period of utility," I believe; even so, since a chimpanzee may live as much as fifty-five years in captivity, public and private laboratories could conceivably become responsible for a quarter of a million dollars per chimpanzee in retirement support alone. An overestimation of chimpanzee "needs" leading to the overbreeding of research chimpanzees could be fiscally disastrous; and one can find plenty of old-fashioned motivation for the continued application of "euthanasia" and "terminal experimentation" to the problem of surplus chimpanzees.

human disease, AIDS. In 1984 chimpanzees were found to be susceptible to the HIV virus; when injected with the virus, chimps produce
the appropriate antibodies, signifying an experience of infection. As
researchers eventually learned, chimps do not come down with the
actual disease, a fact that makes them imperfect for studying AIDS
itself.* They may still be suitable models for testing vaccines, though,
since chimps demonstrate infection by producing antibodies.

Given current developments, I think it is fair to say that chimpanzees are important for AIDS vaccine testing, but not critically so.
There are, first of all, supplementary and alternative animal models.
Some monkey species are susceptible to a related virus and develop a
similar disease, the so-called Simian AIDS. Those monkeys are being
drafted in U.S. laboratories for supplementary or parallel vaccine testing. Very recent research, moreover, seems to demonstrate that at
least one monkey species, the pig-tailed macaque, can also be infected
with the HIV virus, so pig-tailed macaques may find themselves serving as partial alternatives to chimpanzees.

One common argument for using chimps to test candidate AIDS
vaccines refers to the matter of "safety testing" and recalls, as a
shining example, the successful development of a poliomyelitis vaccine. The principle of the polio vaccine was to infect people with a
little polio, just enough to stimulate their production of protective
antibodies. The final vaccines, in other words, were based on material
taken from actual polio viruses that had been killed, or, in the case of a
later vaccine, weakened or attenuated. Safety testing, using rhesus
monkeys as experimental subjects, was required by law and based on
the legitimate fear that, if the "killed" virus was not completely killed
or if the "weakened" virus was not weak enough, the vaccine could
cause rather than prevent the full-blown disease. The polio vaccine
was developed before genetic engineering existed, of course — and an
AIDS vaccine manufactured through recombinant techniques, a vaccine specifically designed to be nonviable, might work like a more
traditional vaccine but would avoid the safety problems associated
with killed or weakened viral material and should not require massive
animal testing for safety purposes.†

* Latency periods for HIV-infected people can be as long as fourteen years. Chimps
infected with the virus since 1984 have not yet developed the clinical symptoms of
AIDS, but it is still possible that they will.

† Polio vaccine research, manufacture, and testing resulted in the deaths of one million

A few researchers are developing AIDS vaccine candidates in the old-fashioned way, proceeding from a whole virus that has been killed or attenuated; but the safety, regulatory, and liability problems of using such a vaccine could be prohibitive. Thus, the leading vaccine candidates currently are based on recombinant work. An NIH representative recently explained to me that animal models are important for testing the "safety and efficacy" of vaccines. The phrase rolls quickly off the tongue. But researchers working with recombinant vaccine candidates believe that the *safety* of engineered vaccines is not really an issue. *Efficacy* is another matter. Testing the *effectiveness* of an AIDS candidate vaccine using a chimpanzee as the animal model may seem both crucial and straightforward. The chimp is shot with the vaccine and then, after the vaccine has sloshed around for a suitable period of time, shot with a measured dose of the virus. Does the vaccine protect the chimp from the virus? The test seems simple enough. But there are several problems with the chimpanzee model, and one of them might be expressed in the following manner. If chimpanzees don't perfectly model humans by acquiring the actual disease, why should we expect that the chimpanzee response to the vaccine will perfectly model the human response? If a vaccine protects a chimpanzee, we still don't know that it will protect a person. If a vaccine does not protect a chimpanzee, we still might imagine that it could protect a person. The response of a chimpanzee will contribute to the background data, but ultimately there is no substitute for testing candidate vaccines on people.

Researchers will learn what they can from what they have. If chimpanzees weren't there, testing would proceed without them. Since chimpanzees are there, testing will proceed with them. In a normal situation researchers would try to learn everything possible from experimenting on nonhumans before proceeding with human trials. But the AIDS pandemic does not present us with a normal situation, and as early as 1987 some scientists began to discuss how they might short-circuit the normal process and move directly to human trials — efficacy studies in which candidate vaccines would be given to large numbers of people known to have a certain clear risk of infection.

to three million rhesus macaques and probably caused a major decline of the species in India. Because the wild-caught source was much cheaper, American laboratories had not bothered to breed rhesus macaques in significant numbers until 1977, when India terminated the trade.

Plenty of people within high-risk populations are eager to volunteer for such tests. Some European researchers appear to have already begun vaccine trials on human populations. One American scientist, Dr. Allan Schultz of the National Association of Infectious Diseases, informed me in 1992 that there was still "a wide range of opinion" in the U.S. research community about testing candidate vaccines on people, but, he said, there "is a strong sentiment that some sort of human trials are needed, appropriate, and ethical." Recently the World Health Organization identified four nations that might provide the most suitable sites for large-scale vaccine efficacy trials on people. Thus, I have been told, the human trials for potential vaccines developed in the United States could begin reasonably soon.

Does human need, even an overwhelmingly obvious need, justify doing anything we wish with whatever species we choose? The issue of whether chimpanzees *ought* to be used for AIDS vaccine testing is a separate issue that must still be addressed by our society at large. But, assuming for the moment that we ought to use apes for AIDS research and vaccine testing, I asked three experts to estimate for me the numbers of chimpanzees currently "needed." One, a highly respected scientist and a laboratory director, explained to me that since there is no danger from the recombinant vaccines, clinical trial sites (for vaccine testing with human subjects) are now being developed all over the world. "This major human trial program will make chimps really not needed. There will be certain things, of course — people who have access to chimps [and] have a vaccine they think is potentially exciting might just use their chimps." As for the number of chimps actually needed, "I'm almost ready to say, 'Zero.' " Another scientist and laboratory director estimated "not more" than forty chimpanzees per year. An NIH representative who is intimately familiar with that federal bureaucracy's allotment plans for research chimpanzees estimated that one hundred to two hundred chimpanzees in the United States would be required for AIDS studies during the next two to three years.* Their numbers vary considerably, in short, but none of these three experts believes that the supply of chimps already sitting in laboratories will fail to meet the demand.

During the mid-1980s researchers may have been slightly more

---

* These would not be fresh or experimentally naive chimps, but rather veterans of considerable experimentation in other projects. For the protection of people who work with them, AIDS is the end of the line in a laboratory chimp's career.

sanguine than they are in the 1990s about the significance of chimpanzees in the war against AIDS. But there was *never* a consensus within the scientific community that too few chimpanzees existed in captivity, or that the species' new importance for research would ever require or justify taking more chimpanzees out of Africa. Some very prominent hepatitis and AIDS researchers — Alfred Prince of the New York Blood Center and Vilab II in Liberia, Jan Moor-Jankowski of LEMSIP, Jorg Eichberg of the Southwest Foundation for Biomedical Research, Huub Schellekens of the TNO Primate Center in Holland, Marc Girard of the Pasteur Institute in France — formally declared in 1988 that plenty of chimpanzees were available for AIDS research. These internationally recognized experts estimated that "conservatively" half the chimpanzees held by research laboratories in the world at that time "could be made available for AIDS research if required." The scientists asserted that, presuming an AIDS vaccine was developed with recombinant techniques, the numbers of chimpanzees required would be "relatively small and well within the numbers available in biomedical research laboratories."

There was never a perfect scientific consensus that chimps were an important model. There was never a scientific consensus that more chimps would be required from Africa for AIDS research. There were many hundreds of chimpanzees in American labs, and hundreds more were available in overseas labs. Furthermore, there were good reasons not to move into the forests and woodlands of Africa for more chimps. Taking more wild chimpanzees could devastate already precarious wild populations in West Africa.* Taking more wild chimpanzees would undermine if not violate outright the CITES treaty and the U.S. Endangered Species Act.

So it remains puzzling why the single best-known AIDS researcher in the United States, Dr. Robert Gallo, should have traveled to Vienna in 1986 and lobbied on behalf of a Viennese pharmaceutical company, Immuno A.G., that had just imported twenty wild-caught chimpanzees from Africa. Immuno's importation was highly controversial at the time. It appeared to many people to challenge the CITES treaty, in

---

* Taking more wild chimpanzees would also violate the policy statement issued in 1982 by the World Health Organization and the European Economic Community: that chimpanzees and other endangered primate species "be considered for biomedical research projects only if they are obtained from existing self-sustaining captive breeding colonies."

spirit and probably in letter. (The CITES Secretariat later confirmed that Immuno's importation did violate the treaty.)* But Gallo appeared to argue publicly, as part of his support for Immuno, that the AIDS crisis justified fetching more chimpanzees from Africa and that anyone who might harbor an alternative opinion on this matter (as he stated succinctly to an Austrian journalist) deserved an unpleasant incarceration: "I will put anyone who prevents us from importing apes into a mental institution or a prison."

Some people were curious about whether Gallo was lobbying for the privately owned Immuno A.G. as an individual who happened to be on vacation in Europe or as a representative of the NIH and therefore, ultimately, of U.S. taxpayers. A little investigation at the time revealed that Robert Gallo had traveled at least once before from the United States to Vienna as a guest of Immuno, receiving reimbursement for travel expenses and an honorarium for speaking. Letters and phone calls to NIH officials in Washington yielded ambiguous comments and finely chiseled denials. NIH director James Wyngaarden deplored Gallo's "exaggerated and intemperate statements." It was true that Gallo's trips to Vienna had been "cleared in advance" by NIH, but he was "not a policy representative." The NIH leadership did not seem interested in further elaboration, but a Freedom of Information request eventually forced into daylight the fact that officers of the U.S. National Institutes of Health and executives of Immuno in Austria had signed on July 23, 1986 (one week before Franz Sitter's twenty chimps arrived on a midnight flight from Freetown), a formal agreement to share recombinant viral material, quite possibly as part of a more extensive plan to conduct AIDS research or to test AIDS vaccines using the Immuno chimps. The single copy of the agreement, moreover, was signed on both sides of the Atlantic by both parties on the same day — a remarkable event considering that the more usual time from signature to signature on such an important document is about six months. Perhaps someone felt an unusual urgency to formalize the NIH-Immuno partnership before those twenty chimpanzees were sent out of Africa. Perhaps the actual re-

---

* Letter of January 24, 1989, from Jacques Berney, deputy secretary-general of the CITES Secretariat: "To conclude, the opinion of the Secretariat is that the chimpanzees should not have been imported into Austria, as the transaction was in violation of CITES and, probably, of Sierra Leone law. However, this opinion does not necessarily reflect that of all the Parties to CITES and certainly not that of Austria." One response (in translation) from Immuno to this statement: "The CITES Secretariat . . . in reality had no competence by CITES rules."

moval of the chimpanzees from Sierra Leone was anticipated in both Austria and the United States.

Gallo returned to the United States and began expressing there his wrenching concerns about a shortage of American laboratory chimpanzees to be enlisted in the fight against AIDS. "We may be further along [in the research] than we know," he told an Associated Press writer late in 1987. "We may not know how well off we are because not enough animal work has been done." He called for extensive breeding of chimps and stated that he had had fewer than a dozen of these apes to use in his research since his 1984 discovery of the AIDS virus. "If we have 50 chimps, we have the materials to test," he added. One month later, according to the *American Medical News,* Gallo's shortage had grown even more acute. The famous scientist declared he needed seventy-five chimps during the next two years and that he would be "lucky to get two or three." Chimps are in "very short supply," he concluded, and "we're up against the animal rights lobby."

Robert Gallo's "shortage" of chimpanzees continues to amaze me. He was believed to be a co-discoverer of the AIDS virus. He was imagined to be Nobel Prize material. He headed a multibillion-dollar U.S. agency's fight against the most terrifying disease of the century. An international registry of laboratory chimpanzees, part of the International Species Inventory System (ISIS), counted three years earlier well over *twelve hundred* chimpanzees held in U.S. biomedical research laboratories. Surely Gallo could have been "lucky" enough to get more than two or three chimpanzees for his most critical research project. Surely not all twelve hundred chimpanzees listed in the ISIS registry were hopelessly distracted by breeding or otherwise previously engaged. The ISIS registry, moreover, underrepresented the American supply of laboratory chimps by a very significant amount, since by that time a small portion of New York State had been scissored out of the U.S. chimpanzee map and set aflutter. The major colony of chimpanzees at LEMSIP was never listed in the registry. In fact, the entire laboratory had been cut out of direct NIH funding well before some NIH people were discovering a terrible chimp shortage. The result was that two hundred to three hundred chimpanzees in New York, ordinarily available for such projects, became remarkably unavailable.*

---

* That there were at least two hundred *uncounted* chimpanzees in New York State at this time makes even more remarkable the Austrian assessment of the world shortage. According to one publication: "It is a fact that in the U.S. there are altogether only approximately one hundred chimpanzees available for animal experiments. Immuno

LEMSIP chimpanzees thus became experimental subjects for French AIDS researchers, who were busy competing with Dr. Robert Gallo and the U.S. research industry for the honor of discovery and the wealth of patent rights.

While Dr. Robert Gallo of the NIH was telling a reporter that "we may not know how well off we are because not enough animal work has been done," Dr. William Gay, director of the Animal Resources Program at NIH, was telling another reporter that he was "not aware of any protocols not being done because we don't have any chimps." While Dr. Robert Gallo was declaring himself "lucky" to get two or three chimps and blaming the "animal rights lobby," Dr. James Wyngaarden, director of the NIH, was deploring the fact that only four hundred to six hundred chimps were available, and Dr. Patricia Fultz of the Yerkes Primate Center was concerned that only seven hundred chimps were available within the U.S. regional primate centers (a category that excludes major chimpanzee holdings at LEMSIP, White Sands, the Arizona Primate Foundation, the Southwest Foundation, Sema, and so on).*

---

alone, however, has more than twenty. This would be sufficient for testing of at most some vaccines, but not for as many as one may want to."

* The precise number of chimps actually residing in U.S. laboratories was a mystery then, and is still a mystery — largely, I believe, because the NIH has made a policy decision to keep the information secret and even to release misinformation on the subject. All this mystery is possible because the principal registry of U.S. laboratory chimps is held in the computerized data base known as ISIS, formerly a government system. According to minutes of an April 11, 1988, meeting of the NIH AIDS Animal Model Committee, some individuals at NIH were concerned about the "Freedom of Information liability of the ISIS system." (By law, government information can be acquired through Freedom of Information requests.) Thus, the NIH leadership at that time encouraged transformation of the ISIS system from a governmental to "an independent, nonprofit organization which will not be subject to FOI [Freedom of Information]." In February 1992 I telephoned Dr. Milton April, director of the NIH AIDS Animal Model Project, and asked him for the current figures on U.S. laboratory chimps. Quoting from his source of "current" figures, he reported some 1,730 chimpanzees altogether in this country, including both zoos and biomedical labs, and about 1,220 in U.S. biomedical laboratories. Incredibly, those figures are nearly identical to published ISIS numbers "current" well before the five-institution breeding project began, in late 1984: 1770 in zoos and labs, with a total of 1,218 in laboratories alone (see Seal and Flesness, 1986). In fact, the 1984 figures did not include LEMSIP chimps or some other chimpanzees in a few independent laboratories — so even in late 1984 there must have been 1,400 to 1,500 or more chimpanzees actually residing in U.S. labs. My own estimate, based on a variety of sources, would be that approximately 1,800 chimpanzees are held in U.S. laboratories as of 1992.

To European reporters, Robert Gallo declared that he had come to Austria "to work with the Austrian firm Immuno AG for the vaccine against AIDS." Referring further to his work with Immuno, Gallo stated that "the chimpanzees are definitely important. In the U.S.A. we do not have enough experimental animals." To an American reporter, the same man pronounced himself "really angry about all the inference and innuendo. They've come to the conclusion that I'm a big backer of Immuno or that I'm all for bringing in chimps from the wild, and I'm not."

Taken out of context, Dr. Gallo's public clamor over the shortage of chimps for AIDS research in the United States and his apparent support, most openly expressed in Vienna, for reopening the trade in wild-caught chimpanzees out of Africa, might seem curious rather than disturbing. But there was a context. Gallo was a famous scientist from the U.S. National Institutes of Health, the world's biggest and most significant consumer of chimpanzees for research. And, gradually, during the period in question, it began to seem as if the NIH leadership had never entirely retired its particular vision of African chimpanzees as a "valuable renewable resource." The protection given to chimpanzees and bonobos by CITES, as implemented by the U.S. Endangered Species Act, had originally been weakened to accommodate biomedical research interests. During the mid-1980s, as a panic about the scope and significance of the AIDS epidemic developed, it began to appear that the NIH leadership would prefer to scrap whatever flimsy protections still remained.

A closed breakfast meeting given for members of Congress, organized by the NIH in February 1988, a few months after Gallo complained of his great shortages, commenced with the pregnant comment that "chimpanzees are not yet an endangered species." A guest speaker at the meeting, Dr. Maurice Hilleman of the Merck Institute of Therapeutics in Pennsylvania, told those present that "there must be maximal effort" to acquire "thousands" more chimpanzees from the wild in Africa. "The U.S. government has an obligation" to do that, Hilleman insisted. It would actually be a charitable wildlife "rescue" operation, because the species is regarded as a "pest" over there. One month later, the minutes of an NIH AIDS Animal Model Committee meeting recorded "frequent suggestions that we comment on the possibility of collaborating with African institutions to do chimpanzee research or to develop sources of these animals." Three months after that, NIH director James Wyngaarden told an Associated Press correspondent that researchers were thwarted by the CITES treaty. "We clearly don't want to get into an international fracas over seeming to subvert rules that apply in this country," the director said — but "we're taking lots of looks at Africa." Not so very long after that, an NIH representative met with Jane Goodall at a dinner in Los Angeles and described the idea of fencing off very large tracts of rain forest in Gabon to protect chimpanzees from all human intrusion except for the "culling" of "surplus" youngsters for biomedical research. Goodall was offered an important position on the committee to oversee this "conservation" effort in Gabon.

After these various events and statements reached a certain level of controversy, however, they were properly denied. Although Dr. Hilleman had spoken to members of Congress at the request of the NIH, he was expressing his views, according to an NIH spokesperson, as "a private citizen." And NIH director Wyngaarden's remarks had been taken out of context. Indeed, the NIH leadership appeared to be deeply hurt, deploring, in the words of one official, the people who had "spun this grand plot that NIH is up to some worldwide sneaky action. It simply is not true."

Denials proceeded from the contradictory to the litigious.

The reader will remember Immuno A.G. as a powerful international pharmaceutical company that polished the silver tools of litigation. The reader will recall the lawsuit in American courts against, among others, Shirley McGreal (who wrote a letter to the editor) and Jan Moor-Jankowski of New York University and LEMSIP (who allowed it to be published). The American background of that lawsuit now becomes relevant. While this seven-year masterpiece of litigious "harassment and coercion" (to recall the language of presiding justice Francis T. Murphy of the Appellate Division of the Supreme Court of New York) was grinding away, the NIH signed contracts with Immuno in Austria and its affiliate in America, Immuno-U.S. During the lawsuit, if we are to believe circumstantial evidence, an official of NIH unofficially provided Immuno's attorneys with information to be used against McGreal and/or Moor-Jankowski.

After Shirley McGreal had dropped out of the lawsuit because her insurance company was unwilling to sustain further legal expense — after every defendant but Dr. Moor-Jankowski had dropped out of the suit, in fact — an organization in the United States known as the National Association for Biomedical Research (NABR) petitioned the court for permission to file its brief in support of Immuno A.G. (Because an officer of the NABR has since denied that this actually happened, one is forced to shuffle back into the court records to find a language of acknowledgment: "This brief is submitted on behalf of the National Association for Biomedical Research . . . in support of plaintiff-appellant Immuno A.G.") Although I have mentioned the attempted entry of the NABR on behalf of Immuno in my earlier chapter on the lawsuit, the nature and role of the NABR deserves sharper focus.

The National Association for Biomedical Research is a lobbying and public relations organization serving the animal research community in the United States. When the NABR stumbled into the *Immuno v. Moor-Jankowski* case, declaring itself "to represent the scientific community in national policy-making concerning the responsible use and humane care and treatment of laboratory animals" and to be "committed to returning civility, morality and, above all, truthfulness in the presentation of and reporting upon the research activities of its membership," it so happened that New York University's School of Medicine counted itself among the NABR membership. Dr. Moor-Jankowski was and is a professor at the NYU School of Medicine, and LEMSIP is owned by that school. I will presume that Immuno had also acquired a membership in the NABR by then, and so my question is very simple: Isn't it curious that the National Association for Biomedical Research should petition to enter a lawsuit to support one of its members against another?

Links between the NABR and the NIH are not, I believe, fully documented. It does seem that Frankie Trull, executive director of NABR, was a personal friend of James Wyngaarden, director of the NIH at the time of the Immuno lawsuit. It does appear that Ms. Trull of the NABR officially met, during the period in question, with "high-level directors and administrators of US government research agencies" specifically to discuss "ways to fight" the "animal rights movement," according to a newspaper in Long Island. (Dr. Frederick Goodwin, now head of the National Institute of Mental Health, commented in 1989 about Trull's special relationship with federal employees: "We're not allowed to lobby. There's a law against it. [But] all federal agencies have linkages to various advocacy groups interested in the business of that agency.") And when in 1990 the U.S. Public Health Service unveiled its plan to spend "millions of dollars" to create an Office of Animal Affairs on the NIH campus, in order to promote its own "fundamental philosophy" on why many more millions of dollars must be spent to use animals in biomedical research, it does appear that the possible involvement of the NABR was discussed. But to speculate that someone from the NIH, a federal agency, directly instructed or encouraged someone at the NABR, a private organization, to enter a U.S. courtroom and attempt to tip the scales of justice in favor of one laboratory against another laboratory, would be to evoke a conspiracy of supermarket tabloid dimensions. I don't intend that. No, I prefer to imagine that this was a case of shared perceptions, interests, beliefs, and orientation — a culture shared by Trull and Wyngaarden, by the NABR and the NIH leadership. Moor-Jankowski, I believe, had committed some unpardonable transgressions. Moor-Jankowski was far too outspoken and unpredictable. Moor-Jankowski was the loose cannon on a tight ship, a heterodox man in an orthodox world. Not only had he publicly questioned the hypothetical need for taking more chimpanzees from Africa to fight AIDS; not only had he staunchly defended the World Health Organization's policies against doing so and the CITES restrictions on doing so; he had actually allowed a serious critic from outside the biomedical research industry to enter a normally closed arena. Yes, I believe Moor-Jankowski's cardinal sin was to associate with Shirley McGreal of the International Primate Protection League and to provide her a small platform for debate.

A larger social context might help to clarify the character and role of Shirley McGreal. People have criticized experiments on animals almost as long as other people have been experimenting on animals — for all practical purposes, starting in the nineteenth century. The contemporary animal-rights movement began in 1975, perhaps, with the publication of *Animal Liberation*, written by an Australian philosopher, Peter Singer. During the 1980s the animal-rights movement acquired significant social and political force, particularly with the growth of an organization called the People for the Ethical Treatment of Animals, or PETA. PETA produced well-documented exposés of some particularly gruesome cases of animal abuse in laboratories, and developed a large membership that funded those activities and a monthly newsletter. After receiving a videotape made by dancer Ottavio Gesmundo in 1989, PETA also documented and publicized its version of Bobby Berosini's orangutan slapstick show in Las Vegas. By the second half of the decade, PETA's annual budget was approaching $5 million, and the organization was part of a larger movement of animal-welfare and animal-rights groups in the United States, whose interests sometimes dovetailed with the traditional conservation groups. Shirley McGreal's International Primate Protection League belongs somewhere within that larger social movement.

That movement, during that period, contained more than its share of passionate proponents. At the extreme, an underground organization calling itself the Animal Liberation Front was then perpetrating laboratory break-ins, smashing equipment, setting fires, "liberating" no doubt very confused little animals. Some researchers were receiving death threats; major research institutions began spending hundreds of thousands of dollars on security measures. Shirley McGreal herself remains a passionate advocate for the primates. But she is not the sort who would smash a microscope or set fire to a laboratory desk. She can be very outspoken, sometimes rash I'm sure, sometimes wrong I expect, but she and her organization have generated so much trouble for so many people for so long precisely because she measures behavior against ethical standards and the law.

With all of these tremendously varied advocacy groups clamoring loudly, threateningly, and in some cases destructively, however, the National Association for Biomedical Research apparently decided at some point to simplify matters by withdrawing all color from the universe. Suddenly, the universe became black versus white. The NABR, which actually represents an entire industry, including wealthy and powerful commercial interests, began by imagining that it represented "science" and "scientists." And the critics — all of the critics, no matter what their angle, no matter what their cause, no matter what their credentials — became (to return to the NABR affidavit in the *Immuno* v. *Moor-Jankowski* case) "a coalition of zealous antivivisectionists who often hide behind innocuous conservationist labels." The NABR wanted to encourage "free and robust debate," it declared then, but suddenly there was no one worthy of debate: "the current movement shares the antivivisectionist abolitionist position," and various members of the movement will do anything they can to achieve this "ultimate goal, frequently by adopting a false moderate stance."

So it was that the NABR declared itself fully in support of Dr. Franz Sitter. Sitter was no false moderate, after all. And so it was that Dr. Frederick King, director of the Yerkes Primate Research Center in Atlanta, could wonder wistfully at the end of 1988, "Where have all the moderates gone?" Most of them had just been defined out of existence. Any few moderates remaining, I would imagine, left in disgust a few months later when Dr. Kenneth Gould of the Yerkes center traveled two thousand miles west to Las Vegas in order to defend the "marvelous" care of orangutans who were still being held in cages a third the minimum legal size and being dressed in clothes every night to dance and engage in slapstick comedy at a casino nightclub.

What remained of a debate was finally transformed from a secular into a spiritual one of Manichean symmetry. The NABR co-sponsored a press conference in which Louis Sullivan, secretary of health and human services, described the animal-welfare and animal-rights crowd as "terrorists" who "will not succeed, because they are on the wrong side of morality. It would be evil to forsake vital animal research when lives hang in the balance." This, of course, was the same sort of language that Bobby Berosini and his main lawyer, Harold Gewerter, were struggling to use over in Las Vegas. Their critics, the PETA people, were wicked "terrorists." In spite of dead birds on Gewerter's doorstep and a mysterious drive-by shooting that missed yet was videotaped, the label never quite stuck in Las Vegas. In the end it didn't matter, as we have seen. Berosini and Gewerter won their suit against PETA — and the National Association for Biomedical Research was impressed enough to invite Harold Gewerter to address a biomedical industry conference it sponsored in November 1990. Mr. Gewerter's subject: "Counterattacking the Animal-Rights Business."

Not long after that conference, Shirley McGreal found herself counterattacked by yet another nasty lawsuit. It seems that three wooden crates stamped "Birds" on the outside were detained at customs in Bangkok, Thailand, having just passed out of Singapore. They were bound for Poland and ultimately, perhaps, the Soviet Union. Thai customs police truncated the journey after they heard crying from inside the crates and passed them through an X-ray. The X-ray revealed not birds but rather mammals inside, six baby orangutans and two gibbons — all without food or water; all sick, emaciated, and dehydrated; three of them dying. The courier, a German animal dealer named Kurt Schafer, was arrested in Singapore and fined $1,200. German wildlife officials became involved, I believe because Schafer was a German citizen; they chose to send McGreal copies of faxes that had been zipping back and forth between Schafer and an apparent associate in the United States. One of the faxed letters was signed with an "M" and included a telephone number. The number has since been disconnected, but at that time it rang a telephone inside the Miami-area home of one Matthew Block, the wealthy and elusive twenty-nine-year-old owner of Worldwide Primates, NIH supplier and importer of roughly a quarter of all the live primates entering the United States each year.

McGreal turned over her information to the U.S. Attorney's office in Miami, which initiated a criminal investigation. The young Mr. Block acknowledged sending the faxes in question but denied that they referred to apes. Then he hired lawyers and sued Shirley McGreal over another issue. Apparently, McGreal had mailed to one of Block's customers, Dr. Peter Gerone, director of the Tulane University Primate Center, several U.S. Department of Agriculture inspection reports on conditions inside Block's facility. In a later letter to Gerone, she referred to the Center for Disease Control's temporary revocation of the importer's federal registration, after Worldwide Primates had been cited for forty-six violations of health standards. Block was not pleased that McGreal had revealed this information, even though it was true. He sued her for intentional, malicious, and unjustifiable interference in a business relationship and asked $5,000 for compensation and another $500,000 for punishment.

Dr. Gerone of the Tulane University Primate Center eventually admitted that he had acquired monkeys from Matthew Block both before and after receiving McGreal's information, and that instead of investigating McGreal's complaints he had simply faxed a copy of one of her letters to Matthew Block. It is hard to see, therefore, how Shirley McGreal had interfered in a business relationship. But Gerone had attended the NABR conference in November 1990 on libel litigation and animal rights, and he had already decided, as he told a reporter for the *Sacramento Bee,* that if an opportunity to "zing" someone like Shirley McGreal came along, he would take it. This lawsuit may have seemed like a prime chance to "zing" Shirley McGreal, and so Peter Gerone seems to have allowed himself to take some time before admitting that McGreal's information had no damaging effect at all.

As the suit entered its discovery stage, each side requesting information and documents from the other, McGreal became concerned because Block and his attorneys were asking for a large number of documents, some of which she believed could compromise the criminal investigation and perhaps endanger some of her sources of information overseas. Actually, during that period, a woman who had helped to expose the wildlife traffickers in Thailand, Claudia Ross of the *Bangkok Post*, was murdered. But McGreal and her attorneys requested some documents from Matthew Block, too. Unfortunately, papers mysteriously disappeared from his Miami warehouse during a burglary so quick and clean it had local police scratching their heads. In the process of not responding to questions and requests from McGreal's attorney, Mr. Block discovered forty-nine times what a refuge the Fifth Amendment to the United States Constitution provides against self-incrimination.

It might seem strange that someone *initiating* a lawsuit should plead forty-nine times a need to avoid self-incrimination, but in any case, on February 20, 1992, Matthew Block was indicted by a federal grand jury on four felony counts related to the smuggling of the six orangutans. Facing a possible twelve years in jail and $700,000 in fines, Block generously dropped his lawsuit against Shirley McGreal. Dr. Peter Gerone went back to directing the Tulane University Primate Center, and Dr. Shirley McGreal returned to her work as chairwoman of the International Primate Protection League, trying to figure out how to pay her litigation insurance bills.

From litigation, the denials diversified into lobbying.

In 1987 (as we saw in an earlier chapter) the Jane Goodall Institute, the Humane Society of the United States, and the World Wildlife Fund formally petitioned U.S. Fish and Wildlife Service to upgrade, in the terminology of the U.S. Endangered Species Act, the status of chimpanzees from "threatened" to "endangered." With the formal petition they submitted a fifty-page report prepared by Geza Teleki and the Committee for Conservation and Care of Chimpanzees that was based on all available field studies in Africa.

Fish and Wildlife solicited responses to the petition between March 23 and July 21 of 1988. During this period the agency received from the general public more than fifty-four thousand letters and postcards supporting the reclassification, as well as forty supporting comments from concerned organizations, experts, and African governments. Seventeen of those forty comments were written by people who had actually studied chimpanzees in the wild. During this same period six people wrote to Fish and Wildlife opposing reclassification.

Now, obviously no one should be faulted for holding a minority view. Minority views often prove to be the most interesting, and in this case I think they are interesting enough. One of the six people represented a circus. Two wrote their protests under the NIH letterhead. And the other three represented organizations — Yerkes and Immuno — that were contractual partners with the NIH, which is, of course, a federal agency entirely funded by U.S. taxpayers. So is the Fish and Wildlife Service. Thus, we find the probably not unusual case of one federal agency moving to influence the actions and policy of another. In fact, the five letters (and more that followed after the deadline) are merely the best bones of a whole corpus of lobbying activity taking place between representatives of the NIH and U.S. Fish and Wildlife during this time.

Of the letters in opposition, that written by James Wyngaarden, then director of NIH, stated the case most reasonably. Chimpanzees are important for research to "improve human health," he wrote. He found "no justification" for the idea that biomedical research was "responsible for an alleged decline" in wild chimpanzee populations, since U.S. laboratories had not been able to import chimps from Africa for the last ten years, and since the NIH had recently begun its own breeding program. He was concerned that an endangered status might "permanently preclude" using any chimps now in captivity or, at the least, would require "volumes of additional paperwork." He claimed strong support for his ideas not only from the biomedical research community at large, but from many major Washingtonian modalities: the Environmental Protection Agency, the National Aeronautics and Space Administration, the National Science Foundation, the Veterans Administration, the Department of Agriculture, the Department of Defense, the Department of Health and Human Services, the Department of Interior, and the Department of State. A formidable segment of the United States government, if we are to be impressed by Wyngaarden's list, was already marching right behind him in order to keep chimpanzees threatened rather than endangered.

Wyngaarden's letter, as I say, was the most reasonable one. If we assume that human needs require experimenting on chimpanzees in laboratories, then at least his concern about more paperwork follows logically. The letter from Frederick King, director of the Yerkes Primate Center, cut less thoughtfully but more directly to the heart of things. Dr. King began with his habitual misspelling of CITES and an important misreading of the same.* Since the United States "already abides by CITIES [sic]," he wrote, and had not imported chimps for ten years, reclassifying chimps as endangered would not further protect them from exportation out of Africa and into the United States. Moreover, "contrary to the rumor campaign conducted by certain animal rights and animal supremacist groups," King could promise and assure that "the National Institutes of Health does not plan to resume importation of wild chimpanzees."

King's important misreading of CITES might be summarized as follows. Yes, the United States signed CITES. Yes, the United States "abides by" that treaty — to the extent that it chooses to do so. The U.S. legal mechanism for abiding by the treaty is the Endangered Species Act. That was the whole point. The U.S. Endangered Species Act, as it so far had been constructed, exempted chimpanzees and bonobos from the full protection that CITES would have otherwise provided.

As further evidence of the goodwill of NIH on this matter of wild chimps in Africa, King quoted Dr. George J. Galasso, chairman of the AIDS Animal Model Committee: "The NIH categorically denies the Jane Goodall allegation that we are planning to get chimpanzees from their natural habitat in Africa to send to Centers around the world. We are signatories to CITIES [sic] and abide by its provision. Our research is limited to chimpanzees already in captivity and their progeny."

By that time, however, few people were worried that the NIH was planning to import wild-caught chimpanzees directly from Africa. People were more concerned that the NIH might move into Africa and begin using wild-caught African chimps through various proxies, or that it would work with contractual partners in Europe and Asia that had acquired chimps from the wild in Africa, thus not violating CITES so much as subverting it. Ultimately these concerns would have remained comparatively minor, at least to an organization of chimpanzee scientists such as the Committee for Conservation and Care of

---

* I mention King's "habitual misspelling" of CITES not out of pettiness, I hope, but because it suggests a cavalier attitude to the treaty. Dr. King appears to be ordinarily very careful about such things, so it is notable that CITES is misspelled three times in this letter and twice again in a 1988 letter to *Science* (see King, 1988).

Chimpanzees (CCCC), had it not been that Immuno's Committee for the Conservation of Chimpanzees (CCC) about then appeared to be moving into Sierra Leone with plans to set up a "captive breeding" operation with dealer Franz Sitter. Some people did not trust Dr. Sitter, and some worried about the possibility that deep inside his captive breeding machinery wild-caught chimps, somewhat protected under law, might conceivably be relabeled as "captive-bred" chimps, which were not protected. Arithmetic did not reassure the skeptics: Sitter had on occasion during the early 1980s claimed to have fifty chimpanzees "in stock," had officially exported at least fifty during the decade, yet still seemed to have enough left over to contemplate a major captive breeding operation.*

George Galasso must have soon realized that he had to clarify the original NIH "policy" statement: "our research is limited to chimpanzees already in captivity and their progeny." As the policy now more precisely articulates, the NIH will not support research on any wild-born chimpanzees pulled out of their dead mothers' arms after 1986. In spite of an apparently adequate supply at home, however, the NIH currently has contracted for research on chimpanzees at a laboratory in Liberia, West Africa.†

---

* As of 1992, Immuno has withdrawn plans to establish a chimpanzee captive breeding colony in Sierra Leone. But Immuno's plans for Sierra Leone were never the full focus of concern. The problem is much broader. Chimpanzee laboratories have now been established in Liberia, Gabon, and Zaire. European biomedical researchers also attempted to establish a chimpanzee laboratory in Uganda; that nation finally chose otherwise. Belgian researchers recently petitioned government officials in Congo for permission to conduct a research project on the wild apes of that nation. In this context the "joint venture" of the White Sands Research Center of Alamogordo, New Mexico, and the Rare Animal Breeding Center near Beijing, China, takes on new significance — the center did not have chimpanzees and would have had to import them. Such operations undermine or have the potential to undermine CITES.

Another reason to discourage research in African chimpanzee laboratories is the possibility of returning experimental infections into wild populations (or spreading human infections into previously uninfected human groups in Africa via infected laboratory chimps). The Immuno lawsuit focused on this concept — Immuno was outraged that McGreal would suggest that research chimps released after hepatitis work might spread hepatitis to wild chimps. I would rather avoid commenting on that controversy here. It is the case, however, that human-induced polio epidemics have swept through wild chimpanzee populations in East Africa, and some wild chimps in Gabon are infected with the human AIDS virus. Luc Montagnier of the Pasteur Institute in Paris once speculated that those wild chimps may have become infected via released chimps that had undergone experimental blood studies in the Gabon laboratory.

† A small number of those chimps could have been taken from the wild after 1986,

3

The battle over the future of chimpanzees in Africa ended with a truce in 1988, when the U.S. Fish and Wildlife Service chose to define chimpanzees as "endangered" in the wild or in captivity in Africa and "threatened" in captivity outside Africa. A second and related conflict began at about this same time largely because Senator John Melcher of Montana, the one member of Congress who had been a veterinarian before becoming a politician, stepped inside a standard laboratory cage for chimpanzees one day and recognized how small it was. It was about as big as a shower stall. Chimpanzees confined in laboratories, Melcher thought, should have "space, exercise and things to make life interesting." This realization ultimately led the senator to insert in a 1985 amendment to the Animal Welfare Act the requirement that federally funded laboratories provide "a physical environment adequate to promote the psychological well-being of primates."

Those dozen or so words, seemingly specific and comprehensible, provoked a five-year battle of interpretation led by the National Association for Biomedical Research. The NABR was concerned partly that redesigning laboratories to provide for the "psychological well-being" of caged primates could turn expensive. Implementation was a problem in part because the category of "primate" includes close to two hundred species of monkeys, apes, and prosimians. About thirty of those species are represented in labs, and their psychological needs could vary not only according to species, but sometimes according to gender, age, and individual personality. Defining requirements for all primates in an overly specific fashion could prove both expensive and wrong.

It was the law of the land, however. The U.S. Department of Agriculture, trying to determine how the new language in the Animal

---

conceivably, but if so probably not enough to matter very much, and since so many were killed and eaten during the recent civil war in Liberia it would be hard to know which ones are still there in any case. This, incidentally, is a well-run lab managed by thoughtful people who behaved heroically during the war, protecting and feeding many refugees. The chimps were infected with hepatitis, not AIDS. The director of the lab tells me that the same hepatitis virus is common among local people, so there was no risk of introducing a new disease to them. Moreover, he said, "Liberians cook their meat to death." The director insists he will never contract for AIDS work on these chimps.

Welfare Act could be implemented, published a set of proposed regulations in March 1987 and solicited opinions on them. That's when it became obvious that many laboratory representatives would deny a need for any significant change at all. Some seemed to believe that their primates were already quite content. Nancy Mello of Harvard Medical School introduced the idea that the psychological well-being of caged primates "exceeds that of primates in the wild since they are not subject to the threat of predators, loss of food supply and loss of living sanctuary." Other experts believed that current conditions were probably satisfactory, because primates are "extraordinarily well adapted to surviving radical environmental change." Still others thought that monkeys and apes might not possess psychological needs in any case. Charles Schuster and Lewis Seiden of the University of Chicago Drug Abuse Research Center imagined that "the reality of psychological similarities between humans and other primates has not been and perhaps cannot be established." Roger Thomas of the University of Georgia reckoned that "there is absolutely no reason to suspect that a nonhuman primate can contemplate its condition, and . . . only with such contemplation could psychological well-being significantly affect the primate."

The latter perspective induces a certain awe. Since the early 1950s, under the leadership of Harry F. Harlow, NIH-funded scientists at the University of Wisconsin had examined what happens to the psychological well-being of monkeys when they are deprived in various ways. Scientists removed newborn monkeys from their mothers and substituted several sorts of surrogates — mechanical surrogate mothers made from wire and cloth, surrogate mothers constructed with ejecting devices, jets of compressed air, spikes, and contraptions to produce violent rocking and extreme changes in surface temperature — to examine psychological reactions to that sort of deprivation. University of Wisconsin scientists studied clinical depression by placing individual monkeys in total isolation at the bottom of steel pits. This technique, according to a 1972 report from university researchers, produced perhaps irreversible "severe behavioral disturbances," such as "elevated self-clasp and huddle and several diminished levels of locomotion, exploration, and social activities of any kind." Later, Wisconsin researchers removed the pits and tried depression-inducing drugs, random and repeated social isolation, and inescapable electric shock to produce in their monkeys what they still thought was clinical depression. And now, from Chicago, we discover that no "reality of psychological similarities" between humans and monkeys has been "established." Now, from Georgia, we find that without self-contemplation, which they lack, primates cannot be significantly affected by "psychological well-being."

In the end, the White House's Office of Management and Budget (OMB), possessing some authority to review and refine proposed federal regulations, reviewed and refined those proposed by the Department of Agriculture for implementing the Animal Welfare Act. With the assistance of lawyer Michael Horowitz (a former OMB staff member hired by the American Council on Education to lobby at the OMB), the OMB, using as one commentator put it "almost every regulatory device at its disposal," essentially scrapped the Department of Agriculture proposals. The National Association for Biomedical Research had objected that the proposals "paint a very detailed picture of laboratory animal care. They tell you point by point — and that's what we object to." This objection was communicated directly to the reviewing group at OMB by other advisers to the executive branch — the Office of Science and Technology Policy for the White House, for example, whose biomedical research desk was by then occupied by Dr. James Wyngaarden, former director of the NIH. Then lawyer Horowitz argued successfully that regulations enforcing the Animal Welfare Act should focus on "performance" and not "engineering" standards, which appears to be another way of stating that as long as laboratories can say they have promoted the psychological well-being of their primates, it matters only a little how they have gone about promoting it.

The law had been enacted by the United States Congress. But the rules to enforce that law were altered so thoroughly that Senator John Melcher, the man who had stepped inside a regulation chimpanzee cage the size of a shower stall and imagined something better, finally declared that he had "never seen anything so misinformed" as what the White House OMB, with a little help from its friends, had done.

4

It was on December 27, 1986, that I watched the videotape that would change the pattern of my life. I had spent a traditional Christmas with my family in Bournemouth, England. We all sat watching the tape, and we were all shattered. Afterward, we couldn't speak for a while. The tape showed scenes from inside a biomedical research laboratory, in which monkeys paced round and round, back and forth, within incredibly small cages stacked one on top of the other, and young chimpanzees, in similar tiny prisons, rocked back and forth or from side to side, far gone in misery and despair. I had, of course, known about the chimpanzees who were locked away in medical research laboratories. But I had deliberately kept away, knowing that to see them would be utterly depressing, thinking that there would be nothing I could do to help them. After seeing the video I knew I had to try.

The videotape had been made a short time earlier by some animal-rights activists calling themselves True Friends, who had managed to break into an anonymous-looking, one-story building situated between a steakhouse and a suburban bank in Rockville, Maryland, U.S.A. The large plate-glass windows were discreetly curtained, and the only hint that about five hundred apes and monkeys lived inside was a very small sign out front embossed with the name of the laboratory: Sema, Inc.

Although Sema, Inc., was funded entirely through federal taxes in the United States ($1.5 million per year, awarded through the National Institutes of Health), the goings-on inside were veiled from the eyes of most American taxpayers as an important national secret. True Friends made an extensive videotape of the conditions inside, removed some animal-care records, and also removed two cages and four young chimpanzees that had been destined for AIDS research. Those chimpanzees were valuable government property. True Friends had apparently broken federal law, and the FBI was called in to investigate. In the meantime, True Friends passed the records and videotape to an organization we have heard about before: the People for the Ethical Treatment of Animals. PETA combined the records with its own investigation to assemble and publicize a report on Sema, simultaneously distributing an edited version of the videotape entitled *Breaking Barriers.*

The report on conditions inside Sema was disturbing enough. The laboratory's own records seemed to indicate an unusually high death rate among its animals: over five years, a total of seventy-eight primates dead. Some of the deaths were simply unfortunate — such as the steaming alive of twenty-six monkeys during a plumbing mishap — but others seemed to indicate faulty veterinary care or husbandry. Four chimpanzees also died during the period in question, and all four deaths might likewise be attributed to inadequate care. Chimpanzee number 56 died in 1981 because, according to the record, a veterinarian was not fully aware of appropriate surgical procedures. Chimpanzee 904 died in February 1983 from apparently untreated "bloat" — untreated because bad weather reduced the number of caretakers coming to work. Chimpanzee A117 suffocated to death in August 1983; when an NIH official formally claimed to be "disturbed" about that death, a representative of the lab declared that the accident occurred because the cage was too small and that the government should "share responsibility" for the event. Chimpanzee A51 choked to death on his own vomit in November 1984; the lab's records blamed that fatality on a "breakdown in normal procedures."

Beyond the high number of accidental deaths occurring within this facility, the records seemed to show that Sema had systematically failed to comply with federal rules governing animal care in laboratories. Inspectors from the U.S. Department of Agriculture (USDA), after five inspections over a two-year period, had reported serious violations of federal laws and regulations in fifteen categories — space requirements, feeding, watering, veterinary care, lighting, ventilation, and so on. Every inspection during that period had charged that the cages were too small for their inhabitants. At various times inspectors also complained of "many" empty drinking receptacles, "grossly contaminated" feeding receptacles, "excreta caked onto the bars" of many cages, "roaches and mouse feces" in all dark corners, and "evidence of vermin . . . everywhere." As if to underscore this government-financed laboratory's disdain for government regulations, several months after PETA issued its investigative report on conditions inside Sema, two veterinarians from the USDA attempted to inspect the laboratory one day and found their car blocked by a security guard's truck; the director of the laboratory threatened them with a lawsuit and demanded that they hand over their cameras and film. A formal complaint was filed by the Department of Agriculture that employees of Sema had "repeatedly threatened, harassed, and otherwise intimidated" government inspectors.

Yet the crucial secret inside this particular laboratory had almost nothing to do with accidental deaths, systematic violation of animal-care regulations, or harassment of government inspectors. The crucial secret was simpler and more basic and far more disturbing. Sema had, over the years, developed the habit or policy of keeping many of its research primates inside containers known as "isolettes."

Isolettes are stainless steel boxes with windows on one side. Designed to filter out airborne viruses, isolettes are hermetically sealed — rather like refrigerators or ovens — and air is forced through filters by powerful fans that are kept running constantly. Sema at that time was using a total of 325 isolettes, of which some 32 were occupied by very young chimpanzees. The laboratory's normal procedure was to acquire chimpanzees taken from their mothers at birth and raised in a nursery for eighteen months at an NIH breeding colony elsewhere in the United States. The eighteen-month-old chimps were sent to Sema in pairs, and they would settle in as pairs for six months, stuffed together inside cages barely large enough to allow serious motion: 24 inches high and less than that on each side. Once research began, these young chimps — now approximately two years old — would be placed individually inside the sealed isolettes (31 inches deep, 26 inches wide, 40 inches high) where they would remain, hardly able to see, quite unable to smell, taste, feel, or even hear another living being, except for the occasional laboratory caretaker, during their entire "research protocol," roughly two and a half to three years.

Officials from Sema defended the isolettes by citing scientific and hygienic concerns beyond the ordinary person's capacity to appreciate. Placing young chimps inside steel boxes was described as an unfortunate but critical sanitary measure for experimental subjects infected, as the Sema chimps were, with respiratory diseases, hepatitis, and the HIV virus. But some of the best experts openly questioned that policy. Dr. Alfred Prince, director of the New York Blood Center's Vilabs in Liberia, discoverer of the hepatitis non-A non-B virus, told a British journalist, "Isolettes are no more necessary for hepatitis or AIDS-infected animals than they would be for similarly infected human patients." Dr. Jan Moor-Jankowski, director of LEMSIP in New York, agreed: "I have visited most, if not all, chimpanzee laboratories in the world, and have never seen isolettes in use like at Sema." To store young chimpanzees individually inside small, windowed refrigerators for up to three years is patently cruel, I believe, and the cruelty was vividly recorded in the videotape *Breaking Barriers*, a copy of which was sent to Jane Goodall on December 23, 1986.

Dr. Goodall was moved to publicize her concerns. In a notarized

statement she declared conditions at Sema to be "totally unacceptable." She charged Sema with failing to meet "even the minimum
standards required by federal and state law" and declared that "the
stark, barren conditions are highly psychologically damaging to the
apes, and inevitably cause profound stress leading to despair." As
might have been expected, Dr. John Landon, president of Sema, Inc.,
denied the existence of serious problems. "We are a superb facility,"
he said to a journalist. "There is no indication that we have any
problems in the treatment of animals. You have to realize that it's an
animal research laboratory." Landon expressed ironic surprise that a
respectable scientist such as Jane Goodall would respond to stolen
documents without first attempting to find out "what the situation is"
firsthand. By late March of 1987, in fact, Goodall had been given
permission to visit Sema.

*Even repeated viewing of the videotape had not prepared me for the
stark reality of that laboratory. I was ushered, by white-coated men
who smiled nervously or glowered, into a nightmare world. The door
closed behind us. Outside, everyday life went on as usual, with the sun
and the trees and the birds. Inside, where no daylight had ever penetrated, it was dim and colorless. I was led along one corridor after
another, and I looked into room after room lined with small, bare
cages, stacked one above the other. I watched as monkeys paced
around their tiny prisons, making bizarre, abnormal movements.*

*Then came a room where very young chimpanzees, one or two years
old, were crammed, two together, into tiny cages that measured (as I
found out later) some twenty-two inches by twenty-two inches at the
base. They were two feet high. These chimp babies peered out from
the semidarkness of their tiny cells as the doors were opened. Not yet
part of any experiment, they had been waiting in their cramped
quarters for four months. They were simply objects, stored in the most
economical way, in the smallest space that would permit the con-
tinuation of life. At least they had each other, but not for long. Once
their quarantine was over they would be separated, I was told, and
placed singly in other small cages, to be infected with hepatitis or
AIDS or some other viral disease. And all the cages would then be
placed in isolettes.*

*What could they see, these infants, when they peered out through
the tiny panel of glass in the door of the isolette? The blank wall*

opposite their prison. What was in the cage to provide occupation, stimulation, comfort? For those who had been separated from their companions — nothing. I watched one isolated prisoner, a juvenile female, as she rocked from side to side, sealed off from the outside world in her metal box. A flashlight was necessary if one wanted to see properly inside the cage. All she could hear was the constant loud sound of the machinery that regulated the flow of air through vents in her isolette.

A "technician" (for so the animal-care staff are named, after training) was told to lift her out. She sat in his arms like a rag doll, listless, apathetic. He did not speak to her. She did not look at him or try to interact with him in any way. Then he returned her to her cage, latched the inner door, and closed her isolette, shutting her away again from the rest of the world.

I am still haunted by the memory of her eyes, and the eyes of the other chimpanzees I saw that day. They were dull and blank, like the eyes of people who have lost all hope, like the eyes of children you see in Africa, refugees, who have lost their parents and their homes. Chimpanzee children are so like human children, in so many ways. They use similar movements to express their feelings. And their emotional needs are the same — both need friendly contact and reassurance and fun and opportunity to engage in wild bouts of play. And they need love.

Dr. James Mahoney, veterinarian at LEMSIP, recognized this need when he began working for Jan Moor-Jankowski. Several years ago he started a "nursery" in that lab for the infant chimpanzees when they are first taken from their mothers. It was not long after my visit to Sema that I went for the first of a number of visits to LEMSIP.

Once I was suitably gowned and masked and capped, with paper booties over my shoes, Jim took me to see his nursery. Five young chimps were there at the time, ranging in age from about nine months to two years. Each one was dressed in children's clothes — "to keep their diapers on, really," said the staff member who was with them. (Someone is always with them throughout the day.) The infants played vigorously around me as I sat there on the soft red carpet, surrounded by toys. I was for the moment more interesting than any toy, and almost immediately they had whisked off my cap and mask. Through a window these infants could look into a kitchen and work area where, most of the time, some human activity was going on. They had been taken from their mothers when they were between nine and eighteen months old, Jim said. He brings them into the nursery in groups, so that they can go through the initial trauma together, which is why some were older than others. And, he explained, he tries to do this during summer vacation so that there will be no shortage of volunteer students to help them over their nightmares. Certainly these boisterous youngsters were not depressed.

I stayed for about forty minutes, then Jim came to fetch me. He took me to a room just across the corridor where there were eight young chimpanzees who had recently graduated from the nursery. This new room was known as "Junior Africa," I learned. Confined in small, bare cages, some alone, some paired, the youngsters could see into the nursery through the window. They could look back into their lost childhood. For the second time in their short lives, security and joy had been abruptly brought to an end through no fault of their own. Junior Africa: the name seems utterly appropriate until one remembers all the infants in Africa who are seized from their mothers by hunters, rescued and cared for in human families, and then, as they get older, banished into small cages or tied to the ends of chains. Only the reasons, of course, are different. Even these very young chimpanzees at LEMSIP may have to go through grueling experimental procedures, such as repeated liver biopsies and the drawing of blood. Jim is always pleading for a four-year childhood before research procedures commence, but the bodies of these youngsters, like those of other experimental chimps, are rented out to researchers and pharmaceutical companies. The chimpanzees, it seems, must earn their keep from as early an age as possible.

During a subsequent visit to LEMSIP, I asked after one of the youngsters I had met in the nursery, little Josh. A real character he had been then, a born group leader. I was led to one of the cages in Junior Africa, where that once-assertive infant, who had been so full of energy and zest for life, now sat huddled in the corner of his barred prison. There was no longer any fun in his eyes. "How can you bear it?" I asked the young woman who was caring for him. Her eyes, above the mask, filled with tears. "I can't," she said. "But if I leave, he'll have even less."

This same fear of depriving the chimpanzees of what little they have is what keeps Jim at LEMSIP. After I had passed through Junior Africa that first day, Jim took me to the windowless rooms to meet ten *adult chimps. No carpets or toys for them, no entertainment. This was the hard, cold world of the adult research chimps at LEMSIP. Five on each side of the central corridor, each in his own small prison, surrounded by bars — bars on all sides, bars above, bars below. Each cage measured five feet by five feet and was seven feet high, which was the legal minimum cage size at that time for storing adult chimpanzees. Each cage was suspended above the ground, so that feces and food remains would fall to the floor below. Each cage contained an old car tire and a chimpanzee. That was all.*

JoJo's cage was the first on the right as we went in. I knelt down, new cap and mask in place, along with overalls and plastic shoe covers and rubber gloves. I looked into his eyes and talked to him. He had been in his cage at least ten years. He had been born in the African forest — shipped to America, probably, by Franz Sitter himself. Could he remember, I wondered? Did he sometimes dream of the great trees with the breeze rustling through the canopy, the birds singing, the comfort of his mother's arms? Very gently JoJo reached one great finger through the steel bars and touched one of the tears that slipped out above my mask, then went on grooming the back of my wrist. So gently. Ignoring the rattling of cages, the clank of steel on steel, the violent swaying of imprisoned bodies beating against the bars, as the other male chimps greeted the veterinarian.

His round over, Jim returned to where I still crouched before JoJo. The tears were falling faster now. "Jane, please don't," Jim said, squatting beside me and putting his arm around me. "Please don't. I have to face this every morning of my life."

I also visited Immuno's two labs in Austria. The first of these, where hepatitis research is conducted and where chimpanzees are used to test batches of vaccine, was built some time ago. There I got no farther than the administration building. I was not allowed into the chimpanzee rooms because I had not had a hepatitis shot. And — how unfortunate! — the closed-circuit TV monitors could not, for some reason, be made to work that day. In the lobby, though, were two demonstration cages, set there so the public could see for itself the magnificent and spacious housing that Immuno was planning for its chimpanzee colony. (This they felt was necessary because of all the criticisms that were being made about the small size of the existing cages, dangerous criticisms leading to expensive lawsuits.) The present cages, I knew, were not very large. The new ones looked identical to those at LEMSIP.

I went into one of those cages and experienced, for the first time, what it is like to be inside a cell that is five feet by five feet by seven feet, with bars all round. I was inside for only a few brief moments, but they have remained with me, keeping me wakeful through many a long night. I have tried to imagine what it would be like to be shut up in one of those prisons for life, without hope of escape.

Because that visit had been planned by the Austrian minister for the environment, and because I had not yet seen any of Immuno's chimpanzees, it was arranged that I should see the brand-new lab, just outside Vienna, where AIDS research was being conducted. I was taken into the infectious disease rooms by Gerald Eder himself — an understandably annoyed Dr. Eder, who had been dragged away from his Friday afternoon at home by an order from the director of the lab (who was probably also annoyed by this request from the ministry). They were to show Jane Goodall their six chimpanzees infected with the AIDS virus.

In order to see these chimps, I had to remove most of my clothes and struggle into a sort of astronaut suit, complete with helmet, gloves, and huge boots. Dr. Eder explained, carefully, how I must attach the nozzle of my breathing tube to air vents each time I moved from room to room. And he gave me an emergency button to press if I got into difficulties, since, he assured me, he would not be able to hear anything I said, nor would I hear him. I admit to a moment of panic as he strapped the helmet over my head. How, with the thick gloves I had pulled on, would I ever be able to attach my nozzle to anything? How easily Dr. Eder could leave me inside!

He preceded me into a little cubicle where a strong chemical shower would totally sterilize his outer self. When a buzzer sounded, I followed. The door to the rational world closed behind me. When the shower clicked off, I went through another door into the dim, unreal world where six chimpanzees would spend the rest of their lives, two cages to a room. Inside the first of these rooms I fumbled desperately with my nozzle, trying to remember how many seconds I had left before my air supply would run out. In the end, Dr. Eder fixed it for me. He began telling me about the chimps in their cages. I could hear him quite well, though his voice was distorted and hollow, as unreal as everything else in there.

The cages were the same size as the one I had been inside. Each had a fiberglass hammock suspended from the overhead bars, shaped to the body of a resting chimpanzee. Two of the prisoners remained in their hammocks, indifferent, seemingly, to the presence of these two bizarre invaders of their solitude. One approached with a big grin on his face. Was it a grin of fear or excitement? I couldn't tell. He pressed his wide-open mouth against the bars, lips drawn back from his teeth. Dr. Eder briefly rubbed his nose. Thirty minutes later we were back in the outside world. Eder and the director could return to their interrupted weekends. I could drive across Vienna to be interviewed on Austrian television. But the six chimpanzees could not leave. Only death would release them from their bleak existence.

The other two labs I have visited, while leaving much to be desired, are definitely more "chimpanzee friendly." TNO is a big laboratory in the Netherlands. I went there with Ignass Spruit of Pro Primates and Dr. Huub Schellekens, a respected Dutch immunologist. The chimpanzees were, with only one exception, housed in pairs or groups. The groups of breeding females were lying on automobile tires, in the morning sun. But the infants who had been taken from their mothers seemed depressed, even fearful. They were crammed together in a sterile wire cage. A new chimpanzee facility is being constructed, however; I hope it will provide better accommodations for these sad youngsters.

The Southwest Foundation for Biomedical Research is in San Antonio, Texas. Dr. Jorg Eichberg, who was director for several years, employed a full-time scientist, Dr. Linda Brent, to enrich the lives of the laboratory's chimpanzees. He did that long before people were complaining about the treatment of chimps in laboratories. And Dr. Eichberg pioneered the idea of a retirement fund, so that chimpanzees no longer useful for research, or between periods of testing, could be moved out of the lab and into "condominiums." These were small rooms, each with an outside run, each built for four chimpanzees. Not my idea of an ideal retirement home, but definitely a step in the right direction. Chimpanzees were still housed alone during most experiments, but windows were being installed in the previously windowless buildings, and fresh air found its way inside. I went to Southwest a second time to see the newly constructed "playground," a very large outdoor enclosure with grass and a high roof, where chimpanzee groups, each comprising one male and his females and youngsters, can play or groom or simply rest outside in the sun. Dr. Eichberg had plans to build similar playgrounds for the "retire-

*ment homes" and for the AIDS research chimpanzees. Unfortu-
nately, he left before they were started. The new management, I am
told, is less sympathetic.*

*When I tell people about my visits to these labs, two questions are
asked most often. The first of these is, "Jane, how can you keep calm?"
And the second is, "Why do they let you in?" I think the two are
interrelated. I keep calm, or try to, partly because I know from experience that once I lose control it becomes difficult to think clearly. If I
get angry and allow it to show, it is hard to have a rational discussion.
The person or persons to whom I am talking become aggressive and
defensive and cannot, or do not want to, hear what is being said. And I
keep calm, or try to, by telling myself that most of the cruelty or
callousness in the labs results from a lack of understanding. This is not
always true, but it often is.*

*Consider Jan Moor-Jankowski. He has very strong beliefs about the
relevant positions of humans and animals in this world. He has dogs,
and he cares deeply for them and is concerned when they are sick.
But only as "animals" — that is, of the nonhuman variety. While he
admits that animals can feel pain, he believes that they do not have
souls. Humans have souls; animals do not. And chimpanzees are
animals. It was not until I gained this insight into his outlook on the
human versus the nonhuman animal world that I understood how a
seemingly humane man could run a lab for our closest relatives that
was so completely lacking in understanding of their social and psychological needs. And that is why he could not understand the feeling of
absolute shock and outrage that seized me when I first visited his lab.
He simply could not and cannot believe that lack of close companionship, boredom, and frustration are as bad for chimpanzees as for
humans — or maybe even worse.*

*Or consider Immuno. If the people involved with public relations at
the Immuno lab in Austria had any concept of the real nature and
needs of chimpanzees, how could they have proudly showed off those
two cages — five-foot by five-foot prisons — as an advertisement to
the general public?*

*Perhaps the story that best illustrates this pervasive lack of under-
standing comes from an underground lab where eight chimpanzees
are stored. My informant, who I promised should remain anonymous,
was walking along a corridor there when he saw soap bubbles floating*

through a doorway. He paused to see what was going on. A young male chimpanzee was sitting in a very small cage, rocking from side to side, desperately banging his head against the bars of the cage. Nearby sat a young woman blowing soap bubbles. "What are you doing?" my informant asked her. "I'm blowing bubbles," she said. "Yes, I can see that. Why are you blowing bubbles?" She told him that she had been instructed to "entertain" the chimpanzees, because there were new regulations about psychological well-being.

That anecdote makes two important points. First, the message about enriching the lives of laboratory chimpanzees has been heard, and heeded, even in secret underground labs. Second, there is an extraordinary lack of understanding. You would not blow bubbles to amuse a psychotic child, locked up and too crazed even to look at the bubbles. You would attempt to console him in very different ways. People still have not realized how closely the emotional and intellectual needs of chimpanzees resemble our own.

I have been allowed into labs partly because those responsible have truly not understood the nature, the full horror, of the crime being perpetrated against the inmates. But times are changing. They are changing in direct response to the bad press generated by the release of information about what actually goes on inside labs, and also because more and more of the lab people themselves are beginning to see things in a different light — beginning, at last, to understand the nature of the beings held in their power. Over the past few years there has been a series of workshops to discuss ways in which laboratory conditions can be improved. The first of these was a direct outcome of my visit to Sema in 1987.

After I emerged from the lab that day, shocked and dazed, I found myself sitting at a conference table surrounded by Sema and NIH personnel. I suddenly realized that everyone was looking at me, questioningly. I experienced a moment of panic and then, as so often happens at moments like that, when one's mind is numb, I knew what I had to say.

"I think you all know what I felt in there," I said. "And since you are all decent, compassionate human beings, I assume you feel much the same." No one said anything. I went on to talk a little about wild chimpanzees, their close family lives, the long and carefree childhood, the excitements of social living. About the challenges that chimps must meet, their use of tools, their love of comfort, the rich variety of *their diet. I described briefly some of our recent insights into the working of the chimpanzee mind. And then, as my gray cells slowly began to function, I broached the idea of a workshop, a meeting at which biomedical scientists and veterinarians and technicians from the labs could discuss, with field scientists and ethologists and animal-welfare advocates, what realistically could be done to improve conditions for the chimpanzees. For there would be little point in planning a laboratory designed in the best interests of the chimpanzees if, at the end, the research scientists stepped in to say well and good, but in such a lab they would be quite unable to conduct the research for which the chimpanzees had been brought there in the first place.*

Initially, the NIH agreed to fund that first workshop, but the relationship soured. So the Jane Goodall Institute (JGI) got together with the Humane Society of the United States, and we held a much smaller meeting than originally planned. Along with those of us representing, as it were, the chimps, we managed to gather into the same room some top-caliber scientists — Jorg Eichberg from Southwest, Jan Moor-Jankowski from LEMSIP, Alfred Prince from the New York Blood Center, and Huub Schellekens from TNO. A second workshop, with some of the same personnel, was hosted by TNO in the Netherlands the following year. And, later that year, a third, much larger meeting, which included the heads of some of the NIH primate facilities, was hosted by Tufts University.

These workshops, representing very diverse interests, resulted in a couple of documents that spelled out, as recommendations, the sort of conditions that we believed appropriate for maintaining our closest relatives in captivity. The proposals were submitted to the United States Department of Agriculture in 1987 in the hope that they might influence the regulations being designed to implement Senator Melcher's amendment to the Animal Welfare Act (specifying that captive conditions for nonhuman primates should promote their psychological well-being). In fact, the USDA took little heed of our suggestions. But the documents are valuable in that they set out guidelines for the least hurtful way of maintaining chimpanzees in biomedical research laboratories, emphasizing their need for space, companionship and stimulation, fresh air, and a view of life beyond the laboratory prison. Each suggestion was based on a procedure that is being used by at least one facility somewhere, for there were labs, such as

Bastrop (University of Texas) and Southwest, that had already insti-
gated improvements on their own initiative.*

   The new animal-welfare regulations are far less comprehensive
than many of us would like. Still, the open discussion of the issues,
along with releases to the press, the airing of concerns on television,
and extensive lobbying on Capitol Hill, has clearly had an impact on
both the administration and scientists from many other labs. Atti-
tudes are changing.

Sema, the NIH-funded laboratory that gained notoriety for keeping
baby chimps inside microwave-oven-style isolettes, is transformed.
The laboratory now operates under the name Diagnon. Most significant, the isolettes are gone. The two dozen very young chimpanzees
now inhabiting this laboratory live not in isolation boxes or even
inside steel-barred cages, but within ample plexiglass cubicles, including areas for day and for night. The rooms are distinctly larger than
current regulations dictate as minimal; the chimps can see and to some
degree hear one another at all times. They have considerable space to
move around. Human caretakers regularly come and hold and play
with the young apes. The chimps still generally live in isolation, but at
some points in their experimental regimen they are allowed to live
together and have physical contact with others.

   I met Dr. John Landon, president of what is now Diagnon, in De-
cember 1991, and he warmly invited me to come and see how much
better off the chimpanzees are. He even thanked me for the part I
had played in making it possible for him to instigate these improve-
ments. For my part, I told him that I understood absolutely why he
had been so angry when, after visiting his lab with his permission, I
had then criticized the conditions inside — in lectures around the
country and in a forum as public as the Sunday New York Times
Magazine. *At the time of my visit to Sema, he had only recently*
become president, so he was in the unenviable position of defending
a situation for which he had not been personally responsible. Let me
take this opportunity to congratulate him on what has been done to
make things so much better for the chimps. I have not yet seen the
newly constructed quarters, but Dale Peterson has — and I plan to
do so when the opportunity arises. I also intend to visit the brand-

---

* A copy of these recommendations appears as Appendix B to this volume.

new facility that has been built for the Immuno chimps in Vienna. Jorg Eichberg tells me that the apes there have much better housing now, even though they are still separated.

The chimpanzees at LEMSIP have not benefited to the same extent. After that first visit I made to the lab, Dr. Moor-Jankowski had agreed that a student, funded by a small JGI grant, could spend six months devising ways to improve the quality of life for his chimps. Mark Bodemar, who had been a pupil of Roger Fouts, worked closely with Jim Mahoney and the lab technicians. Without doubt his presence made a difference. He designed several effective and inexpensive enrichment devices, such as providing the chimps with short, thick tubes stuffed with raisins and marshmallows, along with willow twigs to poke out the treats. And Mark periodically gave the chimps toothbrushes, combs, and mirrors. After Mark left, Moor-Jankowski instructed that enrichment procedures should become part of normal daily routine; but now, I understand, only the more caring of the technicians bother.

Another aspect relevant to this discussion is that many of the scientists who use chimpanzees to test drugs or vaccines have never seen the inside of a chimp lab. They deal not with the whole being, but with protocols on paper and results that arrive in their research labs in test tubes. Take Robert Gallo. His allegations regarding a supposed shortage of chimpanzees for AIDS research are all the more curious in light of the fact that he, personally, used only one chimpanzee once. And he never visited the chimp in his cage. Indeed, only a few months after declaring that progress in understanding AIDS would come to a halt because of wicked legislation that prohibited the import of more chimps from Africa, he presented a paper at an international AIDS conference in Arusha, Tanzania, which announced that progress in AIDS research was now "boxed in by inappropriate results from chimpanzees and gibbons."

At Gallo's invitation I spoke at one of his big AIDS conferences in Washington, D.C. Afterward I received a number of letters from scientists who said that they would never feel quite the same about experimental animals, particularly nonhuman primates. To my mind, it should be required that all scientists working with laboratory animals, whatever the species, not only know something about the animals and their natural behavior, but see for themselves how their protocols affect individual animals. Researchers should observe firsthand any suffering they cause, so that they can better balance the benefit (or hoped-for benefit) to humanity against the cost in suffering to the animal. Laboratory chimpanzees are prisoners, but they are guilty of no crimes. Rather, they are helping — perhaps — to alleviate human suffering. Yet in some of the labs I have described, and in others around the world, they are subjected to far harsher treatment than we give to hardened criminals. Surely we owe them more than that.

Even if all research labs could be redesigned to provide the best possible environment for the chimpanzee subjects, there would still be one nagging question — should chimpanzees be used at all? Are we really justified in putting our closest relatives in the animal kingdom into cages and subjecting them to lives of slavery for the sake of human health? Just because we have decided that it is not ethical to use human "guinea pigs"? We have far more in common with chimpanzees than the physiological characteristics that make them, in the eyes of some scientists, so suitable for certain kinds of research. We should not forget that there are equally striking similarities in the social behavior, intellect, and emotions of human beings and chimpanzee beings. And I personally believe that if we have souls, then probably chimpanzees have them too.

I have been described, by the director of one large chimpanzee colony, as a "rabid antivivisectionist." That kind of language is used regularly by individuals, extremists on both sides of the animal-rights issue, who wish to imply that those holding views in opposition to theirs are irrational, even dangerous. Often such talk is a way of avoiding debate. It certainly is not useful.

Of course I wish I could wave a wand and see the lab cages standing empty. Of course I hate the suffering that goes on behind the closed doors of animal labs. I hate even more the callous attitude that lab personnel so often show toward the animals in their power — deliberately cultivated, no doubt, to try to protect themselves from any twinge of guilt. But it would not be constructive to go around denouncing these individuals as "sadistic vivisectionists" — or whatever may be the counterpart of "rabid antivivisectionist." The animal-rights movement is here to stay, and because scientific investigations have now shown conclusively that the higher animals have minds and feelings and are capable of making complex decisions, the movement will continue to grow in strength. For too long we have used and

abused the nonhuman animals with whom we share this planet, without even pause for thought — not just in the lab, but in the slaughter-
house, the hunting field, the circus, and so on. Our children are gradually desensitized to animal suffering. ("It's all right, darling; it's only
an animal.") The process goes on throughout school, culminating
in the frightful things that zoology, psychology, veterinary, and medical students are forced to do to animals in the process of acquiring
knowledge. They have to quell empathy if they are to survive in their
chosen fields, for scientists do things to animals that, from the animals' point of view, are torture and would be regarded as such by
almost everyone if done by nonscientists.

Animals in labs are used in different ways. In the quest for knowledge, things are done to them to see what happens. To test the safety
of various products, animals are injected with or forced to swallow
different amounts to see how sick they get, or if they survive. The
effectiveness of medical procedures and drugs are tried out on animals. Surgical skills are practiced on animals. Theories of all sorts, ranging from the effects of various substances to psychological trauma, are
tested on animals. What is so shocking is the lack of respect for the
victims, the almost total disregard for their living, feeling, sometimes
agonizing bodies. And often the tortures are inflicted for nothing.
There is an angry debate, ongoing and abrasive, about the role of
animals in medicine. Even though I am not qualified to judge a dispute
of this magnitude, which has become so polarized, it seems obvious
that extremists on both sides are wrong. The scientists who claim that
medical research could never have progressed at all without the use of
animals are as incorrect as the animal-rights activists who declare
stridently that no advances in medicine have been due to animal
research.

Let me return to chimpanzees and to the question of whether we are
justified in using them in our search for medical knowledge. Approximately three thousand of them languish in medical research laboratories around the world, somewhat more than half of this number
(about one thousand eight hundred) in the United States. Today, as we
have seen, they are primarily used in infectious-disease research and
vaccine testing; even though they have seldom shown even minor
symptoms of either AIDS or hepatitis, the experimental procedures
are often stressful, the conditions in which they are maintained typically bleak. Yet they are so like us that some people believe that they

and the other great apes should be reclassified and placed, along with humans, in the genus Homo. *Chimpanzees, instead of being* Pan troglodytes, *would become* Homo troglodytes. *Proponents of this plan believe that such a taxonomic change would result in greater appreciation for the sentient, sapient nature of apes — but I doubt it. It seems more likely that it would backfire, incensing thousands of people, particularly those in certain religious groups.*

I think it is more important to educate people to a better understanding of the true nature of chimpanzees (and other nonhuman animals), particularly an appreciation of the extent to which they can feel — feel pain, feel emotions. Humans are a species capable of compassion, and we should develop a heightened moral responsibility for beings who are so like ourselves. Chimpanzees form close, affectionate bonds that may persist throughout life. Like us, they feel joy and sorrow and despair. They show many of the intellectual skills that until recently we believed were unique to ourselves. They may look into mirrors and see themselves as individuals — beings who have consciousness of "self." Do they not, then, deserve to be treated with the same kind of consideration that we accord to other highly sensitive, conscious beings — ourselves? Granted, we do not always show much consideration to one another. That is why there is so much anguish over human rights. That is why it makes little sense to talk about the "rights" of chimpanzees. But at least where we desist from doing certain things to human beings for ethical reasons, we should desist also from doing them to chimpanzee beings. We no longer perform certain experiments on humans, for ethical reasons. I suggest that it would be logical to refrain also from doing these experiments on chimpanzees.

Why do I care so much? Why, in order to try to change attitudes and actions in the labs, do I subject myself repeatedly to the personal nightmare of visiting these places, knowing that I shall be haunted endlessly by memories of my encounters with the prisoners there? Especially their eyes, those bewildered or sad or angry eyes. The answer is simple. I have spent so many years in the forests of Gombe, being with and learning from the chimpanzees. I consider myself one of the luckiest people on earth. It is time to repay something of the debt I owe the chimpanzees, for what they have taught me about themselves, about myself, about the place of humans and chimpanzees in the natural world.

When I visit JoJo in his tiny steel prison I often think of David Greybeard, that very special chimpanzee who, by his calm acceptance of my presence, first helped me to open the door into the magic world of the chimpanzees of Gombe. I learned so much from him. It was he who introduced me to his companions, Goliath and Mike and the Flo family and all the other unique, fascinating personalities who made up his community at that time. David even allowed me to groom him. A fully adult male chimpanzee who had lived all his life in the wild actually tolerated the touch of a human hand.

There was one especially memorable event. I had been following David one day, struggling through dense undergrowth near a stream. I was thankful when he stopped to rest, and I sat near him. Close by I noticed the fallen red fruit of an oil nut palm, a favorite food of chimpanzees. I picked it up and held it out to David on the palm of my hand. For a moment I thought he would ignore my gesture. But then he took the nut, let it fall to the ground and, with the same movement, very gently closed his fingers around my hand. He glanced at my face, let go of my hand, and turned away. I understood his message: "I don't want the nut, but it was nice of you to offer it." We had communicated most truly, relying on shared primate signals that are deeper and more ancient than words. It was a moment of revelation. I did not follow David when he wandered off into the forest. I wanted to be alone, to ponder the significance of what had happened, to enshrine those moments permanently in my mind.

And so, when I am with JoJo, I remember David Greybeard and the lessons he taught me. I feel deep shame — shame that we, with our more sophisticated intellect, with our greater capacity for understanding and compassion, have deprived JoJo of almost everything. Not for him the soft colors of the forest, the dim greens and browns entwined, or the peace of the afternoon when the sun flecks the canopy and small creatures rustle and flit and creep among the leaves. Not for him the freedom to choose, each day, how he will spend his time and where and with whom. Nature's sounds are gone, the sounds of running water, of wind in the branches, of chimpanzee calls that ring out so clear and rise up through the treetops to drift away in the hills. The comforts are gone, the soft leafy floor of the forest, the springy branches from which sleeping nests can be made. All are gone. Here, in the lab, the world is concrete and steel; it is loud, horrible sounds, clanging bars, banging doors, and the deafen-

ing volume of chimpanzee calls confined in underground rooms. It is a world where there are no windows, nothing to look at, nothing to play with. A world where family and friends are torn apart and where sociable beings are locked away, innocent of crime, into solitary confinement.

It is we who are guilty. I look again into JoJo's clear eyes. I acknowledge my own complicity in this world we have made, and I feel the need for forgiveness. He reaches out a large, gentle finger and once again touches the tear trickling down into my mask.

12 ◆ Our Pardon

PROSPERO:

> Go, sirrah, to my cell;
> Take with you your companions. As you look
> To have my pardon, trim it handsomely.

The light of my hurricane lantern is soft, barely dimming the radiance of the waxing moon as I write these words. The waves of Lake Tanganyika lap the shore, a small animal rustles noisily among the fallen June leaves, and a solitary male baboon barks from his night tree up the slope behind my house — barks at a night prowler, or perhaps a dream.

I have been here only a few days, but what wonderful days. The first morning I spent with Gremlin, her brother young Gimble, and her enchanting son Galahad, now four years old. He is adventurous and full of mischief, stamping and slapping on the ground as he mock charges toward me, then shinnying up a vine and swinging so that his toes touch my hand. With a characteristic mood change, he ducks back into childhood, running to his mother for a quick suckle. Next he is all grown up, practicing grooming techniques on his Uncle Gimble, then using a little leaf sponge to sop up water from a hollow in a tree trunk — just like his mother. And then, overcome by a surge of energy, he pirouettes away and leaps onto Gimble for a game, a game of tickling and mock wrestling that soon has Galahad laughing hysterically. Suddenly Gimble pulls away and runs to greet Wilkie, the new alpha male, who arrives with bristling hair, ready to defend his top position. Galahad greets him too, then goes to embrace the deposed alpha, his own Uncle Goblin.

Fifi and her family gave me hours of fascination yesterday. She now has five offspring, ranging from Freud, who is more than twenty years of age, to little Faustino, only three and a half yet already being vigorously weaned. He is too young for this, but it has to be because his mother is hugely pregnant. Fifi, in fact, is the most reproductively successful female of any I have known at Gombe over the past thirty years. Her eldest daughter, Fanni, gave birth a couple of months ago, and yesterday was my first encounter with her precocious son. As I heard about his birth and his sex by fax, we named him Fax! Flossi, at eight years old, has not yet attained puberty and is still spending all her time with Fifi and Faustino — and Fanni and Fax are usually with them, too. Fifteen-year-old Frodo is the bully of the community, the only chimpanzee who has consistently charged and hit humans at Gombe. He and Freud hang out together a good deal, traveling with other adult males. But yesterday the whole family was together.

On my way back to the house this evening, I stopped near the lake to listen to the evening chorus of the birds, the sweet liquid song of the robin. Suddenly, there was the sound of delicate footsteps. I kept absolutely still. Presently a female bushbuck appeared. She knew I was there — or rather, she knew something was there, but she couldn't make out exactly what I was. When she was some twenty feet away, she stopped and stared from dark, unblinking eyes, ears out-stretched, only her nose twitching up and down as she searched the air for clues. But the breeze, such as there was, wafted my telltale scent away from her. Quite an old lady she was, the hair on her neck sparse, and on her body somewhat moth-eaten. She stayed, motionless save for that questioning nose. Minutes passed, the evening chorus of birds surrounded us, the sun sank lower toward the lake, red now through the trees. Still neither of us stirred.

After twenty-three minutes she began to flick her ears. Then she made a chewing movement. She twitched all along her back where a fly tickled. She blinked. And then she froze again, staring, sniffing, while ten more minutes passed. She turned her head for a moment to look behind her. She chewed again, with quick sideways movements of her lower jaw. She licked her lips with a blackish pink tongue. And then, very quietly, she took three steps and vanished behind a tree. Very, very slowly I leaned sideways to see what she was doing. She was peeping at me from behind the trunk! She barked then, twice. Finally, fifty-two minutes after she had appeared, she began to walk very slowly away. Every so often she stopped, turned, stared back at me, and barked. And then moved on until her barking faded into the dusk. A whole hour I had spent, playing a game with a bushbuck. A battle of

*wills it had been — who could keep still the longest? I had won, and I
felt absurdly pleased as I clambered down the steep slope above the
house, into the sunset. I was indeed back at Gombe. Back, for a brief
moment, into a world where there is enough time between dawn and
dusk to be still and simply exist for one whole hour.*

*The peace of the forest is healing. All of us who lead too-busy lives
need ways to recharge our fading batteries. For me it is these inter-
ludes at Gombe, when, for a while, I can live again according to the
rhythm of the rising and setting of the sun, the waxing and waning of
the moon. Live in a world with real time, not the frenzied and artificial
time that jumps with the hands of the clock. Absorb, through every
pore, the unspoiled beauty of the forest, and its creatures who live
their lives in freedom. Here they need fear no hunter's gun or spear;
they will never know the slow agony of the snare. How privileged I am
to know this place, to call it home, to be able to spend time with
chimpanzees who over the years have become as familiar to me as
members of my own family.*

Yet even in Gombe, the world impinges. In wilderness across
Africa, the world impinges; and, in Africa at least, it is not a world of
betterment for either animals or people. Human populations and
needs are doubling every generation. The forests that sustain chimpanzees are vanishing. The soils that sustain people follow — human
environments are equally vulnerable. The chimpanzees are disappearing from Africa now, and I can visualize those who have been seized,
taken out of the disappearing forests, and flown into the temperate-
zone nations, sitting pathetically inside cages in a laboratory, testing
this or that vaccine for us, or dressed absurdly in clothes to satisfy
some person's appetite for amusement.

Until recently, when "civilized" anthropologists from the Western
world visited "primitive" peoples elsewhere in the world, the anthropologists never thought to ask whether they were welcome or not.
Nobody thought to ask. That attitude has persisted right into very
recent times. We have approached chimpanzees the same way. In
some sense, the barriers are the same — language, culture, and all
those other differences that we didn't know how to deal with and
weren't interested in dealing with. If chimpanzees knew fully what
we are doing to them, and if they had the capacity to speak, what
would they say? Is it possible to see our relationship from the chimpanzee perspective? What do the chimpanzees think of us? Are we welcome?

The questions, I imagine, are too abstract to ask a chimpanzee who knows sign language, even though it is certain that the signing apes develop very distinctive feelings about individual people. Signing apes usually develop a vocabulary of obscenities, typically associated with feces, and they will swear in no uncertain terms at people they don't happen to like. *Signing apes can also indicate how they would like humans to behave toward them. I have always told my students and field staff at Gombe to sit rather than stand when near the chimps, presuming that it is threatening for one ape to tower over another, particularly in view of the fact that a bipedal stance, in ape society, is often a form of threat. And so I wrote to Francine Patterson, the scientist who has taught American Sign Language to two gorillas, Koko and Michael. I asked her to ask Koko if she preferred people standing or sitting. Koko's reply, delivered very emphatically, was that she preferred people to lie down!*

Chimpanzees often make it very clear if they like a person or not. And captive chimps can make quick character assessments. One of my favorite stories concerns Ai. She is, I believe, the most intelligent captive chimp I have met, and this, in large part, is because of the way she has been taught and the sensitivity and gentleness of her "partner," as he calls himself, Tetsuro Matsuzawa. He introduced me to Ai over the wall of the enclosure where she lives with six other chimpanzees. We looked briefly into each other's eyes, then she moved inside to her computer. I was allowed to watch her perform through a small glass window in a tiny cubicle. I was warned that she hated to be watched if she made a mistake; that when she did, she would approach me and hit the glass. It was a long time before she made a wrong choice (she can beat high school students in many of her complicated tasks). But eventually she did, and at once charged toward me. But instead of hitting the window she stopped, stared at me, then kissed me through the glass. She made three mistakes, and she kissed me three times. Everyone in the lab was amazed.

The chimpanzees at Gombe also make it clear when they like some human observers and dislike others. Some are quite definitely interested in people, especially when parties of tourists arrive wearing absurdly inappropriate flowery clothes. Fifi and Goblin, in particular, are likely to approach to within a few yards of such a group, then sit and watch them for minutes on end. When I return to Gombe after a long absence, some of the chimps will come and sit quite close to me when I am with them, out in the forest. And when Goblin was really sick, after being wounded in a fight with Wilkie, he developed a close relationship with the field staff who took turns being with him each day, administering medication. When occasionally they lost him, he would invariably wander toward the camp where they live, as though seeking their company again. When they were sprinkling antibiotic powder on his wounds, he would sometimes take their hands and direct them to a particular spot. It is equally apparent when chimpanzees dislike someone, or get tired of being followed and observed. In particular, they get upset if they are walking quietly and you inadvertently make a noise: then they are likely to turn and make a threatening gesture. One adult male, Humphrey, didn't like women. When I or one of the female students followed him, he often made his irritation very clear by turning and hurling stones at us! Except for one young woman, whom he never threatened at all. And he almost never threatened any of the male observers. It meant that I seldom followed Humphrey, as I felt that it was unfair to impose myself on him and perhaps spoil his day.

In general, the chimpanzees are uneasy in the presence of humans who have loud voices or who make sudden movements. I had one student who had a very high-strung, nervous temperament and who sometimes threw tantrums. She never did so in front of the chimps but they sensed it in her, and Fifi, who was a child then, was always threatening her. Once she even bit the student's finger, warning her to keep her distance.

There is one very common communicative signal used by chimpanzees everywhere — a soft, coughlike sound usually accompanied by a sudden raising of one arm. This arm wave looks like a similar gesture made by humans and, for us and chimpanzees alike, it seems to convey much the same message: "Leave me in peace." If it were possible to make that gesture much larger, in a way that could be understood as a generalized communication from chimpanzees to humans, then perhaps chimpanzees might just say: "Leave us in peace."

1

Human arrogance. Human greed. Human cruelty. And an astonishing ability to close our eyes to the truth, to live in a world of delusions and make-believe. These characteristics, shared to a greater or lesser ex-tent by all of us, have helped to create a sick planet and a great deal of suffering, human and nonhuman alike. We agonize over the mutilated victim of war, the battered child, the cancer patient. Some of us agonize over the neglected, starving dog, the elephant slaughtered and left to rot by ivory poachers, the chimpanzee tethered for life at the end of a two-foot chain. Human nature: cunning, selfish, and full of self-righteous intolerance on the one hand; wise, compassionate, and loving on the other. Which side will gain the upper hand? The question is desperately important to those of us who care about the future of the world. Fortunately, people are beginning to understand the issues at stake, and our attitudes toward the environment and the amazing beings with whom we share it are beginning to change. If changed attitudes then lead not only to changes in our personal lives but also to policy changes at the corporate and governmental level, indeed we have cause for hope.

This is a book about the relationship between humans and chim-panzees, our closest living relatives in the animal kingdom. In our closing chapter, then, perhaps we should speculate a little about their future. Is it likely that our treatment of chimpanzees in captivity will change? Will chimpanzees survive in their wild state? For how long? Can we undo the vast damage we have already done? Can we now grant our "pardon" to an abused species, to our closest relatives?

As an initial step, the attitude of human beings toward nonhuman beings must change. In all parts of the world we find evidence of humanity's grim cruelty toward animals — and I include here the human animal. William Golding's chilling classic, Lord of the Flies, *points directly to the deep-rooted aggressive tendencies in us all, to that cruel streak that leads to "man's inhumanity to man," a part of our genetic inheritance that we are not, unfortunately, very good at controlling. Nonhuman animals, by and large, suffer even more than humans from the inhumanity of man. The pages of this book have described innumerable examples of human inhumanity to chimpan-zees, ranging from kidnapping infants from their murdered mothers in the African forests to imprisoning infants in American laboratories inside cages measuring two feet on a side. Of course, an action that is very cruel when considered from the point of view of the recipient may not be perceived as cruel by the perpetrator. When people excuse a barbarous action with the words, "It's only an animal," they may mean that even though they know they are inflicting pain it doesn't matter because the subject is not human — or they may honestly believe that animals don't experience pain. It is therefore of utmost importance to educate people about the truly sentient nature of chimpanzees and other nonhuman beings.*

Thanks to the dedication of a growing number of advocates for animals around the world, attitudes are changing. Particularly encouraging is the diversity of people who are helping to make this change. They range from animal-rights activists to scientists, from television personalities to veterinarians, from zookeepers to politicians, from teachers to schoolchildren. Yet there is also a network of individuals who hold a vested interest in denying the new order and maintaining the old. These people prefer that the general public continue to regard all nonhuman animals as "mere" animals. Their ranks include greedy and often unscrupulous dealers and traders, entertainers, animal-research scientists, pharmaceutical companies, those running intensive cattle, hog, or poultry farms, and many others whose livelihood depends on the continued exploitation of nonhuman animals. These people have, over the past few decades, caused the deaths of thousands of chimpanzees in Africa and brought thousands more into captivity beyond the African shores. Our inhumanity to man led to the export and degradation of humans during the days of the slave trade. Our inhumanity to beast has, among other crimes, placed hundreds of chimpanzees in bleak cages, tethered them on chains, tortured their bodies and their minds.

What hope is there for these captives, for individuals who have been torn brutally from their African lands or born into human servitude on foreign shores, who serve human masters as pets or entertainers or living test tubes? Given that it is almost impossible to reintroduce them to the wild, what can we do now to improve their lives?

Three new laws would help. First, in recognition of the fact that chimpanzees are our closest living relatives, legislation should be introduced to prohibit private ownership. People do not "own" other people; neither should they "own" conscious beings who are so close to people. I do not mean that chimpanzees currently living with people in their homes should be immediately removed — unless the conditions in which they are kept are very poor. Such an action would only create additional suffering, since the bonds between chimpanzees and their owners are typically close and affectionate. But future sales to private individuals should be prohibited.

Second, we should take legal steps to prevent the use of chimpanzees in entertainment, since that sort of exploitation is too often abusive and debasing. I am not urging that we stop filming chimpanzees behaving naturally, either in the wild or in captivity. But they should not be forced to perform in any routine manner, wearing human clothing, for the circus, for advertising, for picture postcards, calendars, and the like, or for the cinema. Nor should they be exploited to attract customers, either by photographers or by any other business.

Third, chimpanzees should be phased out of medical research as soon as possible. In view of our close relationship with these apes, it is simply unethical to continue exploiting them in this way. Many advances have been made in developing alternatives to the use of living animals. Additional encouragement and reward will undoubtedly produce many more. Once these alternatives exist and have been proved effective and safe, researchers and pharmaceutical manufacturers should be legally compelled to use them.

The ultimate goal, of course, is the adoption of similar measures throughout the world. In fact, there are enlightened places where some of these prohibitions concerning the use of chimpanzees already exist. Cities such as Toronto have banned circuses that include performances by any exotic animals. Sweden has strict laws regarding the use of nonhuman animals in medical research, so chimpanzees are not used in Swedish labs. They are not used in the United Kingdom either, but only because it is expensive to maintain them. British scientists who feel that chimpanzees are important for their particular research use those in the laboratories of other countries.

If the above restrictions are widely introduced, as eventually they must and will be, all captive chimpanzees will eventually be living in zoos or sanctuaries. A good many zoos, however, continue to exhibit chimpanzees (as well as other animals) in quite inappropriate conditions. This is true even in the United States, the United Kingdom, and other wealthy countries of Western Europe. But zoos are improving everywhere, in large part because a better-educated public is lobbying steadily for change. Almost all the zoos I have visited recently that still have unsuitable, old-fashioned cages of the prison-cell variety have plans for new chimpanzee facilities, and some have embarked on the task of trying to raise the money to implement those plans.

I do not enjoy visiting chimpanzees in zoos. I should prefer to see all chimpanzees free in protected African forests. Even in the very best zoos, where chimpanzees have plenty of space, plenty of stimulation, and a sizable social group, their situation is dull when compared with life in a forest such as Gombe. The captives can never know the sheer delight of arriving, after a long journey, at a stand of trees laden with the first luscious fruits of a new crop. They cannot climb high into a tree in the evening and look out, from fresh nests of springy green leaves, over the hills and valleys of their territory. They cannot enjoy the exhilaration and exuberance of being part of a large gathering, when many members of the community join for a while, the males display their prowess, and the young ones play. They will never experience, these captives, the excitement of the hunt, or the spice of danger provided by intercommunity encounters. A male cannot wander away by himself, or with a female consort.

We must remember, though, that life in the wild is not always easy. The chimpanzees at Gombe and elsewhere sometimes suffer agonizing injuries and illnesses. I shall never forget the grim days of the polio epidemic, or Mandy's infant with her broken arm, or Passion's pain during her last days in the grip of an unknown disease. Nor is it always comfortable, especially during the wet season when the chimpanzees may be cold and shivering day after day, night after night. When they may, indeed, catch pneumonia and die. Yes, even in the totally protected area of Gombe, life can be grim. Yet the Gombe chimps live in paradise compared with those in nonprotected areas where there is constant risk from poachers. Not only may those chimpanzees suffer painful mutilations from snares or gun wounds, but particularly mothers of young infants must be constantly alert for the sight or sound or scent of their cunning human enemies. Everywhere across their range, except in the few protected areas, chimpanzees are driven into smaller and smaller areas as, relentlessly, the African forests are felled. I wonder if many — even most — of these increasingly persecuted individuals, given the choice, would not opt for life in one of the better zoos. These thoughts occurred to me the other day as I watched an adult male chimpanzee, his coat sleek and glossy, his demeanor confident and proud, sitting on a high platform of his large enclosure, his females and a couple of subordinate males grooming and feeding peacefully in the late afternoon sun. He looked utterly content with his lot. He was born in captivity; he has never known the zest of life in the wild. He lives in a European zoo.

The fact is that many zoos have built excellent enclosures for groups of chimpanzees. And during the past several years, the practice of enriching the environment of captive chimpanzees has become increasingly widespread. Last year I visited the Tama Zoo outside Tokyo. A large group of chimpanzees inhabit an enclosure that is too small — but one of the most enriched anywhere. They have climbing poles and ropes and tires. A tier of thick cement platforms provides dense shade, and the poles supporting the platforms are drilled with many holes into which, each morning, the dedicated keepers stuff raisins. A rock hammer is chained to a rock anvil, and every so often the chimpanzees are thrown handfuls of hard-shelled nuts for cracking — macadamia nuts the day I was there. For me, though, by far the most fascinating enrichment device was a three-foot-high cylindrical object with a diameter of about eighteen inches. It was hollow, with a number of holes drilled through its outer cement skin. The curator showed me a large notice board near the exhibit, which displayed the painted picture of three chimpanzees industriously poking sticks into this cylindrical object to get at whatever was inside. He translated the Japanese writing, which told visitors that this object served as an artificial termite mound; it had been built after the curator read an account of a young English girl by the name of Jane Goodall who had observed chimpanzees fishing for termites in Africa. He had made it in 1963 — the first artificial termite heap (actually filled with honey) ever installed in a zoo enclosure. Those chimpanzees have another, more realistic mound today, but the original one is still there.

When I first returned to England from Gombe in 1961, with the memory of two poor chimpanzees in a concrete cell of the London Zoo, I designed a "honey fishing box" for them. A friend of mine at the Natural History Museum in London made it for me, with a zinc interior, holes in the lid, and bolts to secure it to the cement floor. With great excitement I presented it to the curator of the London Zoo at that time, Desmond Morris. But the honey fishing box was never used because the head keeper decided it would be too much work to fill it with honey and keep it clean. Indeed, those head keepers of the old school, with their set ways and considerable power, have delayed the introduction of many types of enrichment for zoo chimpanzees. One of the most effective is "browse" — branches and twigs selected from nonpoisonous trees and shrubs. The leaves can be eaten and chewed, crumpled up and used as drinking sponges; bark can be eaten *from the branches; and twigs can be pulled from the stems and used as tools. The introduction of browse has made a big difference to some chimpanzee groups. It has, for example, decreased and even brought to an end the unpleasant habit of coprophagy (the eating of feces). But in many zoos a wall of resistance had to be overcome before this beneficial, inexpensive procedure could be introduced. The debris, it was argued, would block the drains.*

It is still a battle in some zoos to introduce new ideas of any sort, but on the whole the curators and zookeepers are open to change. We know a lot more now about the natural behavior of wild animals, and this makes it easier to provide for their needs — physical, social, and psychological — in captivity. Many keepers have studied animal behavior and are anxious to do the best they can for their charges, even if it means extra work. I remember visiting my great friend the late Sheldon Campbell soon after he was appointed director of the San Diego Zoo. He wanted to show me the new bonobo (pygmy chimpanzee) enclosure. There was an artificial termite mound and also some little hollows in a tree trunk that had just been filled with water. One of the bonobos picked some leaves, crumpled them, and used them as a sponge, to drink. Sheldon turned to me: "Fifteen years ago, Jane," he said, "you and I were looking at these bonobos in their old rock grotto. You said, 'Wouldn't it be nice to make water bowls in the cement, and a termite heap, so they would have something to do?' Isn't it sad that it has taken so long to do such a simple thing?"

We are all conservative in our own ways, resistant to change — just as most chimpanzees are. But the world is changing, and we must change, too.

Zoos in Africa, by and large, are depressing places where animals exist in concrete cells, often with very little to eat. This is not because the directors and staff are necessarily cruel. Sometimes it is because they don't understand the needs of the animals; more often it is a result of the lack of funds. I visited one zoo, the Brazzaville Zoo in Congo, where the management and staff neither understood nor cared, and where the funds were miserably insufficient. The result, for the animals, was horrifying. The director, no longer there, regularly stocked his zoo with animals bought for a few dollars from local hunters. He kept them, to entertain the few weekend visitors, until they died of starvation. Then they were replaced. It was cheaper and much less work that way.

The trouble is, of course, that in cities such as Brazzaville most humans cannot afford to eat more than once a day. The Congolese currency is tied to the French franc, so the cost of living is exorbitant. How, I am continually asked, can we justify providing food for nonhuman beings in a zoo when human beings are starving? The answer, I think, is simple. Humans put these animals into cages. They cannot get out to search for their own food. They rely on us. If we are not to feed them, they must either be freed or be killed.

During my first visit to the Brazzaville Zoo I met Grégoire. It was a while ago, but I can still recall my sense of disbelief and outrage as I gazed at the strange being, alone in his bleak cement-floored cage. His pale, almost hairless skin was stretched tightly over his emaciated body so that every bone could be seen. His eyes were dull as he reached out with a thin, bony hand for a proffered morsel of food. Was this really a chimpanzee? Apparently so: "Shimpanse," announced a notice over the cage, with the added information, "GREGOIRE — 1944." 1944! It was hard to believe. In that dim, unfriendly cage Grégoire had endured for forty-six years.

A group of Congolese children approached quietly. One girl, about ten years old, had a banana in her hand. Leaning over the safety rail, she called out: "Danse! Grégoire — danse!" With bizarre, stereotyped movements, the old male stood upright and twirled around once, twice, three times. Then, still standing, he drummed rapidly with his hands — rat tat, rat tat, rat tat — on the single piece of furniture in his room, a lopsided shelf that was attached to one wall. He ended the strange performance by standing on his hands, his feet gripping the bars between us. The girl held the banana toward him and, righting himself, he reached out to accept payment.

That meeting was just after Nelson Mandela had been released from his long imprisonment by the white South African government. I was with a Congolese official at the time, who knew nothing of chimpanzees. After staring at Grégoire for a while he turned to me, his face solemn. "There, I think, is our Mandela," he said. I was moved by those words, by the compassion that lay behind them.

The gaunt image of Grégoire hung between me and sleep that night. How had he survived those long, weary years deprived of almost everything that a chimpanzee needs to make life meaningful? What stubbornness of spirit had kept him alive? It was as though he, like other starving, neglected chimpanzees in impoverished African zoos, had been waiting for help.

The response of people, once they become aware of a situation such as that at the Brazzaville Zoo, is heartening. Two British organizations, the Royal Society for the Prevention of Cruelty to Animals and the World Society for the Protection of Animals, sent emergency funds. The local community rallied round, particularly the British ambassador and his wife, Peter and Jane Chandley, and the American ambassador and his wife, Dan and Lucie Phillips. We employed a keeper, Jean Maboto, to feed and care for Grégoire and the six other chimpanzees. Jean, who had never worked with animals before, soon developed a wonderful relationship with his charges. Then, as more chimpanzees arrived (including the seven refugees from Zaire mentioned in an earlier chapter), we had to hire two more keepers. And, of course, Graziella Cotman, from Zaire, joined our staff. All the chimpanzees are healthy and well fed now, and Grégoire has a respectable amount of hair covering his respectably plump body.

We cannot rescue all the chimpanzees in all the underfunded, understaffed African zoos. Our slender resources are already strained to the limit. Clearly, a long-term solution must be found to provide relief for so many miserable, starving animals. Nonetheless, we have become involved in other zoos in Africa where our help was solicited — for instance, a very small zoo in Tanzania, where an adult male has lived alone for the past nine years; working with the government we are building a larger enclosure and plan to introduce to him the one infant who is illegally in the country. At the Entebbe Zoo a JGI representative is helping to care for the infants confiscated by the Ugandan government. At the zoo in Luanda, Conoco of Angola is building a large enclosure for the three chimpanzees living there, with the idea of integrating a number of confiscated youngsters and former pets from the forested part of the country in the north. And then there is the so-called zoo in Pointe Noire, in southwestern Congo.

I first heard about the dreadful conditions prevailing in Point Noire from Ian Redmond of BBC Wildlife Magazine. He showed me a photograph of a chimpanzee, emaciated and depressed, who was apparently starving to death. Seven adult chimpanzees were at the "zoo," Ian told me, none of whom received regular food or water, and two infants were close to death. These chimps, along with a few pathetic monkeys and a large turtle, were (fortunately) the only animals there.

As soon as I saw that photo I knew we had to try to help. Karen Pack, fluent in French and with one visit to Congo already behind her, was the ideal person to go on a rescue mission. She arrived in Pointe Noire just ten days after my meeting with Ian. Already one of the infants had died, but the other had been removed from the zoo and was being cared for by a local businesswoman, Aliette Jamart, and her husband.

We had very little money for Karen, and Congo is an expensive place to be. Fortunately for us and the chimpanzees, Roger Simpson, president of Conoco Congo (one of the oil companies with concessions in the area), took Karen under Conoco's wing and provided a good deal of logistical support. It was not long before conditions at the zoo improved enormously. With regular food and water the emaciated female, La Vieux, whose photo started it all, soon filled out, and it became apparent that she was not, after all, so old. Karen could do nothing about the size of the cages, which were much too small, but she opened connecting doors so that at least some of the previously solitary prisoners could socialize. And she worked closely with the keepers, teaching them about chimpanzees, explaining their different personalities. The two men, who had been afraid of the apes, who had teased and baited them rather than feeding and watering them, were gradually transformed into concerned caretakers.

I shall never forget my visit there six months after Karen's arrival. I watched one of the keepers as he approached the cage housing an adult male and two females. The big male immediately went over, reached out with both arms through the bars, drew the once-abusive keeper close, and kissed him. One of the females hurried up for her share of attention. The second female, always shy, remained at the back of the cage. The keeper kept looking toward her, talking to her, and after a few minutes she too approached him, cautiously and diffidently. "Oh, ma chérie," he said, gently reaching out to caress her head. His expression brought tears to my eyes — it was love.

Once things had been stirred up in Pointe Noire, the local government began to enforce the law, confiscating infant chimpanzees from local hunters. The JGI continued to tend the zoo chimps, but Karen could not care for the confiscated babies; Aliette Jamart volunteered to take them. She also accepted former pets from a variety of thankful owners. Before long she was caring for twenty-four youngsters in her house and backyard. We helped her as best we could and began to plan a sanctuary for her charges. Conoco Congo generously agreed to build it. But we took so long getting started (for various reasons we had to abandon the first three sites selected) that Madame Jamart, in desperation, found a river island close to the Gabonese border and released her ape family there. There is not enough for them to eat on the island, but someone has been hired to bring out food every day. As I write, the Conoco/JGI sanctuary is finally being built, and by the time this book is published, the chimps of Pointe Noire Zoo will have a real home at last.

Many conservationists feel that it is a waste of money to improve zoos and to build sanctuaries for orphaned chimpanzees in Africa. They argue that the funds would be better spent in protecting wilderness areas and chimpanzees who are still free. Indeed, sanctuaries are expensive. But there are not many people who, after meeting an orphaned infant and looking into those desperate eyes, can turn away.

In actuality, building a sanctuary can benefit conservation in a variety of ways, in addition to saving the lives of individual chimpanzees. Not until government officials start to confiscate chimpanzees being captured, sold, or held without licenses can we hope to end the illegal trade that still goes on across Africa. Unless there is somewhere that the orphans can be cared for, confiscations can hardly be made. What is vitally important is that no money ever be paid to anyone involved — not to the hunter, not to the middleman in the market, not to the pet owner. For that only serves to perpetuate the trade.

Sanctuaries can encourage a positive sort of tourism and also provide an important educational service. Soon, we hope, the two already established sanctuaries in Africa — Chimfunshi in Zambia and the Chimpanzee Rehabilitation Project in The Gambia — will be supplemented and supported by a network of sanctuaries and rehabilitation projects across the continent. We hope that many people will come to see and learn about the chimpanzees, tourists as well as the local people, especially the children. It is not easy for city children to see the wildlife that is such a magnificent part of their heritage. And children living in the bush tend to think of all animals as bushmeat. We shall establish a conservation educational program in conjunction with each of our sanctuaries. We plan to provide facilities where visitors can see videotapes of animal behavior (not only chimpanzees, of course), read books, and ask questions. The local people need the opportunity to learn about the remarkable beings with whom they share their country.

Sanctuaries are important for saving individuals and necessary for ending the cruel and destructive trade in live baby chimpanzees. That trade has certainly been one of the three major threats to chimpanzee survival in Africa, along with subsistence hunting and habitat loss. But saving the chimpanzee as a species in Africa also requires protecting and saving wild habitat.

Some African nations and governments deserve great credit for preserving pieces of chimpanzee habitat as national parks or forest reserves; yet it is equally important to recognize that action follows understanding — habitat has been preserved as international scientists have demonstrated the importance of so doing. Gombe was already a forest reserve when Jane Goodall first arrived there, but it may have been the international significance of her early work that encouraged Tanzanians to preserve Gombe forever as a national park. And the pioneering research of primatologist Toshisada Nishida may have demonstrated the importance of defining a Mahale Mountains National Park. The people of Ivory Coast have long understood the magic of Tai Forest, but the significance of Tai Forest National Park as the centerpiece for West African conservation is confirmed by the ongoing research of Christophe and Hedwige Boesch on chimpanzee cultures.

Researchers are studying wild chimpanzees elsewhere, within several other fragments of remaining chimpanzee habitat, and one hopes that their presence and work will clarify the necessity for saving those fragments. The Kibale Forest of Uganda is protected by the Ugandan government, of course, yet the presence of Isabiriye Basuta, Richard Wrangham, and other researchers from Harvard and Uganda's Makere University regularly emphasizes the value of Kibale for the international community. In Guinea, the research of Tetsuro Matsuzawa and Yukimaru Sugiyama helps protect a small forest and its fragile chimpanzee community. In Gabon, Michel Fernandez and Caroline Tutin have conducted a series of ecological studies in the Lopé-Okanda Forest Reserve; Lopé remains a pristine wilderness that could become one of Africa's great national parks. In Zaire, once the current political turmoil ends, perhaps the people of that nation will choose to protect the world's seventeen thousand remaining bonobos within areas first studied in detail by primatologists Takayoshi Kano, Richard Malenky, and Nancy Thompson-Handler. And just north of Zaire, Congo possesses what has been called "the last Eden," one large piece of wilderness in the heart of Africa, so isolated from human intrusion that the animals there are not yet afraid of people. That wilderness, the Ndoki, ought to become a national park; if it does, it will remain a credit to the vision of the Congolese people and a handful of Congolese, Japanese, and American scientists — most notably Michael Fay, Suehisa Kuroda, Masazumi Mitami, and Antoine Ruffin Oko.

The 1992 Earth Summit in Rio de Janeiro, Brazil, while it did not achieve the results that environmentalists so desperately hoped for, did demonstrate the increased importance of green issues to governments all over the world. Only too often, though, commitment to conservation measures goes no further than words, spoken or written on paper — actions do not change. In Africa the areas of wilderness yet unspoiled are relentlessly exploited, not only because of the ever-increasing needs of ever-expanding human populations but also to bring in much-needed foreign exchange — for development and to pay off foreign debts. In the developed world, where so much that was wild and lovely has long gone, we point sanctimonious fingers at the developing countries as they sell their timber and their wildlife, yet at the same time we continue to buy these products. We create a large part of the market that is destroying the tropical wilderness. And by exporting our "experts" as well as our technology to those same developing countries, we ensure that they destroy their natural resources ever more quickly, more efficiently, and more destructively, for our own benefit.

Ordinary people in most African nations, by and large, are crushed by a poverty that strangers to the continent find hard to imagine. The villager who fells trees in the neighborhood to grow crops and to harvest building poles and firewood may understand that his actions are destroying the land, may know that soon the soil will be incapable of sustaining any crops at all, but what can he do about it? His overriding problem, one that he faces every morning, is to assuage his hunger and that of his family. He lives from day to day, concerned only with issues of immediate survival. And these same issues confront the leaders, particularly those in the new democracies springing up all over Africa. Politicians would never be reelected if they tried to save areas of nature for animals and birds while local people starved for lack of land to cultivate, or because they were no longer allowed to hunt for bushmeat.

Given the pressing needs of the African people, there is little hope for saving and protecting the few remaining wild places without three critical changes in the human environment. First, there must be a different attitude toward the environment and the importance of conserving it. And attitudes are changing, as we have seen. Second, there must be a stabilization of population growth. Third, there must be responsible development that will help the people of Africa escape the grip of poverty.

Without a doubt, the single most devastating problem faced by most of Africa is human population growth. This is, in many ways, directly attributable to the intervention of colonialists — empire builders and traders and missionaries. The new religions and the new cultures so often swept away indigenous cultures and traditions that had evolved in harmony with the environment. In many traditional African societies, for example, women breastfed their infants for at least three years, and women living on a subsistence diet are unlikely to conceive again while they are lactating. And, as insurance that people did not produce more children than they could care for, more mouths than they could feed, intercourse with lactating women was often prohibited. During the colonial period, however, new technologies resulted in more food and better health care. Women gave birth much more frequently, and although infant mortality remained high in rural areas, modern medicines and mass vaccination meant that many babies lived who would previously have died. Modern medicines and mass vaccination obviously were positive introductions, except that they contributed to a population expansion without precedent in traditional Africa. At the same time, farming, fishing, and hunting methods all changed with the advent of Western technologies, while logging and many other kinds of environmental exploitation became profitable businesses that in many cases depleted a country of its natural resources.

The desolation of the land around Gombe provides, for me, a stark picture of what is happening across the whole of Africa. In another ten years the farmers, now that the trees are gone, will no longer be able to grow crops or catch fish, for the soil will have washed away, and the fishes' breeding grounds silted up. (Not that there will be many fish left to breed, thanks to the use of skein nets introduced with all good intentions by a donor nation of the developed world.) What will these people do? Their numbers are steadily growing even as their resources are decreasing — both at an alarming rate. In other countries where people have hunted and lived on bushmeat for hundreds of years, the *theme is the same, only the details are different. There is the same rapidly growing population and the same depletion of the natural resources, at an ever-faster rate with increasingly sophisticated hunting weapons. The bushmeat is taken not only for the hunter and his family and his village, but for trucking out to the constantly expanding cities. No wonder the animals and the forests are vanishing so quickly.*

For many years it was taboo among conservationists even to mention family planning. And, for ideological reasons, the United States has lately reduced its important governmental aid to international family planning organizations. Additionally, there were those in both the developing and the developed worlds who insisted that any emphasis on family planning was merely an attempt to keep down numbers in the Third World so that the developed world could maintain an upper hand. Today, though, African leaders are well aware of the fallacy of this argument, well aware that it is the accelerating increase of their populations along with the accelerating destruction of their natural resources that hinders positive development and improved living conditions. Throughout Africa attitudes are changing, particularly in the urban centers where large families are an economic drain. Yet many living in rural areas continue to produce larger families than they or their resources can support. Clearly, there is a desperate need to balance improved health care and family planning education with new values that honor the small rather than the large family. In this, as in many other conservation issues, the women's movement gradually acquiring strength across Africa can make a major difference.

Africa is caught in a vicious circle. Only by alleviating the crippling poverty that holds so much of the continent in its grip can people begin to live instead of existing, begin to care about a future for their children instead of being concerned only with the pressures of staying alive from day to day, begin to think and make intelligent choices. Poverty can be alleviated by responsible development. But responsible development is difficult when there is so much poverty. Poverty worsens as resources diminish in response to a rapidly growing population. Explosive population growth is, at least in part, due to the crippling poverty that tends to suppress the determination to improve and develop. Add to this mixture the now-chronic droughts that seem to be spreading across the continent, the revolutions and the wars, and the picture is grim indeed.

Is there hope for the peoples and the chimpanzees of Africa? There is always hope, and in this case it is dependent on fostering what is currently known as "sustainable development" — development that nurtures the environment, the long-term wealth of the continent, rather than exploiting it for short-term profit. This may call for a return to farming methods that once enabled people to live in harmony with nature but were swept aside by Western ideas. Or for the giving up of methods that worked when there were fewer people and less sophisticated machinery, but that are too destructive in the Africa of today. It calls for the introduction of new ideas and the casting aside of some old ones. And it requires a new kind of collaboration between Africa and the developed world, new ways of attracting foreign exchange. The governments of the developed world may need to impose sanctions on the importation of tropical hardwoods, while the African governments, for their part, need to control environmentally irresponsible logging, mining, and oil drilling operations, and penalize those companies that fail to maintain internationally accepted environmental standards. The local people should be involved, in financially meaningful ways, in new developments. When conservation measures prevent people from using land for their own immediate needs, it is not enough merely to explain the ultimate benefits. There needs to be some kind of immediate, tangible benefit in terms of new job opportunities or a share in any new financial gain — from tourism, for example.

If we set aside the constantly increasing demand for land made by the constantly expanding human population and its domestic livestock, the most destructive exploitation of the natural environment is by timber companies. Any kind of logging in virgin tropical forest or woodland is bound to disturb the complex and inherently fragile ecosystem. Some species of plants and animals will vanish. And, unfortunately, once extensive damage has been inflicted, nature will be unable to restore what has gone. Some countries have announced plans to experiment with sustainable, selective logging; and in secondary forests it is indeed possible that trees can be harvested without causing further permanent damage. In Gabon, which still has vast areas of untouched forest and one of the largest chimpanzee populations remaining in Africa, Michel Fernandez, Caroline Tutin, and Lee White are studying the effects of light, selective logging on the movements of nonhuman primates. Certain species are disturbed more

than others by the sudden appearance of men and machinery in the
forest, but in some instances species that flee during the actual logging
eventually return. At the same time, core areas of forest are preserved
intact in Gabon, as part of the country's national heritage and because
our understanding of the functioning of tropical ecosystems is still
incomplete. In Uganda, selective logging has been practiced for years,
with mixed results; but most of the remaining tropical forest in the
west of the country has now been given protected status. Instead of
logging, tourism is being developed in a major way, with each of nine
forest blocks designated as chimpanzee viewing areas.

One way of safeguarding virgin forest is to encourage people to grow
trees and view them as part of their crops — a practice known as
agroforestry. This reduces the need of the peasant farmer to take these
products from the forest. In all the countries where JGI has become
involved — Tanzania, Burundi, Congo, Uganda, and Angola — agroforestry programs are being developed and villagers are discovering the
benefits of planting species for a variety of purposes, such as to provide
building poles, firewood, charcoal, nitrogen fixation, shade, and fruit.

Of course, trees help to prevent erosion and preserve water tables;
and tree planting programs are becoming increasingly popular across
Africa. In Congo, there is a group that teaches schoolchildren the value
of using indigenous species to restock deforested areas. And in
Uganda, the Uganda Women's Tree Planting Association also plants
many indigenous trees. These forceful and determined women organize official tree planting ceremonies as part of almost every public
function — they have even persuaded the Ugandan army to help refor-
est land despoiled by military operations! Obviously, it is not possible
to recreate forests exactly as they were; it is inevitable that much of
the original biodiversity will be gone forever. Nevertheless, the planting of indigenous species is certainly a vast improvement over the
plantations of exotics, such as eucalyptus or pine, that until recently
were sponsored in Africa by the forestry departments of the industrialized nations. (Of course, when a major reforestation effort is needed,
when the devastation is almost total, as it is around Gombe, plantations of exotic species may be necessary; for the donor countries have
experience in planting and growing these trees, and any tree cover is
better than none. But few if any mammals or birds move into these
newly created places. The plantations, other than the trees themselves, are all but devoid of life.)

The discovery of a commercially viable oil field in a previously poor
African nation is comparable to a pauper's finding a bag of treasure
buried in his garden. The sale of the "black gold" will bring in suffi-
cient foreign exchange to enable the country to develop in many ways.
Still, given that so much oil is situated under some of the most
beautiful wild habitats, and given the extent to which the refining of
crude oil and the production and subsequent use of its products
pollutes our environment, among environmentalists the petroleum
industry has a shocking reputation. Rightly so, for their overall envi-
ronmental record is undeniably poor, often hideously bad. But even in
this area there is change. Ever since JGI became involved in trying to
protect chimpanzees and conserve their habitat in Congo, we have
been assisted by Conoco. Many people are horrified at the very idea of
association with an oil company; many tried to convince me that a
relationship with Conoco would do JGI no good. Yet in the developed
world we all use petroleum products. We all use electricity, and we
drive or are driven in cars; many of us fly in airplanes. Even people in
the most remote areas of the developing world today use artifacts that
could never have arrived there unless they had been transported by
motorized vehicles of some sort. Although oil companies have indeed
played a major role in despoiling wilderness areas, they are slowly
improving. All the major international oil companies have outlined
new "green policies" and proclaim (in public) their concern for the
environment. Unfortunately, the operations of some of these compa-
nies in tropical countries, far from watchdog environmental groups,
are often shocking. Huge areas of wilderness are churned up during
exploration; environmental and safety standards in the operation of
drilling rigs, in the refining and transporting of oil, all fall far below
developed-world standards.

Conoco not only has a strong environmental policy in Congo, but as
vice president for exploration Max Pitcher says, "We walk where our
talk is." I have flown over Conoco's seismic drilling lines in Congo and
what I have seen for myself is impressive. Conoco did not use bulldoz-
ers during exploration; the team walked. They did not cut a swath
through the forest; they cut down a few trees, at intervals, so that
helicopters could lower equipment on long ropes. In many other ways
they cared for the environment — even to the extent of hiring bota-
nists to help with replanting trees where, inevitably, some vegetation
had been destroyed or damaged. Six months after one of their seismic

drilling operations, it was virtually impossible to know they had been there. I have met with the managers of some of the Conoco operations in tropical forests in other parts of the world, and I have seen photos that have convinced me that they carry out their stated principles.

Of course, when oil is actually located, rich enough to be used commercially, some destruction is inevitable. In the tropical forest this fact is particularly distressing. Yet explorations will be carried out whatever the environmentalists say, and rather than ostracize the oil companies, it seems more practical and less hypocritical to work with those that are operating in an environmentally responsible way.

Once onshore oil has been found and a company moves from exploration to extraction, one of the first steps is to build a good road. This means, typically, that the forest will be opened up — for hunters and settlers alike. But if the government can be persuaded to create a national park in the area, everyone will benefit. The local people will get jobs from both the oil company and the park service and also find a new market for their products, and the animals and their habitat can be saved. Conservation education projects can be set up. The government, with foreign exchange from oil revenues in its coffers, will also get good marks from the international conservation community. Conoco did not strike oil in Congo and has pulled out (although, honoring Conoco's commitment, an entire team has remained to construct the chimp sanctuary). But we hope to work with Chevron, and perhaps other companies, to create a national park in this lovely part of the continent where there are still chimpanzees, as well as gorillas, elephants, and other forest and savanna fauna.

Tourism can be a major industry for a developing country. In Rwanda, where visitors flock to see some of the last remaining mountain gorillas, tourism is the number one foreign-exchange earner. The gorilla project employs as many local Rwandans as a timber company might have if it had moved into the park and removed all the trees. The difference is that tourism, provided it is well managed, can furnish employment in perpetuity, whereas logging provides employment only until the forests are gone.

The danger of tourism is that there is a temptation to cater to as many visitors as wish to come. After all, the more people who come, the more money will be brought into the country — and, to emphasize the point once more, we are talking about countries that are devastatingly poor. In Rwanda, the per capita income is only equivalent to $290 per year. So why not build more and more hotels, bulldoze

more and more roads into protected areas? We know, of course, that
overexploitation can gradually change a beautiful area into a barren
place that becomes unattractive to visitors and animals alike. But how
difficult for a politician to turn away tourist dollars! While he understands that too many visitors will eventually kill the hen that lays the
golden egg, he needs the money now. It is hard for him to justify a
policy that rejects the prospect of immediate riches, ignoring the immediate needs of the people. Because those needs are often desperate — for food, for hospitals and clinics and medicines, for schools and
teachers and textbooks, for buses, for repair of roads. The list could
become very long.

It is this desperation that has saddled many African countries with
the horrifying burden of foreign debts. Ever since the "white man"
colonized Africa, the wealthy nations of the industrialized world have
shamelessly exploited her vast natural resources. Yet rather than
returning some of those plundered riches in the form of foreign aid,
the wealthy nations typically gave money in the form of loans — loans
accepted in desperation, which leave the recipient nation with a debt
that hangs around its neck like a millstone for years. Even when the
aid comes in the form of a grant, the motive of the donor nation is
seldom purely altruistic; it is usually part of some scheme that will
enable the benefactor to exploit the natural resources of the recipient
country, draining away ever more of its remaining wealth.

There are signs, though, that the developed world is beginning to
realize the need for a more symbiotic partnership with the so-called
Third World in the pressing need to save our planet. The industrialized
nations are more sensitive today than ever before to the interdepen-
dence of human welfare and the natural world. And this sensitivity is
making it possible for leaders in African countries to obtain generous
foreign aid, for a variety of rural development programs, that is condi-
tional on sound environmental practices in the recipient country.
They can therefore more easily enforce regulations pertaining to environmental conservation. "See what good things we get for saving the
forest?" And the many enthusiastic and idealistic young environmentalists who are blossoming in today's Africa can operate in a political
and economic climate that allows them to develop new ideas in their
chosen field.

Immediate and practical solutions to the vast problems of deforestation and the encroachment of the desert must be closely linked with
economic benefits to all concerned, at both the government and the

local level. Perhaps most important of all, we must never forget that the only conservation measures that can hope to withstand the pressures of time are those that are fully endorsed and supported by the people themselves. Not only is autocratic interference by foreigners resented, but there is a long history of projects that have failed because foreigners, arrogant in the assumption that they know best, have failed to listen to the wisdom of the people on the spot. Why is aid of this sort accepted in the first place — for a project that the local people surmise is doomed to failure? Because it provides, at least temporarily, jobs and food for the local people. But it also brings a deep, slow resentment that surfaces as scorn for the condescending hand that is doling out such inappropriate scraps. It hurts self-esteem and national pride.

Thus, to summarize, development is inevitable in Africa, given the ever-expanding needs and the legitimate aspirations of the people living there. Beyond all doubt, mile upon mile of forest and woodland will fall to the chain saws and pit saws, and, through clear cutting, be totally destroyed: the chimpanzees living there are doomed. But if Western greed is curtailed and if lessons from the developed world are heeded, some forests can be preserved intact. And even though human needs are ever more pressing, it is still possible to treat the land and its creatures with respect. There is still hope for the wildlife of the continent, as well as for the human populations, if development goes hand in hand with family planning and sustainable use of natural resources. If people nurture their long-term wealth and attempt to recreate fertility in degraded land instead of cutting down more and more trees to create ever more desert. And if the industrialized nations cease their cruel exploitation.

Chimpanzees — at least some chimpanzees — can survive if humans choose that they do so. And humans will make this choice only when they realize that in fighting for the chimpanzees' survival they are also fighting for their own.

2

At the end of the play, Prospero gives up his magic and arranges to sail back to Italy with his daughter and the other Europeans. His daughter will marry the Prince of Naples. Prospero expects to regain his rightful position as Duke of Milan. As for Caliban, Prospero seems ready to grant him a "pardon," possibly intending to free the slave with the honored shape and to leave him, in peace, on the island.

The Tempest presents a generally coherent and convincing parable of human behavior in certain situations. Least plausible is the concept that Prospero would voluntarily abjure his magic and that the Europeans would voluntarily leave the island and set Caliban free. I can imagine a more realistic outcome: Prospero, with some regrets, holds on to his magic; the Europeans sail home to Italy, but leave their flag on the island and a small contingent of armed soldiers to protect it until they return with merchant ships, beads for trading, and the like. Voluntarily to give up power, voluntarily to free a slave, voluntarily to forsake commerce or to ignore someone or something no doubt marketable, voluntary to pardon a thing of darkness — these are not ordinary human behaviors.

But humans are creative, and while it is true that ethical progress has never been achieved entirely voluntarily, surely it has taken place. History has seen the end (or at least the marked decline) of the worst and most obvious sorts of human exploitation of humans: slavery, imperialism, colonialism. In Africa, let us hope, we are witnessing the final throes of apartheid. To recognize that these achievements in human ethical behavior and understanding have taken place painfully and imperfectly is not to deny their reality or wonder.

The new ethics we seek will not be easy either, but it too will be driven and sustained by necessity. We seek a new respect for the world's wild places and for the sentient beings who inhabit them. Concomitantly, we seek a recognition of the limits of human expansion. We in the West seem to imagine that the planetary larder is limitless: only if we can exploit more cleverly, recycle more thoroughly, our belief seems to be, we can continue to grow indefinitely. Our belief seems to be that an expanding economy is a healthy one, that a stable economy is a stagnant one. Yet unexamined growth in the West has already depleted the earth's ozone layer, created a harmful layer of greenhouse gases in the atmosphere, poisoned rivers and lakes and oceans, destroyed open spaces and the peace they bring. Unexamined growth in Africa is fast depleting the great forests and the wildlife and the soil — the ecological context that has for millions of years sustained Africa and Africans. Even with the most ingenious technological improvements, surely we cannot happily expand our numbers and needs forever. Some people point to very crowded societies — Japan, England, the Netherlands — as examples of how successfully nations can continue to expand. But those small countries sustain themselves by drawing, brilliantly, on resources from outside their own ecological base. They are exceptions, and there is no obvious resource base outside our planet itself. When the earth's atmosphere and seas are fully poisoned, the soils entirely drained, the forests and wilderness permanently destroyed, where then will we turn our energies for consumption?

In the final moments of the play, Prospero, alone on stage, turns and faces the audience. Now that his own magical powers are gone, he tells his listeners, he needs their help to achieve his own freedom from confinement on the island; the wind from their applause and cheers can fill his sails. He pleads, "As you from crimes would pardoned be, Let your indulgence set me free." Both Prospero and Caliban are prisoners and slaves, and both seek freedom — from each other and from the circumstances of the drama.

Prospero and Caliban are, we recognize at last, partners and twins, both slaves, both masters. Slavery violates equally the owner and the owned. By enslaving Caliban we enslave ourselves. Only when we free Caliban will we free ourselves.

APPENDIXES

ACKNOWLEDGMENTS

NOTES

REFERENCES

Appendix A

Conservation Status of the Chimpanzees of Africa, 1990

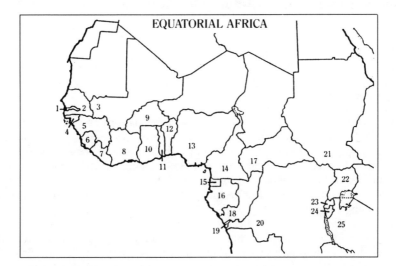

EQUATORIAL AFRICA

POPULATION BY COUNTRY

1. The Gambia	0	14. Cameroon	8,000
2. Senegal	200	15. Equatorial Guinea	2,000
3. Mali	700	16. Gabon	64,000
4. Guinea Bissau	100	17. Central African Republic	900
5. Guinea	3,000	18. Congo	4,000
6. Sierra Leone	2,000	19. Angola (Cabinda)	400
7. Liberia	3,000	20. Zaire	90,000
8. Ivory Coast	11,700	21. Sudan	300
9. Burkina Faso	0	22. Uganda	4,000
10. Ghana	400	23. Rwanda	150
11. Togo	0	24. Burundi	400
12. Benin	0	25. Tanzania	2,000
13. Nigeria	200		

NOTE: These figures are estimates. Estimates apply only to the common species, *Pan troglodytes*. Zaire has about 17,000 additional bonobos, *Pan paniscus*, a species occurring nowhere else.

PREPARED BY: Committee for Conservation and Care of Chimpanzees, 3819 48th St., NW, Washington, DC 20016, USA

SUPPORTED BY: The Jane Goodall Institute, 2200 East Speedway Boulevard, Tucson, AZ 85719, USA

Appendix B

Recommendations to USDA on Improving Conditions of Psychological Well-Being for Captive Chimpanzees*

As currently formulated and applied, federal regulations and guidelines governing the maintenance and care of captive primates used in experimental studies do not adequately address their psychological well-being. A workshop was therefore held on December 1–3, 1987, bringing together a cross-section of professionals experienced in studying both normal and abnormal chimpanzees, to consider this deficiency and to develop sound recommendations on improving the psychological well-being of chimpanzees held in laboratories and other facilities. The collective expertise of this diverse group covered many aspects of chimpanzee behavior and biology, ranging from biomedical research and veterinary care in laboratories to psychological and ethological studies in both wild and captive settings, as well as zoo administration and colony management. Conservation and animal welfare interests were also represented.

Chimpanzees are more like human beings — genetically, physiologically, anatomically, and in the structure of the brain — than are any other living beings. Wild chimpanzees have a long childhood of about seven years followed by six or so years of adolescence during which the skills needed to succeed in adulthood must be learned through experience and from other group members. Lack of opportunity for normal development can severely impair this learning process.

Chimpanzees show many cognitive abilities once viewed as uniquely human. They are, for example, capable of reasoned thought, generalization, abstraction, symbolic representation, and self-awareness. Many of their emotions, such as joy and sadness, fear and anxiety, and even a sense of humor, are highly similar to ours. They also exhibit empathy and friendship, perform acts of true altruism, and mourn the deaths of companions. There are also many similarities in social behavior, including communicative gestures such as kissing, embracing, and holding hands. Close, supportive, friendly bonds

*Reprinted from *Journal of Medical Primatology* 17 (1988): 113–122.

between individuals are maintained and strengthened, via social grooming and many other relaxed social activities, through spending long hours in one another's company. These relationships last for a lifespan of 40–50 years. Separation from a close companion can lead to marked distress, even among adults. Any youngster less than five years in age who loses a mother is likely to become clinically depressed and may even become so ill that death follows. The chimpanzee infant and the human child are alike in many ways, such as their capacity for endless romping and play, their curiosity, their ability to learn by observation and imitation, and above all in their need for reassurance and affection.

All professionals attending the December workshop agreed that, in view of the close evolutionary relationship between chimpanzees and human beings, this sibling species should receive special treatment when used in the laboratory or when maintained in any other captive situation.

Despite the difficulty of adequately defining psychological needs and states for another species, it was further agreed by those attending the workshop, based on their collective expertise and the best available information, that the psychological well-being of the chimpanzee depended on provision of the following: space for vigorous activities such as running, climbing, and swinging to allow adequate exercise; material for making comfortable beds as substitutes for tree nests; frequent social contact with other chimpanzees and human caregivers; opportunity to establish close social bonds in groups of mixed age and sex; variety in basic routine, including diet, social interaction, and object manipulation; and presence of intellectual stimulation and challenge.

It is precisely because chimpanzees are so like humans physiologically that they are used by medical researchers in the attempt to alleviate human beings' suffering and illness. And it is also because they are so like ourselves emotionally, cognitively, and behaviorally that we must improve the quality of their lives during those long years of imprisonment and servitude.

In order to assist the USDA in formulating regulations that are in keeping with the spirit of the new legislation on psychological well-being for chimpanzees and other primates held in captive conditions, we offer the following recommendations:

GENERAL ISSUES Scientists intending to perform experiments on chimpanzees must be able to prove, beyond all reasonable doubt, that the experimentation cannot be performed by using a lower species, via nonanimal alternative methods, or through carefully controlled clinical research. Chimpanzees should only be used for laboratory research of exceptional importance. All proposals for work involving chimpanzees must be subject to rigorous and independent professional scrutiny, with due consideration of whether similar studies have been undertaken previously or are already in progress elsewhere. Evaluation of the scientific merit of the proposed work and the benefits likely to accrue from it must be set against the likely adverse effects on the chimpanzees to be used. Unnecessary and unjustified duplication of experimentation is scientifically and ethically unacceptable, as are terminal studies on chimpanzees. Once a project using chimpanzees has been approved by the proper authorities, changes in protocol that potentially affect the psychological well-being of the experimental subjects must be periodically reviewed and reapproved under the same set of standards.

The use of chimpanzees in laboratory research is an international problem, and should not be considered solely in a national context. It is deemed unacceptable for individual scientists, institutions, corporations, or funding agencies to be involved in research on chimpanzees carried out in other countries having lower standards of scientific scrutiny or animal housing, care, and acquisition. Moreover, the taking of chimpanzees from Africa for any reason is unacceptable.

Any chimpanzee used once for painful and/or extremely stressful experimentation should be exempt from further experimentation of a painful or stressful nature.

PERSONNEL TRAINING   Scientists whose work involves the use of chimpanzees for any purpose must have an understanding of the nature of chimpanzees, so that the effects of experimental protocols on individual chimpanzees can be properly assessed in the course of planning the research.

Caregivers responsible for chimpanzees must receive special training, over and above the standard training required in caring for other laboratory species, including other primates, to fit them for the very special task of attending to the physical and psychological needs of chimpanzees. These special training procedures must be established at every facility housing chimpanzees. Evidence must be provided that training has been undertaken and successfully completed. In addition, a national accreditation scheme must be established, providing for professional certification by the USDA. The National Agriculture Library, in cooperation with the National Library of Medicine, should facilitate training by providing manuals, videotapes, and other books and papers that must be read by those working with chimpanzees.

During the selection of caregivers, emphasis must be placed on the qualities of compassion, dedication, and empathy with chimpanzees, in addition to the usual qualifications demanded of such laboratory personnel. The adult chimpanzee to caregiver ratio must never fall below ten to one. With youngsters below the age of seven years, additional caregivers are required in order to maintain frequent interaction.

The director of any facility must be responsible for ensuring that all institution personnel, including caregivers, are fully aware of the rules and regulations of USDA Veterinary Services and other pertinent governmental agencies that apply to the maintenance and experimental use of chimpanzees. Any violations of these regulations must be reported to the USDA and any funding agency involved.

HOUSING CONDITIONS   Chimpanzees must be kept in compatible groups, at a minimum of two individuals together. Separation from close companions typically induces psychological stress leading to physiological as well as behavioral changes, and in addition to threatening well-being may skew the results of experiments performed on that individual.

Chimpanzees must never be housed singly unless sick and in need of special treatment. If under exceptional circumstances the experimental protocol necessitates single housing, then the scientist must prove the need for this beyond all reasonable doubt. There is no known or justifiable medical or scientific reason for a chimpanzee to be kept in an isolette — i.e., a chimpanzee must never be maintained without aural and visual contact with other members of the same species, on at least two sides of the enclosure.

Chimpanzees must be housed in areas of not less than 400 square feet, with a minimum height of 7 feet, consisting of two to four interconnecting enclosures in different rooms. The structure and furnishings of the enclosure must provide ample opportunity for vigorous activity as well as privacy, and for varying the size of the social group.

The size of enclosures should increase on a sliding scale as a function of the number of chimpanzees being housed in a group. Two adult chimpanzees require 400 square feet of usable space, but in cases of demonstrated compatibility four adults or six juveniles can be maintained in enclosures of this size. If a scientist can confirm an empirical need for individual housing for experimental purposes, the enclosures must never be smaller than 196 square feet (14 feet × 14 feet) with as much height as is reasonably possible within a standard room (minimum 7 feet).

In all newly built facilities chimpanzees must be provided with an outdoor activity area. Chimpanzees should never be confined to rooms without windows through which to view the outdoors.

Existing facilities which cannot immediately comply with the new regulations pertaining to enclosure size must nevertheless provide chimpanzees with exercise rooms of 200 square feet floor area until the standards mentioned above can be fully implemented.

ENVIRONMENTAL FACTORS Chimpanzees must be provided with a variety of occupations and opportunities for object manipulation in the effort to improve their lives of confinement to the greatest extent possible. This must include variety in food items, variation of routine with surprise treats and events, provision of items such as magazines, empty egg cartons, etc. A series of problem-solving devices will enable them to work for their food instead of picking it out of a feeder bin. They must be given the opportunity to exercise some control over their environment. As an example, a series of buttons, connected to a computer terminal, can provide, when pushed, a drink, a raisin, a toy, etc. Such machines could be activated at irregular times and the chimpanzees informed by a caregiver or some signal device. Detailed records must be kept of the different enrichment procedures used each day, and made available to USDA (APHIS) inspectors. A regular exchange of information about enrichment procedures should also be promoted among facilities.

Mechanical enrichment devices or procedures, such as those noted above, should not be regarded as substitutes for social activity with caregivers.

Bedding materials, such as blankets, are essential. Young chimpanzees can readily be taught to hand over such items for washing in the morning in exchange for, for example, a treat.

Handling procedures such as anesthetization, capture, introductions, moving to new enclosures must be done in ways that minimize stress, fear, and physical harm. For example, chimpanzees living in large cages can be taught to enter smaller separate handling cages for experimental procedures, such as injections. If chimpanzees routinely sleep in small cages attached to the larger enclosures, they can then be easily handled in the morning if needed for experimental purposes.

For young chimpanzees, friendly interaction with the caregiver is also of tremendous importance, and must be encouraged on a regular basis so as to develop bonds which help to reduce stress when individuals must be handled in experimental protocols.

The Institutional Animal Care and Use Committee shall establish, in consultation with the attending veterinarian, written procedures and guidelines for ensuring the psychological well-being of primates in accordance with established regulations and standards, and a record system to permit evaluation of compliance.

SOCIAL CARE FACTORS   The mother-infant bond is essential to normal psychological development of an infant chimpanzee. In addition, relationships with other chimpanzees during infancy lead to the acquisition of normal social and parental skills. Therefore, every effort must be made to raise infants in multimother groups that also include compatible adult males.

Infants must remain with their mothers as long as possible, at least to the age of 18 months. If earlier separation is necessary because the mother is unable to care for the infant, fostering of the infant to another lactating female should be attempted. If that is not possible, the infant must be placed with compatible youngsters of similar age. Infants under the age of 18 months who are separated from their mothers and raised by human caregivers must receive individual care around the clock for several months. When mother-infant separation is required by experimental protocol, this should be done so as to provide time for the gradual transfer of emotional attachment from the mother to the human caregivers.

Youngsters of any age who are separated from their social groups for use in any experiment must be given a minimum period of 3 months for adjustment to their new conditions, before placement in any experimental situation.

Careful attempts must be made to reunite juveniles and infants with their mothers in their original social group at the completion of experiments.

RELOCATION   The transfer of chimpanzees between research facilities should be avoided unless absolutely necessary. If it becomes necessary to relocate individuals or groups, then chimpanzees should be accompanied by a familiar caregiver who must remain with them until they have begun to adjust to the new facility and formed new affinitive attachments with the new caregivers.

RETIREMENT Chimpanzees who are no longer useful to biomedical research must be retired and when necessary rehabilitated so that they may live out their lives in conditions that guarantee their psychological well-being until they die of natural causes. No research projects involving the experimental use of chimpanzees should be initiated without prior guarantee of adequate funding to endow a program of retirement designed to provide normal lifetime support for each subject.

Acknowledgments

Without the generous help of many individuals this book could not have been written. It is impossible for us to name everyone, but those whose cooperation was most significant are mentioned below.

In the United Republic of Tanzania, chimpanzees are well protected now owing to the conservation policies of the government. We especially thank the president of Tanzania, Hassan Ali Mwinyi. And the director of wildlife, Costa Mlay; the director of national parks, David Babu; park warden Stefan Qoli and his staff; also Dr. Anthony Collins, Ramji Dharsi, Asgar Remthulla, and Jayant and Kirit Vaitha. Invaluable data have been provided by Dr. Janette Wallis and the Gombe field staff, among whom we should especially mention Yahaya Alamasi, Hilali Matama, Hamisi Mkono, Eslom Mpongo, Gabo Paulo, and the late David Mussa; also by David Gardner-Roberts, Sally Anne McOwan, Wolfgang Knoepfler, Bill Wallaner, and James Murray; and by Dr. Toshisada Nishida and members of his team at Mahale Mountains National Park.

Elsewhere in Africa, we are indebted to many field researchers, wildlife officers, and other experts for sharing their knowledge about wild chimpanzee behavior and conservation issues: in Burundi, Peter Trenchard (U.S. Peace Corps and New York Zoological Society Biodiversity Program); in Gabon, Michel Fernandez and Dr. Caroline Tutin of the Lopé-Okanda Forest Reserve; in Guinea, Dr. Yukimaru Sugiyama (Kyoto University); in Ivory Coast, Drs. Christophe and Hedwige Boesch (Centre Suisse de Recherches Scientifiques and University of Basel in Switzerland), Denis Lia (CSRS), and Dr. Paul and Natalie Marchesi (CSRS); in Liberia, Alexander Peale (director of the Forestry Development Authority); in Uganda, Dr. Isabiriye Basuta (Kibale Forest Research Project and Makerere University), Dr. Kevin D. Hunt (KFRP and Indiana University), and Dr. Richard Wrangham (KFRP and Harvard University); in Zaire, Dr. Takayoshi Kano (Kyoto University). We also thank Mike Garner of Mike Garner Safaris in Nairobi, Kenya; Dr. Franz Sitter of Horseshoe Farm near Freetown, Sierra Leone; and Peter the Little Hunter.

We must thank those involved in zoos and sanctuaries for orphaned chimps. In Burundi, we have received much help from the government of President Mbuyoya, and also from the minister of the environment, Hon. Louis Nduwimana, and the director general of INECN, Laurent Ntahuga; as well as from Dr. Susanne and Dean Anderson (JGI representatives), Geoff Cresswell, Dr. Ken Pack, Johnna Wenburg, Susan Stenquist, Charlotte Uhlebroek (now at Gombe Wildlife Research Institute), Karen Winter, and the Burundian staff who are helping to care for the chimpanzees. In Congo, we are specially grateful to Graziella Cotman, who rescued the seven young chimpanzees from Kinshasa after the riots, and who is now the JGI representative in Congo, caring for twenty-four chimpanzees in the Brazzaville zoo, as well as Jean Mabotot and the other keepers at the zoo. We are also grateful for the support of the British Ambassador Peter Chandler and Jane Chandler, the German Ambassador Adolf Ederer, Vince Smith, and John Stronge. We also thank Jean Jacques Bazonguisa, Aliette Jamart, Steven Matthews, Serge Ouamba, Karen Pack, André Picque, and Patrice Simon. In The Gambia, we were provided information and assistance through the courtesy of Dr. Camara (Wildlife Conservation Department); and Janis Carter, Boiro Samba, and Jim Zinn (The Gambia's Chimpanzee Rehabilitation Project). We are grateful for the efforts, in Tanzania, of Maria Finnigan (Sanaane Island Sanctuary); in Uganda, of Tim Holmes (formerly with the Entebbe Zoo), Christine Manning (Entebbe Zoo), and Oscar and Linda Rothen (JGI representatives in Kampala); in Zambia, of David and Sheila Siddle (Chimfunshi Wildlife Orphanage); and in Zaire, of Richard Hamer (Chevron Oil), Dr. Delfi Messenger, and Chris Rules (American School of Kinshasa, Kinshasa and N'Sele Zoos).

We should like to express our gratitude to the U.S. Department of State, in particular to Secretary James A. Baker III, for his invaluable support in many ways both in the United States and in Africa. Special thanks to Ambassador James "Dan" Phillips and Lucie Phillips for their wonderful support, first in Burundi and second in the Republic of Congo; in Tanzania, Ambassador Edmund de Jarnette and Katia de Jarnette, and Ambassador Don Petterson and Julia Petterson; in Burundi, Ambassador Cynthia Perry; in Zaire, Ambassador William C. Harrop and Janet Harrop. Many of the embassy staff in these countries have volunteered their help as well and deserve recognition, particularly Christopher Bane, Ralph and Barbara Bressler, Mimi Brian, Dr. Cedric Dumont and Ruth Dumont, Stevenson and Penelope McIllvaine, Sarah Rosenberry, and Sarah and Lawrence Stone.

Very special thanks to our friends at Conoco, who have done so much to help: to Dino Nicanderos, president; Max Pitcher, vice president for exploration; and Jack Blackshear, Mike Johnson, Mary Lewis, Ladislau Silva, Dee Simpson, and Terry Thoem; and especially to those who are helping with the sanctuary in Pointe Noire, including Roger Simpson, who began the work but has since moved on, Michel Bercut, René Beghara, Marco Besseling, Klaus Dinse, Rod MacAllister, and Rodrigue Tiaku.

For so generously providing information, assistance, and advice, we also wish to thank many people in the United States and other parts of the world beyond Africa: Dr. Milton April, director of the NIH AIDS Animal Models Program in Bethesda, Maryland; Bob Barker in Hollywood, California; Dr. Donald Barnes of the National Anti-Vivisection Society in Washington, D.C.; Elaine Bennett in Lefaria, Texas; Bobby Berosini in Las Vegas, Nevada; Gwenna Blackmore in Rolling Hills Estates, California; Tim Bleach, frequent volunteer at Chimfunshi Orphanage; Dr. Sarah T. Boysen of the Primate Cognition Project at Ohio State University; Connie Braun in Festus, Missouri; Nancy Burnet of the Coalition to Protect Animals in Entertainment in Riverside, California; Adele Caramanian in Cincinnati, Ohio; Dr. and Mrs. Russ Cochran in West Plains, Missouri; Jon Cohen in Washington, D.C.; James Cronin of Monkey World in Dorset, England; Pat Derby of the Performing Animal Welfare Society in California; Roseanne D'Ercole in Ramsey, New Jersey; Bob Dunn of Bob Dunn's Animal Rentals in Sylmar, California; Lee Ecuyer of "Zippy the Chimp" in St. Petersburg, Florida; Dr. Jorg Eichberg, formerly with the Southwest Foundation for Biomedical Research in San Antonio, Texas; Dr. Joseph M. Erwin of Diagnon Corporation in Rockville, Maryland; David Fischer, formerly of Rent-a-Chimp in West Palm Beach, Florida; Jo Folger in Cincinnati, Ohio; Dr. Roger Fouts of the Department of Psychology at Central Washington University; Tony Gentry, owner of Cheeta in Thousand Oaks, California; Ottavio Gesmundo in Las Vegas, Nevada; Cherie Gray in West Palm Beach, Florida; Ken Harris, owner of Sam at the Train Stop Inn in Foster, Ohio; Philip and Roberta Herman, owners of "Charlie the Chimp" and Party Productions in Hillburn, New York; Liam Hussey of Marine World/Africa USA in Vallejo, California; Susan Hyndman of Monterey, California; Marvin Jones of the San Diego Zoo; Dr. John Landon of Diagnon Corporation in Rockville, Maryland; Dr. Bernie Levine of Parrot Jungle in Miami, Florida; Linda Levine of PETA in Las Vegas, Nevada; Greg Lille of Lille's Performing Animals in Auburn, California; Franklin Loewe, dean, Tufts School of Veterinary Medicine; Dr. James Mahoney of the Laboratory for Experimental Medicine and Surgery in Primates in Tuxedo, New York; Stacey M. Maloney of the Southwest Foundation for Biomedical Research in San Antonio, Texas; Dr. Tetsuro Matsuzawa of the Primate Research Institute at Kyoto University; Shirley McGreal of the International Primate Protection League; David McKenna in Rumford Point, Maine; Dr. Jan Moor-Jankowski of the Laboratory for Experimental Medicine and Surgery in Primates in Tuxedo, New York; Dr. Thomas Moser of the Department of English at Stanford University; Tina Nelson, formerly with the Humane Society of the United States in Ohio; Mae Noell of the Noell's Ark Chimp Farm in Tarpon Springs, Florida; Carol Noon, Gainsborough University; Dr. John Oates of the Department of Anthropology at Hunter College; Gloria and Allen Painten, owners of Denyse in Jacksonville, Florida; Dr. Alfred Prince of the New York Blood Center and Vilab II in Liberia; Ian Redmond of *BBC Wildlife* in England; Sled Reynolds of Hollywood Animal Rentals in Los Angeles, California; Valerie Rohy of the Department of English at Tufts University; Dr. Andrew Rowan of the Tufts Center for Animals and Public Policy at Tufts University; Robert Rush of the Los Angeles City Department of Animal Regulations; Dr. Albert Sabin in Washington, D.C.; Dr. Huub Schellekens of TNO Primate Center in The Netherlands; Les Schobert of the North Carolina Zoo; Gene and Rusty Schuler of the Wild Animal Retirement Village in Waldo, Florida; Dr. Allan Schultz of NIH NAID in Bethesda, Maryland; Ignass Spruit, Pro-Primates, The Netherlands; Dr. Martin L. Stephens of the Humane Society of the United States in Washington, D.C.; Christine Stevens of the Animal Welfare Institute in Washington, D.C.; Michael Stower, formerly of Rent-a-Chimp in Richardson, Texas; Wally Swett of Primarily Primates in San Antonio, Texas; Dr. Geza Teleki of the Committee for Conservation and Care of Chimpanzees; Simon Templar in Spain; Virginia Valbuena of Valbuena Chimps in Clearwater, Florida; Mr. and Mrs. Vivier of Simian Lodge in Tennessee; John Waugh of the International Union for the Conservation of Nature in Washington, D.C.; Daniel Westfall, owner of the Marquee Chimpanzees in Palm Springs, California; Ron Winters, owner of Mr. Jiggs in Ramsey, New Jersey; and Jean Wright, formerly with the Marquis Chimpanzees.

Much of the content of this book has depended on access to the files of the Committee for Conservation and Care of Chimpanzees. The CCCC is a professional organization with representatives in more than twenty-five countries working on survival problems of wild and captive chimpanzees. In addition to its primary role as a scientific adviser to government agencies and private organizations focusing on wildlife and wildlands protection, the CCCC assesses population status, monitors trade trends, promotes conservation and rehabilitation projects, provides guidelines for captive care, supports legislative action, and encourages public education. We are deeply indebted to the scientists who have contributed information and assistance to this organization.

I am grateful to the staff and directors and trustees, past and present, of the Jane Goodall Institute. In the United States our officers are Princess Genevieve di san Faustino, founder; Mary Smith, president of the board; Edward P. Bass, vice president; and Leslie Groff, secretary. Robert Edison, who is treasurer and also executive director, has devoted himself single-mindedly to the development of the Tucson office, JGI International headquarters, and it is hard for me to find words to thank him. I am also grateful to Nick Leon, financial officer, as well as to Susan Butterfield, Gillian Dundas, Cathy Frachey, Jennifer Kenyon, Lorraine Robinson, and Dr. Virginia Landau. I thank board members Anthony Athaide, Larry Barker, Dr. Eugene Bonham, Hugh Caldwell, Roger Caras, Joan Cathcart, Bart Deamer, Robert Fry, Gordon Getty, Vanne Goodall, Margaret Gruter, Dr. Sally Kirkham, Dr. Henry Klein, Claire Pollack, and Elizabeth Strode; and our legal advisers in the United States, McCutcheon, Doyle, Brown & Emerson. In the United Kingdom I thank our officers: Dr. Karsten Schmidt, OBE, chairman; Guy Parsons, treasurer; and Robert Vass, secretary. I am extraordinarily indebted to Dilys Vass, administrative officer, who has often worked single-handedly to keep JGI-UK afloat. And I thank also Andrea Jones and Rebecca Wood-Robinson. Other trustees, to whom I am most grateful, are Clive Hollands, Steve Matthews,

Michael Neugebauer, Virginia Pleydell-Bouverie, Susan Pretzlick, David Shepherd, and John Tandy. In Tanzania I am most grateful to our officers Jeetu Patel, treasurer; Steven Sabaini, secretary; and our trustees Girish Chande, Ramji Dharsi, Abdul Haji, Addie Lyaru, Oosha Sehmi, Iddi Simba. The commitment and efforts of all the staff and officers, past and present, of JGI internationally have made it possible for me to initiate many projects that today are saving the lives of chimpanzees and that are helping to educate people and change attitudes toward nature and animals in many countries. A big thank-you to all the members of JGI around the world.

Certain people have helped me with fund raising, moral support, and friendship during the period when this book was being written. I thank them all: Robert Bateman, Dr. Eugene and Alynda Bonham, Dr. James Caillouette, Toni Carmichael, Dr. John "Jack" Conaghan, Dr. John Conaghan, Jr., Neva Folk, Neil Furman, Milton Harris, Dr. Junichero Itani, Chitra and Jagan Jagannathan, Olwen "Olly" Joseph, Drs. Wayne and Sally Kirkham, Gary Larson, Dr. Martin Lazar, Jack and Felicia Lemmon, Ambassador Christopher Liundi, Cecilia Liungman, Dimitri Mantheakis, Stevie Nicks, Guy Odom, Robert Schad, Virginia Schwien, Austin and Marta Weeks, Richard and Mollie Williford. And, it goes without saying, I owe everything to my amazing mother.

No one but the authors is responsible for opinions expressed in this book, of course, but we must thank the experts who read and commented on sections of the manuscript: Professor Kevin Hunt of Indiana University, Dr. Wyn Kelley of the Massachusetts Institute of Technology, Professor Ron Rebholz of Stanford University, Dr. Andrew Rowan of Tufts University, Dr. Mark Savin in Minneapolis, Minnesota, Dr. Geza Teleki of the Committee for Conservation and Care of Chimpanzees, and Professor Richard Wrangham of Harvard University.

Other experts contributed in other ways and equally deserve our sincere thanks: Peter Matson of Sterling Lord Literistic and Harry Foster of Houghton Mifflin, for launching this book in the first place; Barbara Williams, for battening the hatches; Dwight Peterson, for tending the galley and trimming the sails; and Wyn Kelley, for conducting important celestial navigation in all kinds of weather. The Jane Goodall Institute, the Baker Foundation, and Arlington Arts/Massachusetts Arts Lottery provided grants at critical times during the writing of this book, and so we are most grateful to those organizations as well.

Notes

2. MAN OR FISH?   The Bauman material on chimpanzee strength is from Bauman, 1926. The quoted remarks of the Premacks may be found in Premack and Premack, 1983, p. 2.

It is my own idea that Andrew Battell's arrival in England in 1607, speaking of two humanlike "monsters" alive in Africa, influenced Shakespeare's 1610–11 creation of Caliban. I don't know that anyone else has suggested it before, and I am almost surprised that the best current study of Caliban (Vaughan and Vaughan, 1991) did not. Some actors' interpretations of the character of Caliban, particularly during the time when a Darwinian vision predominated, have stressed an apish appearance and style. It is a commonplace observation that European zoology and mythology (the two were not perfectly distinguishable) from ancient times into the Renaissance also referred, with varying degrees of seriousness, to any number of humanoid creatures. It is certainly clear that Shakespeare relied on contemporary travelers' tales, most obviously the accounts of a shipwreck in the Bermudas. For one good survey of the play's known sources, see Langbaum, 1987 (1964); for a survey of possible origins of Caliban, see Vaughan and Vaughan, 1991, which I have relied on. My more general ideas about *The Tempest* find their most inspired origins in Leo Marx's illuminating essay of 1964. The brief footnote concerning historical portrayals of Caliban is mostly based on Barnet, 1987 (1964) and Vaughan and Vaughan, 1991.

Vaughan and Vaughan, incidentally, use the "honored shape" passage to confirm their idea that the Caliban character was ultimately human and therefore perhaps modeled on some sort of real-life human precursor. I believe they have unnecessarily limited their thinking on this subject as, possibly, does Bernheimer, 1979 (1952). We do know from the "honored shape" passage that Caliban had a humanlike physical form. Obviously he was not intended by his creator to be a half-fish or some sort of tortoise, as some interpreters of the play have mistakenly supposed. But Vaughan and Vaughan ignore for no evident reason the fact that a being can possess the honored shape and still not be human (see Vaughan and Vaughan, 1991, pp. 10, 11, 248).

The Battell quotation is from Purchas, 1905 (1625), vol. 6, p. 398. Vaughan and Vaughan refer to Shakespeare's reliance on Hakluyt; the quotation about Shakespeare as an "apparently avid reader of histories and travel accounts" is on page 44 of that source. For more on Hakluyt, see Masefield, 1927. It is possible that Battell's report found publication before Purchas took it, but I have not been successful in locating an earlier version of Battell. Tyson is quoted in Yerkes and Yerkes, 1929, pp. 14, 15. The Darwin quotation is from Darwin (1872), p. 34. Information on Gallup's mirror experiments are from Gallup, 1970; see also Gallup, 1977. Köhler may have been the first to suggest the ape mirror issue, in Köhler, 1925.

The "emergence of humankind from the rest of the natural world" is obviously a bigger subject than this chapter can treat properly. My vast generalizations found wind and I hope will find anchor in Calder, 1983; Diamond, 1984, 1989; and Ronan, 1982. See also Byrne and Whiten, 1988; Ciochon and Corruccini, 1983; and Sibley and Alhquist, 1984. Anthropologist Kevin Hunt of Indiana University informs me that the record is unclear on the history of the development of speech; the idea that language and the capacity to symbolize account for our emergence from nature is, of course, fanciful. Hunt would prefer to examine the effects of settled agriculture, "where humans pretty much ceased entering into nature and began subduing natural flora so that they could inject domesticated plants into the situation. In such a world view natural flora and fauna become weeds and pests, and human cultural interests are completely outside nature." The words of Martin Luther I took from Ronan, 1982, p. 330.

3. TO SNARE THE NIMBLE MARMOSET   The brief survey of animal tool-using behavior (polar bears, sea otters, etc.) is paraphrased from Griffin, 1984, pp. 118–127. The material on the assassin bug's termite fishing is from McMahan, 1983. Boesch, 1990, and Boesch and Boesch-Achermann, 1990, provide some material on the variety of chimp hunting techniques. Hunting and meat eating are rare behaviors to begin with, and they would be affected by factors such as availability of prey and alternative foods, and the presence of competing predators. A thorough study by William McGrew comparing long-term data from six different field sites in Africa found widely varying meat diets among chimpanzee groups, even when the same prey species were present, which generally confirms Boesch's 1990 observations about prey species. Geza Teleki studied the predatory behavior of chimpanzees at Gombe for a year, during 1978 and 1979, and reached conclusions about collective hunting and meat sharing after a hunt that might seem to contradict some of Boesch's conclusions about the Gombe chimps. Of twelve successful kills observed during that period, Teleki noted that in eight cases the hunts were carried out collectively by several males who divided the meat among themselves afterward (Teleki, 1973). What Boesch reports specifically about the Tai chimps is not debatable.

Material on Richard Wrangham and chimpanzee medicines is based on a 1990 interview with Wrangham; also Maugh, n.d.; Merewood, 1991; Newton and Nishida, 1989; Wrangham and Goodall, 1989; Wrangham and Nishida, 1983; and Wrangham and Rodriguez, n.d. The first quotation (Wrangham's) is from the 1990 interview; the quotation of Rodriguez is from Merewood, 1991, p. 56; the second Wrangham quotation is from page 58 of the same source. Newton and Nishida, 1989, provide the basis for my commentary on buccal administration. Specific material on nutcracking comes from interviews; see also Boesch and Boesch-Achermann, 1990.

4. CALIBAN'S ISLAND   This chapter considers the conservation problems for chimpanzees (*Pan troglodytes*); for a general consideration of the somewhat parallel problems facing the critically endangered bonobos, sometimes called pygmy chimpanzees (*Pan paniscus*), see especially Malenky, Thompson-Handler, and Susman, 1989; see also Badrian and Badrian, 1977; Mubalamata, 1984; Kano, 1984; MacKinnon, 1976; Susman and Mubalamata, 1984; and Susman and others, 1981.

Marx (1964) clarifies that in *The Tempest* the debate about the island reconstructs opposing Elizabethan ideas and images about nature in the New World. For Marx the debate in the play takes place only among the Europeans; I feel the debate also occurs between Caliban and the Europeans. I am grateful to Newman, 1990, p. 14, for pointing out the etymology of "jungle." Myers (1980, 1984) provided some well-respected data on deforestation, from which he concluded that the tropical forests were being *altered* at the rate of 80,000 square miles a year, of which some 36,000 square miles consists of permanent alteration — total deforestation. The estimate of one million species extinct by the end of the century was originally calculated by Norman Myers; it is cited in Newman, 1990, p. 129. The Rodriguez quotation is from Newman, 1990, p. 129; the other three quotations are from page 10 of the same source. Data on fuelwood in Africa, Nigeria's timber export figures, and Ethiopia's rates of topsoil loss are also taken from Newman, pp. 117, 140, 153. All my population statistics (doubling times) are from "World Population Data Sheet," 1990. Data on cutting of ancient forests in North America will be found in Connelly, 1991, and Zuckerman, 1991.

The assumption that chimpanzees are found solely in primary tropical forest (Hartmann, 1886; Hill, 1969) has been replaced by the recognition that they can survive in a variety of African habitats and, conversely, that they will not necessarily be found in every area of primary forest. (See, for example, Kortlandt, 1972; McGrew, Baldwin, and Tutin, 1981; Teleki, 1980.) Chimpanzees are much more adaptable than was previously believed. But the destruction of the African rainforest (MacKinnon and MacKinnon, 1986; Myers, 1979, 1980, 1984, 1985; Salati and Vose, 1983) has been accompanied by the decline of chimpanzees throughout their once broad and protective range. Some individuals associated with biomedical research speculate that vast numbers of chimpanzees remain in the still largely unstudied Zaire Basin (Johnsen, 1987), but virtually everywhere in Africa, available information tells the same story of collapsing habitat.

For overall information on the endangerment of chimpanzees in Africa, see

Teleki, 1986, 1989. See also "Chimpanzee Experts," 1978; Harrisson, 1971; Mack and Mittermeier, 1984; Oates, 1985; Suzuki, 1971; Wolfheim, 1983. For more specific reports, see the following. For the eastern range: Baldwin and Teleki, 1973; Ghiglieri, 1984; Goodall, 1986; and Hiraiwa-Hasegawa, Hasegawa, and Nishida, 1984; see also Harako, 1981; Hart, 1978; and Hart and Thomas, 1986. For the western range: Albrecht and Dunnett, 1971; Boesch and Boesch-Achermann, 1981; Bournonville, 1967; Kortlandt and Holzhaus, 1987; McGrew, Baldwin, and Tutin, 1981; Struhsaker and Hunkeler, 1971; and Sugiyama, 1984; see also Jeffrey, 1977; Robinson and Peal, 1981; Teleki, 1980; Teleki and Baldwin, 1980; and Teleki and Bangura, 1981. For the central range: Jones and Sabater Pi, 1971; Kortlandt, 1962, 1963; Sabater Pi, 1978; Sabater Pi and Jones, 1967; and Sugiyama, 1985; see also Gandini, 1979; Harcourt and Stewart, 1980; Sabater Pi, 1979; and Tutin and Fernandez, 1988. General research combined with survey work (Albrecht, 1976; Baldwin, McGrew, and Tutin, 1982; Bournonville, 1967; Jones and Sabater Pi, 1971; Kano, 1972; Moore, 1985; Sugiyama and Souman, 1988; Teleki, 1980; Trenchard, 1988; Tutin and Fernandez, 1983, 1984) and incidental studies by scientists more focused on other species (for example, Carroll, 1986, and Fay, 1987) yield reliable information on thirty-two different areas located within more than half the nations where chimpanzees still survive. The studies consistently document an alarming decline.

General information on subsistence hunting in Africa is available in many places. My sources include Asibey, 1974; Goodall and Teleki, n.d.; Mittermeier and others, 1986; also Jeffrey, 1970, 1977; and Lowes, 1970. For more on European sport hunting of great apes see Merfield and Miller, 1956; also Du Chaillu, 1861. Most of the information on Liberian hunting is from Robinson and Peale, 1981; the background on Liberian hunters moving into Sierra Leone is from Teleki, 1980. Kortlandt's comments on Ivory Coast are cited in Wolfheim, 1983, p. 709. For details about hunting in northern Ghana see Sabater Pi and Groves, 1972, p. 242; see also Asibey, 1978. Carroll, 1990, discusses the situation of the BaAka; Hart, 1978, reports on the Mbuti. Harcourt and Stewart, 1980, report on great ape consumption in Gabon; Tutin and Fernandez, as cited in Ghiglieri, 1988, p. 273, add information on the effects of subsistence hunting in Gabon. The story of the killing of crop-raiding chimps in western Uganda is from Ghiglieri, 1988, pp. 266, 267.

"Chimpanzees are in many places protected by law . . . But laws not backed by tradition are usually ineffectual." See, for example, Asibey, 1978; Dossi, Guillaumet, and Hadley, 1981; Happold, 1971; Harcourt and Stewart, 1980; Jeffrey, 1975; Lamotte, 1983; Spinage, 1980; Struhsaker, 1987; and Suzuki, 1971. Ghiglieri's discussion of the effects of snares on chimpanzees in Kibale is from Ghiglieri, 1988, pp. 166–172; quotation from p. 166. Rahm's work is described in Rahm, 1967; quotations are from pp. 195, 206.

5. WHAT, HO! SLAVE! Information on "keeping primates as pets or servants" is from Morris and Morris, 1966, pp. 240–247. The Dapper and Garner quotations are cited in this source, p. 246, as is the information on Meunier's ideas, including the quotations, pp. 240, 241.

6. NO DOUBT MARKETABLE Much information in this chapter is taken from materials not regularly published — interviews, personal and business correspondence, customhouse and court records, and so on — and therefore not listed in References and not fully described in these notes. I have the materials on file.

Franz Sitter's television interview was in "Brutal Kinship," a *National Geographic Explorer* documentary shown in 1987. Estimates on the number of chimpanzees in biomedical research laboratories are from Institute, 1986; Prince and others, 1988; Seal and Flesness, 1986; see also my comments in Chapter 11 and its notes. A summary of the best scientific estimates of wild chimpanzee populations in various parts of Africa can be found in Teleki, 1989. Franz Sitter does not agree that his trade has damaged wild chimpanzee populations. In fact, when a journalist for *Geo* magazine wrote in 1981 that Sitter was responsible for reducing the chimpanzee population in Sierra Leone from an estimated one hundred thousand to approximately two thousand, Sitter sued. The statement that one hundred thousand chimpanzees originally lived in Sierra Leone was indeed an error, as everyone agreed; but Sitter was unable to convince the court that the full account was serious enough to require a payment of money. He lost the suit and paid for court expenses.

Yerkes' original article is Yerkes, 1916, and the quotes are from pp. 233, 234, 232. His later work is Yerkes, 1943; see pp. 1–11. J. L. Buck's story is from Buck, 1927. In support of my contention that Africa at this time served as a "convenient field of dreams" for Americans and Europeans, I refer the reader to "Along the Trail," 1927, which occurs in the same publication as Buck's piece, but a different month. Editor Mary Hastings Bradley poses in a photograph as "the guest of jolly, carefree villagers in the Belgian Congo"; we are informed that Carl Akeley, licensed by the Belgian colonial government to kill ten mountain gorillas for the American Museum of Natural History in New York, only killed five, "so strongly did he disapprove of the destruction of the rare ape"; and so on. One doesn't have to look hard for this sort of thing. A few African tribes, at least until recently, have hunted gorillas in roughly the same fashion as Buck describes capturing chimpanzees, except that nearly all the apes were killed. See Denis, 1963, and Merfield and Miller, 1956. Perhaps Rahm's (1967) description of an expensive and thoroughly organized capture expedition in eastern Zaire comes closest to sustaining Buck's fiction. Local methods for acquiring live primates in Sierra Leone were actually very bloody; see Robinson, 1971; Tappen, 1964; and Teleki, 1980. Yerkes' final quote about Buck is from Yerkes, 1943, p. 23.

Much of my biographical information on Sitter comes from material not regularly available — the biographical statement on his application for a degree at the University of Vienna, papers retrieved from the Berlin Archives, various remarks he himself made in personal correspondence, and so on. The few regularly published accounts that refer to his background, such as Duberley, 1988, rely on some of this same material. Customhouse records on Sitter's exports of live chimpanzees out of Sierra Leone have been noted in Teleki, 1980, tables 1 and 2.

Most of the biographical background on Teleki and Moor-Jankowski is taken from interviews. The story of permit applications by Merck Sharpe and Dohme and Albany Medical College in 1977 is based in part on Teleki's recounting of the event; I have also examined the original U.S. Fish and Wildlife documents on those applications. The Kortlandt survey was mentioned there.

Data on the situation in Sierra Leone during the mid-1970s were sketchy, and Kortlandt's study seems to have been the best at that time. But there were other reports: Tappen, 1964, did not mention chimpanzees in his survey of potential primate exports from the country; Jones, 1966, stated that chimpanzees there were "not often seen except in captivity"; Robinson, 1971, noted that "all the signs are that chimpanzees are decreasing in most parts of their range that I visited"; Harrisson, 1971, referred to a personal communication from Kortlandt and a report from the chief conservator of forests in Sierra Leone in her confirmation of the dire situation. More theoretical studies, based on known figures for local densities and available habitat, confirmed the overall picture of an unsustainable exploitation (Bournonville, 1967; Harrisson, 1971; Kortlandt and van Zon, 1969; Robinson, 1971; Teleki, Hunt, and Pfifferling, 1976).

Merck's assurances that "humane" capture methods would be used remain based merely on what Franz Sitter in Africa and his middleman in the United States, Mike Nolan of Primate Imports, were telling them. Other reports of capture techniques in the area suggest a far bloodier and more destructive picture: Tappen, 1964, described the technique of driving other primates into nets and then clubbing them to death; Robinson, 1971, noted the same technique used to gather chimpanzee babies, with the unmanageable older animals "usually being killed on the site." Descriptions of "the typical West African problems" of Sierra Leone are cited in Teleki, 1980, pp. 2, 6, 60, 61.

The problems of West Africa are described in many other sources, some of which I refer to in earlier chapters. Additional problems are cited in Teleki and Baldwin, 1981; see also Teleki, 1980, pp. 10, 19. Information specifically on Sitter's methods is cited in Teleki, 1980, pp. 10, 34–36; Teleki and Baldwin, 1981; and Teleki and Bangura, 1981. Teleki's conclusion that two thousand plus or minus five hundred chimps remained in Sierra Leone, incidentally, reconfirmed a private and never released report provided by other field experts (T. S. Gartlan, C. J. Jones, A. Kortlandt, and T. T. Struhsaker) to the NIH in 1978, which indicated not only "very few" chimps in Sierra Leone but also smuggling out of Guinea to sustain the still considerable trade from Sierra Leone: "Most exports of Guinean origin."

For a summary of the background and meaning of CITES, see Dunlop, 1989; see also Inskipp and Wells, 1979, and Mack and Eudey, 1984. U.S. policies on the importation of live animals are also affected by the Lacey Act of 1900, which was modified to prohibit the import of any animal exported in violation of another country's laws. The Code of Federal Regulations 42, Public Health, was amended in 1975 to prohibit importing *any* wild-caught primates for the pet trade. Kavanagh and Bennett, 1984, p. 30, mention the changes in Sierra Leonean laws.

Much of the interesting correspondence between Sitter, Stehlik, Bieber, and others became a matter of public record during Immuno's extensive litigation in the United States after a court order of secrecy was lifted. Most of the correspondence between Bieber and Stehlik was originally in German, and I am working from translations. Everything to and by Sitter was written in English, including Dr. Eder's letter. The Immuno plan also became a matter of public record during court proceedings. Some of Bieber's background is cited in Teleki, 1983, p. 2; see also Greisenegger, 1986, p. 4. A synopsis of what went on in Vienna in 1986 may be found in Teleki, 1986, including the paraphrase of what Gallo said. Other documents and materials were assembled by the Austrian World Wildlife Fund and others and have been passed my way. It is possible to find many secondary descriptions in English and German, including Greisenegger, 1986, and "Immuno: Neue Entwicklung," 1986. The extended quotation criticizing Dr. Moor-Jankowski ("now again shrill shouts emanate") is translated from "Tödlich," 1986. The 1986 importation brouhaha, incidentally, was preceded by another. Two days after Austria's CITES membership became effective (in April 1982), Immuno tried to import two wild-caught chimps from Africa via Belgium; those were confiscated and placed with the Vienna Animal Protection Society. See "Chimpanzees in Danger," 1989.

McGreal's letter to the editor is McGreal, 1983. For the reaction of Dr. Prince, discoverer of hepatitis non-A non-B virus, see Prince, 1984. Summaries of and commentaries on this case appear in Cherfas, 1989; "Decision of the Day," 1989; Frey, 1992; Gest, 1988; Lewis, 1991; Redmond, 1986; Schmidt, 1992; and Strausbaugh, 1991. Later arguments in court would on occasion suggest that Shirley McGreal deliberately and maliciously ignored Immuno's plans to establish a captive breeding operation on Franz Sitter's chicken farm, outside Freetown. But, as I have already noted, McGreal composed the letter sometime before the April 18, 1983, meeting, where apparently Abass Bundu introduced the dream of a captive breeding operation, probably as a way of countering future objections from conservationists. McGreal clearly focused her attention on the original 1982 document, and so was spared the exercise of pointing out just how tenuous the captive breeding dream was.

Sitter never, at any one time, had more than a few dozen baby chimps on his farm — he claimed at various times to have as many as fifty chimps "in stock." But his modus operandi was to fill orders by capturing more animals when the demand arose. In any event, at approximately the time Bundu was discussing with Immuno how a breeding operation in Freetown based on fifty to sixty chimps would start producing sixty to eighty new chimps per year within three years, American scientists with the National Institutes of Health, also discussing the potential for breeding chimpanzees, imagined that a population of three hundred fifty adults might under multimillion-dollar circumstances be persuaded to produce fifty new chimpanzees per year. By what rough magic would Sitter's few dozen chimpanzee babies, generally ten years from breeding age, produce sixty to eighty new chimps per year within three years on what was still fundamentally a chicken farm?

Libel law in the United States distinguishes between opinion and fact. Statements of opinion are protected, as are statements of true fact. Even false statements of fact are not recognized to be actionable if they are made about public figures or issues of public interest as long as they are not made with "actual malice," that is, with knowledge that the statements are false or with reckless disregard as to whether they are true or false. McGreal's letter seems to state the facts precisely. When opinions are presented, the letter generally clarifies that they are opinions, using qualifiers such as "presumably" and "appears to be" and "could well become" and "should be." (A weakness of McGreal's letter, as Immuno recognized, was the contention that releasing hepatitis-infected chimpanzees might spread hepatitis infections into wild chimpanzee populations. McGreal stated that "there is no way to determine that an animal is definitely not a carrier of the disease." Practically, I believe that was true; technically, it may not have been. A person can take blood from a possibly infectious chimp and inject it into a noninfected chimp. If the second becomes infected, the first is infectious. The problem, of course, is that this procedure can wipe out the healthy chimps. Today, a better method of determining infectiousness exists.) Moreover, that her comment was published as a letter to the editor might have clarified that much of it was opinion, a citizen's contribution to the free exchange of ideas on important subjects such as ethics, conservation, and the subversion of an international treaty meant to protect endangered species. Moreover, Immuno was given substantial opportunity to reply to McGreal's letter or to challenge her facts, and it did not. It is difficult to imagine how a single letter to the editor could cause so many millions of dollars of damage. It is also difficult to imagine why American courts all the way to the United States Supreme Court should become deeply engaged for almost six and a half years in responding to the complaint of an Austrian-based company.

Milkovitch v. *Lorain Journal* arose out of an altercation at a wrestling match at the Maple Heights High School in Maple Heights, Ohio. Ultimately the Maple Heights wrestling coach, a man named Milkovitch, and the local superintendent of schools, Donald Scott, appeared at a hearing before a state court. That appearance led a local journalist to write in a newspaper owned by the Lorain Journal Company statements such as "Anyone who attended the [wrestling] meet . . . knows in his heart that Milkovitch and Scott lied at the hearing after each having given his solemn oath to tell the truth." Those statements led to a libel suit against the journalist. After a tortured history in the Ohio courts, *Milkovitch* v. *Lorain Journal* eventually found a place before the U.S. Supreme Court. In a majority opinion authored by Chief Justice William Rehnquist, the Court ruled in favor of Coach Milkovitch and against the journalist, on the grounds that (after a reading close enough to inspire any graduate student in literature) the tenor of the article and the quality of the language (which was not loose or figurative or hyperbolic) suggested not *as an opinion* that Milkovitch and Scott lied in court but rather suggested *as fact* that Milkovitch and Scott had perjured themselves. As I understand it, then, First Amendment protection can now be assured only after a sophisticated examination of the quality of the language in any contentious statement. If the language is wild enough (loose or figurative or hyperbolic enough) to indicate opinion, the statement is protected; if the language is temperate and reasonable enough to suggest fact, then libel may have occurred.

Raymond S. Fersko, Immuno's principal lawyer in the United States, declared in his own letter to the editor, printed by the *New York Times* on June 15, 1991 (see Fersko, 1991), that the case raises "the critical First Amendment question, 'Who's the boss?' " Fersko had thought the U.S. Supreme Court was the boss, but the New York State Court of Appeals appeared to be "making a grab" for that title. Aside from raising that significant First Amendment question about who the boss really is, Fersko believes that this and other similar cases teach us some "important lessons" regarding the "inefficiency of our legal process." He would like us to "look more critically at a system in which time-consuming and expensive adversarial procedures, such as lengthy depositions and lengthy appeals, as opposed to a quick trial, are imposed on both sides." As late as 1992, Immuno continued to dispute many details of this story — demanding, for example, major retractions from an article by journalist Marc Frey in the *Frankfurter Rundschau*. Among several other complaints, Immuno's attorney was concerned that Frey had described Franz Sitter as an animal dealer with a questionable reputation; that Frey had overestimated Immuno's wealth; that Frey had exaggerated Moor-Jankowski's exspenses in defending himself; and so on. Frey and *Frankfurter Rundschau* resisted this bullying.

The quotations from the Austrian and Liberian delegations to the 1987 CITES conference are taken from conference documents. The CCC proposal is an unpublished document; Redmond, 1991, summarizes much of it, but I have worked primarily from the original. Statements of Fersko's legal associate are quoted and paraphrased in Strausbaugh, 1991. Sitter's document is in my possession; I have relied on a translation by Dr. Linda Frisch.

7. THE STUFF OF DREAMS   This chapter includes material from several interviews with trainers and owners around the country. My report on the David Letterman show's "monkey cam" episode is based on a videotape of that event. Lee Ecuyer, the creator and still owner of Zippy the Chimp, told me that he trained his chimps with affection only and that he never used an electric shock device. I do not wish to contradict him. But Ecuyer, while he owned the business, also relied on several other people as trainers and managers. My information about what went on during that particular Letterman show is based on interviews with people who were there.

Any producer of any Shakespeare play will consider whether to present it plain or fancy, but *The Tempest* is particularly suited to the second kind of interpretation. It was first performed at court during the fall of 1611 and then, in the winter of 1611–12, during celebrations preceding a royal wedding; so its original productions were probably very fancy indeed. The text of the play provides many opportunities for visual and auditory elaboration. Prospero manipulates the characters with hypnotic-like magic, so that they sleep and wake, dream and hallucinate, are frozen in midaction and then freed to act. The characters describe for us dreamlike and wondrous experiences. The stage directions call for the playing and singing of music, a "tempestuous noise of thunder and lightning," a "strange, hollow, and confused noise," "the noise of hunters" (and probably of dogs). Stage directions also call for characters to be invisible to other characters; for the vanishing of characters; for the miraculous disappearance of a banquet from a tabletop by means of some "quaint device" (stage mechanism); and for some obviously elaborate costumes. Thomas Shadwell's 1674 version of *The Tempest* was actually an opera, complete with a devils' chorus and a ballet of Tritons and winds. William Charles Macready's 1838 version brought a large ship onto the stage and flew one of Prospero's slave-spirits around in the air. Charles Kean's 1857 version used enough stage machinery to advertise "scenic appliances of a more extensive nature than have been attempted in any theater in Europe." Gaslight in 1817, limelight two decades later, electric light toward the end of the century, all increased the nineteenth-century potential for theatrical elaboration. By 1904 Herbert Beerbohm Tree was producing a *Tempest* that included a shipwreck, a sudden blackout, and purple light gradually shifting to amber during a scene in which actors playing nymphs, suspended by wires, floated in the air behind a screen of gauze. See Barnet, 1987 (1964).

The concept of Prospero as a hypnotist will be supported by any scientific consideration of hypnotic phenomena. My own favorite discussion is Haley, 1967. See Ellenberger, 1971, for the best historical discussion of hypnosis, mesmerism, and precursors of mesmerism. At least a few speeches in *The Tempest* are excellent examples of hypnotic inductions, including a type of embedded hypnotic induction the American psychiatrist and clinical hypnotist Dr. Milton Erickson described as his "interspersal hypnotic technique" (Erickson, 1966). See also Erickson, 1964.

For more information on the Noells' "Gorilla Show," see Noell, 1979. My information is supplemented by an interview with Mae Noell. Some material on the use of ape costumes in the movies can be found in Sibley, 1990. For an example of the trainer's emphasis on the "soft technology" of control, see Belcher, 1992. I cannot say that soft technology alone — "love" and "humane" training — has never worked, since I do not know the full history of every ape show. I can only extrapolate, based on many interviews and other research into the backstage situation of several shows. Kenneth DeCroo, on the beating of Buddha, is quoted in O'Neill and Fitz, 1985; other quotations are taken from affidavits signed by the relevant parties. A brief history of animal protection in the movies can be found in Pequet, 1989, and Donner, 1989. The suggestion that the American Humane Association in Hollywood also served as a "job referral service" was made in a private letter from an investigating government employee to an officer of AHA. A more detailed summary of the story behind *Project X* appears in Peterson, 1989, pp. 267, 268, 273–275. Producer Walter Parkes was quoted in a promotion press release; other material in this section on *Project X* is taken from or based on various affidavits and my own interview with Bob Barker. See also Caulfield,

1987, and Klein, 1987. The "shocked" Parkes and Lawrence Lasker described themselves that way according to Caulfield; and an AHA representative, speaking of the association's "in-depth investigation," was quoted there as well.

My suggestion that "few great apes would voluntarily submit to a life" loosely paraphrases a statement made by Cooper, 1989. The brief comments about training methods used on one chimp character and the chimpanzees on a television show are based on Burnet, 1989; I have chosen to be less specific than Burnet about the identities of the character and the television show because I am not yet convinced by the evidence. Nick Connell, 1986, reminisces about Mickey Antalek; see also Johnson, 1990. For more on Spanish beach chimps see Boroviczeny, Carwardine, and Watkins, 1985; also Elliott, 1992; "List," 1991; and "A Visit," 1985.

Where does legitimate control end and abuse begin? The astute exotic animal trainer will argue that we are ignorant about what exotic animals require, that because of our ignorance we are not entitled to serious opinions on the subject, and that animal trainers are a special class of people informally licensed to create certain pleasing effects without revealing any messy details of how those effects are created. For more on what the astute animal trainer might say, see Hearne, 1986, p. 175, whose comments there I have loosely paraphrased here.

Dunn is quoted in Schlosberg, 1988. For more on Bubbles at Dunn's, see Castro, 1991. A close associate who blabs to the tabloids is described in "Michael Jackson," 1991.

8. TO LAUGH, TO BEAT   This chapter is based in part on several interviews. My account of the orangutan show at the Stardust is based on memory, refreshed by close examination of a videotape taken of the show itself some months earlier. The quotations obviously are from the videotape, although I recognize them to be extremely close to statements made during the show I saw. My report of the interview with Berosini is based on extensive notes made immediately after the interview. I believe it reproduces fairly and accurately the content and style and, where quotation marks are used, the actual language.

The expression "cowards" was quoted in Harris, 1989a. The article in the *Las Vegas Sun* containing Berosini's early disclaimer is "No Aping," 1989; the later article is Shemeligian, 1989a. The statements by various experts, dancers, stagehands, and the like are part of the legal documentation compiled by PETA and should be available from that organization. I have listed in the text only a sampling of expert opinions. Many other specialists also submitted opinions. For example, Robert Stone, in private veterinary practice for more than thirty-five years and experienced in treating primates, concluded from watching the tape that the orangutans were "petrified" and "beaten into submission." Veterinarian Robert Agramonte, in private practice for twenty years, wrote of "physical and psychological abuse" and "blatant and regular cruelty." Michael Wolff, a veterinarian completing an internship at the National Zoo in Washington, D.C., wrote as his "professional assertion" that the videotape shows "clear cases" of "excessive, unprovoked acts of violence, intimidation, and behavioral deprivation" to inflict "fear, pain, and anxiety." Glenn Benjamin, a veterinarian in practice for twenty-seven years and thoroughly familiar with the treatment of exotic animals in zoos and entertainment, wrote that although "occasionally force" is necessary in the training of exotic animals, what he saw on the videotape "appeared to be abusive." Dr. Benjamin seemed particularly disturbed by the repeated striking with what looked like a metal bar, the yanking of hair, and the kicking and kneeing of the orangutans. Michael Fox, a veterinarian and author of more than thirty books, concluded that the videotape documents the "deliberate, calculated, and methodical infliction of physical and psychological harm to these innocent and benign creatures." Alan Boessman, licensed and practicing veterinary medicine for more than eight years, saw in his "professional opinion" scenes of "gross abuse and cruelty via unprovoked systematic physical beatings and psychological intimidation."

The two Dick Maurice articles are Maurice, 1989a and b. The *Showbiz* article is "Bobby Berosini," 1989; the Christmas card is "Thank You, Las Vegas," 1989; the testimonies of schoolchildren may be found in "Kid Talk," 1990. For a review of the language used to describe Berosini's critics, see Frederick, 1990; Harris, 1989a; Kerr, 1989a; Maurice, 1989a; "Rush to Judgment," 1989. For language during the trial, see Bates, 1990a and b. The article describing Las Vegas as "rallied behind" Berosini is Bates, 1990a.

I have examined the Department of Agriculture report and a later letter from a USDA official (sent in November 1989) to the Berosinis, neither of which is generally available and therefore not listed in the references. The November 1989 letter stated that the USDA investigation found "no violations" of the Animal Welfare Act. However, as the official pointedly mentioned in the same letter, "physical abuse" in the training and handling of animals was not actually illegal until an October 30, 1989, alteration in the Animal Welfare Act. Articles that refer to the report include Roderick, 1990, which contains Berosini's comments about how the orangs lie down. "USDA: No Sign of Orangutan Abuse" is Kerr, 1989b. For another example of how this complex USDA inspection became twisted into a simple vindication, see Gang, 1990a. On the Humane Society of Southern Nevada inspection, Anthony is quoted in Kerr, 1989a; Brink is quoted in Harris, 1989b. Anthony's later admission about his qualifications is quoted in Bates, 1990c, which also refers to Anthony's background.

Soon after Brink's description of the Humane Society of Southern Nevada's official examination, incidentally, he was either fired or he resigned, complaining that he had been unaware of the "depth of magnitude of financial instability, bad debts, and court judgments" against the organization. Within a few days of his departure in late October, someone burglarized the society's offices on West Tropicana Street in Las Vegas and made off with $10,000 worth of records and computer equipment and software. Some of the records soon were placed in the hands of a local journalist, who reported that from the organization's total expenses of more than $200,000 between 1983 and 1985, less than 1 percent was actually spent on "animal welfare." Brink's complaint is quoted in "Humane Society Exec," 1989; earlier information on the theft is mentioned in Shemelgian, 1989b. Greenspun refines this information and comments on what she knows of Anthony in Greenspun, 1989b.

The inspection by Berosini's experts from the University of Nevada and Yerkes is described by Finnigan, 1989. For the sake of journalists present during the examinations, Dr. Richard Simmons of the University of Nevada at Reno turned the spotlight of his own expertise onto the shadowy credentials of PETA's experts. "I think they're not unqualified," he sniffed. "But I don't think they'd be classified as world class experts." Presumably, that meant that Simmons himself was enough of an expert to distinguish the "world class" variety. But he could not have been much of an expert on orangutans per se, since, as he was to admit almost a year later (as cited in Bates, 1990b), he had never actually examined one before that day.

Concerning terrorism, the article in the *Washingtonian* is McCabe, 1990. For PETA's lawsuit against McCabe and the *Washingtonian*, see "PETA Wins," 1991. For the retraction by the *Washingtonian*, see "Correction and Clarification," 1991. For one reference to the "death threats" see Harris, 1989b. Early on, the Berosini version of reality would be temporarily bolstered by a shadowy figure, a young woman who first appeared on television anonymously and disguised, apparently fearful of retaliation for the testimony she was willing to provide against "animal-rights terrorists." This young woman turned out to be the sister of Linda Levine, the Las Vegas member of PETA who was being sued. Levine's sister never testified at the trial — perhaps because she began to seem like a tainted witness after the PETA attorneys complained that she and Berosini's lawyer Harold Gewerter were having an affair. For one comment on this relationship, see Gang, 1990a; see also Bates, 1990a. The shooting and dead birds are mentioned in Bates, 1990a; Berosini's complaints on the witness stand are quoted in Bates, 1990d. The recently widowed woman's statement is included in an affidavit acquired by PETA.

Concerning capitalism and charges that the tapes had been altered, see Bates, 1990e; on charges that the tapes had not been altered, see Bates, 1990h. On PETA and PAWS "dashing for cash," see Bates, 1990e. Money in Las Vegas is discussed by Leerhsen and Burbank, 1990; most of my other information about the Boyd Group and Judge Leavitt's relationship with Bill Boyd can be found in various court documents, including most obviously the Motion of Appeal filed by PETA attorneys. See also Gang, 1990e. The editorial describing PETA as "spoiled children" is "PETA Becomes Shrill," 1990. For more on the ramifications of Judge Leavitt's Boyd connection, see Gang, 1990c and f; German, 1990, 1991.

Concerning the testimonies of the veterinarian for PETA, see Bates, 1990g, and of veterinarians for Berosini, see Bates, 1990b. The testimonies of Michael Bradshaw and Jill Milane are in Gang, 1990b. For more on the nature of the disappeared baton, see Gang, 1990a. The "trial by ambush" comment is quoted in Bates, 1990f.

Berosini won. See Gang, 1990d, for some of the material I have quoted. Joan Berosini is quoted in McKinnon, 1990; additional quotations of Bobby Berosini are from the same source. Later references to *Review-Journal* editorials: the question of whether orangutans have psyches was raised in an editorial entitled "Berosini Gets Bum Rap"; my torn copy is missing an exact date; Greenspun, 1989a, refers to that editorial. The statement "to anthropomorphize non-sentient creatures is absurd" was made in the editorial "Rush to Judgment," 1989. Konrad Lorenz' speculations about canine laughter were in *Man Meets Dog* (1954), which is described and referred to by Douglas, 1975. The expert from the San Diego Zoo is Marvin Jones.

A further note on ape humor. People will imagine that only humans play practical jokes, but it is not clear to me that the distinction holds. There is the story about a chimpanzee who was a pet in West Africa and still young enough to enjoy the freedom of her owner's house and garden. One day when an older woman was visiting, this ape rummaged in the visitor's handbag and pulled out a pair of sunglasses. When people noticed her with the sunglasses, of course they ran after her. During the chase she ran over to the swimming pool and accidentally dropped the sunglasses into the water, subsequently witnessing the wonderful commotion of several people frantically fishing for a rapidly sinking object. That was the end of the incident; she was reprimanded. About two weeks later the chimpanzee raided someone else's handbag and retrieved another pair of sunglasses. She made straight for the swimming pool. When she got there, she stopped, waited until she saw people running toward her, then with some deliberation held the glasses out over the water and dropped them. Then she bounded off, laughing.

People imagine that only humans can tell jokes, and since wild apes cannot talk, of course they don't tell jokes. But there is evidence to suggest that the several sign language–using apes in captivity have expressed humor. One episode involves Koko, the gorilla who was taught American Sign Language by Francine Patterson. Koko was having an idle conversation with a woman, Barbara Hiller, who had recently come to work with the project. Koko had made a nest of white towels, and Hiller asked her to name the color of the stack. Koko signed, "Red." The young woman said, "No, Koko, that's wrong. What color is it?" Koko signed back, "Red." So Hiller scolded Koko for being naughty and asked the gorilla once again, "What color is it?" Still Koko signed "Red." By this time Hiller was getting cross because she knew that Koko knew the color was white, so she gave some kind of mild ultimatum. Koko, grinning, picked up a tiny speck of red fluff from the middle of the pile of white towels, held up the speck, and signed: "Red, red, red."

9. IN MINE OWN CELL   This chapter is largely based on material acquired in several interviews, formal and informal, and a few books and articles. Russ Cochran's autobiographical piece will be found in Cochran, 1990. The story of the Primate Foundation of Arizona is largely based on Fritz, 1975, and Hahn, 1988. The quotations from Fritz are from all three pages of that short piece. The quotation from Hahn occurs on page 165. Information on Gus and

Gabbie comes from interviews and two short pieces: Berryman and Berryman, 1977, 1978. See also Koenig, 1991. Regarding the age of Gabbie, Connie Braun told me she had had five offspring and was eighteen years old in the fall of 1990. I tend to believe her age was closer to fifteen at that time, since the Berrymans, who described her as two years old in the summer of 1978, were more likely to know her true age. Regarding the basement facilities, Braun told me she hopes to expand her breeding group's indoor area with a section that will allow them to go outdoors in good weather.

The story of Chuck and Judy was written with reference to a personal letter (by the "witness") and a number of articles. The former Bel-Aire Coiffures employee was quoted in Lackey, 1985. The Lafayette Zoo superintendent, Ochsenbein, was quoted in Alley, 1985. The articles that transformed "rehabilitation" into "psychotherapy" include (in the order I discuss them in the text) Maddry, 1986a and b; Novek, 1986; Eisen, 1986; Landers, 1986.

The details concerning a young adult male chimp in a Texas pawnshop come from an unpublished account given me. The woman who visited Daphney and Sam at a game park in the northwestern United States made her comments in a personal letter. The story of Sam and Rudy comes from several interviews and articles. Tina Nelson described for me the appearance of Sam's cistern; I have also relied on a private report written by animal behaviorist Sarah Boysen of Ohio State University. The lawyer's worries that Sam would be "locked in a stainless steel cage" are quoted in Wright, 1987b, as are his concerns that Sam will come to expect quiche and chablis. The four articles with pseudohumorous titles I refer to are Love, 1987; Switzer, 1987; and Wright, 1987a and b. For additional commentary on the case I have relied on Beyerlein, 1987; "Case of Chimp," 1987; "Chimp Returning," 1987; "Judge Orders," 1987; "Judge Signs," 1987; Turmell, 1987; and Wright, 1987c.

10. ENDOWED WITH WORDS, CONFINED IN ROCK I am particularly indebted to Eugene Linden's excellent book, *Silent Partners* (1986), which first brought to my attention the general outlines of this story. I have, of course, developed my own version by, among other things, interviewing some of the people involved — most obviously Janis Carter, Roger Fouts, James Mahoney, Jan Moor-Jankowski, and Mae Noell. Herbert Terrace missed our appointment for an interview by telephone.

The story of Lucy, in the first section, relies heavily on Temerlin's *Lucy* (1975). Mae Noell provided some background for me on Lucy's sale. Specific material from Temerlin, 1985: "most ingenious use of tools," p. 104; Jewish mother, pp. 31–45; Lucy's emotions, p. 164; language, pp. 113–125; exchange with Roger Fouts, pp. 122, 123; "my daughter's story," p. xxii; "She was my daughter," p. 127; drinking, p. 49; masturbation in front of her, p. 89; "like owning another human being," p. 89; "to live normal lives," p. 212; "chimpanzee madness," p. 210; "contributing to science," p. 211; "actualize her potential," p. 211; "virginal daughter," p. 212. Stella Brewer's early work with rehabilitating chimps in The Gambia is described in Brewer, 1978; see also Duberley, 1988a. For a closer examination of Carter's contribution in The

Gambia, see Carter, 1988; "We shared the island," p. 39. See also Linden, 1986, p. 183; Linden was the "journalist" who provides the long quotation from Carter, pp. 85–86.

Were there thirty chimps at the Institute for Primate Studies at that time? Linden states there were more than thirty language-using apes throughout the country (Linden, 1986, p. 30); Mahoney, whose laboratory purchased the institute's chimps, told me there were "about thirty" at the institute, and that "they all had some degree or other of signing." The most precise number I can find is in Minty, 1991: "An estimated twenty-seven." Crail, 1983, pp. 87–90, provides some general background on Washoe's early education, as does Linden, 1986, p. 45. The story of Fouts leaving with Washoe and Loulis is told by Linden on p. 106. Fouts has clarified some of these events for me. Terrace, 1987, p. ix, denies he is limited by behaviorism. For a popular review of the Premacks' work, see Premack and Premack, 1983; see Hayes, 1951, for the Hayeses' story; see Patterson and Linden, 1981, for background material on Koko. On quoted material from Terrace, 1987: "Nim was socialized," p. v; "non-professional," p. 134; "felt more affection for Nim," p. 41; "meager amount of time," p. 41; "few hours," p. 46; early vocabulary statistics and comment on Nim's motivation, pp. 137, 145; sign combinations, p. 179; words as substitutes for acts, p. 150; misrepresentations, p. 150; invented signs, p. 154; "many spontaneous signs," p. 39; extended descriptions of Terrace's reversal, p. vi. For this discussion presented in the full panoply of academic jargon, see Terrace, 1985. For material on Washoe and Loulis, see Fouts, 1987; see also Fouts and Fouts, 1989; Fouts, Fouts, and Van Cantfort, 1989; Gardner and Gardner, 1989; and Stokoe, 1989. Terrace's comments about Savage-Rumbaugh are in Terrace, 1987, p. x.

For Linden's damaged digit score, see Linden, 1986, p. 107. For the story of Bob Noell's injury, see Noell, 1979, pp. 89–96. Washoe's signing "sorry" is mentioned in Crail, 1983, p. 90. See Linden, 1986, p. 107, for further background on the Pribram fiasco. My brief comments on Pribram's career as a monkey experimenter are based on "Chimpanzee Center," 1981.

Robert Yerkes' analysis of chimpanzee emotional expression will be found in Yerkes, 1943, pp. 28, 29. Linden's story of meeting the signing chimps before they went to LEMSIP is told in Linden, 1986, pp. 144, 145. Terrace mentions being awakened by a telephone call in Terrace, 1987, p. x; see also Linden, 1986, pp. 155, 156. Ally as a "scholarly-looking, freckle-faced chimp" is depicted in Linden, 1986, p. 143. Ally's habit of signing a cross is mentioned in that source, p. 49. White Sands advertising: "Chimpanzees," 1988. On Harry and Midge at White Sands, see Linden, 1986, pp. 159, 160.

Hardy's early work on xenografting is mentioned in Eyre, 1988; Reemtsma's heart transplant is mentioned in Bluestone, 1989; McManus' work is described in Manning, 1988; the NIH agreement to contribute money is mentioned in Taylor, 1987. My footnote includes material from "Don't Use Chimps," 1977, about Christiaan Barnard. The background on severed-head research is based on material in Thompson, 1988, and McNulty, 1981. The quotations are from Thompson, 1988. Thompson's story of White's work on severed monkey heads appeared in the *Washington Post.* I am not quite ready to believe the report published in *Weekly World News* that a Soviet surgeon, recently emigrated to Germany, described the experimental transfer of a chimp's head onto a man's body at a Moscow research institute. According to a diagram accompanying the article, the man kept his own head, which must have been defunct, and the chimp's head was attached on top of it with the assistance of various tubes and cables. See Dunn, 1988. More information on White comes from Tidyman, 1992. As far as I can tell, Bruno and Booee are finished with their experiments at LEMSIP; an Oklahoma man who once worked with the chimps, Bob Ingersoll, has been trying to find a home for them. The Oklahoma City Zoo has turned down an offered donation of the two, purportedly because they don't know how to breed. See Minty, 1991, 1992; and "Ex-Trainer," 1991.

11. I ACKNOWLEDGE MINE This chapter is based on material acquired from several interviews, published and unpublished government reports, unpublished correspondence, and published books and articles.

The NIH head-smashing study is described in Ommaya, Corrao, and Letcher, 1973, also in Letcher, Corrao, and Ommaya, 1973. The researchers' objections to a proposed script for *Quantum Leap* are quoted in Rosenberg, 1991. Trull's worry is expressed in "Scientists Fear," 1991.

My comments on the linguistic habits of biomedical research scientists versus those of field scientists derive from my own observations. As anyone familiar with the subject will recognize, the expression "a cat is a mouse is a rat is a chimpanzee" closely paraphrases (with a very significant twist) an infamous statement made by Ingrid Newkirk of PETA. "Animals" and "animal models" are, of course, common categories for chimps, reflecting our usually oversimplified thinking on the subject. On occasion, chimpanzees have been called "subhuman primates" (Swyers, 1990a, p. 4), which suggests a hierarchy of value more firmly than the usual "nonhuman primates."

On the numbers of animals in laboratories cited in my footnote, King and others, 1988, provide a standard, albeit conservative, estimate on the numbers of animals in U.S. laboratories, a total of 20 million. I would not be surprised if the actual number is closer to the carefully constructed estimate given by Rowan, 1984, p. 71: a total of 71 million. Everyone agrees that the number is very large.

Trefflich gives his trade figures in Trefflich and Anthony, 1967, p. ix. The two Trefflich quotations are from that book, pp. 10 and 172. Wild gorillas have been encountered as far north and west as southeastern Nigeria. (Nigeria is approximately a thousand miles from Sierra Leone.) Buck's self-serving fantasy can be found in Buck, 1927. Phil Carroll's concerns are described in Noell, 1979, back pages. For background on my footnoted comments about the reproductive limitations of chimpanzees, see Clark, 1977; Goodall, 1983; Hiraiwa-Hasegawa, Hasegawa, and Nishida, 1984; Nishida, 1985; Sugiyama, 1984; Teleki, 1989; and Teleki, Hunt, and Pfifferling, 1979. For general background on the brutality of the live-animal trade, see Domalain, 1978.

Information on the Pasteur Institute is from Harrisson, 1971; and Kortlandt, 1965, 1966. Sabater Pi's account is in Sabater Pi, 1979; Teleki's is in Teleki, 1980. For some comparable information on the hunting and capture of gorillas, see Denis, 1963; Merfield, 1954; Merfield and Miller, 1956; and Schaller, 1963, 1964. George Galasso's angry denial was quoted in Booth, 1988.

For a summary of the design of CITES, see especially Dunlop, 1989. See also Inskipp and Wells, 1979, pp. 83, 84. Karno, 1991, mentions the problem of imprecise language in CITES. The "valuable renewable resource" language is quoted by Booth, 1988, p. 778; I have examined the original source as well. If chimpanzees were a "valuable renewable resource," incidentally, it would appear that monkeys were a cheap renewable resource. According to Roy Henderson, chief of lab animal care at the University of Berkeley at California (as quoted in Blum, 1991a): "When I first started, 20 years ago, monkeys were $25 each. You'd use one once and you'd throw it away." The words of Dr. Creamer of Merck Sharpe and Dohme are mentioned in "Merck," 1978; the original Fish and Wildlife memo about that conversation, which I have also examined, was reproduced accurately.

Deliberations of the NIH Special Task Force are recorded in Interagency Committee, 1978. The NIH 1978 National Primate Plan and its need for 180 new chimps per year is cited by Whitney, Wolfle, and Blood, 1991. For more on the five-institution breeding project, see Johnsen, 1987; see also *Progress Report*, 1990, and Swyers, 1990b. The 1990 language and figures from the NIH Working Group on Chimpanzees are cited in an unpublished draft report. The 1991 language and figures from an NIH AIDS Animal Model Committee meeting are taken from minutes of March 21, 1991. The 1992 quoted remarks of Milton April are based on an interview.

On the issues of "euthanasia" and "terminal experimentation," see Eckholm, 1985; the NIH representative is quoted there. Wolfle is also quoted in Eckholm, 1985. Galasso's comments on "terminal experimentation" will be found in Luoma, 1989, p. 57. The footnoted "humane alternative" (that is, retirement funds and so on) is described in Eichberg and Speck, 1988. Jorg Eichberg, director of veterinary resources at the Southwest Foundation, is quoted in Little, 1990: The retirement program "comes out of compassion for the animals . . . Once you have worked with these animals a long time, you get very attached. You see the similarities that exist between them and humans. After what they have done for mankind, we should give them a good home — as good as possible in captivity." In earlier NIH discussions about "euthanizing" those "surplus" chimps, incidentally, someone recommended that before they were killed the chimps should be placed in some final scientific study, "even a trivial study." See Linden, 1986, p. 205.

On the value of the breeding project as a "sound and reasonable plan," to the degree that this project reduced pressure to take more chimpanzees from the wild, it was good. However, those chimpanzees will never contribute to wild stocks. Full reintroduction into wild populations has worked with a number of bird species and at least one monkey species, but not with chimps — for several clear reasons. Later claims made by various people in the biomedical research industry that they are somehow actually contributing to conservation is stretching the point. At best, it can be said that the breeding project has reduced the usual drain on conservation. One does find strange ideas, though. As her laboratory acquired several chimps from a domestic source for vaccine testing, one manager expressed the following logic: "In a way, this testing is how the chimps pay their dues to a society that is saving them from extinction" (as quoted in Linden, 1986, p. 150).

For some of the background on AIDS and chimpanzees, see Alter and others, 1984; also Barnard, 1988. See also "Chimps Suffer," 1988; Cohen, 1989, 1991; Swyers, 1990a and b. On the story of polio, see Dowling, 1977, pp. 202–219. Much of my information on the current situation is based on interviews. Dr. Anthony Fauci, head of the National Institute of Allergy and Infectious Diseases, announced in 1987 that vaccine testing would begin ahead of schedule on human volunteers (see "AIDS Vaccine Tests," 1987). Human volunteers from very high-risk populations in France and Zaire were being used to test an AIDS vaccine as early as the summer of 1987, according to Boffey, 1987. By the summer of 1989, Robert Gallo was publicly objecting to Jonas Salk's old-fashioned attempt to develop an AIDS vaccine from killed virus (see "Dr. Salk's Research," 1989; also Altman, 1989; and Specter, 1989).

On the lack of consensus about the importance of chimps during the mid-1980s, see, for example, Montgomery, 1988, who quotes Robert Couch of the Baylor College of Medicine in Houston: "There is no consensus on the role of chimpanzees in the evaluation of vaccine candidates at present." It was not even clear that chimps were appropriate or necessary as models for vaccine testing. Arie Zuckerman, British virologist at the London School of Hygiene, for example, concluded that there was no case for using chimps at all: "There is no suitable animal model for AIDS research" (as quoted in Woolf, 1988). The formal declaration that there would be enough chimps is in Prince and others, 1988. The policy statement of the World Health Organization has been quoted in several places. See, for example, Prince and others, 1988. Gallo's famous statement ("I will put anyone who prevents," etc.) was quoted in *Ein Herz für Tiere* (1986). See Luoma, 1989, for additional comments by Gallo on the collaboration with Immuno. For the "shortage" in the United States, Gallo is quoted first in "Chimpanzee Shortage," 1987, and "Animal Shortage," 1987, then in Bree, 1987. The European version of the shortage (footnote) is translated from Gergely, 1987a.

William Gay is quoted in Junkin, 1987, p. 28; James Wyngaarden is quoted in Rosenblum, 1988; Patricia Fultz is quoted in Thompson, 1988b. Gallo's comments in Europe appeared in Gergely, 1987b; they are quoted in translation by Lumoa, 1989, who also quotes Gallo's comments in the United States. See also "Immuno AG," 1987.

Regarding my footnote on the mystery of chimpanzee numbers in U.S. labs, Seal and Flesness, 1986, give a fairly standard figure for the number before the breeding program began, but we should remember that the ISIS figures never included LEMSIP chimps or those from some other private laboratory colonies; see also "Chimpanzees an Important Model," 1990; Institute of Medicine, 1986; and *Progress Report,* 1990. The most accurate published estimate on current numbers, in my opinion, is cited in a small journal with apparent access to ISIS figures, the *AIDS Research Exchange* (see "Chimpanzees an Important Model," 1990).

Maurice Hilleman at the breakfast meeting was quoted by Montgomery, 1988, p. 21. Luoma, 1989, p. 46, includes more. See also "NIH Holds Briefing," 1988. The minutes of an NIH AIDS Animal Model Committee meeting are quoted in Luoma, 1989, p. 45. For "taking lots of looks at Africa," see "AIDS Research," 1988, or Rosenblum, 1988. NIH reaction to these comments is mentioned in Rovner, 1988; also Luoma, 1989, p. 46. The "grand plot" is mentioned on page 47 of Luoma.

For more on the Immuno lawsuits in Europe, see "Slama Acquitted," 1989; see also Wrussnig, 1986. Immuno, of course, has always maintained that its lawsuits were entirely justified. More on the "American connection" of the Immuno lawsuit: Richard Parsons, identifying himself as the former director of the Federal Wildlife Permit Office, presented his own affidavit in support of Immuno against Shirley McGreal. Parsons would have been ultimately responsible for regulating the U.S. importation of endangered and threatened species, but by the time he submitted the affidavit against McGreal he seems to have shifted allegiance. He became executive director of the Fur Retailers' Information Committee (FRIC), a fur merchants' promotional organization; at one point he represented the Safari Club International, a big-game-hunters' society that had astonished many people in 1978 by applying to import animal trophies from forty endangered species, including gorillas and orangutans (see "Revolving Door," 1988; also "Secret Memo," 1988).

The National Association for Biomedical Research (NABR), quite naturally, emphasizes the most idealistic end of its spectrum of interests. But the spectrum surely reaches into commerce as well as human health. The NABR was founded in 1979 by a coalition of animal breeders and users in the research industry, including particularly the Charles River Breeding Laboratories. At 20 million vertebrates per year by 1988, Charles River was and is the world's biggest breeder and purveyor of laboratory animals. The chairman of the board of NABR during the lawsuit in question was Craig Burrell, who doubled as vice president of Sandoz Pharmaceuticals in East Hanover, New Jersey. I am convinced that Charles River and Sandoz completely and absolutely favor science, rationality, and human health. Of course. Rightly so. They are nevertheless primarily commercial ventures, and the NABR is solidly funded by the commercial branch of scientific progress. The connection between Charles River and the NABR is mentioned in Society for Legislation, n.d., which also declares that the NABR was the "brainchild" of Charles River, that Frankie Trull was at one time an employee of Charles River, and that the NABR was "created in her livingroom when she was working for Charles River." A person who has reason to know some of this background informs me that Trull never actually worked for Charles River, but that the original organization was "started with a lot of help from Charles River." The size of Charles River is mentioned in Stevens, 1984; see also Minetree and Guernsey, 1988, p. 159.

On the association between NABR and NIH. The personal friendship between Trull and Wyngaarden is mentioned in Society for Legislation, n.d., and has been confirmed. Trull's attendance at a meeting of "high-level directors and administrators of U.S. government research agencies" is referred to in "Mental Health Shake-up," 1992, and "Dr. Frederick Goodwin," 1989; the latter simply quotes an earlier article in *Long Island Newsday*. The U.S. Public Health Service proposal is referred to in Anderson, 1990b. For background material on the history of antivivisectionism and the current animal-rights/animal-welfare movement, see Rowan, 1984.

For more on PETA's beginnings, it is necessary to turn back to the Edward Taub and Silver Spring monkeys story: see Kilpatrick, 1984; Minetree and Guernsey, 1988; Torrey, 1984. For more general background on the animal-rights movement, see Cowley and others, 1988; also Zak, 1989.

Obviously, biomedical research using animals has brought some tremendously valuable knowledge. For a popular review of the benefits of primate research, see King and others, 1988. The animal-rights and animal-welfare protesters were indeed creating a serious public-relations problem at best; at worst, some groups were perpetrating destructive attacks on property (see Budiansky, 1987, for example). See Kaplan, 1988, for a reasonable statement of the "animal-rights" threat from a researcher's perspective. My point is not that the animal-rights people were right and the researchers were wrong, or vice versa. The situation has always been far more complex. Opportunists on both sides found life easier once they had simplified the picture. I have taken Dr. King's comments ("Where have all the moderates gone?") from "Animal Activists," 1989. Louis Sullivan is quoted in "June 1990 Press Briefing," 1990. (See also Sullivan's address to the Vatican, as described in "Pope," 1991.) This discussion of the "morality" of all animal experimentation when "lives hang in the balance" is exaggerated to begin with; it becomes completely twisted in the case of the extensive research on animals, including primates, that was once sponsored by the U.S. Department of Defense for the development and testing of biological warfare and delivery systems (see Hatch, 1991).

Labbee, 1991, provides nearly all the material on Matthew Block's lawsuit against Shirley McGreal; but see also "Worldwide Primates," 1992, and "Peter Gerone's Deposition," 1992. Peter Gerone's "zing" speech (as quoted in Blum, 1991b): "People like Shirley will stop at nothing to make research look bad. And what I say is, if I get an opportunity to zing them back — why not?" I judge Block to be "elusive" based on my own brief encounter with him in Miami during the summer of 1989: Matthew Block was the person who told me that Matthew Block was temporarily out of the country.

The six opposing letters to the NIH, unpublished but a matter of public record, complained of the inadequacy of the CCCC report. Immuno's letter deplored "bias," "lack of objectivity," and so on. The U.S. Fish and Wildlife formally responded to these complaints in the Federal Register: "the Service is satisfied that the report by the Committee for the Conservation and Care of Chimpanzees is reliable and contains much valuable information derived in large part from parties who have observed firsthand the situation in the wild . . . The indicated errors seem to be mostly minor typographical ones.

The report acknowledges that data are limited for some areas and that additional survey work is urgently needed. However . . . major new field surveys would take years to complete, and the Act requires that classification be based on the best data available." An alternate "field study" that Wyngaarden suggested in his letter would have taken years; moreover, it surely would have been conducted in the spirit with which the NIH was informally describing it, as a survey of potential resources: "An additional suggestion was to do a field study of the chimpanzee population in various parts of Africa. It was the consensus of the Committee that a RFP [Request for Proposals] be developed to do an African field survey to provide us with numbers of animals, serological information, and the condition of the chimpanzees" (as cited in "HSUS Works," 1988).

The "policy" statements issued by George Galasso (also Robert Whitney) have been quoted in several places. See Rovner, 1988, and "NIH Denies," 1988. The more precise NIH "policy" statement is mentioned in Booth, 1988, p. 777, and elsewhere. On the NIH contract in Liberia, see Junkin, 1989, p. 26. Information on the Rare Animal Breeding Center in China is from "Chimp Lab," 1988; Chuan, 1988; "Local Firm," 1988. Wild chimps infected with HIV are discussed in Kingman, 1988.

The critical language of the amendment to the Animal Welfare Act can be found in several places; see, for one, "Pressure," 1988. Some of the background on the Animal Welfare Act controversy is from Montgomery, 1988; see also Anderson, 1990a. The NABR provided alarmingly expanding estimates of cost, starting with $150 million and growing finally to $2 billion: see Montgomery, 1988, p. 20; Holden, 1987, p. 881; Holden, 1988, p. 1753; and Haveman, 1989. At one point, the Department of Agriculture's Plant and Animal Inspection Service estimated that the new rules would involve, for improvement of primate facilities, a capital expenditure of $111 million. The new rules could also have required improving facilities for dogs, estimated to require another $138 million. Changes in cages for cats, guinea pigs, hamsters, and rabbits would have pushed the expenses much higher, ultimately contributing to a total one-time "capital expenditure" of $885 million, with another $207 million per year in additional operating expenses (see Holden, 1988).

The figure of about thirty primate species in labs is according to King and others, 1988. Comments by Nancy Mello and others are cited in McArdle, 1987. For more on responses to the proposed regulations, see "Storm," 1990. For material on the depression experiments, see "Monkey Depression," 1981; "Sumoi," 1981. Good science probably has no particular correlation with love for animals. Harry Harlow says (as quoted by Torrey, 1984): "The only thing I care about is whether the monkeys will turn out a property I can publish. I don't have any love for them. Never have. I really don't like animals."

For more on the debate about the psychological well-being of primates, see Bloomsmith, Alford, and Maple, 1988; Bloomsmith, Keeling, and Lambeth, 1990; Fajzi, Reinhardt, and Smith, 1989; Maki and Bloomsmith, 1989; Markowitz and Spinelli, 1986; Moor-Jankowski and Mahoney, 1989; Novak and

Suomi, 1988; and Prince and others, 1989. The "one commentator" (on the OMB) is Anderson, 1990a. The NABR objections are quoted in Rubinstein, 1990; the other material about lobbying at the OMB also appears there. Melcher's comment is quoted in Anderson, 1990a.

The background material on Sema and conditions therein is from Dumanoski, 1987c; Goodall, 1987; and PETA, 1986. The story of Sema's harassment of USDA inspectors will be found in Levy, 1988. Prince and Moor-Jankowski's opinions on the isolettes were quoted in Redmond, 1988, p. 188. Officials from the NIH denied that anything was amiss inside Sema. As Katherine Bick of NIH wrote in her letter to Senate Majority Leader Robert Byrd in December 1987: "there is no evidence that SEMA failed to comply with established laws, regulations or policies relating to the conduct of research involving non-human primates, including chimpanzees." In the end, the U.S. Department of Agriculture was demoted. Reorganization reduced the agency's total number of inspectors to forty-two. One of the inspectors heavily involved in the Sema case was reorganized entirely away. The administrator in charge of USDA inspections at that time, Bert Hawkins, found himself replaced by a more congenial sort, James Glosser. And Glosser introduced his department's new mood with the statement (according to Society for Legislation, n.d.): "We need to take away the enforcer concept." John Landon, president of Sema, was quoted in Redmond, 1988, p. 188. For expert opinion on the issue of housing chimpanzees alone during AIDS or hepatitis studies and on the related issue of air filtration, see Prince and others, 1989. The Jane Goodall Institute recommendations for the treatment of chimpanzees in labs are reproduced in Appendix B. See "Maintenance of Chimpanzees," 1988; see also Holden, 1988.

12. OUR PARDON   For more on the African parks and reserves that protect chimpanzees, see Heltne and Marquardt, 1989; for more especially on Ndoki, see Linden, 1992.

References

Adler, Jerry, and Mary Hager. 1988. "Emptying the Cages." *Newsweek*, May 23, pp. 59, 60.

"African Rainforest Threatened." 1991. *EDF Letter* 22 (2): 8.

"AIDS Research Plan Threatens Last Wild Chimps, Experts Say." 1988. *Tucson Citizen*, June 10.

"AIDS Vaccine Tests on Humans May Come Soon, Scientists Say." 1987. *Boston Globe*, Jan.

Albrecht, Helmut. 1976. "Chimpanzees in Uganda." *Oryx* 13 (July): 357–361.

Albrecht, Helmut, and S. C. Dunnett. 1971. *Chimpanzees in Western Africa.* Munich: Piper Verlag.

Alley, Jerry. 1985. "Animal Lovers Join to Send Chimps to 'Paradise.' " *Virginian-Pilot*, Jan. 29.

"Along the Trail with the Editor." 1927. *Asia* 27 (2): 89.

Alter, Harvey J., and others. 1984. "Transmission of HTLV-III Infection from Human Plasma to Chimpanzees: An Animal Model for AIDS." *Science* 226 (Nov.): 549–552.

Altman, Lawrence K. 1989. "Salk Says Tests of Vaccine Show Halt of AIDS Infection in Chimps." *New York Times*, June 8.

Anderson, G. Christopher. 1990a. "White House Says No." *Nature* 344 (Apr. 26): 804.

———. 1990b. "U.S. Takes the Offensive on Animal Research." *Nature* 344 (Apr. 5): 477.

"Animal Activists." 1989. Associated Press, Jan. 3.

"Animal Shortage May Slow AIDS Vaccine — Dr. Gallo." 1987. *American Medical Association News*, Nov. 13.

Animal Welfare Institute. 1985. *Beyond the Laboratory Door.* Washington, D.C.: Animal Welfare Institute.

Asibey, Emmanuel O. A. 1974. "Wildlife as a Source of Protein in Africa South of the Sahara." *Biological Conservation* 6 (1): 32–39.

———. 1978. "Primate Conservation in Ghana." In *Recent Advances in Primatology: Conservation*, vol. 2, ed. D. J. Chivers and W. Lane-Petter, pp. 55–74. New York: Academic Press.

Badrian, Alison, and Noel Badrian. 1977. "Pygmy Chimpanzees." *Oryx* 13 (Feb.): 463–468.

Baldwin, Lori A., and Geza Teleki. 1973. "Field Research on Chimpanzees and Gorillas: An Historical, Geographical, and Bibliographical Listing." *Primates* 14: 315–330.

Baldwin, P. J., William C. McGrew, and Caroline E. G. Tutin. 1982. "Wide-ranging Chimpanzees at Mt. Asserik, Senegal." *International Journal of Primatology* 3 (Dec.): 367–385.

Barnard, Neal D. 1988. "AIDS Research: Problems with the 'Animal Model.'" *Reverence for Life* (Mar.–Apr.): 4–7.

Barnet, Sylvan. 1987 (1964). "The Tempest on Stage." In *William Shakespeare, The Tempest*, ed. Robert Langbaum, pp. 217–226. New York: New American Library.

Bates, Warren. 1990a. "Ill Will Flows as Berosini Trial Starts." *Las Vegas Review-Journal*, July 9.

———. 1990b. "Veterinarian Applauds Berosini's Care of Apes." *Las Vegas Review-Journal*, July 24.

———. 1990c. "Ex-Producer Says Berosini's Image Tainted." *Las Vegas Review-Journal*, July 26.

———. 1990d. "Berosini Says He 'Wanted to Die.'" *Las Vegas Review-Journal*, July 29.

———. 1990e. "Charges Dismissed in Berosini Trial." *Las Vegas Review-Journal*, July 31.

———. 1990f. "Renowned Ape Expert Jane Goodall Approved as Witness in Berosini Trial." *Las Vegas Review-Journal*, Aug. 2.

———. 1990g. "Veterinarian Claims Apes Ill-Treated." *Las Vegas Review-Journal*, Aug. 4.

———. 1990h. "Berosini Ends Four Days on the Witness Stand." *Las Vegas Review-Journal*, Aug. 1.

Bauman, John. 1926. "Observations on the Strength of the Chimpanzee and Its Implications." *Journal of Mammalogy* 7 (1): 1–9.

Beck, B. 1980. "Chimpocentrism: Bias in Cognitive Ethology." *Journal of Human Evolution* 11: 3–1.

Belcher, Walt. 1992. "'Today's 'Missing Link.'" *Tampa Tribune*, Jan. 14.

Bernheimer, Richard. 1979 (1952). *Wild Men in the Middle Ages: A Study in Art, Sentiment, and Demonology*. New York: Octagon Books.

"Berosini Gets Bum Rap." 1989. *Las Vegas Review-Journal*. Nov. 29.

Berryman, Ernst, and Cheryle Berryman. 1977. Letter to the editor. *Simian* (Feb.): 12.

———. 1978. Letter to the editor. *Simian* (July): 13.

Beyerlein, Tom. 1987. "Humane Societies File Suit for Custody of Chimpanzee." *Dayton Newshn,,5/hn,,5Journal Herald*, June 17.

Bloomsmith, M. A., P. L. Alford, and T. L. Maple. 1988. "Successful Feeding

Enrichment for Captive Chimpanzees." *American Journal of Primatology* 16: 155–164.

Bloomsmith, M. A., M. E. Keeling, and S. P. Lambeth. 1990. "Videotapes: Environmental Enrichment for Singly Housed Chimpanzees." *Lab Animal* (Jan./Feb.): 42–46.

Bluestone, Mimi. 1989. "Spare Parts for Humans: Science Steps up the Search." *Business Week*, Feb. 27, pp. 65–66.

Blum, Deborah. 1991a. "The Monkey Wars." *Sacramento Bee*, Nov. 25.

———. 1991b. "Protester Runs into Foes Who Play Hardball." *Sacramento Bee*, Nov. 25.

"Bobby Berosini Sets Record Straight." 1989. *Showbiz*, Dec. 10.

Boesch, Christophe. 1990. "First Hunters of the Forest." *New Scientist* (May 19): 38–41.

Boesch, Christophe, and Hedwige Boesch-Achermann. 1981. "Sex Differences in the Use of Natural Hammers by Wild Chimpanzees: A Preliminary Report." *Journal of Human Evolution* 10: 585–593.

———. 1990. "Adventures in Eating." *BBC Wildlife* (Oct.): 668–672.

Boffey, Philip M. 1987. "U.S. Announces Decision to Test AIDS Vaccines." *New York Times*, Aug. 19.

Booth, William. 1988. "Chimps and Research: Endangered?" *Science* 241 (Aug. 12): 777, 778.

Boroviczeny, Imre de, Mark Carwardine, and Victor Watkins. 1985. "IUCN Calls Spain to Stop Chimp Trade." *TRAFFIC Bulletin* 7 (Apr. 19).

Bournonville, D. de. 1967. "Contribution à l'étude du chimpanzee en République de Guinée." *Bulletin de l'Institut Français d'Afrique Noire* 29: 1188–1269.

Bree, Dennis. 1987. "Robert C. Gallo, M.D." *American Medical News* (Dec. 4): 3, 21, 22.

Brewer, Stella. 1978. *The Chimps of Mt. Asserik.* New York: Alfred A. Knopf.

"Brutal Kinship." 1987. *National Geographic Explorer.* Film documentary.

Buck, J. L. 1927. "The Chimpanzee Shaken out of His Nest." *Asia* 27 (4): 308–313, 326, 328.

Budiansky, Stephen. 1987. "Winning through Intimidation?" *U.S. News and World Report*, Aug. 31, pp. 48, 49.

Burnet, Nancy. 1989. "And That's Entertainment?" *Animals' Voice* 2 (5): 27–28.

Byrne, Richard W., and Andrew Whiten, eds. 1988. *Machiavellian Intelligence: Social Expertise and the Evolution of Intellect in Monkeys, Apes, and Humans.* Oxford: Clarendon Press.

Calder, Nigel. 1983. *Timescale: An Atlas of the Fourth Dimension.* New York: Viking Press.

Carroll, Richard W. 1986. "Status of the Lowland Gorilla and Other Wildlife in the Dzanga-Sangha Region of Southwestern Central African Republic." *Primate Conservation* 7: 38–41.

———. 1990. "In the Garden of the Gorillas." *Wildlife Conservation.* 93 (May/June): 50–63.

Carter, Janis. 1988. "Freed from Keepers and Cages, Chimps Come of Age on Baboon Island." *Smithsonian*, June, pp. 36–49.

"Case of Chimp Still Hangs in Balance." 1987. *Columbus Dispatch*, July 1.

Castro, Tony. 1991. "Bubbles Dumped!" *Globe*, Nov. 12.

Caulfield, Deborah. 1987. "New Charges of Animal Abuse in 'Project X.' " *Los Angeles Times*, Nov. 2.

Cherfas, Jeremy. 1989. "Pharmaceuticals Company 'Coerced' the Press." *New Scientist* (Apr. 22): 32.

"Chimp Lab Planned for China." 1988. *International Primate Protection League Newsletter** 15 (Aug.): 4.

"Chimp Returning to Bar after Verdict on Abuse." 1987. *Newark Advocate*, June 15.

"Chimpanzee Center of Multi-Million Dollar Lawsuit." 1981. *IPPL Newsletter* 8 (Sept.): 10.

"Chimpanzee Experts Meet." 1978. *IPPL Newsletter* 5 (Aug.): 14.

"Chimpanzee Shortage May Hurt Research." 1987. *Los Angeles Times*, Oct. 22.

"Chimpanzees an Important Model for HIV." 1990. *AIDS Research Exchange* (Jan./Feb.): 6–9.

"Chimpanzees and Other Non-Human Primates Available for Biomedical Research." 1988. *Alamogordo Daily News*, May 22. Advertisement.

"Chimpanzees in Danger." 1989. *IPPL Newsletter* 16 (Dec.): 7.

"Chimps Suffer in AIDS Tests, Doctor Warns." 1988. *Rochester Times-Union*, June 17.

"Chimps to Be Half-Upgraded?" 1989. *IPPL Newsletter* (Mar.): 15.

Chuan, Yan. 1988. "Rare-Animal Breeding Center." *China Reconstructs*, Nov., p. 17.

Ciochon, Russell L., and Robert S. Corruccini, eds. 1983. *New Interpretations of Ape and Human Ancestry*. New York: Plenum Press.

Clark, C. B. 1977. "A Preliminary Report on Weaning among Chimpanzees of the Gombe National Park, Tanzania." In *Primate Bio-Social Development*, ed. Suzanne Chevalier-Skolnikoff and F. E. Poirier. New York: Garland.

Cochran, Russ. 1990. "Tarzan of the Ozarks." *Inside Collector* 1(4): 42–48.

Cohen, Jon. 1989. "Shots in the Dark." *Washington City Paper* 9 (Oct. 13–19): 18ff.

———. 1991. "Is NIH Failing an AIDS 'Challenge'?" *Science* 251 (Feb.): 518–520.

Connell, Nick. 1986. "I Remember . . . Those Circus Chimps." *Hudson News*, Aug. 8.

Connelly, Joel. 1991. "The Big Cut." *Sierra* 76 (May/June): 42–53.

"Correction and Clarification." 1991. *Washingtonian* 27 (Dec.): 35, 36.

Cowley, Geoffrey, and others. 1988. "Of Pain and Progress." *Newsweek*, Dec. 26, pp. 50–59.

* Hereafter cited as *IPPL Newsletter*.

Crail, Ted. 1983. *Apetalk and Whalespeak: The Quest for Interspecies Communication.* Chicago: Contemporary Books.

Darwin, Charles. 1872. *The Descent of Man.* New York: D. Appleton and Company.

"Decision of the Day." 1989. *New York Law Journal* (Jan. 30).

Denis, Armand. 1963. *On Safari: The Story of My Life.* New York: E. P. Dutton.

Diamond, Jared. 1984. "Making a Chimp out of Man." *Discover* 5 (Dec.): 55–60.

———. 1989. "The Great Leap Forward." *Discover* 10 (May): 54–60.

Dolan, Carrie. 1989. "Life Is a Jungle for Some Animals Kept behind Bars." *Wall Street Journal,* Jan. 12.

Domlain, Jean-Yves. 1977. *The Animal Connection: The Confessions of an Ex–Wild Animal Trafficker.* New York: William Morrow.

Donner, Jill. 1989. "Lassie, Stay Home." *WGAW Journal* (Apr.): 23, 47.

"Don't Use Chimps, Top Scientist Tells Barnard." 1977. *Cape Times,* Sept. 10.

Dossi, H., J. L. Guillaumet, and M. Hadley. 1981. "The Tai Forest: Land Use Problems in a Tropical Forest." *Ambio* 10: 120–125.

Douglas, Mary. 1975. "Do Dogs Laugh?" In *Implicit Meanings.* London: Routledge & Kegan Paul.

Dowling, Harry F. 1977. *Fighting Infection: Conquests of the Twentieth Century.* Cambridge, Mass.: Harvard University Press.

"Dr. Frederick Goodwin." 1989. *Animal Welfare Institute Quarterly* 38 (Spring): 4.

"Dr. Salk's Research on AIDS Important But No Breakthrough." 1989. *Williamsport Sun-Gazette,* June 9.

Duberley, Linda. 1988a. "Sanctuary of the Apes." *Mail on Sunday,* Mar. 27.

———. 1988b. "The Evil Trade of Dr. Sitter." *Mail on Sunday,* Apr. 3.

Du Chaillu, Paul B. 1861. *Explorations and Adventures in Equatorial Africa: With Accounts of the Manners and Customs of the People . . .* London: John Murray.

Dumanoski, Dianne. 1987a. "Chimps Mistreated at Md. Lab, Researcher Goodall Charges." *Boston Globe,* Jan. 31.

———. 1987b. "Goodall Going Public in Chimp Rights Fight." *Detroit Free Press,* Mar. 17.

———. 1987c. "The Animal-Rights Underground." *Boston Globe Magazine,* Mar. 22.

———. 1988. "Researchers Grapple with Primate Law." *Boston Globe,* Sept. 18.

Dunlop, Becky Norton. 1989. "Endangered and Threatened Wildlife and Plants; Proposed Endangered Status for Chimpanzee and Pygmy Chimpanzee; Proposed Rule." *Federal Register* (Feb. 24): 8152–57.

Dunn, Ragan. 1988. "Medical World Enraged at Latest Soviet Experiment." *Weekly World News,* Oct. 18.

Eckholm, Erik. 1985. "Will There Be Enough Chimps for Research?" *New York Times,* Nov. 19.

Eichberg, Jorg W., and John T. Speck. 1988. "Establishment of a Chimpanzee Retirement Fund: Maintenance after Experimentation." *Journal of Medical Primatology* 17: 71–76.

Eichberg, Jorg W., and others. 1988. "In Utero Infection of an Infant Chimpanzee with HIV." *New England Journal of Medicine* 319 (Sept. 15): 722.

Eisen, Jack. 1986. "Electronic Intrusion." *Washington Post*, Mar. 6.

Ellenberger, Henri F. 1971. *The Discovery of the Unconscious: The History and Evolution of Dynamic Psychiatry.* New York: Basic Books.

Elliott, Harvey. 1992. "Benidorm Ends Chimpanzee Abuse." *Times*, Jan. 15.

Elon, Amos. 1991. "Report from Vienna." *New Yorker*, May 13, pp. 92–102.

Erickson, Milton H. 1964. "The 'Surprise' and 'My-Friend-John' Techniques of Hypnosis: Minimal Cues and Natural Field Experimentation." *American Journal of Clinical Hypnosis* 6: 293–307.

———. 1966. "The Interspersal Hypnotic Technique for Symptom Correction and Pain Control." *American Journal of Clinical Hypnosis* 8: 198–209.

Eudey, Ardith, and David Mack. 1984. "Use of Primates and Captive Breeding Programs in the United States." In *The International Primate Trade*, vol. 1, ed. David Mack and Russell A. Mittermeier, pp. 153–180. Washington, D.C.: Traffic (U.S.A.).

"Ex-Trainer of Chimps Hopes They'll Be Freed." 1991. *Dallas Morning News*, Dec. 30.

Eyre, Kathy. 1988. "Animal-Human Transplants." Associated Press, Sept. 5.

Fajzi, K., V. Reinhardt, and M. D. Smith. 1989. "A Review of Environmental Enrichment Strategies for Singly Caged Nonhuman Primates." *Lab Animal* (Mar.): 23–25.

Fay, J. M. 1987. *Partial Completion of a Census of the Lowland Gorilla (Gorilla g. gorilla Savage & Wyman) in Southwestern Central African Republic.* St. Louis: Washington University. Special report.

Fersko, Raymond S. 1991. Letter to the editor: "Chimpanzee Case Tests Libel Jurisdiction." *New York Times*, June 15.

Finnigan, David. 1989. "Berosini's Orangutans Get Clean Bill of Health after Inspection by Vets." *Las Vegas Review-Journal*, Sept. 13.

Fouts, Deborah H. 1987. "Signing Interactions between Mother and Infant Chimpanzees." *Friends of Washoe* 6 (Winter): 4–8.

Fouts, Roger S., and Deborah H. Fouts. 1989. "Loulis in Conversation with the Cross-Fostered Chimpanzees." In *Teaching Sign Language to Chimpanzees*, ed. R. Allen Gardner, Beatrix T. Gardner, and Thomas E. Van Cantfort, pp. 293–307. Albany, N.Y.: SUNY Press.

Fouts, Roger S., Deborah H. Fouts, and Thomas E. Van Cantfort. 1989. "The Infant Loulis Learns Signs from Cross-Fostered Chimpanzees." In *Teaching Sign Language to Chimpanzees*, ed. R. Allen Gardner, Beatrix T. Gardner, and Thomas E. Van Cantfort, pp. 280–292. Albany, N.Y.: SUNY Press.

Fouts, Roger S., and others. 1989. "Signs of Enrichment toward the Psychological Well-Being of Chimpanzees." In *Housing, Care, and Psychological*

Well-Being of Captive and Laboratory Primates, pp. 376–388. Park Ridge, N.J.: Noyes Publications.

Frederick, Sherman R. 1990. "Animal Crackers." *Las Vegas Review-Journal,* Feb. 11.

Frey, Marc. 1992. "Affen für den Nobelpreis." *Frankfurter Rundschau,* Apr. 11.

Fritz, Jo. 1975. "Dream or Nightmare — Which Will It Be?" *Simian* (Aug.): 3–5.

Galdikas, Biruté M. F., and Geza Teleki. 1981. "Variations in Subsistence Activities of Female and Male Pongids: New Perspectives on the Origins of Hominid Labor Division." *Current Anthropology* 22 (3): 241–256.

Gallup, George G., Jr. 1970. "Chimpanzees: Self-Recognition." *Science* 167 (Jan.–Mar.): 86–87.

———. 1977. "Self-Recognition in Primates." *American Psychologist* 32: 329–338.

Gang, Bill. 1990a. "Berosini: As the Judge's Temper Turns." *Las Vegas Sun,* July 25.

———. 1990b. "Berosini's 'Punch' Told." *Las Vegas Sun,* Aug. 2.

———. 1990c. "Lawyers Facing New Battle." *Las Vegas Sun,* Aug. 9.

———. 1990d. "Berosini Case Not Over." *Las Vegas Sun,* Aug. 13.

———. 1990e. "Leavitt Charged with Boyd Conflict." *Las Vegas Sun,* Dec. 14.

———. 1990f. "PETA Motion against Leavitt Tossed Out." *Las Vegas Sun,* Dec. 27.

Gardner, R. Allen, and Beatrix T. Gardner. 1989. "A Cross-Fostering Laboratory." In *Teaching Sign Language to Chimpanzees,* ed. R. Allen Gardner, Beatrix T. Gardner, and Thomas E. Van Cantfort, pp. 1–28. Albany, N.Y.: SUNY Press.

Gergely, Stefan M. 1987a. "Wettlauf mit dem Tod." *Profil* (Mar. 16): 34–36.

———. 1987b. " 'Ich Werde den Ersten Aids-Impfstoff Entwickeln.' " *Profil* (Nov. 9): 87.

German, Jeff. 1990. "Free Speech Attacked in Berosini Case." *Las Vegas Sun,* Aug. 12.

———. 1991. "Judge Purges PETA Fines in Berosini Case." *Las Vegas Sun,* Apr. 30.

Gest, Ted. 1988. "A Chilling Flurry of Lawsuits." *U.S. News and World Report,* May 23, pp. 64–65.

Ghiglieri, Michael P. 1984. *The Chimpanzees of Kibale Forest: A Field Study of Ecology and Social Structure.* New York: Columbia University Press.

———. 1988. *East of the Mountains of the Moon: Chimpanzee Society in the African Rain Forest.* New York: Free Press.

Goodall, Jane. 1971. *In the Shadow of Man.* Boston: Houghton Mifflin.

———. 1983. "Population Dynamics during a 15-Year Period in One Community of Free-Living Chimpanzees in the Gombe National Park, Tanzania." *Zeitschrift für Tierspsychologie* 61: 1–60.

———. 1986. *The Chimpanzees of Gombe: Patterns of Behavior.* Cambridge, Mass.: Harvard University Press.

———. 1987. "A Plea for the Chimps." *New York Times Magazine,* May 17, pp. 108–110, 118, 120.

———. 1990. *Through a Window: My Thirty Years with the Chimpanzees of Gombe.* Boston: Houghton Mifflin.

Goodall, Jane, and Geza Teleki. N.d. "Chimpanzee Survival: A Global Challenge." Unpublished.

Gore, Al. 1992. *Earth in the Balance: Ecology and the Human Spirit.* Boston: Houghton Mifflin.

Greenspun, Janie. 1989a. "Horizons." *Las Vegas Sun,* Aug. 10.

———. 1989b. "Horizons." *Las Vegas Sun,* Nov. 2.

Greisenegger, I. 1986. "Tarzans Geschäfte." *Profil* (Oct. 20): 60–62.

Griffin, Donald R. 1984. *Animal Thinking.* Cambridge, Mass.: Harvard University Press.

Hahn, Emily. 1988. *Eve and the Apes.* New York: Weidenfeld & Nicolson.

Haley, Jay, ed. 1967. *Advanced Techniques of Hypnosis and Therapy: Selected Papers of Milton H. Erickson, M.D.* New York: Grune & Stratton.

Happold, David C. D. 1971. "A Nigerian High Forest Reserve." In *Wildlife Conservation in West Africa,* ed. David C. D. Happold. Gland, Switzerland: International Union for the Conservation of Nature.

Harako, Reizo. 1981. "The Cultural Ecology of Hunting Behavior among Mbuti Pygmies in the Ituri Forest in Zaire." In *Omnivorous Primates,* ed. R. S. O. Harding and Geza Teleki, pp. 499–525. New York: Columbia University Press.

Harcourt, A. H., and K. J. Stewart. 1980. "Gorilla-Eaters of Gabon." *Oryx* 40 (3): 248–251.

Harris, Warren. 1989a. "Strip Show Must Go On, But without Orangutans." *Las Vegas Sun,* July 29.

———. 1989b. "Witness Disputes Berosini's Claim of Animal Harassment." *Las Vegas Sun,* Aug. 2.

Harrisson, Barbara. 1971. "Conservation of Nonhuman Primates in 1970." In *Primates in Medicine,* vol. 5. Basel: S. Karger.

Hart, John A. 1978. "From Subsistence to Market: A Case Study of the Mbuti Net Hunters." *Human Ecology* 6 (3): 325–353.

Hart, John A., and S. Thomas. 1986. "The Ituri Forest of Zaire: Primate Diversity and Prospects for Conservation." *Primate Conservation* 7: 42–43.

Hartmann, R. 1886. *Anthropoid Apes.* New York: D. Appleton.

Hatch, Richard. 1991. "Cancer Warfare." *Covert Action* 39 (Winter): 14–19.

Havemann, Judith. 1989. "Animal Rules Uncage Scientists' Complaints." *Washington Post,* July 9.

Hayes, Cathy. 1951. *The Ape in Our House.* New York: Harper & Brothers.

Hearne, Vicki. 1986. *Adam's Task: Calling Animals by Name.* New York: Alfred A. Knopf.

Heaton, Tom. 1989. *In Teleki's Footsteps: An East African Journey.* London: Macmillan.

Ein Herzfür Tiere. 1986. Dec.

Hill, W. C. O. 1969. "The Nomenclature, Taxonomy, and Distribution of Chimpanzees." In *The Chimpanzee,* vol. 1, ed. Geoffrey H. Bourne. Basel: S. Karger.

Hilts, Philip J. 1988. "Mice Implants Create Model of Human Immune System." *Washington Post,* Sept. 15.

Hiraiwa-Hasegawa, M., T. Hasegawa, and T. Nishida. 1984. "Demographic Study of a Large-Sized Unit-Group of Chimpanzees in the Mahale Mountains, Tanzania: A Preliminary Report." *Primates* 25 (4): 401–413.

Holden, Constance. 1987. "Animal Regulations: So Far, So Good." *Science* 238 (Nov.): 880–882.

———. 1988. "Experts Ponder Simian Well-Being." *Science* 241 (Sept.): 1753–55.

"HSUS Works to Prevent the Taking of Chimpanzees from the Wild." 1988. *HSUS News* (Fall).

"Humane Society Exec Resigns." 1989. *Las Vegas Review-Journal,* Oct. 29.

"Immuno: Neue Entwicklung in der Affen-Affäre." 1986. *Kurier,* Nov. 8.

"Immuno AG Seeks to Test AIDS Vaccine on Humans." 1987. *Wall Street Journal,* June 16.

"Immuno's New York Lawsuit Dismissed." 1989. *IPPL Newsletter* 16 (Mar.): 9–10.

Inskipp, Tim, and Sue Wells. 1979. *International Trade in Wildlife.* London: Earthscan.

Institute of Medicine/National Academy of Sciences. 1986. *Confronting AIDS: Directions for Public Health, Health Care, and Research.* Washington, D.C.: National Academy Press.

Interagency Primate Steering Committee. 1978. *Report of the Task Force on the Use of and Need for Chimpanzees.* Bethesda, Md.: National Institutes of Health.

Jackson, Joe. 1986. "Norfolk Praised for Funds to Help Rehabilitate Chimps." *Ledger-Star,* Mar. 18.

Jeffrey, Sonia M. 1970. "Ghana's Forest Wildlife in Danger." *Oryx* 10 (May): 240–243.

———. 1975. "Ghana's New Forest National Park." *Oryx* 13 (Apr.): 34–36.

———. 1977. "How Liberia Uses Wildlife." *Oryx* 14 (Dec.): 168–173.

Johnsen, Dennis O. 1987. "The Need for Using Chimpanzees in Research." *Lab Animal* (July–Aug.): 19–23.

Johnson, Peter. 1989. "Melcher Says He's 'Nosing Around, Looking for Ways to Help.' " *Great Falls Tribune,* Jan. 11.

Johnson, William. 1990. "Happy Menageries and Flying Pigs." *BBC Wildlife* (May): 320–325.

Johnston, Robin. 1988. "Using Chimpanzees for AIDS Study." *Christian Science Monitor,* July 12.

Jones, Clyde, and Jorge Sabater Pi. 1971. "Comparative Ecology of *Gorilla*

gorilla (Savage and Wyman) and *Pan troglodytes* (Blumenbach) in Rio Muni, West Africa." *Bibliographia Primatology* 13: 1–96.

Jones, T. S. 1966. "Notes on the Commoner Sierra Leone Mammals." *Journal of the Nigerian Field Society* 53 (Jan.): 4–18.

"Judge Orders Return of Smoking Chimp to Owner." 1987. *Cleveland Plain Dealer,* July 8.

"Judge Signs Release for Smoking Ape." 1987. *Cleveland Plain Dealer,* June 23.

"June 1990 Press Briefing." 1990. *Foundation for Biomedical Research Annual Report,* p. 5.

Junkin, Elizabeth Darby. 1989. "Solomon's Child." *Buzzworm: The Environmental Journal* 1 (Spring): 20–29.

"Jury Says Chimp Was Not Abused." 1987. *Mansfield News Journal.* June 15.

Kano, Takayoshi. 1972. "Distribution and Adaptation of Chimpanzees on the Eastern Shore of Lake Tanganyika." *Kyoto University African Studies* 7: 37–129.

———. 1984. "Distribution of Pygmy Chimpanzees *(Pan paniscus)* in the Central Zaire Basin." *Folia Primatologica* 43: 36–52.

Kaplan, John. 1988. "The Use of Animals in Research." *Science* 242 (Nov.): 839, 840.

Karno, Valerie. 1991. "Protection of Endangered Gorillas and Chimpanzees in International Trade: Can CITES Help?" *Hastings International and Comparative Law Review* 14 (4): 989–1015.

Kavanagh, Michael, and Elizabeth Bennett. 1984. "A Synopsis of Legislation and the Primate Trade in Habitat and User Countries." In *The International Primate Trade,* vol. 1, ed. David Mack and Russell A. Mittermeier, pp. 19–48. Washington, D.C.: TRAFFIC (U.S.A.).

Kerr, John. 1989a. "Berosini Plans to File Lawsuit." *Las Vegas Review-Journal,* Aug. 1.

———. 1989b. "USDA: No Sign of Orangutan Abuse." *Las Vegas Review-Journal,* Aug. 3.

"Kid Talk." 1990. *Las Vegas Sun,* Feb. 27.

Kilpatrick, James J. 1986. "Caged in Poolesville." *Washington Post,* May 12.

King, Frederick A. 1987. Letter to the editor. *New York Times Magazine,* June 21, p. 86.

———. 1988. Letter to the editor: "Chimps and Research." *Science* 242 (Dec.): 1227.

King, Frederick A., and others. 1988. "Primates." *Science* 240 (June): 1475–81.

Kingman, Sharon. 1988. "Virus Develops Even with Antibodies Presenthn,,5/hn,,5Chimpanzee Theory." *New Scientist* (May 26).

Klein, Karen E. 1987. "No Criminal Charges Filed against Trainer." *Daily News,* Nov. 13.

Koenig, Marcia L. 1991. "Apes Are All in the Family." *St. Louis Post-Dispatch,* Jan. 10.

Köhler, Wolfgang. 1925. *The Mentality of Apes*. London: Routledge and Kegan Paul.

Kortlandt, Adriaan. 1962. "Chimpanzees in the Wild." *Scientific American* 206 (5): 128–138.

———. 1965. "Some Results of a Pilot Study on Chimpanzee Ecology." Amsterdam: University of Amsterdam. Unpublished.

———. 1966. "Chimpanzee Ecology and Laboratory Management." *Laboratory Primate Newsletter* 5: 1–11.

———. 1972. *New Perspectives in Ape and Human Evolution*. Amsterdam: Stichting voor Psychobiologie.

———. 1983. "Marginal Habitats of Chimpanzees." *Journal of Human Evolution* 12: 231–278.

Kortlandt, Adriaan, and Ewald Holzhaus. 1987. "New Data on the Use of Stone Tools by Chimpanzees in Guinea and Liberia." *Primates* 28 (Oct.): 473–496.

Kortlandt, Adriaan, and J. C. J. van Zon. 1968. "The Present State of Research on the Dehumanization Hypothesis of African Ape Evolution." *Proceedings of the Second International Congress of Primatology* 3: 10–13.

Labbee, William. 1991. "The Primate Debate." *New Times* 6 (Nov. 20): 20–26.

Lackey, Patrick K. 1985. "Chuck the Chimp Loves His TV." *Virginian-Pilot/Ledger-Star*.

Lamotte, M. 1983. "The Undermining of Mt. Nimba." *Ambio* 12: 174–179.

Landers, Ann. 1986. "Ann Landers Says Norfolk Has Gone Ape over Chimps." *Virginian-Pilot/Ledger-Star*, May 25.

Langbaum, Robert. 1987 (1964). "The Source of 'The Tempest,' " in *William Shakespeare, The Tempest*, ed. Robert Langbaum, pp. 125–139. New York: New American Library.

Leerhsen, Charles, with Jeff Burbank. 1990. "Gambling on the Future." *Newsweek*, Oct. 29, pp. 82, 83.

Letcher, Frank A., Paul G. Corrao, and Ayub K. Ommaya. 1973. "Head Injury in the Chimpanzee. Part 2: Spontaneous and Evoked Epidural Potentials as Indices of Injury Severity." *Journal of Neurosurgery* 39 (Aug.): 167–177.

Levy, Claudia. 1987. "Rockville Lab Accused of Threatening Inspectors." *Washington Post*, Dec. 1.

Lewis, Anthony. 1991. "Abusing the Law." *New York Times*, May 10.

Linden, Eugene. 1986. *Silent Partners: The Legacy of the Ape Language Experiments*. New York: Times Books.

———. 1990. "The Last Eden." *Time*, July 13, pp. 62–68.

"List of Chimpanzee Sightings Available." 1991. *IPPL Newsletter* 18 (Nov.): 23.

Little, Linda. 1990. "Swinging Singles: Lab Chimps Retire to Condos in the Sun." *American Medical News* (Jan. 19): 9–10.

"Local Research Firm to Develop Chimp Facility in China." 1988. *Alamogordo Daily News*, May 22.

Love, Steve. 1987. "Was Life Too Wild for Sam?" *Akron Beacon Journal,* June 21.

Lowes, R. H. G. 1970. "Destruction in Sierra Leone." *Oryx* 10 (Sept.): 309, 310.

Luoma, Jon R. 1989. "The Chimp Connection." *Animal Kingdom* (Jan./Feb.): 38–51.

Mack, David, and Ardith Eudey. 1984. "A Review of the U.S. Primate Trade." In *The International Primate Trade,* vol. 1, ed. David Mack and Russell A. Mittermeier, pp. 91–136. Washington, D.C.: TRAFFIC (U.S.A.).

Mack, David, and Russell A. Mittermeier, eds. 1984. *The International Primate Trade,* vol. 1. Washington, D.C.: TRAFFIC (U.S.A.).

MacKinnon, John. 1976. "Mountain Gorillas and Bonobos." *Oryx* 13 (4): 372–382.

MacKinnon, John, and K. MacKinnon. 1986. *Review of the Protected Areas System in the Afrotropical Realm.* Gland, Switzerland: International Union for the Conservation of Nature.

Maddry, Lawrence. 1986a. "Bachelor Swings to the Aid of 2 Chimps." *Virginian-Pilot.*

———. 1986b. "Chimps Deserve Guided Tour of San Antonio Digs." *Virginian-Pilot.*

"Maintenance of Chimpanzees in Captivity for Biomedical Research." 1988. *Journal of Medical Primatology* 17: 113–122.

Maki, S., and M. A. Bloomsmith. 1989. "Uprooted Trees Facilitate the Psychological Well-Being of Captive Chimpanzees." *Zoo Biology* 8: 79–87.

Malenky, Richard K., Nancy Thompson-Handler, and Randall L. Susman. 1989. "Conservation Status of *Pan paniscus.*" In *Understanding Chimpanzees,* ed. Paul G. Heltne and Linda A. Marquardt, pp. 362–368. Cambridge, Mass.: Harvard University Press.

Manning, Joe. 1988. "Transplants of Monkey Hearts Aim at Organ Shortage." *Milwaukee Sentinel,* Sept. 8.

Markowitz, H., and J. S. Spinelli. 1986. "Environmental Engineering for Primates." In *Primates: The Road to Self-Sustaining Populations,* ed. Kurt Benirschke, pp. 489–498. New York: Springer-Verlag.

Marx, Leo. 1964. *The Machine in the Garden: Technology and the Pastoral Ideal in America,* chap. 2. Oxford: Oxford University Press.

Masefield, John. 1927. Introduction. In Richard Hakluyt, *The Principal Navigations Voyages Traffiques and Discoveries of the English Nation Made by Sea or Overland to the Remote and Farthest Quarters of the Earth at any Time within the Compass of These 1600 Years,* vol. 1, pp. v–xviii. New York: E. P. Dutton.

Maugh, Thomas. N.d. "Search for New Medicine Leads Scientists to the Plants of Apes." *Los Angeles Times.*

Maurice, Dick. 1989a. "Lido's Bobby Berosini's Orangutan Story a 'Monkey Smear.' " *Las Vegas Sun,* Aug. 1.

———. 1989b. "Vegas Animal-Lover Forced to Sue to Protect His Name." *Las Vegas Sun,* Aug. 14.

McArdle, John. 1987. "Primate Psychological Well-Being: Passive Suffering in Research Laboratories." *Reverence for Life* (May–June): 8–10.

McCabe, Katie. 1990. "Beyond Cruelty." *Washingtonian* (Feb.): 73–77, 185–195.

McGreal, Shirley. 1983. Letter to the editor: "A Project with Potential to Spread Non-A, Non-B Hepatitis in West Africa." *Journal of Medical Primatology* 12: 280–281.

McGrew, William C. 1983. "Animal Foods in the Diets of Wild Chimpanzees (*Pan troglodytes*): Why Cross-Cultural Variation?" *Journal of Ethnology* 1: 46–61.

McGrew, William C., and Caroline E. G. Tutin. 1978. "Evidence for a Social Custom in Wild Chimpanzees." *Man* 13: 234–251.

McGrew, William C., P. J., Baldwin, and Caroline E. G. Tutin. 1981. "Chimpanzees in a Hot, Dry, and Open Habitat: Mt. Asserik, Senegal, West Africa." *Journal of Human Evolution* 10: 227–244.

McKinnon, Shaun. 1990. "Berosini Awarded $4.2 Million." *Las Vegas Review-Journalhn,,5/hn,,5Las Vegas Sun*, Aug. 12.

McMahan, Elizabeth. 1983. "Bugs Angle for Termites." *Natural History* 92 (5): 40–47.

McNulty, Timothy. 1981. "Human Chimp." *Miami Herald*, Feb. 12.

"Mental Health Shake-up." 1992. *Animal Welfare Institute Quarterly* 41 (Spring): 15.

"Merck Sharp and Dohme Applies to Import 125 Chimpanzees." 1978. *IPPL Newsletter* (Apr.): 9, 10.

Merewood, Anne. 1991. "Plants of the Apes." *Wildlife Conservation* 94 (2): 54–59.

Merfield, Fred G. 1954. "The Gorilla of the French Cameroons." *Zoo Life* 9 (Autumn): 84–94.

Merfield, Fred G., and Harry Miller. 1956. *Gorilla Hunter*. New York: Farrar, Straus and Cudahy.

"Michael Jackson Fires Bubbles — And He's Bringing in a Lookalike for Liz's Wedding." 1991. *Star*, Sept. 3.

Minetree, Harry, and Diane Guernsey. 1988. "Animal Rights — And Wrongs." *Town and Country* (May): 158–161, 230–238.

Minty, Chip. 1991. "Norman Man Urges Ex-OU Chimps EscApe." *Daily Oklahoman*, Dec. 29.

———. 1992. "City Zoo Rejects Chimps Trained in Sign Language." *Daily Oklahoman*, Jan. 15.

Mittermeier, Russell A., and others. 1986. "Primate Conservation." In *Comparative Primate Biology*, ed. G. Mitchell and J. Erwin, vol. 2A, pp. 3–72. New York: Alan R. Liss.

"Monkey Depression Experiments at University of Wisconsin." 1981. *IPPL Newsletter* 8 (May): 8, 9.

Montgomery, Cy. 1988. "Chimpanzees: Endangered by Demand." *Animals* (May–June): 17–22.

Moor-Jankowski, Jan, and C. James Mahoney. 1989. "Chimpanzees in Captivity: Humane Handling and Breeding within the Confines Imposed by Medical Research and Testing." *Journal of Medical Primatology* 18: 1–26.

Moore, J. 1985. "Chimpanzee Survey in Mali, West Africa." *Primate Conservation* 6: 59–63.

Morris, Ramona, and Desmond Morris. 1966. *Men and Apes.* New York: McGraw-Hill.

Mubalamata, Kabongo Ka. 1984. "Will the Pygmy Chimpanzee Be Threatened with Extinction like the Elephant and the White Rhinoceros in Zaire?" In *The Pygmy Chimpanzee: Evolutionary Biology and Behavior,* ed. Randall L. Susman, pp. 415–419. New York: Plenum Press.

Myers, Norman. 1979. *The Sinking Ark: A New Look at the Problem of Disappearing Species.* New York: Pergamon Press.

———. 1980. *Conversion of Tropical Moist Forests.* Washington, D.C.: National Academy of Sciences.

———. 1984. *The Primary Source: Tropical Forests and Our Future.* New York: W. W. Norton.

———. 1985. "Tropical Deforestation and Species Extinctions." *Futures* 17 (Oct.): 451–463.

Newman, Arnold. 1990. *Tropical Rainforest.* New York: Facts on File.

Newton, Paul N., and Toshisada Nishida. 1989. "Possible Buccal Administration of Herbal Drugs by Wild Chimpanzees, *Pan troglodytes.*" *Animal Behavior* 39 (4): 798–801.

"NIH Denies Plans to Import Chimps for AIDS Research." 1988. *ILAR News* 30 (Summer).

"NIH Experimenter Tortures Chimpanzee." 1988. *PETA News* (Sept./Oct.): 19.

"NIH Holds Chimpanzee Briefing." 1988. *IPPL Newsletter* 15 (Apr.): 13.

Nishida, Toshisada. 1985. "The Mahale Mountains Declared a National Park." *IPPL Newsletter* 12 (Dec.): 9.

Nishida, Toshisada, and Shiego Uehara. N.d. "Import and Use of Anthropoid Apes in Japan before Her Signature to the Washington Convention (CITES): A Preliminary Report." Unpublished.

"No Aping Berosini's Orangutans." 1989. *Las Vegas Sun,* Feb. 10.

Noell, Anna Mae. 1979. *The History of Noell's Ark Gorilla Show.* Tarpon Springs, Fla.: Noell's Ark.

Novak, M. A., and S. J. Suomi. 1988. "Psychological Well-Being of Primates in Captivity." *American Psychologist* 43 (10): 765–773.

Novek, Ellie. 1986. "City Will Spend $25,000 to 'Rehabilitate' Chimps." *Virginian-Pilot,* Mar. 5.

Oates, John F. 1985. *Action Plan for African Primate Conservation: 1986–1990.* Washington, D.C.: IUCN/SSC PSG. Special report.

Oldfield, Margery L., L. Joseph Folse, and Duane German. 1992. "Population Dynamics and Demography of the Common Chimpanzee *(Pan troglodytes)* in West Africa." Unpublished.

Ommaya, Ayub K., Paul G. Corrao, and Frank S. Letcher. 1973. "Head Injury in the Chimpanzee. Part 1: Biodynamics of Traumatic Unconsciousness." *Journal of Neurosurgery* 39 (Aug.): 152–166.

O'Neill, Bill, and Reginald Fitz. 1985. "TV and Movie Animal Stars Beaten and Abused." *National Enquirer*, May 14.

Patterson, Francine, and Eugene Linden. 1981. *The Education of Koko*. New York: Holt, Rinehart and Winston.

Pepys, Samuel. N.d. *Diary and Correspondence of Samuel Pepys*. New York: Bigelow, Smith.

Pequet, Barbara. 1987. "Animals in the Movies." *Animals' Agenda* (May): 26–28.

"PETA Becomes Shrill in Berosini Lawsuit." 1990. *Las Vegas Review-Journal*, Aug. 6.

PETA Department of Research and Investigations. 1986. *Investigative Report: SEMA Laboratory, Rockville, Maryland.*

"PETA Wins One." 1991. *Nature* 353 (Oct. 24): 687.

"Peter Gerone's Deposition." 1992. Special Supplement to *IPPL Newsletter* 19 (Apr.): 7–12.

Peterson, Dale. 1989. *The Deluge and the Ark: A Journey into Primate Worlds*. Boston: Houghton Mifflin.

Piccoli, Sean. 1986. "Theft of Four Chimps Puzzles Lab Officials." *Washington Times*, Dec. 9.

"Pope Urged to Support Animal Experimentation." 1991. *IPPL Newsletter* 18 (Apr.): 15.

Premack, David, and Ann James Premack. 1983. *The Mind of an Ape*. New York: W. W. Norton.

"Pressure for Better Care for Chimpanzees in Captivity." 1988. *ATLA: Alternatives to Laboratory Animals* 15 (3).

"Primate Centre Ready to Begin Tests." 1987. *New Scientist* (Dec. 10): 21.

Prince, Alfred M. 1984. Letter to the editor. *Journal of Medical Primatology* 13: 169–170.

Prince, Alfred M., and others. 1988. "Chimpanzees and AIDS Research." *Nature* 333 (June): 513.

———. 1989. "Appropriate Conditions for Maintenance of Chimpanzees in Studies with Blood-Borne Viruses: An Epidemiologic and Psychosocial Perspective." *Journal of Medical Primatology* 18: 27–42.

———. 1990. "Enrichment, Rehabilitation, and Release of Chimpanzees Used in Biomedical Research." *Lab Animal* 19 (July/Aug.): 29–37.

Progress Report: NIH Chimpanzee Breeding and Research Program. 1990.

Purchas, Samuel. 1905 (1625). *Hakluytus Posthumus, or Purchas His Pilgrimes, Contayning a History of the World in Sea Voyages and Lande Travells by Englishmen and Others*. Glasgow: James MacLehose and Sons.

Rahm, Ursula. 1967. "Observations during Chimpanzee Captures in the Congo." In *Progress in Primatology*, ed. D. Starck, R. Schneider, and H. J. Kuhn, pp. 195–207. Stuttgart: Gustav Fischer Verlag.

Redmond, Ian. 1986. "Law of the Jungle." *BBC Wildlife* (June): 300.

————. 1988. "Aren't Chimps God's Children Too?" *BBC Wildlife* (Apr.): 187–191.

————. 1991. "A Tale of Seven C's." *BBC Wildlife* (Apr.): 285–286.

"The Revolving Door." 1988. *IPPL Newsletter* 15 (Aug.): 15.

Robinson, Phillip T. 1971. "Wildlife Trends in Liberia and Sierra Leone." *Oryx* 11 (Sept.): 117–122.

Robinson, Phillip T., and Alexander Peale. 1981. "Liberia's Wildlife: The Time for Decision." *Zoonooz* 54 (10): 7–20.

Roderick, Kevin. 1990. "Spectacle, Complete with Apes, in Las Vegas Courtroom." *Los Angeles Times*, Aug. 8.

Ronan, Colin A. 1982. *Science: Its History and Development among the World's Cultures.* New York: Facts on File.

Rosenberg, Howard. 1991. " 'Quantum' Leaps into Biomedical Fray." *Los Angeles Times*, Aug. 12.

Rosenblum, Mort. 1988. "U.S. Institute May Go 'Offshore' with AIDS Research on Chimps." Associated Press wire report, June 8.

Rovner, Sandy. 1988. "Humans, Chimps, and AIDS: Matters of Survival." *Washington Post*, June 14.

Rowan, Andrew N. 1984. *Of Mice, Models, and Men: A Critical Evaluation of Animal Research.* Albany, N.Y.: SUNY Press.

————. 1989. "The Development of the Animal Protection Movement." *Journal of NIH Research* 1 (Nov.–Dec.): 97–100.

————. 1991. "Animal Experimentation and Society: A Case Study of an Uneasy Interaction." In *Biosciencehn,,5/hn,,5Society,* ed. D. J. Roy, B. E. Wynne, and R. W. Old, pp. 261–282. New York: John Wiley & Sons.

Rubinstein, Gwen. 1990. "Creature Discomforts." *Government Information Insider* (June).

"Rush to Judgment in Orangutan Affair." 1989. *Las Vegas Review-Journal,* Aug. 2.

Sabater Pi, Jorge. 1978. *El Chimpance y los Origenes de la Cultura.* Barcelona: Promocion Cultural.

————. 1979. "Chimpanzees and Human Predation in Rio Muni." *IPPL Newsletter* 6 (Aug.): 8.

Sabater Pi, Jorge, and Colin Groves. 1972. "The Importance of Higher Primates in the Diet of the Fang of Rio Muni." *Man* 7 (June): 239–243.

Sabater Pi, Jorge, and Clyde Jones. 1967. "Notes on the Distribution and Ecology of the Higher Primates of Rio Muni, West Africa." *Tulane Studies in Zoology* 14 (Sept.): 101–109.

Salati, E., and P. B. Vose. 1983. "Depletion of Tropical Rain Forests." *Ambio* 12 (2): 67–71.

Schaller, George B. 1963. *The Mountain Gorilla: Ecology and Behavior.* Chicago: University of Chicago Press.

————. 1964. *The Year of the Gorilla.* Chicago: University of Chicago Press.

Schimmell, Wolfgang. 1988. "Der Schimpanzen-Krimi." *Express* (Oct.).

Schlosberg, Suzanne. 1988. "Chimps Bred for Show Business Are Stars of Animal-Rights Battle." *Los Angeles Times*, July 20.

Schmidt, Christian. 1992. "Sieben Jahre Affentheater durch Alle Gerichtsin-stanzen." *Weltwoche* (Apr. 16): 27, 28.

"Scientists Fear TV Show Will Be Backward Leap for Animal Research." 1991. *FBR Newsletter* 8 (Sept./Oct.): 1, 2.

Seal, Ulysses S., and Nathan R. Flesness. 1986. "Captive Chimpanzee Popula-tions — Past, Present, and Future." In *Primates: The Road to Self-Sus-taining Populations*, ed. Kurt Benirschke, pp. 47–55. New York: Springer-Verlag.

"Secret Memo Made Public." 1988. *IPPL Newsletter* 15 (Apr.): 10.

Seidenberg, Mark. 1983. Letter to the editor. *New York Times Magazine*, Jan. 23.

Shakespeare, William. 1987 (1611). *The Tempest*, ed. Robert Langbaum. New York: New American Library.

Shemeligian, Bob. 1989a. "Animal Abuse Charges Devastate Berosinis." *Las Vegas Sun*, Aug. 1.

———. 1989b. "Stolen Papers Raise Humane Society Payment Questions." *Las Vegas Sun*.

Sibley, Adrian. 1990. "Ape Actor: Peter Elliott." *Premiere* (Sept.).

Sibley, Charles G., and Jon E. Ahlquist. 1984. "The Phylogeny of the Homin-oid Primates, as Indicated by DNA-DNA Hybridization." *Journal of Molecular Evolution* 20: 2–15.

Singer, Peter. 1975. *Animal Liberation: A New Ethics for Our Treatment of Animals*. New York: Avon Books.

"Slama Acquitted." 1989. *IPPL Newsletter* 16 (Mar.): 11.

Smith, Richard. 1986. "Up-Tight Chimps Coming Here for a Cure." *San Antonio Express News*, Mar. 7.

Society for Animal Protective Legislation. N.d. *The Animal Welfare Act Is in Danger*. Brochure.

Specter, Michael. 1989. "Work on AIDS Vaccine Showing More Promise." *Washington Post*, June 9.

Spinage, C. A. 1980. "Parks and Reserves in Congo Brazzaville." *Oryx* 15 (3): 292–295.

"State Department Papers Show How U.S. Tried to Overturn India's Primate Ban." 1979. *IPPL Newsletter* 6 (Dec.): 7–9.

Stevens, Christine. 1984. "Mistreatment of Laboratory Animals Endangers Biomedical Research." *Nature* 311 (Sept. 27): 295–297.

Stokoe, William C. 1989. "Comparative and Developmental Sign Language Studies: A Review of Recent Advances." In *Teaching Sign Language to Chimpanzees*, ed. R. Allen Gardner, Beatrix T. Gardner, and Thomas E. Van Cantfort, pp. 308–316. Albany, N.Y.: SUNY Press.

"Storm over Primate Housing Standards." 1990. *IPPL Newsletter* 17 (Nov.): 7–27.

Strausbaugh, John. 1991. "Monkey Business." *New York Press* 4 (Mar. 6–12): 17ff.

Struhsaker, Thomas T. 1987. "Forestry Issues and Conservation in Uganda." *Biological Conservation* 39: 209–234.

Struhsaker, T. T., and P. Hunkeler. 1971. "Evidence of Tool-Using by Chimpanzees in the Ivory Coast." *Folia Primatologica* 15 (3–4): 212–219.

Sugiyama, Yukimaru. 1984. "Population Dynamics of Wild Chimpanzees at Bossou, Guinea, 1976–1983." *Primates* 25: 391–400.

Sugiyama, Yukimaru, and Aly G. Soumah. 1988. "Preliminary Study of the Distribution and Population of Chimpanzees in the Republic of Guinea." *Primates* 29 (Oct.): 569–574.

"Suomi Denounces Harlow Techniques." 1981. *IPPL Newsletter* 8 (Sept.): 13.

Susman, Randall L., and K. M. Mubalamata. 1984. "Update on the Pygmy Chimpanzee in Zaire." *Primate Conservation* 4: 34–36.

Susman, Randall L., and others. 1981. "Pgymy Chimpanzee in Peril." *Oryx* 16 (2): 179–183.

Suzuki, Akira. 1971. "On the Problems of Conservation of the Chimpanzees in East Africa and the Preservation of Their Environment." *Primates* 12 (Dec.): 415–418.

Switzer, John. 1987. "Sam the Chimp to Leave Vices Behind in 6-Week Quarantine." *Columbus Dispatch*, Apr. 18.

Swyers, James P. 1990a. "Animal Models Offer Hope for AIDS Vaccines." *Research Resources Reporter* 14 (Apr.): 1–5.

————. 1990b. "Successful Breeding Program Benefits Chimpanzee Conservation and Research." *Research Resources Reporter* 14 (June): 1–6.

Tappen, N. C. 1964. "Primate Studies in Sierra Leone." *Current Anthropology* 5 (4): 339–340.

Taylor, Nick. "Heart to Heart: Can a Chimp Transplant Save a Human Life?" *New York Magazine*, July 13, pp. 44–48.

Teleki, Geza. 1973. *The Predatory Behavior of Wild Chimpanzees.* Lewisburg, Penn.: Bucknell University Press.

————. 1980. "Hunting and Trapping Wildlife in Sierra Leone: Aspects of Exploitation and Exportation." Report submitted to Office of President, Sierra Leone; World Wildlife Fund–U.S.; World Wildlife Fund–International.

————. 1981. "The Omnivorous Diet and Eclectic Feeding Habits of Chimpanzees in Gombe National Park, Tanzania." In *Omnivorous Primates*, ed. R. S. O. Harding and Geza Teleki. New York: Columbia University Press.

————. 1983. "Confidential Supplement to Progress Report #3," *IUCN/WWF Project 1993.*

————. 1986, 1989. *Threats to the Survival of the No Longer "Common" Chimpanzee (Pan troglodytes) of Equatorial Africa.* Washington, D.C.: Committee for the Care and Conservation of Chimpanzees. Special report.

————. 1989. "Population Status of Wild Chimpanzees *(Pan troglodytes)* and Threats to Survival." In *Understanding Chimpanzees*, ed. Paul G. Heltne and Linda A. Marquardt, pp. 312–353. Cambridge, Mass.: Harvard University Press.

Teleki, Geza, and Lori Baldwin. 1981. "Sierra Leone's Wildlife Legacy: Options for Survival." *Zoonooz* 54 (10): 21–27.

Teleki, Geza, and Ibrahim Bangura. 1981. "Outamba-Kilimi National Park: Cornerstone for Conservation." *Zoonooz* 54 (10): 28–31.

Teleki, Geza, E. E. Hunt, Jr., and J. H. Pfifferling. 1976. "Demographic Observations (1963–1973) on the Chimpanzees of Gombe National Park, Tanzania." *Journal of Human Evolution* 5: 559–598.

Temerlin, Maurice K. 1975. *Lucy: Growing up Human.* Palo Alto, Calif.: Science and Behavior Books.

Terrace, Herbert S. 1985. "In the Beginning Was the 'Name.' " *American Psychologist* (Sept.): 1011–28.

———. 1987 (1979). *Nim.* New York: Columbia University Press.

"Thank You, Las Vegas." 1989. *Las Vegas Sun,* Dec. 18.

Thompson, Larry. 1988a. "The Eerie World of Living Heads." *Washington Post,* Feb. 14.

———. 1988b. "The Absence of a Good Animal Model Stymies Vaccine Researchers." *Washington Post,* June 21.

Tidyman, John. 1992. "Brain Man." *Cleveland Edition* (Jan. 30): 1, 6, 8.

"Tödlich: Das 'Affen-Theater' und die Immuno AG!" 1986. *Bezirksjournal* 10: 6, 7.

Torrey, Lee. 1984. "The Agony of Primate Research." *Science Digest* (May): 70–72.

Trefflich, Henry, and Edward Anthony. 1967. *Jungle for Sale.* New York: Hawthorne Books.

Trenchard, Peter C. 1988. *Ecology and Conservation of the Kibira National Park, Burundi.* Washington, D.C.: U.S. Peace Corps. Special report.

Turmell, Mike. 1987. "Chimp's Release Delayed." *Cincinnati Enquirer,* June 17.

Tutin, Caroline E. G., and Michel Fernandez. 1983. "Gorilla and Chimpanzee Census in Gabon." *Primate Conservation* 3: 22–23.

———. 1984. "Nationwide Census of Gorilla (*Gorilla gorilla*) and Chimpanzee (*Pan troglodytes*) Populations in Gabon." *American Journal of Primatology* 6: 313–336.

Vaughan, Alden T., and Virginia Mason Vaughan. 1991. *Shakespeare's Caliban: A Cultural History.* Cambridge: Cambridge University Press.

"A Visit with the Beach Chimps." 1985. *IPPL Newsletter* 12 (Apr.): 3.

Whitford, Walter A. 1976. "Sweating Responses in the Chimpanzee (*Pan troglodytes*)." *Comparative Biochemistry and Physiology* 53A: 333–336.

Whitney, Robert A., Thomas J. Wolfe, and Benjamin D. Blood. 1991. "Planning and Development of the Chimpanzee Breeding and Research Program" (abstract). In *Chimpanzee Conservation and Public Health: Environments for the Future.* Rockville, Md.

"William Elementary Students Enjoy Berosini Visit." 1990. *Las Vegas Sun,* Feb. 27.

Wolfheim, Jaclyn H. 1983. *Primates of the World: Distribution, Abundance, and Conservation.* Seattle: University of Washington Press.

Woolf, Gerry. 1988. "Chimps Are No Use to AIDS Workers." *Laboratory News* 399 (June 13): 3.

"World Population Data Sheet." 1990. Washington, D.C.: Population Reference Bureau.

"Worldwide Primates versus Shirley McGreal: Anatomy of the Block Lawsuit." 1992. *IPPL Newsletter* 19 (Apr.): 1–6. Special supplement.

Wrangham, Richard, and Jane Goodall. 1989. "Chimpanzee Use of Medicinal Leaves." In *Understanding Chimpanzees*, ed. Paul G. Heltne and Linda A. Marquardt, pp. 22–37. Cambridge, Mass.: Harvard University Press.

Wrangham, Richard, and Toshisada Nishida. 1983. "*Aspilia* spp. leaves: A Puzzle in the Feeding Behavior of Wild Chimpanzees." *Primates* 24: 276–282.

Wrangham, Richard, and Eloy Rodriguez. "Zoopharmacology: Can Animals Doctor Themselves?" Unpublished.

Wright, Irene. 1987a. "Monkeyshines Rile Animal Lovers." *Cincinnati Enquirer*, Apr. 18.

———. 1987b. "Owner Fears Good Habits for His Chimp." *Cincinnati Enquirer*, Apr. 22.

———. 1987c. "Judge Delays Ruling on Custody of Chimp." *Cincinnati Enquirer*, July 1.

Wrussnig, Manfred. 1986. "Geheimimport für 'Immuno': 13 Affen kamen nach Wien." *Kurier*, Aug. 13.

Wurtz, Robert. 1991. "Different Groups, Common Goal." *Foundation for Biomedical Research Newsletter* 8 (May/June): 5, 8.

Yerkes, Robert M. 1916. "Provision for the Study of Monkeys and Apes." *Science* 43 (1193): 231–234.

———. 1925. *Almost Human.* New York: Century.

———. 1943. *Chimpanzees: A Laboratory Colony.* New Haven: Yale University Press.

Yerkes, Robert M., and Ada W. Yerkes. 1929. *The Great Apes: A Study of Anthropoid Life.* New Haven: Yale University Press.

Zak, Steven. 1989. "Ethics and Animals." *Atlantic Monthly*, Mar., pp. 69–74.

Zonana, Victor F. 1988. "Monkey Doctors on Front Line in War against AIDS." *Los Angeles Times*, Dec. 4.

Zuckerman, Seth. 1991. *Saving Our Ancient Forests.* Los Angeles: Living Planet Press.